The publisher and the University of California Press Foundation gratefully acknowledge the generous support of the Fletcher Jones Foundation Imprint in Humanities.

Age of Coexistence

Age of Coexistence

THE ECUMENICAL FRAME AND THE MAKING OF THE MODERN ARAB WORLD

Ussama Makdisi

UNIVERSITY OF CALIFORNIA PRESS

University of California Press, one of the most distinguished university presses in the United States, enriches lives around the world by advancing scholarship in the humanities, social sciences, and natural sciences. Its activities are supported by the UC Press Foundation and by philanthropic contributions from individuals and institutions. For more information, visit www.ucpress.edu.

University of California Press
Oakland, California

First Paperback Printing 2021

Library of Congress Cataloging-in-Publication Data

Names: Makdisi, Ussama Samir, 1968– author.
Title: Age of coexistence : the ecumenical frame and the making of the modern Arab world / Ussama Makdisi.
Description: Oakland, California : University of California Press, [2019]
|
    Includes bibliographical references and index. |
Identifiers: LCCN 2019016593 (print) | LCCN 2019021598 (ebook) |
    ISBN 9780520971745 (e-book)
    ISBN 9780520258884 (cloth : alk. paper)
    ISBN 9780520385764 (pbk. : alk. paper)

Subjects: LCSH: Cultural pluralism—Middle East—History. |
    Middle East—History—Religious aspects.
Classification: LCC DS62.4 (ebook) | LCC DS62.4 .M345 2019 (print) |
    DDC 305.0917/4927—dc23
LC record available at https://lccn.loc.gov/2019016593

Manufactured in the United States of America

27   26   25   24   23   22   21
10   9   8   7   6   5   4   3   2   1

For Karim and Saree

Contents

Maps

Acknowledgments

I began writing this book in Berlin in 2012, when I was a Fellow at the Institute for Advanced Study in Berlin. I completed it in 2018 when I spent a semester as a Fellow at the American Academy in Berlin. I acknowledge both these institutions for providing me the opportunity to work on the manuscript. I also acknowledge the generous support I have received from my home institution in those years, Rice University. While my experiences in Berlin bookended this project, my time in Houston and Lebanon largely define it.

There are far too many people to thank for the making of this book. I list here those who read and commented on chapters or entire drafts of the book, each of whom knows the degree of my individual debt to them: Hosam Aboul-Ela, Toufoul Abou Hodeib, Seda Altug, Fareed Armaly, Orit Bashkin, Michelle Campos, Nathan Citino, Leena Dallasheh, Dima de Clerck, Esmat Elhalaby, Nathaniel George, Zeina Halabi, Jens Hanssen, Gale Kenny, Dina Khoury, Ilham-Khuri Makdisi, Bruce Masters, Christine Philliou, Amy Remensnyder, Shira Robinson, George Sabra, Grace Said, Kirsten Scheid, Aziz Shaibani, Malek Sharif, and the anonymous readers for UC Press. Their criticisms and insights have been invaluable in helping me clarify my argument. I have taxed the patience of Niels Hooper, the executive editor at UC Press who has accompanied the progress of the manuscript for years. I acknowledge, as well, the assistance of Kamal Boulatta and Lily Farhoud in securing Steve Sabella's permission to use his photograph of the evocative painting on the book's cover. Boulatta alerted me to the Palestinian painter Nicola Saig's circa 1920 depiction of Caliph 'Umar at Jerusalem Gates, an oil on canvas at the Islamic Museum, Jerusalem. In his book *Palestinian Art*, Boulatta writes that the dismounted, Christ-like caliph is raising his arms in peace while looking at the Christian patriarch Sophronius. He adds that this painting represents Saig's own experience of Jerusalem's interfaith harmony. To me, the painting captures the profound importance and ambiguity inherent in the ecumenical frame—a strikingly modern interpretation of historic coexistence that elides much in order to achieve a composite of unity.

My friends Abdel Razzaq Takriti, with whom I co-organized a conference on "Arab Traditions of Antisectarianism" in December 2017, Fady Joudah, and Hicham Safieddine have been key readers of and interlocutors for this work during our years together in Houston. I am also indebted to the fact that I come from an academic family. My parents, Jean Said and Samir Makdisi, have provided crucial feedback, as has my spouse, Elora Shehabuddin. My brothers Karim and Saree know well what I have tried to accomplish, having participated in the work's elaboration by reading and commenting on the manuscript from its earliest drafts. It is to them I dedicate this work. I alone am responsible for any errors of fact or judgment contained herein.

Houston, April 2019

Note on Transliteration

Arabic words and names have been transliterated according to a simplified system based on that used by the *International Journal of Middle East Studies*. Diacritical marks have been omitted. The prefix "al-" is used the first time a transliterated name appears but is omitted later (e.g., al-Husri, Husri). I have not changed the transliterations of names adopted by authors who write in either English or French (e.g., Rabbath, not Rabbat). I have transliterated names to conform as closely as possible to common usage. Arabic words and proper names widely used in English, such as Quran and Beirut, are left in the familiar form.

Introduction

THE ECUMENICAL FRAME

And all the prophets are my kin, but the sky
is distant from its land,
and I am distant from what I speak . . .

— Mahmoud Darwish, "A Canaanite Rock in the Dead Sea" (1992)

Every history of sectarianism is also a history of coexistence. This book reveals how a complex, and now obscured, modern culture of coexistence first developed in the modern Middle East, which today appears to be little more than a collection of war-torn countries and societies. In particular, I question two stories that have traditionally dominated the perception of the Middle East. The first stresses a continuous history of sectarian strife between allegedly antagonistic religious and ethnic communities; the second idealizes coexistence as communal harmony.

More fundamentally, I dispute an entire way of looking at the Middle East, and the Arab world in particular, as some kind of pathological place consumed by the disease of sectarianism. Sectarianism is a real problem, but it is no more real, and no less subject to change over time, than are analogous problems of racism in the West and caste politics and communalism in South Asia. There is a key difference between orientalizing the Middle East (thinking of it as strange, aberrant, and dangerously different) and historicizing it (putting it in context and in dialogue with analogous experiences in other parts of the world). Once we understand this, we can, I believe, study the history of coexistence in the Middle East

1

the system

without defensiveness and without the misplaced paternalism that so often dogs pronouncements about the region.

The conventional usage of the term "coexistence" is admittedly limited. Typically, it vaguely describes what has been one of the most distinguishing characteristics of the long sweep of Arab and Islamic history; it often nostalgically refers to the golden age of Muslim Spain. During the Cold War, the phrase "peaceful coexistence" denoted the toleration of otherwise incompatible communist and capitalist systems that threatened each other with annihilation; in Lebanon, coexistence indicates the allegedly harmonious relationship between separate and notionally age-old communities; in the United States, it suggests an anodyne dialogue between monotheistic faiths in a secular republic. The contemporary usage of "coexistence" hints at an equality between people of different faiths that is not warranted by historical scrutiny. Nevertheless, the term remains resonant and it evokes for me a specific age, and a new kind of political intimacy and meaningful solidarity that cut across Muslim, Christian, and Jewish religious lines. These together define a hallmark of modern Arab history.

Rather than taking sectarianism or coexistence for granted, or assuming either of them to be age-old features of the Middle East, I am interested in historicizing both notions. At what point was "sectarianism" first identified as a political problem? How did parceling out public office along sectarian lines become an expression of equality? Why was this done in some parts of the Middle East but not in others? When was "coexistence" first celebrated as a national value? And how and why did religion go from being a key element of an inegalitarian Ottoman imperial politics discriminating between Muslim and non-Muslim, and privileging Sunni orthodoxy over other Islamic denominations, to a key component of post-Ottoman national politics affirming the equality of all citizens irrespective of their religious affiliation? These are just some of the questions this book will answer.

My interest lies principally in clarifying how different understandings of the relationship between religious diversity, equality, and emancipation have legitimated and cohered radically divergent and highly experimental political orders across the area during the century from roughly 1860 until 1948, an era that first saw the Ottoman Empire reform itself, and then saw European powers destroy and divide the empire into various post-Ottoman states that enjoyed only a nominal sovereignty. This book is specifically focused on the Mashriq—that is, the region that today encompasses Lebanon, Syria, the occupied Palestinian territories, Israel, Jordan, Egypt, and Iraq, all of which were once under a common Ottoman rule.

The Mashriq is a region in which Arabic-speaking Muslim, Christian, and Jewish communities were tightly and densely interwoven during and following the collapse of the Ottoman Empire. It is also the region of the Middle East that has seen the most sustained attempts to forge political solidarities among men and women of different faiths. Thus, it is different from Turkey itself, where the non-Muslim presence was largely expunged [to strike] during and after World War I. It is also different from North Africa or the Gulf, where the indigenous non-Muslim presence was less influential in the region's cultural development. The Mashriq has witnessed constant internal resistance and reaction to the secular implications of national solidarities. Last but far from least, it has been the setting for relentless European, and more recently U.S., interference that both speaks for and exploits the historical diversity of the region. The work to imagine and build societies that transcend sectarian difference has been multifaceted and contradictory. It has received its fair share of setbacks, in our own age perhaps more than in others. But, as I see it, this work has also continued for over a century. I am especially interested in how the idea of modern coexistence as equality between Muslim and non-Muslim went from being unimaginable at the beginning of the nineteenth century to unremarkable by the middle of the twentieth century. This history deserves an empathetic telling.

DEMYTHOLOGIZING THE SECTARIAN MIDDLE EAST

[existing] The ubiquitous representation of a sectarian Middle East consistently medievalizes the region. It conflates contemporary political identifications with far older religious solidarities. The historian Bruce Masters insists, for example, that "as long as religion lay at the heart of each individual's worldview, the potential for society to fracture along sectarian lines remained."[1] Perhaps. But between the potentiality of sectarian violence and its actuality lies the history I tell: how a modern political culture emerged that valorized religion and coexistence, and demonized sectarianism. It was only in the twentieth century, after all, that the Arabic terms for "sectarianism" and "coexistence"—*al-ta'ifiyya* and *al-'aysh al-mushtarak*—were coined as an integral part of a new imagination that accepted Muslim and Christian and Jew as equal citizens within a sovereign political frame.

"Sectarianism," indeed, is not simply a reflection of significant fractures in a religiously diverse society. It is also a language, an accusation, a judgment, an imagination, and an ideological fiction that has been deployed by both Middle Eastern and Western nations, communities, and individuals to create modern political and ideological frameworks within which supposedly innate sectarian problems can be contained, if not overcome. No organization or movement, after all, actually describes itself as "sectarian," just as no modern government anywhere claims to be against "coexistence." The perception of a sectarian problem can reflect an idealistic attempt to build a radical new political community that transcends religious difference. It can denote a way that members of long marginalized communities make political, cultural, and economic claims to resources and privileges in any given nation. It can also justify a cynical mode of colonial or reactionary nationalist governance that exploits religious or ethnic diversity in a given region.

Sunni, Shi'i, Maronite, Jewish, Armenian, or Orthodox Christian identifications are not etched uniformly into the fabric of the past and present. They are historical designations whose meanings have changed and whose salience has ebbed and flowed. At any given moment, communal identities may appear to be entirely genuine and palpable. They may be positive or negative, open-minded or insular. These identities, nevertheless, are not recovered from some container of the past that preserves an unadulterated sense of self and other. They are, instead, produced over and over again in different forms and for different reasons. They manifest only after having been riven by innumerable schisms and after having undergone repeated redefinitions throughout their long histories.

Anyone who has lived in the Middle East, of course, will know that stubborn sectarian problems exist in countries such as Lebanon, Syria, Egypt, Bahrain, and Iraq, just as anyone who lives in the United States will likewise perceive an obvious racial problem there. Imagine, for example, hypothetically, a situation in which a foreign power removed the U.S. federal government, abolished the U.S. Army, and encouraged the division of the United States along racial lines—similar to how the United States acted in Iraq in the aftermath of its invasion of that country in 2003. The race problem in America would inevitably be exacerbated and its implications changed. This is not because the racial identities in America are unchanging or "age-old," but rather because their meaning and transformation, like sectarian ones, are so clearly dynamic products of specific historical, material, and geopolitical contexts.

To demystify the modern problem of sectarianism is to understand how it is far more an expression of a global tension between sovereignty, diversity, and equal citizenship than a restaging of a medieval religious schism. It may indeed be helpful for readers to think about communal and sectarian outlooks, actions, and thoughts in the modern world as analogous to racial and racist outlooks, actions, and thoughts in the United States. The most interesting scholars of American history have grappled with the immense salience of race by historicizing it, not by taking it for granted. They have examined how the notion of race has been produced and reproduced in the context of a U.S. republic that embraced democratic freedoms and justified perpetual bondage.[2] Neither modern racism nor modern sectarianism, in other words, is intelligible outside of the richness of its respective context. Invariably, both are expressed with the full knowledge that there are powerful and meaningful antiracist and antisectarian currents that oppose them. This does not mean that sectarianism is the same as racism, nor that the historical experience of Sunnis, Shi'is, Christians, and Jews in the Arab world is the same as that of Latinos, Anglos, and African Americans in the United States.

What this juxtaposition involves, rather, is understanding how different communal, racial, and sectarian formations—and, just as importantly, different antiracist and antisectarian commitments—were, as I will explain more fully below, common legacies of a global nineteenth-century political revolution. This revolution introduced the profoundly important and historic principle of political equality among citizens, many of whom had been historically and legally discriminated against or classified as inferior in centuries past, in very different circumstances and contexts—Jews in Europe, blacks in the United States, and non-Muslims in the Ottoman Empire, to name a few cases. I recognize, of course, that the vast divergence in the historical experiences of Ottoman Christians and those of oppressed slaves in America can make a direct comparison of the two groups misleading if not mendacious. However, it is important to appreciate how each became vital to the unfolding of parallel yet distinctive politics of emancipation and citizenship in the nineteenth century. What is manifestly clear is that this revolution of equality was deeply contested in every part of the world, including in the United States and Europe. Political equality, after all, is never simply a noble principle that merely spreads from the West to the rest of the world. Rather, its introduction *anywhere* has always been complex.

Perhaps most obviously, the meaning of equality has depended heavily on the quality of political sovereignty, and often on power. Napoleon emancipated Jews in occupied German states; European powers pressured the Ottomans to concede the equality of Muslim and non-Muslim during the Crimean War; and the Union freed slaves in its war against the Confederacy and passed the important Reconstruction Amendments to the U.S. Constitution during the era of Radical Reconstruction when northern soldiers occupied the South. I recognize, moreover, that equality is not an uncomplicated good, for its emergence in different parts of the world has invariably excluded certain groups—slaves in the antebellum United States being only the most obvious example (one can add colonized subjects, women, Native Americans, and African Americans during Jim Crow). Yet, while scholars have recently underscored how modern secular states have excluded minority groups and communities, many of those same states, and the struggles for meaningful self-determination that often accompanied their creation, also legitimated hitherto unimaginable forms of secular affiliation and solidarity. The terms of inclusion are my interest in this book.

EXPLAINING THE ECUMENICAL FRAME

The contemporary obsession, in scholarship and media, with the so-called sectarian Middle East has almost totally obscured a parallel modern development that began to take shape in the Ottoman Empire after 1860. The late Ottoman and modern Arab worlds witnessed the first attempts to cohere modern political solidarities—and to reconcile those solidarities with the reality of religious and ethnic difference in the region. These attempts unfolded within complex geopolitical shifts that saw the Arab region pass from Ottoman dominion to European colonial rule.

I call this modern form of coexistence the *ecumenical frame*. I use the term "ecumenical" because I think it indicates the relevance of religion, which has always maintained a strong public presence in the Middle East. By "frame," I am referring to the scaffolding of a project being built. This ecumenical frame was made out of eclectic Ottoman, European, and Arab materials. Its construction commenced during a specific nineteenth-century moment (hence we could also think of this as the beginnings of an *ecumenical age*); it included many people of the region who belonged to different religious communities; it could and did change over time; and it was neither permanent nor impervious to its social and political environment. The ecumenical frame suggests the rich diversity of the Mashriq that has stubbornly confounded repeated attempts to reduce the region to one religious hue.

The Greek word *oikoumenē*, from which the term "ecumenical" derives, means the whole of the inhabited earth. Scholars of Islam have also invoked the notion of the ecumenical to describe the great shared but also diverse "Islamicate" culture that developed and spread across much of the world.[3] I am aware, of course, that in modern Christian ecclesiastical usage the term "ecumenical" means the cooperation among various separate Christian denominations in the pursuit of a common ideal, the universal church, and is typically distinguished from the term "interfaith," which indicates cooperation between different religions.[4] Nevertheless, I adapt the term "ecumenical" here to capture the shared sense of the universal, transcendent ideal of a modern political community in which explicit religious differentiation was transformed from being a marker of imperial culture to being a crucial aspect of national culture.

In using the concept of the ecumenical frame, I am referring to three things: (1) a body of thought that sought to reconcile a new principle of secular political equality with the reality of an Ottoman imperial system that had historically privileged Muslim over non-Muslim, but that was also attempting to integrate non-Muslims as citizens; (2) a system of governance that often retained vestiges and signs of Islamic paramountcy while upholding the equality of all citizens irrespective of religious affiliation; and (3) a new political and legal order that has consistently upheld

both the constitutional secularity of citizens *and* the necessity of religiously segregated laws to govern marriage, divorce, and inheritance that
have actually denied the secularity and equality of citizens.

An appreciation of the ecumenical frame provides a lens through which
to understand the emergence of a new norm of coexistence rooted in the
principle of secular equality—that is to say, the cultural and constitutional
commitment to the equality of citizens of different faiths. But the ecumenical frame is also the subject of this book because it was built, it was
redesigned, and, in some instances and areas, it was destroyed. It supported several overlapping, and sometimes contradictory, Muslim, Arab,
Ottoman, Christian, and Jewish subjectivities. Some were more secular,
others more pious; some were republican and others monarchical; some
were communalist and others radically dissenting; some were liberal and
others Marxist. For this reason, I do not see the ecumenical frame as
reducible to "liberalism" or as a cognate for a "liberal age," a term that I
have always found deeply inadequate to describe the sectarian and nationalist violence of the late Ottoman era, the dawn of post–World War I
European colonialism across the Arab Mashriq, and the variety of anti- as
well as philo-colonial, secular as well as Islamist, mobilizations that have
defined Arab politics in the twentieth century.

Arab Christians played a major role in the elaboration of this frame, out
of proportion to their demographic weight (similar, in a sense, to the roles
that German and American Jews have played in the elaboration of pre-
Nazi German culture and contemporary American culture, respectively).
By the same token, as the demographic majority, Muslim Arabs in the
Levant were indispensable to making the principle of political equality
with non-Muslims ubiquitous in mainstream political culture. In its most
radical incarnation, this frame encouraged forms of equality and solidarity that denied the political significance of religiosity; in its most conservative formulation, it merely accepted religious diversity and engaged in
what Moroccan philosopher Muhammad 'Abed al-Jabri referred to as a
"traditional understanding of tradition."[5]

The story I tell about the ecumenical frame is, at first glance, primarily
an intellectual one, insofar as those who first wrote, imagined, and inculcated coexistence were typically literate Ottoman Arab subjects between
1860 and 1920. These individuals were, for the most part, not directly

connected to statecraft. Although the history of the ecumenical frame should be explored from the vantage point of many different social classes and experiences, this book begins with what I believe is still an extraordinarily underappreciated story that has never had its proper telling: for the first time in the late Ottoman period, literate Arab Muslims, Christians, and Jews collectively denounced "religious fanaticism," which they construed to be an unnatural deviation from a normative "religion" and the "coexistence" that religion allegedly engendered. They did so while many, though by no means all, of their Ottoman Turkish and Balkan peers and analogues fought existential wars to define new nation-states denuded of meaningful religious diversity.

The story of this book is also a political one. The act of imagining new forms of political equality was neither obvious nor inevitable. I use the term "Arab" in this history to indicate a conscious modern identification among Arabs that transcends religious affiliations. I categorically do not mean the term to be an anachronistic cognate for "Arab nationalist," although of course Arab nationalists of the twentieth century did use the term in precisely that manner. For the earlier periods in Ottoman history, I generally refer to Arabic-speaking Christian or Muslim or Jewish subjects of the Ottoman Empire.

Although the ecumenical frame emerged amid massive political, economic, and technological transformations in the empire, it continued to be modified long after the demise of the sultanate. When the Ottomans were overthrown, their former subjects in the Mashriq were pressed to articulate and express new sovereign, political forms of the ecumenical frame. They did so in a variety of conservative monarchical, consociational, and republican ways. Rather than dismissing their labor as a reflection of the derivative, predictable, and self-serving schemes of native nationalists who were only interested in power, this book situates the different ways that Arabs went about rebuilding the ecumenical frame in their post-Ottoman world.[6]

At the same time, I argue that during the century in question, sharp religious and social differentiation remained visibly at the heart of a new shared public order that ostentatiously abjured religious discrimination among equal citizens. The role of Islam in public life and the relationship between the legacies of the imperial Islamic past and the realities of

Western colonialism that habitually favored minorities were immensely fraught topics. By the middle of the twentieth century, nevertheless, an overlapping consensus, to borrow the phrase of philosopher John Rawls, had been secured in the Mashriq concerning the necessity of political independence, the principle of religious diversity, the equality of all citizens, *and* the codification and maintenance of highly gendered and unequal sectarian regimes of "personal status." These regimes have governed marriage, divorce, and inheritance for all citizens and have prevented the introduction of even an optional secular marriage code anywhere in the Arab world. This interplay between and among dynamic and variegated groupings of secularists and communalists in the Middle East has contributed to the inherently conservative nature of the ecumenical frame and suppressed its more radical implications.

NINETEENTH-CENTURY BEGINNINGS

The modern ecumenical frame reflected a major ideological and political departure from the older imperial model of Ottoman Muslim privilege. Its beginnings lay in the imperial proclamation of nondiscrimination between Muslim and non-Muslim subjects in 1839, and of equal citizenship between them following the promulgation of the Ottoman Constitution of 1876— the period in Ottoman history known as the Tanzimat.[7] The breakdown in the nineteenth century of a long-standing and profoundly unequal Ottoman imperial system that had ruled for centuries over a vast multireligious, multiethnic, and multilinguistic landscape opened the ideological and political space for new political horizons and vocabularies—some of which were more inclusive and some far less so.

It is important to acknowledge the fact that the legal and ideological disestablishment of Ottoman Muslim hegemony occurred under enormous European pressure. This disestablishment was *not* the result of Ottoman Muslim grappling with the implications of a system of pervasive discrimination that (in different ways and with different intensities) affected dress, architecture, forms of address, and sociability across the Islamic Middle East. Nor was this disestablishment the consequence of social movements that identified such discrimination as a problem. Many Muslim subjects in the empire viewed the ending of Islamic privilege as a concession at a time of aggressive Western military and missionary assault on Islam itself. This defensiveness affected and shaped the contours of the post-Tanzimat ecumenical frame.

By the same token, as alluded to above, it is vital to recognize how many cultures around the world in the nineteenth century struggled with new ideas of secular citizenship, national unity, and political equality. Many states at the time strove to reconcile these notions with long-standing convictions of religious and racial difference. The Ottoman Empire contributed its distinctive part to a much larger global problem of citizenship and equality that pulled in several different and often deeply contradictory directions. The rapprochement between Protestant and Catholic (and eventually Jewish) Americans went hand in hand with the systematic racist exclusion of black Americans and staggering antiblack violence and inequality. The integration of Jewish Germans in modern German culture was another example, though it was vitiated by pressures to assimilate that Arab Christians never faced. The emergence of Hindu and Muslim collaboration in Bengal even before the rise of the Congress movement in India points to still another example of cross-communal solidarity, but in this case the British Empire never offered its colonial Indian subjects citizenship, nor was there a corresponding Mughalism that was the equivalent to Ottomanism under which Arab subjects of the Ottoman Empire thrived.[8]

The conjoined problems of coexistence and sectarianism in the modern Middle East emerged at roughly the same time as those of nationalism and racial anti-Semitism in modern Europe, and those of emancipation and segregation in the postbellum United States. The point of any juxtaposition is inherently heuristic. The comparisons historians typically make involving the Ottoman Empire are between large multiethnic empires (the Ottomans and Russians for instance) that collapsed during World War I. These comparisons can obfuscate the fact that European empires such as Britain and France were also multiethnic and multireligious, and that the United States itself constituted a vast multiethnic, multilinguistic, and multireligious expanding state in this same period.[9] They also obscure the fact that the challenge of political inclusion has plagued every secular state in the modern era—whether democratic republics or empires. The Ottoman and American cases might well be juxtaposed, in fact, to emphasize their coevalness. They each refracted older discourses and practices of discrimination through a radically new lens of equality and citizenship. The United States, after all, endured the Civil War and many bouts of antiblack race rioting at roughly the same time that the Ottoman Empire witnessed unprecedented fragmentation and sectarian mobilizations and massacres involving the emancipation of non-Muslims.[10]

My point is to suggest that what race has been to America, religion has been to the Middle East in one specific way: both are perceived as stable and obvious problems, but their political implications have, in fact, changed radically across a century. My point is not to pretend that non-Muslims in the Ottoman case had the same economic, social, racial, or political status as black slaves in America or Jews in European ghettos. Islamic imperial rule that legitimated Muslim ideological, legal, and cultural privilege over non-Muslims (while guaranteeing them protection and religious autonomy) is not the same thing as the baleful ideology of white supremacy that posited the innate, biological, and perpetual supremacy of one group over all others and that was elaborated in the context of chattel slavery and settler colonialism in the United States. Rather, my point is that if in America the question of race defined, undergirded, contradicted, and rendered ambivalent the meaning of U.S. citizenship, in the Ottoman Middle East the question of religious difference haunted an incomplete, paradoxical, and often contradictory nineteenth-century project of equal citizenship.

The key difference between the Middle East and the United States (and the West more generally), however, is that the inhabitants of the Middle East have hardly affected, intervened, and transformed modern Europe or the United States in the manner that Europeans and Americans have transformed, and still transform, the Middle East. Western powers went from being increasingly important factors, players, and agents in what remained a sovereign Ottoman polity to being the *hegemonic* architects of the post-Ottoman Arab world. Western powers claimed to protect non-Muslim minorities in the Middle East at the same time that those same powers encroached aggressively on the Ottoman Empire. There is a brute reality of Western involvement that simply cannot be denied, nor should it for a moment be obfuscated as secondary to the "self-inflicted wounds" that allegedly really "mattered," as Fouad Ajami tendentiously put it.[11] Yet to reduce modern sectarian problems to a question of colonial "divide and rule" is also to ignore the powerful legacies of the nineteenth century that *predated* direct European colonial rule. It also shunts aside the agency of Arabs, Turks, Armenians, Kurds, and others who were most invested in these problems.

The effects of Western imperialism were not monolithic. As much as British and French officials used the fact of religious diversity and theories of religious freedom and innate Eastern sectarianism to justify their interventions in the nineteenth-century Ottoman Empire, they also inadvertently helped consolidate the ideologically antisectarian and nationalist Arab states in Syria and Iraq. Unlike the case of colonial Uganda and South Africa that Mahmood Mamdani has studied, in which a "politically enforced ethnic pluralism" was a hallmark of apartheid and a strategy for European colonial rule,[12] in the Ottoman Empire the situation was not nearly as binary, and European hegemony was far more diffuse. Muslim and non-Muslim Arab subjects in the Mashriq had far more latitude to build an ecumenical frame that was not merely a copy of some European original but coeval to what other subjects of the Ottoman Empire—and many Europeans, Americans, and Indian colonial subjects—were trying to achieve for themselves but in vastly different circumstances.

RECALIBRATING HISTORIOGRAPHY

When my first book, *The Culture of Sectarianism*, was published in 2000, sectarianism was thought of as mainly a Lebanese problem. Although the topic was debated intensely, especially during that country's long civil war between 1975 and 1990, the framework of analysis was often parochial and national. Some scholars defended a sectarian paradigm of politics in Lebanon; others saw in it a lamentable native malady; still others viewed it as a consequence of foreign intervention in Lebanese affairs or as a consequence of the nature of the Lebanese state structure.[13] Historians of the modern Middle East, more generally, have described various economic or political developments that, in their estimation, provoked a sectarian backlash. They suggest that the sectarian layer of identity is the deepest

and most meaningful layer, and yet at the same time they treat it as ana-
lytically insignificant. For them, as for so many other scholars, it simply
exists. In an older orientalist literature, sectarian violence exposed an
allegedly enduring Islamic or native fanaticism that was unable to accept
the principle of secular equality.[14]

Admittedly, I do flag the religious identity of individuals in this book,
either because they have made their religion central to how they read the
world or to underscore an often overlooked point when it comes to the
Middle East: religious identity does not automatically or necessarily dic-
tate political belief. Ideological diversity is often far more important than
ethnic or religious or sectarian diversity: one cannot merely equate being
Sunni or Shi'i, Druze or Alawi, Maronite Christian or Jewish with having
one predetermined communal outlook. I also sometimes use the phrases
"sectarian violence," "sectarian mobilizations," and "sectarian institutions"
in their conventional usage. In these instances, I am referring to tangible
antagonisms between members of different religious or ethnic communities; to networks of affiliation, patronage, resource distribution; or to how
political, social, and economic claims are made in a multireligious or multiethnic society.

Since the U.S. invasion of Iraq in 2003, interest in sectarianism has
increased massively around the world—in large part because of the deplor-
able state of affairs in Iraq, Syria, and the Gulf region.[15] Some of the recent
work that contextualizes sectarianism in the region has been excellent,
and the best of this work is motivated by genuine antisectarian commitments (in much the same way as the best critical writing on racism or
communalism is by those clearly *opposed* to these phenomena). Yet the
deeply problematic comparative view that I have already alluded to in this
introduction remains firmly in place: there is an assumption of a uniformly secular West against which the allegedly sectarian Middle East is
implicitly or explicitly compared and judged.

In this sense, I find Talal Asad's call for an anthropology of the secular
important because he argues strongly against the alleged universalism of
one kind of secularism, and against the idea of the neutrality of the secular
public sphere in Western states.[16] I also appreciate William Cavanagh's
observation that the modern secular era invented a "myth of religious violence."[17] Also crucially important is criticism by Asad and Cavanagh, and

by several other scholars, including Saba Mahmood and Wendy Brown, of the universal and colonial pretentions of Western discourses about religious freedom and tolerance, and about how embedded violence has been in the project of the secular state.[18]

Yet the criticism of Western secularity does not explain the nature of the sectarian problem in the Middle East. Asad, in fact, defines what he regards as a "millennium-old [Islamic] discursive tradition," specifically against what he breezily dismisses as a "Western-derived" discourse of secular Arab nationalism.[19] His necessary criticism of Western secularity as a project that both invents the idea of religion and seeks to privatize it seamlessly becomes a criticism of secular Arab nationalism. But secular Arab nationalism did not simply mimic its Western counterpart; it was one among several reactions to the historical transition from Ottoman Islamic to Western colonial supremacy. For her part, Mahmood refers to secular nationalist Arabs in Syria as "Christians" and asserts that their Egyptian counterparts "ventriloquize" the certitudes of a condescending Western, Christian-derived secularism.[20] For these scholars, it appears that secularity has only one authentic iteration, one provenance, and one history. They miss the fact that secular Arab nationalism and modern Islamism reflected contending antisectarian responses to the same set of problems involving sovereignty, citizenship, and equality.

Like several of my colleagues who work on the modern Middle East, I think it is necessary to question the stark segregation of the Westernized "secular" against the traditional "Islamic" that pervades the literature—as if these two groupings are always segregated communities in the modern era.[21] But to do this empathetically (to feel this history as if it were our own as opposed to narrating sympathetically the history of others), we must also understand how and why a dichotomy between secular projects and religious ones has been key, at times, for the elaboration of, or bitter resistance to, the modern ecumenical frame.

The other problem that stems directly from the extraordinarily copious scholarship produced about Islam—and from those works, such as Asad's and Mahmood's, that use Islam to criticize the universal claims of Western secularism—is that they elide the abundant, obvious, and meaningful signs of Arab Christian (and, for a significant while, Arab Jewish) fellowship with Arab Muslims that has occurred on multiple scales and that is one of the defining features of modern Arab history. I concur with Aziz al-Azmeh's criticism of the "over-Islamization of Islam."[22] The fixation on the study of "Islam," "the Muslim," "the Muslim woman," and "Islamic piety" has ignored secular Arabs, or those Muslim Arabs for whom piety does not signify something publicly political. It also effaces the visibility and importance of Kurds, non-Muslim Arabs, Armenians, and others who have lived, interacted with, and shared a culture with Muslims across the Arabic-speaking Mashriq.

After breaking with the shibboleths of secular nationalism, I hardly see the point in romanticizing Islamic fundamentalism or valorizing minoritarian consciousness in the Middle East. One of the claims of this book is that just as one might use the experience of Arabs and Muslims in the West to understand the limits and pretensions of the secular West and its universalist claims, likewise one might use the experience and history of Arab Christians (and others of different faiths and ethnicities) as points of departure for understanding the modern history of the Middle East, and for thinking about the nature of coexistence within a predominantly Muslim world.[23]

FACING DENIAL

To undertake this criticism of coexistence fairly, one has to roll back the taboos and the deep denial at the heart of Arab, Turkish, and Zionist historiographies. Zionist partisans, for example, routinely invoke the demise of Jewish communities in the Arab world to justify the Israeli dispossession of the Palestinians. Arab nationalist historians, for their part, routinely point to the ills of colonialism but have virtually nothing to say about the myriad inequities that non-Muslims had to endure for centuries, and that continue to be inscribed in various forms in most postcolonial Arab states. Similarly, until very recently, most Turkish historians have routinely denied—and the Turkish state continues to deny—the Armenian Genocide by pointing to the expulsions of Muslim subjects from the Balkans and the Caucasus.

The story of the ecumenical frame is aggregative. It encompasses different histories, each of which has its own genealogy and specificity. This book juxtaposes various episodes of Ottoman and post-Ottoman, Arab and Armenian, Zionist and Kemalist, imperial and local histories that have almost always been narrated separately, segregated by fields of scholarship that have developed their own specialized audiences, literatures, and burning questions. The story of the ecumenical frame I tell is unrecognizable from within the confines of each historiographical tradition. As it now stands, Ottoman history flows seamlessly into that of Kemalist Turkey as if Ottoman history were only a Turkish concern. Arab historians are rarely in conversation with their Balkan or Armenian colleagues. Zionist historians, in turn, often flatten a complex Jewish diasporic past into an anti-Semitic prelude to Zionism.

The Arab-Israeli conflict did not erupt in a timeless empty space. It occurred in a dense historical field that had seen massive demographic and political shifts as a once mighty Ottoman Empire sought to remake itself, under the extraordinary pressure of Western imperialism, into a modern state of nominally equal citizens—and to do so in the context of near constant warfare and ethno-religious nationalisms that took hold in the Balkans and then eventually in Istanbul and Anatolia. Historians such as Benny Morris perversely deny what is so obvious about Israel: that it reflects the forcible grafting of a particular European nationalism, and a European response to European intolerance, onto a multireligious society that was located *outside* of Europe and outside the history of Western anti-Semitism.[24]

The emancipatory aspects of anticolonial Arab nationalism, similarly, were not simply false, *pace* the poet and critic Adonis, who lamented at the end of the twentieth century the failure of the Arabs to secularize and modernize.[25] Rather, anticolonialism was a product of an entangled Ottoman and Arab historical experience that made possible new forms of solidarity that brought together Muslim and Christian Arabs of different denominations. Yet, at the same time, these solidarities depended on obfuscating histories that had previously pushed Muslims and non-Muslims apart and that continued to affect the quality of the post-Ottoman ecumenical frame. Once the political project of Arab nationalism faltered badly in the late twentieth century, perhaps even fatally in our present time, Adonis and countless others have capitulated to despair, while others have turned to a chauvinistic Islamism or have clutched more strongly to a minoritarian outlook, seeking salvation from the West.

My point here is that without grappling with the meaning and implications of Ottoman Muslim imperial rule, it is difficult to reflect truly critically on the effects of Western colonialism, or of Israeli Zionism, on the region. To my mind, it is astonishing that an event such as the Damascus massacre of 1860, the largest single massacre of Christians in the Arab provinces of the Ottoman Empire across four centuries of Ottoman rule, has not been the subject of a *single* major study in Arabic. To the extent that it is acknowledged at all in Syria today, the massacre is typically described as a *haditha* (an event) and is routinely blamed on an Ottoman or Western colonial conspiracy or, at any rate, on non-Damascenes who manipulated the ignorant lower classes to commit terrible acts. More perversely, these events are also referred to as *tawshat al-nasara,* or the "hubbub of the Christians."[26] One result of this elision is the often brittle and flagrantly apologetic nature of the limited historical studies on sectarian violence and discrimination in Arabic.[27] Another result is that much of the writing of Arab history has been ceded to (better paid, equipped, and institutionally supported) academic scholars in Western academies who often answer to theoretical or historiographical debates that are totally unrelated to the concerns of the people of the region.[28]

The answer to this state of affairs is not nativism. Rather, it might be more contrapuntal reading of the sort outlined by Edward Said in *Culture and Imperialism,* "in which various themes play off one another, with only a provisional privilege being given to any particular one, yet in the resulting polyphony there is concert and order, an organized interplay that derives from the themes, not from a rigorous melodic or formal principle outside the work."[29] Indeed, the American historian Thomas Bender challenged U.S. historians "to restore some sense of strangeness, of unfamiliarity, to American historical experience." He wrote that "American historiography has become too familiar, too technical and predictable."[30] I think that the same, more or less, applies to the history of the Middle East. By relating facets of Ottoman and post-Ottoman history—that is, by putting side by side what until now have been told as entirely separate stories—we can far better appreciate, I think, the chronology, ironies, and tragedies of coexistence in the modern Middle East.

THE CHRONOLOGY OF COEXISTENCE

This book is divided into two parts. Part I takes up the Ottoman nineteenth century, in which the ecumenical frame was first constructed. Part II focuses on the post-Ottoman Arab Mashriq in the twentieth century, during the era of Western colonialism.

Chapter 1 begins with a portrait of coexistence in the Ottoman era before the nineteenth century. Unlike the clichéd description of the Ottomans as "tolerant" compared to the Christian empires of Europe that consistently persecuted Jews, it seems to me far more important to appreciate how Ottoman imperial rule distributed privileges across communities in the empire at the same time that it celebrated Muslim primacy over non-Muslims, and Ottoman supremacy over non-Ottomans. In this regard it is misleading, I think, to use the treatment of Jews as the barometer of toleration in the Ottoman Empire, as conventional scholarship on Ottoman toleration has done.[31] There was no "Jewish question" in the Ottoman world. Non-Muslim religious communities unquestionably suffered from a range of formal disabilities—from what ordinary Christians and Jews could wear, to the places of worship they could build, to the *jizya* (poll tax) they had to pay, and, above all, to an Islamic legal system that discriminated blatantly against non-Muslims. However, the ecclesiastical leaderships of these non-Muslim communities also clearly formed an auxiliary to Ottoman imperialism through the "millet system" that effectively guaranteed various Christian and Jewish communities across the empire religious and civil autonomy in return for social, fiscal, and political subordination.

Chapter 2 explains how the nineteenth century shattered the logic of a triumphalist Ottoman Muslim rule. The Ottomans had lost wars before, but they had never experienced nationalist revolts on the part of Christian subjects in the Balkans that so totally repudiated every assumption of Ottoman supremacy. Aggressive Western imperialism in the name of civilization and the protection of non-Muslims further diminished Ottoman sovereignty and forced the empire to undertake major reforms, including promulgating the principle of nondiscrimination during the Tanzimat. The chapter explores the cases of unprecedented anti-Christian sectarian violence in places such as Aleppo, Damascus, and Mount Lebanon between 1840 and 1860. It illustrates how an imperial Ottoman and European interpretation of these disparate episodes of violence legitimated a new sectarian paradigm of politics. New confessional institutional arrangements in Mount Lebanon and the Balkans signaled undemocratic, imperial commitments to religious and ethnic diversity. Crucially, however, this chapter also explores how the violence of 1860 encouraged the first coherent indigenous Arab vision of what ecumenical equality between Muslim and non-Muslim might look like in the shadow of a reforming Ottoman state.

Chapter 3 narrates the bifurcation of the Ottoman Empire between its Balkan and Anatolian north, which was convulsed by the questions of nationalism and ethnic cleansing, and the Arabic-speaking Mashriq, which witnessed no such nationalism. The first major slaughters of Armenian Christians in Anatolia occurred in the 1890s amid the rise of systematic, exclusionary, ethno-religious nationalisms in Balkan countries such as Greece and Bulgaria that spurred, in turn, the rise of a xenophobic Ottoman Turkish Muslim nationalism. In the Mashriq, however, the sectarian violence of 1860 became a catalyst for a new ecumenical sensibility rooted in a diminished, but still viable, Ottoman sovereignty. This sensibility produced a modern ideal and language of coexistence between Arabic-speaking Muslims and Christians and Jews—during a period known as the *nahda,* or "renaissance," of Arabic thought, when a new Arabic press, new professions such as journalism, and new schools and colleges were established across the Arab provinces of the empire.

This great divergence at the end of the Ottoman Empire is something scholars have never properly acknowledged, let alone bothered to explain, but for me it is a central paradox, upon which this book turns. Only by appreciating this divergence can we understand the subsequent stunning irony of a secular Turkish state whose secularism was predicated on ethnic cleansing and genocide, and the emergence of an antisectarian tradition in the Arab world that preserved a wealth of religious diversity. I do not romanticize the ecumenical Arabic nahda, for I see it as an expression of a new, highly gendered, elitist, conservative but nevertheless viable form of coexistence; it legitimated religiously segregated personal-status communities as a precondition for secular male citizenship; it acknowledged a crucial, public role for religion in cohering an elitist idea of a civilized male citizenry; and it instilled a taboo against any open discussion of the history and legacy of Islamic primacy over non-Muslims. The nahda was not in any significant sense militaristic, and still less was it tied directly to any coercive machinery of state. That was both its boon and its bane. My contention is that nahda ecumenism emerged as a counterpoint to Turkish nationalism, and that both manifested the limits and possibilities of a *modern* nationalist age.

Just at the moment of its consolidation, however, the ecumenical frame was shaken by the sudden collapse of Ottoman rule during World War I. The establishment of British and French colonial rule on the ruins of the partitioned Ottoman Empire led directly to the creation of several new Arab states and to the transplantation of Zionism into Palestine, fueled by the desire of European Jewish nationalists to build an exclusively Jewish state.

Part II takes up the post-Ottoman era. Chapter 4 introduces this era by briefly sketching the nature of British and French colonial pluralism. This was the pivotal moment immediately after World War I when the Arab world became the last place in the world to be colonized by Western empires, and yet also the first to be colonized in the name of self-determination and the protection of religious freedom. But this period also provoked contending Arab visions about how to define and structure nominally independent mandate states. I suggest that for all their obvious differences, the mandate states of Iraq, Syria, Jordan, and Lebanon drew on a common late-Ottoman ecumenical heritage. They struggled with its contradictions and largely accepted its taboos.

Chapter 5 contrasts the case of the sectarian state of Lebanon under French colonial auspices with that of the nationalist state of Iraq tied to the British Empire and focuses on how two major figures—Michel Chiha in Lebanon and Sati' al-Husri in Iraq—sought to transform very specific imaginations of coexistence between Muslim and non-Muslim into contrasting ideologies of communalism and secular nationalism. Despite major variations in their internal demographics and political systems—and quite different affiliations to European power—Egypt, Syria, Lebanon, and Iraq each embraced a secular concept of citizenship that constitutionally did not distinguish between the rights and obligations of Muslim and non-Muslim citizens. At the same time, they upheld, while also reforming and elaborating, segregated religious personal-status spheres. This dualism defined the modern ecumenical frame in the Arab East. So too did the attempts to nationalize religion as a pillar of coexistence and national unity.

Finally, chapter 6 examines the advent of British-backed colonial Zionism in Palestine that sought to transform the multireligious land of Palestine into a national Jewish state led by Ashkenazi European settlers. Significantly, Zionism germinated not in Ottoman soil but in that of a highly racialized Europe. Indeed, it was during the British mandate that the terms "Arab" and "Jew" became irreconcilable antonyms, and when the first major intercommunal Arab-Jewish violence occurred. No serious scholar today denies the *nakba* of 1948, during which hundreds of thousands of Palestinian Arabs were expelled from their homes and properties to make way for a Jewish state. My interest is to situate the nakba within the story of the ecumenical frame: to see how the Arab-Israeli conflict not only destroyed Palestinian society but also placed enormous strain and pressure on Jewish communities elsewhere, including, as Orit Bashkin has described, in Baghdad itself.[32] The eviction of hundreds of thousands of Muslim and Christian Palestinian Arabs perversely and tragically sealed the fate of Jewish communities in the Arab world. The loss of a multireligious Palestine was a terrible blow that was compounded by the end of Jewish life in most of the Arab world. The destruction of the idea that one could be simultaneously Arab and Jewish still scars the Arab world.

The epilogue to my story reflects on the Arab world after 1948. The struggle between military and civilian rule, between commitments to unity and to pluralism, between a fear of the exploitation of minorities and the reality of historical and ongoing discrimination and inequality, and between material development and democratic development vitiated the ecumenical frame. As pressures have built on this world, the inherent tensions within the ecumenical frame have revealed themselves more starkly.

A NEW AGENDA BEYOND "SECTARIANISM"

The construction of the nineteenth-century ecumenical frame was not inevitable, but it was, and remains, the deliberate work of men and women. The current and looming wars in the Arab world—whether in Iraq, Syria,

Bahrain, Saudi Arabia, or Lebanon—attest to its fragility, and yet also to its enduring importance. The nomenclature of a "sectarian" war hides more than the political, economic, and material stakes and the range of foreign interventionism that are very much at the heart of the struggle over the region. It also obscures how, over a century and a half, the scholarly gaze has constantly discovered different "age-old" conflicts—from "Muslim" and "non-Muslim" in the nineteenth century to "Arab" and "Jew" in the first half of the twentieth, to "Muslim" and "Christian" during the Lebanese Civil War to "Sunni" and "Shi'i" today—while missing the broader story of the construction and persistence of the ecumenical frame.

I do not, therefore, see it as my task in this book to explain or account for every instance of sectarian violence in the Middle East. Nor do I explore the myriad economic, material, environmental, social, urban, and kinship ties that make sectarian politics viable and meaningful in every instance. I freely admit that far more research needs to be done to put into specific context each and every sectarian act, and of course every instance of antisectarian compatriotship and solidarity that crosses, ignores, or undermines sectarian lines. Sectarianism in the modern world, after all, presupposes a political space that is contested, but also shared, by several competing religious or ethnic or other communities.

The cases I do not take up in this book (such as Hashemite Jordan) and the regions of the modern Arab world I do not delve into (such as the Gulf or the Maghreb) will undoubtedly complicate my thesis. So too will more focus on the gendered, economic, and material foundations of the ecumenical frame in labor unions and other voluntary societies that I do not adequately explore. My focus on (relatively) well-known male figures such as Butrus al-Bustani, Michel Chiha, and Sati' al-Husri is based on what I see as their constitutive role as architects and interpreters of the ecumenical frame. I do not pretend to be exhaustive. Nor does this initial work preclude future study of many other male and female figures who contributed to the story of the ecumenical frame. More knowledge of these aspects, groups, and individuals that I have not been able to cover will provide important and useful counterpoints and corrections to my conceptualization of the ecumenical frame.

What we need, nevertheless, and what I hope this book begins to offer, is a new research agenda that can explore the dialectic between sectarian animosities in whatever part of the Middle East and the now beleaguered, but nevertheless stubborn, will to coexistence on the basis of secular equality. To do this with a measure of humility, we need to always bear in mind the fact that analogous, often desperate, still unconsummated, but nevertheless ongoing struggles for equality take place across the world: in Asia, Latin America, and Africa, and also in Europe and North America.

The sectarian realities that confront the world today are products of modern forces and circumstances that also produced ecumenical and secular solidarities. Their conjoined development reflects a history that after 1856, and certainly after 1920, can no longer be thought of as purely Middle Eastern, Arab, or Islamic. Insofar as there is a story to be told about sectarianism and coexistence in the modern Middle East, it ought to humanize rather than add to the degradation of a tragic part of the world.

PART I

1 Religious Difference in an Imperial Age

Evliya Çelebi was a prolific chronicler of his seventeenth-century Ottoman world. Evliya's father was the chief goldsmith of the Ottoman court and his mother an Abkhazian slave girl. Evliya's patron was also his kinsman, Melek Ahmed Pasha, who had risen from his lowly status as a slave of the sultan to become an important statesman in a vast empire that stretched into three continents. In his *Book of Travels*, Evliya recalls how in 1640 Melek Ahmed Pasha oversaw a great victory over the "Yezidis and Bapiris, dog worshipers, worse than infidels, a band of rebels and brigands and perverts, resembling ghouls of the desert, hairy heretic Yezidi Kurds." Evliya's anecdote of slaughter of the Yezidis by the "army of Islam" is exultant. He writes that the Ottoman soldiers "invested Mt. Saçli with one heart and one mind, intent on avenging upon these Yezidi devils the blood of Imam Hüseyn and the martyrs of Kerbela, and determined to shave off the heads of all the unshorn Yezidis with their keen swords and to win booty, virgin maids and splendid boys." Modern readers brought up on a diet of stories about the implacable hostility of "Sunni" and "Shi'i" might well be confused by this description. For here was the Sunni Ottoman invoking the name of the great Shi'i martyr Husayn—the son of Caliph Ali and grandson of the Prophet Muhammad—to justify the killing of "accursed" Yezidis.[1] And here was an empire that constantly glorified Islam and yet also managed, without too much fanfare, to rule over a landscape filled with heterodox and ostensibly heretical subjects.

For centuries, all around the world, religions of all kinds had provided a vocabulary for faith and for politics. Religion legitimated empires in an age before secularism. And in the Ottoman Empire, it provided one of the most obvious and salient ways that the Ottoman state designated and discriminated between its many subjects. The sultan—the *padishah*, or king of kings—was a Muslim. He styled himself a defender of Islam. If we are to believe Ottoman chroniclers such as Evliya Çelebi, he was ever ready to annihilate unbelievers. Religion was also unquestionably important to how many Ottoman subjects viewed their world, though just how important has been a matter mostly of conjecture. Bruce Masters, a distinguished historian of the Ottoman Empire, writes in his book *Christians and Jews of the Ottoman Arab World* that "religion was at least the primary basis of identity, beyond family, clan, or gender, for members of the Muslim and non-Muslim communities alike for most of the Ottoman period."[2] But the fact of religion's importance has often gone, seamlessly and hastily, hand in hand with an assumption about the deep nature of sectarianism in the Middle East. It is as if there are some basic sectarian types that define the Ottoman landscape, each waiting to emerge, like desert locusts, to devastate the land in periodic, but inevitable, eruptions.

The Ottoman Empire was religiously diverse, and the discrimination between Muslim and non-Muslim was a defining paradigm of Ottoman rule. Even the most cursory reading of Ottoman chronicles such as the *Book of Travels* reflects a world imagined by the Ottomans to be divided between believers and infidels, and an imperial landscape marked by piety and unbelief, obedience and rebellion, benevolence and punishment. The superiority of Islam over Christianity and Judaism was a central tenet of an imperial Ottoman ideology. As Evliya's description of the extirpation of the Yezidis indicates, the empire was both multiethnic and multireligious. Since difference rather than uniformity defined Ottoman subjecthood, diversity was not something to be feared or celebrated. It was simply assumed. Evliya's writings repeatedly emphasized the importance of locality, recognizing how the diversity of foods, crafts, manners, and geography defined the social and political fabric of the empire every bit as much as its

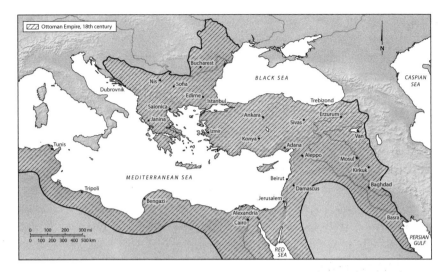

Map 1. The Ottoman Empire in the eighteenth century. (Bill Nelson Cartography).

grand administrative religious delineations. The empire is often referred to as a "mosaic" in the sense that distinct and separate religious and ethnic communities composed a whole. A tapestry might be an equally apt metaphor: the various communities were knotted together in intricate patterns whose colors occasionally bled into one another. As we shall see, the empire could fray at its edges without necessarily unraveling.

Before the nineteenth century, the idea of being Ottoman assumed being Muslim—though, until the conquest of the Arab lands in 1516–17, the majority of tax-paying Ottoman subjects were Christian. "Ottoman," in any case, was a dynastic term, not a religious one—it referred to the ruling House of Osman. Taxation without political representation was the general law of the land for most Muslim and Christian subjects. Arab, Turkish, Circassian, Bosnian, Albanian, Georgian, and Abkhazian Muslims may have been legally and ideologically privileged as Muslims, but none of these groups were politically sovereign. Sovereignty was tied to the person of the sultan, "Shadow of God over all Peoples, Sultan of the Sultans of the Arabs and the Persians"[3]—vassalage alone was universal. Being Ottoman connoted privilege, power, and authority. It implied proximity, and subordination, to the absolute sovereignty of the Ottoman sultan whose function was to preserve an Islamic empire that included large non-Muslim communities.

These communities, which included large numbers of Orthodox, Armenian, Catholic, Syrian Orthodox, Maronite, and Coptic Christians, among others, as well as Sephardic, Romaniote (Greek-speaking), Ashkenazi, and Arabic-speaking Jews, were granted religious and civil autonomy in return for their total political and fiscal subordination to the Ottomans. Local Jewish and Christian religious leaders, therefore, organized marriage and conducted funerals. They mandated the proper forms of religious ritual. They reserved for themselves the right to excommunicate and to ostracize those who strayed into heresy. These same authorities also remitted taxes to the imperial government on behalf of their respective communities. To the extent that they provided education, they did so in a parochial manner that reinforced separate communal identities.

In Ottoman eyes, Christians and Jews were defined as *dhimmis* (protected, inferior, non-Muslims) subject to Muslim law and dominion. In principle, if not always in practice, dhimmis were constrained by various explicit disabilities: from how they dressed, to the prohibition on the construction of new churches or synagogues, to the *jizya* (poll tax) they had to pay to confirm their protection by, and submission to, Islam. Legally, there were not two types of dhimmis. The empire's Islamic courts identified and categorized non-Muslims into what were presumably unchanging legal classifications that held whether one was in a court in Istanbul or a provincial court in Anatolia. Pervasive discrimination was a reality to which Christian and Jewish individuals seeking justice or redress had to adapt. Court scribes routinely emphasized this discrimination even in the manner in which they recorded the names of the litigants; they used the pejorative *walad* to denote a dhimmi and reserved *ibn* for Muslims. But these same non-Muslims nevertheless continually accessed these courts *for* justice and were allowed, indeed encouraged, to constitute themselves as autonomous communities, and these communities varied tremendously across the empire.[4]

The system of non-Muslim autonomy eventually came to be known in the nineteenth century as the millet system insofar as each religious group constituted a separate "nation" or *millet* in the empire. This system is often attributed to the Ottoman sultan Mehmed II, who conquered

Constantinople in 1453. He recognized the ecclesiastical and administrative authority of the Greek patriarch of Istanbul as paramount over all Orthodox Christians of the empire. By doing this, however, the sultan effectively elevated one patriarchate in the Orthodox Church over all others; he subsumed Slavic and—later, when the empire had expanded dramatically after the conquest of the Arab provinces in 1516 and 1517—Arab Orthodox Christians under the authority of the Greek patriarchate. He assumed a single Orthodox community where none actually existed.[5]

Much the same occurred with the establishment of the Armenian patriarchate in Istanbul in 1461. The Ottomans reportedly granted the Armenians a separate millet status in return for Armenian support during the conquest of the Arab provinces.[6] Ottoman Jewish communities also flourished in the Ottoman Empire, especially in Istanbul and in Salonika, as well as among older Middle Eastern Jewish centers in Safad, Jerusalem, Baghdad, Damascus, Aleppo, and Cairo. The absence of a single, unified Jewish religious authority in the empire accentuated the linguistic diversity of the Greek, Arabic, Ladino, Yiddish, and Spanish-speaking Jews in the empire. Other communities, like the Coptic, Syrian Orthodox, and Maronite Christians—none of which were formally recognized as separate millets—all occupied an ambiguous space within this Istanbul-centric vision of a multireligious empire. Their communities did survive, though, and—in the case of the Maronite Christians—even flourished under Ottoman rule.

For all its ambiguity, the millet system pointed to an important imperial reality. In Istanbul and other urban centers directly under Ottoman control, the ecclesiastical leaderships of non-Muslim communities became auxiliaries of Ottoman imperial rule. Both the Ottoman state and the Greek patriarchate in Istanbul, for example, were invested in the same fiction that constituted far-flung, ethnically and linguistically diverse religious communities into monolithic groups of Muslims and non-Muslims.[7]

However, the existence of different religious communities did not translate—and has never translated—axiomatically into a single communal consciousness or identity, and still less into an explicit relationship between communal identity and the right to political representation. Although both were dhimmi subjects of a Muslim state, Orthodox Christians in Crete lived in a vastly different environment than Orthodox Christians in Damascus. They spoke different languages, inhabited manifestly different cultures, were subordinated to separate administrative imperial regimes, and, above all, related in different ways to their Muslim neighbors. For the Christian minority in Damascus, the Ottoman conquest of Syria had substituted one Muslim dynasty for another; for the Orthodox Cretans, the Ottoman conquest ushered in Muslim rule of the first time, and with it an impetus to convert on a large scale. Such differentiation within a religious "nation," of course, applied just as obviously to the Muslims of the empire as to the Christians. The Ottoman Shiʻa were legally recognized as Muslims, not as specifically "Shiʻa"—a term that was hardly used by the Ottoman government. According to the leading historian of Ottoman Shiʻism, Stefan Winter, in certain instances and regions the Shiʻa were discriminated against, but they were not systematically persecuted. And as the historian Tijana Krstic has shown in her work on the early modern Ottoman Empire, the struggle to define Muslim piety and orthodoxy was a constant one.[8]

Because the Ottoman state saw itself as the legitimate successor to previous Muslim dynasties, and as a defender of the faith of Muhammad, it accepted the idea of a multireligious empire in a manner that the Spanish or Portuguese empires never did. With the exception of the occasional enthusiastic moment of empire—such as the Kadizadeli fundamentalism that swept over Istanbul following the Great Fire of 1660, or the related and equally short-lived (though much-discussed) messianism of the Jewish Shabbatai Zvi—the idea of the enduring reality of religious difference between Muslim and non-Muslim remained fundamental to how the Ottoman Empire defined itself. The historical sociologist Karen Barkey identifies this premodern Ottoman system as one in which the Ottoman state "managed" religious difference under the rubric of what she describes as *"separate, unequal and protected."*[9]

Coexistence was not an aspiration or a reflection of a secular public sphere, since no such sphere existed. Before the mid-nineteenth century, there was no elite trying to promote notions of uniform citizenship. Rather, coexistence was predicated on the deep formal inequality within *every* community of the empire and, of course, on the Muslim-dominated spaces of most cities in the empire. There was, therefore, no perceived need to celebrate coexistence. It was taken for granted at the level of everyday life; it surely informed the lives of many, if not most, of the inhabitants of the empire in myriad ways. Coexistence was evident in the urban geography of most major cities in the empire that included churches, mosques, and synagogues; it was evident in the law courts of the empire and in the markets, squares, and bazaars that defined the rhythm of life in cities such as Salonika, Istanbul, and Aleppo. The closeness of strangers— the "chaos of confessions" is how the Rome-educated Maronite patriarch Istifan Duwayhi described coexistence[10]—may have been a problem that preoccupied some religious scholars trying to figure out the proper way of maintaining purity among pollution, and overseeing religious ritual, but it was the overwhelming, unremarkable reality of the empire.

PATTERNS OF EMPIRE

The Ottoman landscape was simply too large, too variegated administratively, to describe the empire as either "tolerant" or "intolerant" *tout court*.[11] On a more regional and local level, however, patterns did emerge that defined particular experiences of toleration in different regions of the empire. In most parts of the Balkans, for example, a Christian majority remained despite several centuries of Ottoman rule. At the same time, these provinces also witnessed a far greater force of conversion from Christianity to Islam than did, for example, the Arab lands. Approximately two hundred thousand Christians from the Balkans were forcibly converted to Islam over the centuries of Ottoman rule as part of the notorious *devshirme* (or "collecting") system that inducted, or rather compelled, Christian youths into the Ottoman imperial system, made them Muslim, but also gave them opportunities to rise high, as high as the rank of grand vizier, in the service of Ottoman sultans.[12] Arabic-speaking Christians experienced nothing even remotely comparable to the devshirme.

The dynamic of Muslim rule over Christians was far more novel in the Balkans than in the Arab provinces, where Muslim rule had been the norm since at least the early eighth century, and where coexistence had existed between Muslims and non-Muslims long before the arrival of the Ottomans. Whereas the Ottoman conquest of Serbia in the fourteenth century was part of an explicit war against infidels, the Ottoman conquest of Syria in 1516 involved war against fellow Muslims, the Mamluks. The rationale for Balkan conquest was extending Muslim rule. The conquest of the Arabs was ostensibly about preserving Islam.

Some historians have focused on the treatment of the Jews as an indicator of toleration in the empire. Bernard Lewis is the most notable example, with his classic account *Jews of Islam*. Scholars have often juxtaposed the expulsion of Jews from Granada in 1492 with the toleration afforded their descendants in the Ottoman Empire. Jews were never systematically expelled by the Ottomans or the Arab medieval dynasties as they were from England, France, and Spain, and so Lewis was not necessarily wrong in his comparison between the treatment of Jews in medieval Europe and the Islamic world. But such a comparison, in and of itself, is of only limited heuristic use in surveying the landscape of toleration in the empire, because toleration was one of several strategies of rule that included coercion.

More so than any other group until the nineteenth century, those inhabitants of the eastern frontiers of the empire identified as "Kizilbash" (redheads, because of the red headgear they wore) were singled out for repeated bouts of oppression. Initially, the term was specifically associated with Turcoman subjects who allied themselves or were suspected of being in alliance with the rival imperial dynasty of the Persian Shi'i Safavids. However, the term was used to stigmatize Shi'i subjects in other parts of the empire, especially in the aftermath of the Ottoman conflict with the Safavids. When asked whether it was licit to kill the "followers of the Safavids," and whether death in battle against them constituted martyrdom, Sheykhulislam (chief jurist of the empire) Ebu's-su'ud Efendi replied, "Yes, it is a great holy war and a glorious martyrdom." More expansively, the same jurist and ideologue of Ottoman supremacy insisted that these followers were both "rebels and, from many points of view, infidels."[13]

In medieval Europe, the Cathars—or, rather, those who were subsequently labeled Cathars—were made into a main heretical community that had to be suppressed. Similarly, in the sixteenth- and seventeenth-century Ottoman Empire, those marked as Kizilbash—and, by extension, all other heterodox groups—found themselves marked by the taint of heresy.[14] It was they, not Christians or Jews more broadly, who bore the brunt of suspicion, occasional heresy trials, bouts of repression, and state terror before the nineteenth century. In November 1694, for example, the sultan ordered his governor of Tripoli to discipline a Druze leader by the name of ibn Ma'n (Fakhr al-Din al Ma'ni), saying, "If he rebels and fights you, do not hesitate to fight back and to punish him and his followers without mercy, for they are villains, accustomed to continuous trouble making and wickedness. Send their heads to my abode of felicity. Clean and purify the area of the filthy presence of the *Kızılbaş* troublemakers and villains. Exert your best efforts in this important service, as befits the Faith and my exalted state."[15]

The outwardly anti-Kizilbash ideology was built upon the basic juxtaposition of believer and infidel that had structured imperial ideology from the outset of the empire. As Stefan Winter has correctly insisted, even this evident anti-Kizilbash ideology has itself to be historicized. In Eastern Anatolia and Iraq, the Ottomans crushed signs of Kizilbash discontent in the sixteenth century, whereas in Mount Lebanon, Shi'i families were incorporated into Ottoman rule until the eighteenth century.

The mandate to persecute heretics was, in effect, routinely trumped by the exigencies of imperial rule. In his excoriation of the marginal Yezidis, the Ottoman Evliya Çelebi clearly indicated that the reason for the punitive campaign against them was not their heretical religious beliefs per se, but their raids on towns and their refusal to pay "respect" and to offer the necessary gifts that indicated their submission to imperial authority.[16] The vocabulary of heresy was potent, but it was also hyperbolic, cynical, and supremely political and tactical. It could be deployed and withdrawn, manifested or obscured by other vocabularies of tranquility and obeisance.

This last point is crucial to understanding a domain of obedience and loyalty that bound Muslim Ottomans and their non-Muslim subjects together. This domain represented a form of politics and ritual that was constantly manipulated at both ends of the imperial spectrum. Karen Barkey refers to this as "deal making" and "consensual politics" in which imperial rulers often sought to co-opt dissidents, mercenaries, and rebels within the empire in a manner fundamentally different from how they ostentatiously extirpated so-called Kizilbash as "heretics" associated with a dangerous, rival imperial power.[17]

The important point here is that the language of religious separation and segregation, with all its attendant symbolic and legal humiliation of non-Muslims, was spoken alongside other voluble languages of obedience and fealty that emphasized a common Muslim and non-Muslim submission to imperial will. Istanbul-based Greek Orthodox Phanariot families may have been "infidels" from a strictly Islamic religious perspective, but they were also active agents of Muslim empire. They were intimately allied with Ottoman Muslims, so much so that they dominated important positions in the Ottoman administration—the governorships of Wallachia and Moldavia and the offices of imperial dragoman (translator but also liaison between European envoys and the imperial court, as well as between the Orthodox patriarchate and the court) and dragoman of the fleet.[18] And when, in the early nineteenth century, the Ottoman governor in Acre, Suleyman Pasha, invested the young Christian emir Bashir Shihab with lordship over Mount Lebanon, he not only granted him a sable fur "to elevate your person over your peers and to subdue your enemies," he also overlooked the Shihab family's apostasy from Islam—for branches of the Shihab were known to have converted to Catholicism in the eighteenth century.[19] Suleyman Pasha specifically praised Bashir Shihab because he remitted imperial revenues in a timely fashion. So long as he kept control of a mountainous hinterland of the empire, and submitted unconditionally to Ottoman sovereignty, Bashir Shihab could be treated as a legitimate Ottoman vassal. His subordination to the House of Osman erased from view, if never totally from mind, the inconvenient history of a Muslim family's conversion to Christianity. The masking and unmasking of religious difference within the empire was a politics that both Ottomans and their non-Muslim and heterodox subjects and vassals often played with adroitness.

SHARED TEMPORALITY: DON'T ASK, DON'T TELL, OTTOMAN STYLE

Such pragmatism—"Don't ask, don't tell," Ottoman style—was reinforced at both ends of the imperial spectrum. Both the sultan and his representatives, as well as provincial notables and religious leaders, accepted the fiction of the permanence of Ottoman sovereignty, a sovereignty that Suleyman Pasha reminded Bashir Shihab would last "for the duration of time and ages."[20] The domain of obedience banished religious fantasies that one religion might completely overtake all others to the realm of the publicly unspoken. The so-called Kadizadeli moment of the seventeenth century, in which Muslim clerics obsessed with the end times sought to convert Jews and Christians, ran its course quickly. In Istanbul, Jewish families were forced out of certain districts around what would become the Valide Sultan mosque after the Great Fire of 1660, while in Syria and Salonika, where Jews also thrived, no such oppression manifested itself. For the preacher Vani Efendi, the leader of the Kadizadeli movement, the main impetus was to end what he saw as the transgressions of Jews and Christians rather than to extirpate or expel them from the empire.[21]

Until the nineteenth century, the idea of "improving" and "civilizing" imperial subjects per se was absent from Ottoman political thought, though assuring the security, well-being, and tranquility of tax-paying subjects and the maintenance of roads and communications were essential attributes of a legitimate ruler. There was certainly no notion of citizenship or political equality. Instead, the emphasis lay in the status quo of an Islamic order already achieved, which had to be defended and regulated.

The ecclesiastical leaderships of Christian communities, as well as most Jewish rabbis in the Ottoman Empire, subscribed to this same dynamic of protecting a status quo in a religiously diverse empire. They too divided the world into believers and unbelievers. They too warded off threats to their established pieties, and they resigned themselves to the enduring reality of religious difference, and to the inevitable proximity, if not actual intermingling, of their followers with those of different faiths. When the Jewish Shabbatai Zvi from Salonika proclaimed himself the messiah in 1648, Jewish rabbis in Izmir protested vigorously about the heretic in their midst whose enthusiastic followers had threatened to destabilize the religious, and hence social and political, order of things. In 1666, Shabbatai Zvi was brought before Sultan Murad IV. He was offered the choice of conversion to Islam or death. This choice was not dictated by a sudden Ottoman revocation of toleration of Jews (though that particular sultan's reign was especially puritanical). Rather, it was because Shabbatai Zvi had declared that 1666 was the year that would see him depose the sultan— that is, overturn the political order of things. Some Jews, two hundred to three hundred families, continued to believe in the messianism of Shabbatai Zvi and, following his example, converted to Islam. They laid the basis for a new community of Jewish converts to Islam known as the Dönme.[22]

For their part, Ottoman Christian patriarchs, bishops, and priests, far more than the laity, fought strenuously against what they regarded as the nefarious, heretical, and foreign French Catholic missionaries in eighteenth-century Aleppo. In turn, Armenian, Maronite, Greek Catholic, and Coptic patriarchs denounced American protestant missionaries on the same grounds in the nineteenth century.[23] The creation of a Catholic community in Syria, whereby the clear majority of Aleppo's Christians became Catholic—Greek Catholics or Melkites (that is, followers of the Greek rite in communion with and subordinate to Rome) and Latin Catholics—by 1750 involved an unquestionably bitter struggle between an Istanbul-centered Greek Orthodox Church, European missionaries, and Arabic-speaking Christians in the city.[24]

The notion of a single communal identity among the Orthodox was exposed by linguistic, geographic, and cultural tensions that pitted many Arabic-speaking Christians in Syria attracted to Jesuit and other Catholic missionaries against a distant, Greek-speaking clergy based in Istanbul. The Ottoman state, in any case, did not recognize the Greek Catholics as a separate millet until 1848. When their representatives in Aleppo informed the city's Ottoman governor in 1818 that they were indeed "Rum" (Orthodox) but that they were now in communion with Rome, he replied in exasperation and incomprehension, "Well, if you are not Christians, have you become Muslims or Jews? If you are still Christians, you have to be obedient to the head of the *millet-i Rum*."[25] Until the outbreak of the Greek War of Independence in 1821, the Ottomans repeatedly upheld the supreme ecclesiastical authority of the Greek patriarch in Istanbul. To flee his wrath, Greek Catholic clerics often found refuge in Mount Lebanon.

The Ottoman attitude toward intra-Christian conversions was nevertheless deeply ambivalent. On the one hand, Muslim jurists in the empire contended that "unbelief constitutes one nation."[26] They exhibited disdain for what they regarded as insignificant squabbles among unbelievers. On the other hand, Ottoman authorities remained concerned with the practical implications of conversions among Christians. They worried about social disorder and threats to tax revenue that was collected on a communal basis. They were also anxious to stem Western intrusion into their affairs and were willing to concede certain privileges to Catholic France to work with Eastern Christians, for example, to counter what they regarded as a more dangerous Russian threat.

As a result, throughout the eighteenth century, Ottoman authorities temporized when it came to foreign missionary work. They lacked a coherent strategy to deflect missionaries, in large part, because of their own disinterest toward their non-Muslim subjects. They were plied with and accepted gifts by both Orthodox and Catholic factions in Istanbul and in the provinces. On the one hand, Ottomans authorized Catholic missionary work among Orthodox, Armenian, and Coptic Christians in 1690, work that would eventually create vibrant Greek Catholic communities. They did this, in part, because the education and private beliefs of their subjects, and the religion of non-Muslims in general, was not an affair of state. On the other hand, in 1728 they reacted to the vociferous protests of the Greek Orthodox patriarch by banning European missionaries from visiting the homes of Orthodox Christians in Damascus or from teaching their children.[27] The Greek and Armenian Orthodox patriarchs were far more cognizant of the foreign European missionary danger to their spiritual and temporal authority than were Ottoman Muslims. Eastern Christian patriarchs, not Ottoman Muslim officials and jurists, constituted the first line of defense for the status quo in a multireligious Ottoman Empire.

The conversions, the subsequent ostracizing and persecution of converts, and the struggle over ecclesiastical office in Syria that ensued were certainly a form of sectarianism in the narrow sense that these actions all involved dissension within sects and the creation of new ones. Bruce Masters has described these struggles as "millet wars."[28] But these wars scarcely involved the Muslim or Jewish inhabitants of Syria. In April 1818, for example, Ottoman troops killed eleven Greek Catholics in an effort to protect the Orthodox metropolitan appointed by the Greek patriarch in Istanbul.[29] In Damascus, the following year during Ramadan, when the Orthodox patriarch of the city was allegedly accosted by Greek Catholics, the Ottoman governor dispatched his soldiers to arrest and imprison Catholics. "It was a dreadful night for the Christians of Damascus, even the Orthodox," relates the chronicler Mikhayil Mishaqa mischievously, "because the musketeers could not distinguish between a Catholic and a non-Catholic, and refused to believe anyone who told them he was of another sect, thinking it was just a ruse to escape."[30] Murder, intrigue, intimidation, bribery, and excommunication were all used in these so-called millet wars. They sharpened quite dramatically the awareness among Christians of belonging to one or another community, but these tensions did not usually entail riots or mob violence on any major scale, nor did they lead to population removal. Rather, this form of sectarianism operated primarily at two levels: a war of petitions to win the favor of Muslim judges and Ottoman authorities (and which the Catholics eventually won), and the elaboration of new notions of religious identities among Greek Catholic Arab and Armenian Catholics in Syria. Ultimately, this sectarianism amplified rather than reduced the multireligious nature of the Ottoman Empire.

The ambivalence of Ottoman authorities regarding the Greek Catholics reflected the ambiguity of the millet system itself, and a deep ambiguity in trying to classify what was "internal" to the Ottoman Empire before the nineteenth century. Borders defined the limits of the sultan's "well-protected domains." The appellation *dhimmi* or *zimmi* to describe non-Muslim subjects denoted that they were clearly subordinate to Muslim rule and subject to discrimination as a price of religious and cultural autonomy and physical security. However, because the particular set of beliefs of their Jewish and Christian subjects were not the concern of imperial authorities, foreign Catholic and Protestant missionary work among non-Muslims was routinely tolerated within the empire. The irony, of course, lay in the fact that this missionary work sought to undo both Ottoman Muslim rule and the intricate system of coexistence without equality that it legitimated. Bernard Heyberger, eminent scholar of the Catholic missionary encounters in the Ottoman Empire, insists correctly that for the Catholic Church, the notions of mission and crusade were inextricably intertwined. He refers to the *"espoirs de croisade,"* or the hopes and fantasies on the part of Catholic missionaries of reclaiming the Holy Land from Muslim rule.[31] This missionary crusade was accompanied by a Catholic obsession with purifying Eastern Christianity from the taint and influence of Islam. Far more consistently and obviously than any local Christian groups, European missionaries sought to create what they believed were pure communities in lands and landscapes that were often mixed.

In his major seventeenth-century work *Théâtre de la Turquie*, the Capuchin missionary Michel Febvre noted that there were precisely fourteen "Sects or Nations" in the Ottoman Empire, seven of which were "infidel" and seven Christian. He accompanied his enumeration of the various ethnic and religious communities in the empire with a declaration that a major problem in the empire—other than Islam itself—was its "diversity," which made it a "true Babylon of confusion." According to Febvre, the various groups hated each other but were nevertheless "mixed and mingled amongst each other."[32]

Febvre's disgust with the Ottoman Empire illustrates more than mere bias. It underscores a major difference in outlook and scale between Western missionaries and Eastern Christians. The Latin (and later Protestant) missionaries not only viewed the landscape in singularly religious terms; they acted on these views and set about trying to purify, order, and rationalize the Ottoman Empire. They wanted to descramble what they believed was an intermingled Muslim-dominated Orient. Western missionaries were overwhelmingly alien to (and alienated by) the Ottoman Empire, and their major interlocutors and patrons were all located in Europe or the United States. One could, of course, suggest that Eastern Christian priests, monks, and hermits were similarly absorbed by religion. But these figures either tended to withdraw from society or sought to manage and sustain their own communities. Western missionaries desired, above all else, to change *other* communities and societies. The vernacular Christianity of the Ottoman Empire was as foreign to the European and American missionary societies as was Islam.

My point is not that Eastern Christians of the empire were in any sense more liberal than missionaries. That notion is belied by the violent reaction of many Eastern Christian patriarchs to the missionaries themselves and to nascent Ottoman Catholic communities in the eighteenth century and Protestant ones in the nineteenth. Ottoman Christian and Jewish religious leaders consistently exploited, legitimated, and drew strength from a world without citizenship, secularism, or equality. Yet it is also true that Western missionaries generally operated on a different theological and temporal register. They were obsessed with the end of Muslim rule, as opposed to being resigned to it. There was nothing in the Orient that came close to matching the prodigious literary output in the West prophesying, proclaiming, fantasizing about, and working toward the end of Islam. For those few Jesuit or Protestant missionaries who made peace with the

Ottoman social world, such as Cornelius Van Dyck, there were many others in Europe (and the United States) who laid new plans and hatched new schemes to overturn the Ottoman order of things.

Moreover, Capuchins, Jesuits, and other Western missionaries could always—and often did—claim that they were ultimately free of politics and the social Ottoman world. They did not have to learn Ottoman, nor did they have to, until much later in the nineteenth century, communicate with Ottoman officials in the manner of urban Eastern Christian and Jewish leaders who routinely had intercourse with the Ottoman state. They were also protected by foreign consuls and by the Capitulations, treaties that initially were intended to protect European merchants in the Ottoman Empire but that by the eighteenth century were interpreted by Europeans to provide them with extraterritoriality in the Ottoman Empire. The synod convened by Jesuit missionaries in the secluded monastery of Luwayze in Mount Lebanon in 1736, during which the Maronite Church was reformed and tightly bound to Rome, or the Jesuit inquisition that the Vatican ordered against the Aleppine-born Maronite female mystic Hindiyya later in the century were striking because they suggested the complete absence of the Ottoman state in its own non-Muslim periphery.

Missionaries, in short, read the empire in *extraordinarily* sectarian terms. Whether they were Catholic or Protestant, they deployed a militant language of conquering and purifying and cleansing infidel space. They did not seek to manage or exploit religious difference as much as to abolish it altogether as part of a divinely inspired plan to reorder the world. They took advantage of Ottoman religious tolerance in order to undermine the Ottoman Empire itself. The American Protestant missionary Eli Smith acknowledged as much in a fascinating essay he published in 1840 titled "Toleration in the Turkish Empire." His point was that contrary to Western stereotypes about a ferocious Orient and Islam, missionaries actually thrived in the security afforded them by Ottoman "toleration" of Christians.[33] The crusading hopes of Catholic missionaries, and the spiritual belligerence of their Protestant counterparts, constituted a counterpoint to Ottoman religious pluralism.

By themselves, Western missionaries could describe Ottoman coexistence, name it even (*diversité* or "toleration"), but they could not substantially undermine it. The Ottomans did not name diversity, but they regulated it dynamically. The significance of the missionaries lies in their anticipation of a Western *political* will to reshape the Ottoman Empire. This will was not monolithic, but it was remarkably pervasive in the nineteenth century. The intersection of this will with the emergence of the problems of nationalism and citizenship in the Ottoman Empire led directly to the great sectarian crisis of the mid-nineteenth-century Ottoman Empire to which I shall presently turn.

The breakdown of the coherence and legitimacy of Muslim-dominated Ottoman rule was protracted. It created the space for a new politics defined largely across ethno-religious lines—a struggle for power, representation, and access to resources circumscribed by the language of civilization, nondiscrimination, and, eventually, political equality. It witnessed incessant European interventionism on behalf of the Christian subjects of the empire, the emergence of an independent Greek state in the Balkans, the birth of a new language of Ottoman nondiscrimination, and the sudden lashing out against ostensible compatriots in Syria in an era of urgent Ottoman reformation. At the same time, this great sectarian crisis consecrated something fundamentally new. The outlines of a modern culture of coexistence between Muslim and non-Muslim became visible in this same era. This culture flourished in the final decades of a waning Ottoman sovereignty—and in certain parts of the empire far more than others. Thus was the modern ecumenical frame born as the contemporary recasting of the historical diversity of the region.

2 The Crucible of Sectarian Violence

The only surviving portrait of Butrus al-Bustani is an oil on canvas said to have been painted a week before his death. It has him dressed as a proud Ottoman subject. His hair is white, and his face hints at equanimity. A red fez, or *tarbush*, adorns his head and a large Ottoman medallion is pinned to his chest. The fez and the medallion mark Bustani as living during the great Ottoman reformation known as the Tanzimat, which attempted to remake a troubled empire into a modern centralized state. The fez, worn by Muslims, Christians, and Jews alike, was a recent introduction to the wardrobe of urban Ottoman notables and bureaucrats. It obscured religious difference in an empire that had long upheld the primacy of Muslim over non-Muslim. Although there was no way to tell from this portrait the religion to which Bustani belonged, the finery of his clothing indicates that he lived in comfort.

Bustani was born in 1819 in a small village in Mount Lebanon when the sultanate was still legally and politically an empire of unequal subjects; he died in 1883 in the bustling port city of Beirut when the "sick man of Europe" (a term allegedly coined by Tsar Nicholas I of Russia) had reconstituted itself as a great and "civilized" state of nominally equal citizens. In between these two points of Bustani's life and death, the Ottoman Empire was transformed almost beyond recognition. The empire was battered by major internal upheavals and relentless colonial pressure. It went bankrupt, lost huge swaths of territory in the Balkans, and witnessed unprecedented sectarian turmoil in Bustani's homeland of Syria. But these calamitous conditions also, paradoxically, provoked entirely new ways of thinking about coexistence; indeed, they inspired a new antisectarian consciousness. They precipitated, in fact, the beginnings of the modern ecumenical frame.

Conventional histories of the nineteenth-century Ottomans tell their stories with the empire's ultimate demise very much in mind.[1] They explain the advent of separatist nationalist violence in the Balkans and the unprecedented bouts of intercommunal, sectarian violence between Muslim and Christian subjects in the Levant between 1840 and 1860 as testaments to Ottoman decline, and to the crisis of sovereignty that, allegedly, fatally and inevitably undermined the great premodern multiethnic and multireligious empire. They cast probing light on the machinations of great-power diplomacy and European imperialism that continually encroached upon Ottoman territorial integrity. And they do this within a singularly narrow and unimaginative interpretive prism that has, in effect, naturalized sectarianism in the Middle East. For far too long, violence that pitted Muslim against Christian Ottoman subjects has been regarded as evidence of the irrepressible reality of notionally ancient religious and ethnic differences. Whereas the West is assumed to be essentially and unproblematically secular, the Middle East is depicted as a region where an angry God and his zealous partisans were (and are still) very much alive. This, at least, is what we are encouraged to believe.

But this conventional view skips over two crucial points. The first is that the nineteenth century was as much a laboratory for new ways of thinking about coexistence as it was the setting for intercommunal violence and separatist nationalisms. The idea of Muslim-Christian coexistence, and the particular ecumenical frame that it legitimated, found evocative expression in the Ottoman lands more than anywhere else in the world. The second point is that the crisis of sovereignty that afflicted the empire did not necessarily have to end in the empire's demise. While the Russian and Austro-Hungarian empires collapsed during World War I, the American, British, and French empires did not. And yet each of these multiethnic and multireligious empires was riven by urgent and vexed questions about the nature of religious difference, political equality, citizenship, and subjecthood. In fact, in the case of the United States, the massive crisis over the question of slavery was contemporaneous with the Ottoman sectarian crisis that engrossed the empire in 1860.

This chapter narrates how and why, under the threat of internal rebellions and external threats, the Ottoman sultanate embarked on an urgent set of political, legal, and administrative Tanzimat reforms between 1839 and 1876. The introduction of the discourse of political equality in the empire did not stem from an internally initiated debate about the immorality of discrimination against non-Muslims. Rather, it stemmed from the imperative to resuscitate a faltering empire. It occurred amid aggressive European claims to intervene on behalf of the Christians of the Orient. In a desperate bid to appease circling European powers, the Tanzimat had as its core mantra the declaration of nondiscrimination between Muslim and non-Muslim subjects of the empire.

The Tanzimat, in truth, represented the advent of a profoundly ambiguous new political culture that valorized national unity at the same time that it repudiated religious "fanaticism," but it did so in different ways and with different effects across the empire—some of which actually sharpened, rather than moderated, the problem of religious difference. Indeed, the Ottoman crisis of sovereignty and European intervention produced competing ways of organizing coexistence in the diminished empire. In some regions, like the provinces that would become the independent Greek state, European intervention in the 1820s was highly militarized, and Ottoman rule was violently overthrown. In other parts of the empire, such as Samos and Mount Lebanon, the nineteenth century witnessed the elaboration of new sectarian quota systems mediated by European interference that continually undercut, without actually abolishing, Ottoman sovereignty. By far the most famous of these quota systems, but by no means the only one, was established after the outbreak of an intercommunal war in Mount Lebanon in 1860 and the eruption of the single largest anti-Christian urban riot in the Arab provinces during the entirety of Ottoman rule, namely the Damascus massacre of July 1860. The so-called Règlement Organique of 1861 created the autonomous region, or Mutasarrifiyya, of Mount Lebanon. It distributed administrative posts along notionally equitable confessional lines under a nonnative Ottoman Christian governor.

The second part of this chapter, therefore, examines how the violence of 1860 gave birth to radically different interpretations of the meaning of sectarian violence and the nature of religiosity in the Ottoman Empire. The imperial European-Ottoman deliberations that led to the concoction of the Mutasarrifiyya enshrined a rigid and highly politicized form of coexistence organized along explicitly sectarian lines in the name of equity and good government. In this moment, Bustani issued the earliest anti-sectarian call for compatriotship between Muslim and non-Muslim subjects. In a series of eleven anonymous pamphlets signed by a "patriot" and printed between November 1860 and March 1861, Bustani imagined a very different kind of nation than anything most of his contemporaries, European diplomats or Ottoman overlords, would have contemplated.

The contrast between the imperial machinations of high politics and Bustani's individual overture encapsulated precisely what was at stake in the divergent *modern* interpretations of what, after all, were highly localized and contingent episodes of sectarian violence. I cannot claim, obviously, that Bustani's plea for an enlightened citizenship—and it was a plea—was more important than the administrative structures that sought to reconcile a notion of equity with the exigencies and compromises of diplomacy and power. But I do think that his desperate printed appeals illustrated how the idea of ecumenical equality was the product of its Ottoman moment. It was not an act of ventriloquizing an abstract Western secularism. Rather, it was a creative act of conscious, critical affiliation that was as locally rooted, and as foreign from the Ottoman past, as were the extreme sectarian affiliations that hemmed it in. Its importance lay not in its ultimate effect but in its very existence.

That Bustani was a Protestant convert who deliberately cast himself apart from the communal currents, and from the actual politics of Mount Lebanon, rendered him at one level a marginal figure. Like many other individuals before and after him, he was shaped by trauma, and like a small minority among them, he refused to succumb to its darkest implications. In this he was perhaps exceptional—and in his call for the separation of religion and statecraft in the Middle East, he was perhaps a "pioneer," in the language of older scholarship. But his importance does not lie in his being a prophet or a pioneer. It lies in how he *became* emblematic of an entire generation of Arabic-speaking intellectuals who could take for granted that Muslim and non-Muslim compatriots could and should be equal. He was, in effect, part of the stunning story that has been systematically overlooked in the conventional historiography of sectarianism: the story of how the crisis of Ottoman sovereignty and the sectarian mayhem of 1860 actually inspired the nascent ecumenical frame.

THE GREEK WAR AND THE DIMINISHMENT OF OTTOMAN SOVEREIGNTY

The violence of the Greek war of independence fought between 1821 and 1829 shattered the fiction of an everlasting imperial sultanate. The Greek insurrectionaries, fighting for what they called the "Motherland" and the "Cross," indiscriminately attacked Muslims whose presence was equated with Ottoman sovereignty.[2] In Tripolitsa in October 1821, for example, they massacred several thousand Muslims and Jews. Muslims were also slaughtered in Athens in 1822.[3] The overwhelming majority of the fifty thousand Muslims who inhabited the Peloponnese at the beginning of the war were forced to leave by its end.[4] The object of massacres like those in Tripolitsa, however, was hardly religious, that is to say hardly doctrinal. Nor was the object punitive. These moments of gross violations did not represent *punctuations* of an otherwise stable system of coexistence. Rather, they were political insofar as the war embodied an imagination of newly liberated Greece, or at any rate of its political future, emptied as much as possible of Muslims. They defined the beginnings of a pattern in which the triumph of cobbled-together Balkan Christian nationalism was routinely, if not axiomatically, intertwined with the flight or expulsion of Muslims from liberated territory. The extirpation of Muslims in the Peloponnese paved the way for a new nationalist imagination in the region that stood in stark opposition to the religious tolerance enforced by the Ottoman imperial order. Whatever the raw passions displayed, religious passion—if this is what various acts of killing actually represented—was clearly in the service of the political and not the other way around. As Paschalis Kitromilides has put it, the emerging Greek state gradually constructed the nation.[5] The problem of coexistence that had been managed by the Ottomans was apparently resolved by the modern Greeks: exit the Muslims; religion was nationalized; neo-Hellenism cannibalized Orthodoxy.[6]

The Ottomans recoiled in fury at the blatant Greek challenge to their imperial might. Initially, Sultan Mahmud II could not fathom the idea of Greek liberation. Instead, he and his government insisted on viewing the Greeks within preconceived paradigms of the contemptible "infidels" in rebellion against the Ottoman "state of Muhammad" (*devlet-i Muhammediye*).[7] Incredulity was quickly followed by savage retribution and the scapegoating of the Orthodox Christians in Istanbul itself. The state-sanctioned persecution of Greeks in Istanbul during 1821 pointed to the breakdown of the Ottoman imperial system rather than its affirmation. The chief jurisconsult of the empire, the head of the *ulema* (religious and legal scholars) in Istanbul, for example, refused to sanction the indiscriminate persecution of Greeks because he believed that such persecution violated Islamic law. He was duly exiled and replaced by a more pliant creature of the sultan.

An atmosphere of terror pervaded the capital as Janissaries, and Muslims as a whole, were encouraged to demonstrate their zeal by arming themselves and fighting "infidels." Hundreds of Greeks of all classes were hunted down and murdered in the streets of Istanbul.[8] The Greek Patriarch Gregory V was held responsible for the rebellion. He was formally deposed and hanged. The Ottomans accused him of failing to control his flock and therefore failing in his primary duty as the Christian eyes and ears of the Muslim state. He was executed not because he was an infidel, but because he was a *hain* (traitor). He allegedly betrayed the empire of which he had been a fundamental part.[9]

The patriarch was put to death on Easter Sunday, and his body was left hanging in public for three days as a warning to all Greeks of the dire consequences of rebellion. The patriarch's body was allegedly delivered to Jewish subjects before it was dumped in the waters of the Golden Horn. There could be no more dramatic demonstration of the ideology of Ottoman Muslim supremacy that justified the old regime than the hanging of a Christian patriarch on Easter Sunday. But there was also no greater departure from its general tenor. The persecution of Greeks continued between April and December 1821. In June, the town of Ayvalık was burned to the ground, its male inhabitants massacred and its women and children sold into slavery. The massacre of Chios in the spring of 1822 commanded headlines in Europe. The reports of plunder and massacre issued by Ottoman commanders in Greece, meanwhile, which spoke of "booty and slaves in quantities never seen and heard of before," read very much like the triumphalist account of the killing of Yezidi Kurds by the seventeenth-century Ottoman chronicler Evliya Çelebi referred to in the previous chapter.[10]

Yet the old order, and the form of unequal coexistence that it had nurtured, could not be sustained. As much as the purpose of this imperial terror was to humiliate the Greeks, its goal was not to eradicate dhimmis more generally but to compel them back into a state of subjecthood. Even following the naval battle of Navarino in 1827 that ended any Ottoman hope of pacifying the Greeks, the Ottomans refused to take seriously the idea of a Greek revolution. They rejected as "unspeakable nonsense" the notion that there could be such a thing as a "Greek government."[11] Indeed, Greek resistance in the face of punitive expeditions exasperated Sultan Mahmud II. It was irrational to him because the Greek rebels refused to play the traditional game of Ottoman politics and rejected Muslim sovereignty totally. The sultan demanded the restoration of a world turned on its head by revolution; he wanted to compel back into the domain of obedience the Greek Christian subjects of the empire who had dared to usurp the place of Muslims. Hence, neither Jews nor Armenians nor Arab Christians were persecuted in this period, though restrictions were placed on non-Muslims in coastal towns across the empire.[12]

The Ottomans were not present at the London Conference of 1832 where the fate of the Greek rebellion was decided by Britain, France, and Russia. The Ottomans were adamant that the Greek question was an internal problem, not an international question. However, when the European powers recognized a Greek kingdom headed by a nonnative Christian prince (and, in the event, a Bavarian Catholic), the breach of Ottoman sovereignty was formalized. The Ottoman Empire acknowledged its defeat when it recognized the new Greek kingdom a year later. Henceforth, the survival of the sultanate depended as much on European policies as on Ottoman agency.[13] Christian subjects across the Balkans, moreover, recognized the potential efficacy of appealing to European Christian sympathy;

and the Ottoman state understood, more urgently than it ever had, the need for an overhaul of the empire in order to save the substantial parts of it that remained.

THE TANZIMAT AS A NEW SECTARIAN QUESTION

In one sense, the Greek war internationalized Ottoman politics, as historian Christine Philliou has argued.[14] The politicization of Christian subjects of the empire either as objects of European intervention, as potential rebels, or as wards of a reforming Ottoman state was the inaugural moment of a new sectarian question in the East. The initial impetus for Ottoman reform, however, had little to do with the condition of its Christian subjects. Rather, the imperative was squarely a military and fiscal one. The famous Janissary regiments, for example, were abolished in 1826; several thousand Janissaries, in fact, were massacred in an attempt to break the back of the old military order. Dress codes were also reformulated in 1829. In a bid to reassert his imperial authority over his sprawling empire, Sultan Mahmud II made the plain fez compulsory for various ranks of Ottoman officials and distinguished them from the equally new cloth-wrapped fez that his new army, the Victorious Muslim Soldiers, wore during the latter stages of the Greek war.[15]

The Ottomans also kept a close eye on the military and economic reforms initiated by their erstwhile governor of Egypt, Mehmed (Muhammad) Ali, who had initially been dispatched to Egypt in the aftermath of Napoleon's invasion of the province in 1798. His conscripted soldiers had been instrumental in Ottoman attempts to retake the Peloponnese and to pacify Arabia. But Mehmed Ali turned on his Ottoman sovereign by invading and occupying Palestine and Syria in 1831. Had it not been for Russian intervention at the time, he would very likely have overthrown the Ottoman sultanate. In 1838, in return for their assistance to the beleaguered sultan, the British coaxed the Ottoman government into acceding to a free-trade agreement that privileged British manufactures. This increased pressure on textile workers across the Ottoman Empire.[16]

Mahmud II died in July 1839, just as his sultanate was again under threat from Mehmed Ali of Egypt. In return for its crucial military and diplomatic assistance to prop up the sultanate, Britain immediately pressured the new sultan, Abdülmecid, to "ameliorate" the conditions of Christian subjects in the empire. At Gülhane Park in Istanbul in early November 1839, the young sultan accordingly announced before European ambassadors and high-ranking Ottoman officials the first of a series of major reform decrees that together constituted the Tanzimat. These included the abolition of the discriminatory *jizya* (poll tax) in 1855 and the major promulgation in 1856 known as the Islahat Fermani.

Issued under tremendous British pressure in the midst of the Crimean War, the Islahat Fermani explicitly declared the equality of all subjects in the eyes of the sultan. The Ottoman ruler pledged that "every distinction or designation pending to make any class whatever of the subjects of my empire inferior to another class, on account of their religion, language, or race, shall forever be effaced from administrative protocol." The sultan also announced that all public employment was open to all groups; that all laws were to be redrawn to conform to the principles of communal equality; that the tax burden of empire was to fall equally on Muslims and non-Muslims; and that the "heads of each community" were to attend, participate in, and vote in meetings of a newly established Supreme Council of Justice, on questions affecting the "generality of the subjects of my empire."[17]

Equivocation and ambiguity were at the heart of the Tanzimat. The sultan's immediate concern was pacifying and appeasing foreign powers. Yet the object of the decrees was his vast and disparate subject population. The Tanzimat reforms were couched in language of total sovereignty, but in their timing, content, and concessions they actually underscored Ottoman dependency on Britain. They affirmed the secularizing intent of the state but were justified as consistent with the sharia. Scholars of the Ottoman Empire have suggested both Western and Islamic roots for this edict, but the question of the precise provenance obscures a more important point.[18] The Tanzimat reflected a coercive and defensive modernization project that was formulated as an engagement with, and response to, parallel and rival European imperial projects and, to a lesser extent, Balkan national projects. Toleration of non-Muslims, which had long been a sign of Ottoman Muslim primacy, now became a sign of Ottoman Muslim coevalness with modern European statecraft and "civilization."

As strongly as the Tanzimat reforms emphasized nondiscrimination and civilizational parity with Europe, they quite clearly also rejected a new democratic social or political contract with the empire's own subject population. The Tanzimat did not intend or imply the granting of any political rights to the empire's subjects. Not until 1876, amid yet another international crisis in the Balkans, were any of them declared to be citizens. The Tanzimat mandated, in effect, the equality of inequality of all communities before a theoretically absolutist sultan. The mid-century Ottoman state was not an emancipatory state; rather, it launched a new authoritarianism that sought to catch up to what Ottoman officials recognized as Western material, economic, political, military, and educational superiority. The new imperial discourse of nondiscrimination corresponded with European imperial penetration that habitually favored—at least at the level of rhetoric—the Christians of the empire. Muslim subjects initially gained little except more conscription, a higher tax burden, more foreign missionaries and foreign missionary schools (there was no comprehensive Ottoman educational system stipulated until the 1870s), and less economic security.[19]

No major reformation of the ideological basis of any society occurs without controversy or complications. The Ottomans attempted to co-opt their erstwhile Christian dhimmi subjects into a new "civilized" and secularized Ottoman sovereignty, and in the process to invent, piecemeal, a new secular sense of being Ottoman; European powers, however, beckoned these same Christians to join transnational systems of sectarian patronage and dependency by marking them as objects of their solicitude. Whether as objects of imperial concessions by an ostensibly benevolent sultan, or of concern and protection by European powers, the non-Muslim communities were set apart from the Muslim subjects of the empire.

This new coexistence was rooted far less in a clear commitment to secular equality than in a set of exceptions that consistently and pervasively distinguished between Muslim and Christian in the empire. Christian subjects were not to be discriminated against, they were to maintain their "ancient" privileges while Muslims had to forgo theirs, and they were to become ever more the object and pretext for a European curtailment of Ottoman sovereignty. The April 1856 Treaty of Paris that concluded the Crimean War made the well-being of the "Christian population of [the sultan's] empire" a barometer of Ottoman progress.[20] Muslim subjects were no longer ideologically privileged in the eyes of the sultan by virtue of their Islamic faith, and yet at the same time were not singled out for protection or alleged solicitude by European powers because they *were* Muslim. The Ottoman abandonment of a centuries-old system of legal and ideological discrimination was a drastic measure, not a democratic one. Imperial fiat appeared to turn its back on a symbolic language of Islamic primacy. However abstract or remote from the actual lived experience of the tens of millions of its diverse Muslim population, the overt language of primacy had nevertheless long legitimated Ottoman imperial rule and defined the social, political, and legal contours of a vibrant multireligious empire.

EPISODES OF SECTARIAN VIOLENCE, 1841–1860

Unprecedented sectarian violence between Muslim and non-Muslim subjects marked the breakdown of Ottoman order in the mid-nineteenth-century Levant. In Aleppo in 1850, an anti-conscription riot left twenty Christians dead, and six churches, thirty-six shops, and 688 homes damaged or destroyed. A decade later, across three days in July 1860, mobs in Damascus rampaged through the Christian quarter of Bab Tuma following the arrest of Muslim boys who had been drawing crosses on the streets of the city. European consular and missionary sources estimated that approximately three thousand Christians were slaughtered; eleven churches and three convents belonging to Franciscan, Lazarist, Capuchin, Maronite, Greek Catholic, Greek Orthodox, Armenian Orthodox, and Syrian Orthodox communities were plundered; European chancelleries were attacked; and some fifteen hundred homes were looted. The Damascus massacre constituted the single largest anti-Christian riot to occur in any Arab city during four centuries of Ottoman rule.[21]

This mid-century crisis in the empire's major urban centers in Syria was magnified by serious bouts of intercommunal fighting between Maronite Christian and Druze villagers that had erupted across Mount Lebanon in 1841, 1845, and 1860. These, in turn, ended in the burning and plunder of hundreds of villages, the creation of thousands of refugees, and, ultimately, an all-out war in June 1860 that led to the massacre of Christian males in four principal towns: Dayr al-Qamar, Hasbayya, Rashayya, and Zahle. Taken together, the events of 1860 in Mount Lebanon and Damascus invited yet more European interference in Ottoman affairs in the name of providing succor to the Christian victims of the turmoil. Interventionism on behalf of Christians that had begun during the Greek war of independence had now become a European habit.

The crisis of Ottoman order in Syria reflected the significant discrepancy between a Tanzimat language of nondiscrimination and a historical reality of discrimination, just as antiblack or anti-Catholic riots in the United States, or anti-Jewish sentiment and action in parts of Europe, indicated analogous problems within a global nineteenth-century discourse of citizenship and equality. Bruce Masters draws a direct parallel between white reactions to "uppity" blacks during the Jim Crow era in the United States and Muslim resentment of Christians in Syria.[22] But Muslims were not of one outlook, and the sectarian violence was not of one kind. It was not even primarily religious in nature: class, ethnicity, region, political economy, Ottoman policy, and foreign intervention, as much as the reality of religious difference itself, played their part in provoking the conflagrations that reverberated across the mid-nineteenth-century Levant.

In Aleppo, for example, Jews were not attacked at all, Muslim neighbors or friends intervened to save many Christians, and, perhaps most important, the actual spark for the riot that occurred during 'Id al-Adha (the Islamic feast to commemorate Ibrahim's willingness to sacrifice his son and thus submit to God's will) had nothing to do with the Christian communities of Aleppo, but rather had to do with resistance to the imperial order for conscription and new taxes that would have fallen most heavily on the Muslim lower classes of Aleppo. The first place attacked by the Aleppine rioters was the government barracks. They also attacked the homes of wealthy Muslims *before* they turned on the homes of Christians in the city's suburbs. The rioters demanded first and foremost the rescinding of conscription orders and the dismissal of the unpopular chief of police. They also, secondarily, demanded that Christians "must not ring bells nor carry crosses in processions" or "employ [black] Muslim slaves, male or female."[23] The rebels scapegoated Christians because they had become the most obvious symbol of the new Europe-oriented Ottoman order of things. The city boasted wealthy Christian merchants and a new monumental Catholic church that had been completed in 1843. In 1849, every major Christian sect in the city engaged in construction work in churches after the Ottoman sultan authorized such work without requiring local permission. At the same time, the Muslim inhabitants of the city were exposed to new material demands of conscription.[24]

In Mount Lebanon, moreover, the nature of the fighting was from its outset deeply colored by competing religious vocabularies; by a struggle over resources, land, and status; and, most of all, by conflicting interpretations about the meaning of a European-mediated Tanzimat. The violence across sectarian lines was often matched by open struggles within the competing sects themselves. Thus, the major uprising of Christian peasants in 1858–59 that precipitated the war of 1860 was initially directed against their Christian feudal lords.[25] In the case of Damascus in 1860, a general pattern of Muslim financial indebtedness to Christians and the significance of the destruction of many Christian-owned looms by the rioters underscored the nature of economic dislocation of craftsmen that may well have been a factor in the riot.[26] Equally significant was the fact that the Russian, French, Austrian, Belgian, and American consulates were attacked and that foreign missions and missionaries were targeted as well.[27] The British and Prussian consulates located outside the Christian quarter were not attacked. And, as was the case in Aleppo a decade earlier, many Muslims often helped Christians escape from the fury of the anti-Christian mob, hid them in their houses, and took to the streets to curb the bloodletting.[28]

What interests me here about these sanguinary episodes, in any case, is less their details than how they unfolded at precisely the moment of transition from a premodern Ottoman Muslim imperial culture to a modern imperial culture based on the mantra of nondiscrimination. This transition was defined—and distorted—by European interventionism. This was the period, in other words, when coexistence among Muslims and Christians was first identified as a problem that had to be managed, contained, and manipulated for contending Ottoman and European imperial ends. Indeed, what most interests me is how, in reaction to the sectarian violence, the rival European powers and the reforming Ottoman sultanate built a new political order in Mount Lebanon that distinguished it from the rest of Syria, and also from the separatist nationalist example of Greece.

The Tanzimat saw certain areas of the empire, and their Muslim populations, subjected to the often brutal, direct, and largely unmediated Ottoman authority, while other areas such as Mount Lebanon, because of its Christian population, saw the authority of the Ottoman state hemmed in by the European powers.[29] Aleppo was subjected to draconian state violence in the name of a reinvigorated central Ottoman authority in 1850 that left, according to Ottoman reports cited by Masters, nearly thirty-four hundred "rebels" dead (a figure that, if true, vastly exceeds the number of those killed in the riots and yet is routinely passed over by historians obsessed with sectarianism). Meanwhile, rural and heterodox Mount Lebanon, which had always lain at the fringes of Ottoman imperial imagination, but which had long been a hub for European and American religious missions and was dotted by monasteries and churches, was inexorably pulled away from direct Ottoman authority.[30]

INTERPRETING SECTARIANISM IN 1860

On July 17, 1860, the Ottoman Empire's minister of foreign affairs and one of the luminaries of the Tanzimat, Fuad Pasha, arrived in Syria accompanied by an Ottoman army.[31] Fuad Pasha announced to the people of Syria that the violence of 1860 had shocked "the public conscience of the civilized world." He blamed Muslim Damascene elites for not doing enough to restrain the "ignorant" Muslim inhabitants of their city and for sullying the image of Islam and the Ottoman state. He told his troops that the sultan cared deeply for all his subjects and, repeating one of the central refrains of the Tanzimat, insisted that, "without exception," all imperial subjects are your "compatriots."[32]

Fuad Pasha then meted out terror. He authorized the hanging and mass shooting, on August 20, of 167 Muslims—mainly from the lower classes—deemed culpable in the city's riots. He imprisoned and exiled many more. He also oversaw the banishment or execution of senior local Ottoman officials because of the massacres, and levied a massive fine on the city's Muslim population. Although an extraordinary Ottoman military tribunal sentenced the Druze feudal lords of Mount Lebanon to death for their alleged roles in the intercommunal violence, their sentences were not carried out due to British pressure. No Maronite Christian leader in Mount Lebanon was tried.[33]

Fuad Pasha's draconian measures in Damascus notwithstanding, France deployed its own army to the Levant to "assist" the sultan in restoring order. More significantly, an international commission was established to investigate the causes of the violence in Syria and to recommend appropriate disciplinary and political measures in its aftermath. The commission was made up of Ottoman, British, French, Austrian, Russian, and Prussian representatives. It convened for fifty-one sessions between October 5, 1860, and April 23, 1862.[34]

The legal basis for the commission was dubious at best. Its fundamental assumption was that a peculiar outrage in a non-European part of the world had to be investigated.[35] No such international commission was established to look into the appalling treatment of blacks or Native Americans in the United States, or the violence perpetrated against Indians by the British Empire, or the violence against Algerians by the French in Algeria or, a little later, by Russians against Poles. Unlike the Conference of London of the early 1830s that had arrived at a settlement for the Greek state and from which the Ottomans had been absent, now they actively participated in formulating a "civilized" response to the violence in their own periphery. At the same time, the creation of the international commission in Beirut confirmed the degree to which Europe had become a fundamental, and from an Ottoman standpoint disturbing, point of reference in its sovereign space.

The Ottomans needed to appease European powers far more than they needed to legitimate the Tanzimat to the inhabitants of Syria. Fuad Pasha and his Armenian Christian deputy, Abro Efendi, used the language of conciliation, reason, rule of law, equality, and courtesy with European commissioners. Toward Ottoman subjects, Fuad Pasha contented himself with a strict paternalism. Dialogue was reserved by Tanzimat statesmen for what they publicly described as "friendly" Christian European powers, not because they trusted these powers—far from it—but because they feared and sought to emulate them.

The upshot was that Mount Lebanon became a center of the "Eastern Question" and a laboratory for producing a new, imperially managed model of coexistence between mostly heterodox Muslims and non-

Muslims within a diminished Ottoman sovereignty. Beirut, not Damascus, was the primary location of the extraordinary commission. Mount Lebanon, not Syria, was its principal concern in articulating a post-1860 regime. There, European and Ottoman representatives concocted the most famous and ostensibly equitable sectarian quota system in the name of nondiscrimination. They regarded this quota system as the best mechanism for stabilizing an area of the empire that had a significant Christian population that mattered to Europe. In putting together this sectarian quota system, the European powers borrowed on prior experiments in places such as the Aegean island of Samos that had been governed after 1832 by a nonnative Christian prince. They also drew on their prior interventions in Mount Lebanon dating back to 1840.[36]

However, unlike Samos, where the overwhelming majority of the population was Orthodox Christian, or Serbia, or other parts of the Balkans that remained under nominal Ottoman sovereignty in this period, Mount Lebanon was far more religiously heterogeneous. It became, therefore, *the* paradigmatic case for a new discourse of communally adjudicated and defined coexistence. But as with Samos, European powers and the Ottoman state viewed Mount Lebanon as a place gripped by age-old tribal solidarities and irreligious fanaticism that had to be pacified from above. They took a dim view of the possibilities and viability of native agency. As much as they understood the need to break with the overtly discriminatory Islamic imperial past, both the Ottoman state and the meddling European powers rejected out of hand the principle that secular Ottoman subjects were actual citizens endowed with rights or the capacity for critical consciousness. The most they were willing to concede is that they were subjects whose communal interests had to be represented equitably and by their respective elites. Mirroring its imperial framers, the sectarian quota system was deliberately designed to be antidemocratic and conservative.

For the European powers, the secular Ottomanism of the Tanzimat (unlike, say, secular Americanism, French nationalism, or a sense of Englishness) was a chimera, if not a travesty. In European eyes, the violence of 1860 confirmed that Ottoman reform, and the Ottoman Empire itself, required European tutelage.[37] For the Ottoman state, on the other hand, the vaguely defined secular Ottomanism of the Tanzimat was a vehicle through which to maintain imperial hegemony, to subordinate all in the name of a nondiscriminatory but also antidemocratic Ottomanism, and to privilege the state over any of its constituent communities, including, of course, its many Muslim and Christian communities.

The commission's deliberations were marked by compromises. The imperative was to find an acceptable solution that the various powers could agree to and that the Ottoman state could formally accept. At first, the commissioners toyed with the idea of outright partition. They echoed the logic of the infamous British ambassador to Istanbul, Stratford Canning, who in 1843 had confessed that "to draw a geographical line between the respective masses of the Druse and Maronite population" represented the "least objectionable" approach to the problem of coexistence.[38] This partition had proved unworkable because the actual human geography of Mount Lebanon did not mirror Canning's imperial and sectarian view of it. Far too many villagers and townsmen of different faiths lived in close proximity, and partition, in any case, left no clear sense about who was ultimately meant to represent Christians and Druzes and on what grounds, nor did it propose to reconcile established privileges of social standing and rank with newer vocabularies of sectarian rights.

In 1860, nevertheless, the majority of the commissioners, including Fuad Pasha, initially regarded the necessity of a partition along "ethnic" lines as a reasonable solution to the problem of Mount Lebanon's religious diversity. The words in the official French-language record of the tribunal were *separation ethnographique* and *désagrégation*.[39] The terms suggested the obvious: to make a sectarian order required unmaking the previous social order in which families and communities had never been defined and classified along purely sectarian lines.

On March 21, 1861, the commissioners debated a forty-seven-point partition plan for Mount Lebanon. The first article of the plan stated "the principle of partition between Christians and Druze on an ethnic basis"; it was followed immediately by the assertion that "in implementing partition, the interests of all sects will be respected equally." That Druzes and Maronites belonged to the same ethnicity and spoke the same language was beside the point. The commission saw what it wanted to see: a ruined landscape in Mount Lebanon inhabited by what it regarded as essentially hostile sects incapable of coexisting without foreign intervention. The recent internecine wars framed the past; they became the principal perspective for imperial deliberations about the future of Mount Lebanon. The fact that Maronite and Druze villagers had coexisted, and that their elites had jointly benefited from an intricate, hierarchical, and nonsectarian social order during the previous three centuries of Ottoman rule, was ignored.

The crucial point is that the commission debated *other* people's futures in a manner that anticipated subsequent and much larger partition schemes such as the 1947 United Nations Special Committee on Palestine. It spoke about the Maronites and the Druzes as if these had always constituted, and thus must always constitute, separate political communities. The French commissioner, at least, reminded his colleagues that the principle of partition had already been tried in 1842 and had proved a failure. Largely because of his objections, in fact, the other commissioners ruled out "ethnic" partition. Yet his own counterproposal to create a single "Christian" government with unspecified guarantees for "minorities" did not garner support.[40] The commissioners could not agree on how to divide Mount Lebanon in a way that would satisfy each of the Great Powers. They hammered out, instead, a blueprint for a new government that rejected the principle of partition and adopted the principle of communal parity. Throughout these negotiations, they did not bother to consult formally with the inhabitants of Mount Lebanon.

In June 1861, representatives of the Ottoman state and European powers unveiled in Istanbul their so-called Règlement Organique for Mount Lebanon. Although it was invoked in the name of the sovereign will of the Ottoman sultan, the special autonomous regime of Mount Lebanon was, in reality, the product of an international protocol. This protocol called, for the very first time, for a "Christian governor" of non-Lebanese origin to rule Mount Lebanon, just as Samos had previously been placed under the control of a high-ranking Ottoman Greek Phanariot. The very term "Règlement Organique" placed Mount Lebanon within a genealogy of European-mediated regulatory regimes in the Ottoman Empire. Although these regimes underscored the European view that unfettered "Muslim" rule over Christians was unacceptable and illegitimate, they were primarily focused on pacifying what the imperial powers regarded as troublesome Christian-inhabited districts and regions. Formal Ottoman sovereignty was retained in order to stave off a potentially destabilizing "balkanization" of the Ottoman Empire. The autonomy of Samos and Crete in 1830 and the Règlement Organique instituted for Moldavia and Wallachia in 1834 were designed as alternatives to outright independence. They represented expedient sectarian fixes to hold together the "sick man of Europe," not to lead to its revitalization.

The great difference from the Balkan regions that had hitherto preoccupied Europe lay in the fact that Mount Lebanon's specific *règlement* constituted a showpiece of the ostensibly nondiscriminatory ethos of the Tanzimat. The first article of the Règlement Organique declared that "constitutive elements of the population shall be represented before the Governor by an Agent appointed by the chiefs and notables of each community." A Central Administrative Council charged with assessing taxes and administering revenues was to be made up of twelve members chosen by the heads of their respective communities: "two Maronites, two Druzes, two Greek Orthodox, two Greek Catholic, two Matawilah [Shi'i], and two [Sunni] Muslims." Article 6 spelled out even more clearly how much of a break with tradition this sectarian system was. "[There shall be] equality of all before the law; all feudal privileges ... are abolished." A Higher Judicial Council, also made up of twelve members, two from each of the major communities, was to be established. To ensure that the democratic possibilities of sectarian representation were nullified, the Règlement Organique specified in Article 11 that "all the members of Judicial and Administrative Councils, without exception, and the justices of the peace, will be chosen and designated by the heads of their respective communities after consultation with the notables and will be appointed by the Governor."[41]

The sectarian paradigm for conflict resolution on the basis of communal parity had virtually nothing to do with tradition and had still less to do with democratic expression. Although there were antecedents for non-Muslim representation in earlier Ottoman reforms, never was the question of non-Muslim representation meant to reflect unambiguously the equality of all *communities* in the manner that the post-1860 Mount Lebanon reforms did.[42] Yet by linking religious affiliation explicitly to equitable secular representation on the administrative and judicial councils, European and Ottoman statesmen transformed belonging—however passively—to a particular religious community into an indispensable marker of a modern politics of nondiscrimination and, ultimately, a modern politics of equal citizenship in the secularized Ottoman public sphere.

Because the Règlement Organique was confined to Mount Lebanon, it left open the question of how the Ottoman commitment to nondiscrimination was going to be translated in other parts of the empire. The Provincial Law of 1864 that reorganized Ottoman provinces, for example, mandated administrative assemblies that consisted of the governor, department heads, and six representative members, three Muslim and three non-Muslim. It also reorganized judicial affairs into separate courts: the sharia court, a criminal court and a commercial court (the latter two with mixed membership), and a court of appeals composed of three Muslims and three non-Muslims presided over by an inspector judge appointed by the leading religious authority in the empire who resided in Istanbul. Moreover, provincial general assemblies were henceforth to include two Muslims and two non-Muslims elected by each district within the province.[43]

While rational in the sense that such transformations built upon an Ottoman imperial stratification of the empire's population along religious lines, the sectarian political arrangements set in place in Mount Lebanon and elsewhere across the empire during the Tanzimat politicized religious diversity in a manner that entrenched, magnified, and made central the idea of the sectarian community: a notionally stable basis upon which to build a nondiscriminatory politics. Being Muslim or Christian or Jewish was made the indispensable venue through which to demand specific rights, tax relief, financial appropriation, and political representation.

By insisting that the violence in Mount Lebanon was a manifestation of allegedly immutable and age-old sectarian antagonisms, the European powers and the Ottoman state ignored, or even obfuscated, the massive contradictions of the Tanzimat project that had explicitly upheld Christian "privileges" at the same time as it secularized and de-Islamized Ottoman statecraft. They upheld a nominal Ottoman sovereignty at the same time that they consecrated European interference in Ottoman affairs. They encouraged transnational patronage networks that undercut a cohesive Ottomanism—so that Orthodox Ottoman subjects might look for protection to Russia, and Catholic subjects to France, because both those powers openly presented themselves as protectors of Christian subjects in the East. In so doing, they left Muslim subjects of the empire, who had no

European patron, even more dependent on the Ottoman state, and ultimately made the late Ottoman Empire view them as its most natural and
important constituency.

Above all, both the European powers and the Ottoman Empire pre-
tended that they themselves had not played crucial roles in sectarianizing
the political landscape of a region such as Mount Lebanon. Europeans
and Ottomans had, in effect, created the conditions for a sectarian storm.
When it inevitably blew in, they each looked to blame someone else. The
sectarian solution transformed an acute crisis into a chronic modern
malady.

THE BEGINNINGS OF THE ECUMENICAL FRAME

Crucially, however, the killings of 1860 precipitated the beginnings of the
antisectarian ecumenical frame. The publication of eleven anonymous
Arabic epistles between October 1860 and April 1861 marked this moment
when coexistence between men and women drawn from different religious communities was consciously valorized. These epistles were entitled
Nafir Suriyya, the "Clarion of Syria," and, taken together, they constituted
the first deliberately ecumenical text in the modern Ottoman Empire—
that is to say, the first to insist on the equal validity of different religions in
relationship to the common, overarching nation. *Nafir Suriyya* made the
war of 1860 the crucible for a new kind of ecumenical society. Their author
urged "the sons of the nation" to "awaken" and to cast away "fanaticism."
He called on all the inhabitants of Syria to understand that they were
"brothers, sons of Adam, and our compatriots" who breathed the same air,
drank the same water, and spoke the same language.[44]

The didacticism and religious allusions of the epistles suggested a missionary zeal, and the "patriot" who authored these pamphlets was, in fact,
the translator, printer, and Protestant convert Butrus al-Bustani. Although
he is today known as an iconic "secular" Arab cultural figure, Bustani was
at the time closely collaborating with the American missionaries who had
made Beirut their base of evangelical operations. Bustani was from the
small village of Dibiyya in Mount Lebanon. His family was Maronite
Christian and he had been educated at the leading modern Maronite

Catholic seminary of 'Ayn Waraqa. He converted to American missionary Protestantism around 1840 and settled in Beirut.

In Beirut, he was employed by the missionaries as a translator and a printer at their press—a stable job that allowed him the financial means and the technological wherewithal to express his ecumenical convictions in print. Bustani reflected a moment when the Levant, and the city of Beirut specifically, was incorporated into a European-mediated Ottoman modernity; he was inevitably exposed to and mingled with Muslims and Christians of different rites. And he recognized how greatly the advent of steamships, telegrams, schools, printing presses, newspapers, and commerce represented the fruits of a global "civilization" made up of dense commercial, missionary, and diplomatic networks that connected Beirut to Marseille, Boston, and Istanbul.

Political, cultural, and economic transformations in Bustani's contemporary world provided the impetus for Bustani's urgent appeal for coexistence in 1860, but none of these in and of themselves explained its form or dictated its content. That Bustani was a Protestant convert in a place where Protestantism had barely a foothold in local society was deeply significant. Bustani was no secular Jacobin. His rejection of inherited faith and his estrangement from the reigning communal orthodoxies contributed directly to his understanding of the possibility of coexistence. This required, first and foremost, a critical awareness of self; second, it required the crucial distinction between individual, uncompromising piety and the realization of belonging to a social body that included, for the first time on equal terms, adherents of different faiths.

But unlike most evangelical American missionaries, whose conversion experiences generally resulted in their embrace of a militant zealotry against "native" societies, Bustani understood the complexity of local society. He identified with it but refused in this moment to cover up or obscure its ills. He did not see Syria as a landscape of perpetual barbarism, and he did not pretend that Protestantism or Western civilization held the only keys to improvement, redemption, and salvation. Nevertheless, the scale of the violence in Mount Lebanon and Damascus, and the reality of massive foreign and Ottoman intervention that was apparent all around the country, forced Bustani to realize that his native land was at a crossroads. Its diversity (*ikhtilaf*) could either pull Syria apart or become the basis of a new kind of society that could propel a unified Syria up what Bustani described as the rungs of the ladder of civilization.

Bustani drew on allegories and injunctions from the Bible and alluded to Muslim hadiths and Quranic verses. He emphasized a Christian fraternal "love" (in contrast to the spirit of anti-Druze vengeance that he perceived among certain Maronites) and referred to the Islamic commandment to promote virtue and prevent vice, and to its commitment to unity irrespective of tribal, sectarian, or ethnic differences. "Hubb al-watan min al-iman," he wrote, citing the apocryphal saying of the Prophet Muhammad, which declared that the "love of the nation stems from faith."[45] This same hadith had been gaining currency in the empire in this period and would eventually adorn the masthead of Bustani's journal *Al-Jinan* in 1870.

This hadith had been used earlier by the Egyptian Muslim Azharite Rifaa al-Tahtawi. But Tahtawi had used the hadith to legitimize the centralizing imperatives of his patron Mehmed Ali, the Ottoman governor of Egypt, and had little to do with coexistence between Muslim and Copt. More significantly, the same hadith was invoked in 1851 by the powerful Ottoman Greek Phanariot, and former governor of Moldavia, Stephanos Vogorides on the occasion of his daughter's wedding, which Sultan Abdülmecid promised to attend. Historian Christine Philliou notes that this was the first time an Ottoman sultan would attend a ceremony in a Christian church.[46] Vogorides sought to ingratiate himself with his patron. Bustani's ecumenism was far less instrumental and far more deliberate in its contemplation of what an antisectarian society might look like.

The beginnings of Bustani's ecumenical self-consciousness were located in his realization that God spoke through multiple religions—and in this sense, perhaps, he built upon his earlier work, published just before the war of 1860, advocating freedom of conscience and rehabilitating the reputation of the first Arab Protestant convert, As'ad Shidyaq, who had died in captivity in the late 1820s at the hands of the Maronite Church. His inference in the *Nafir* was that different "real" religions were equidistant from a universal God. He suggested, moreover, that the measure of their validity lay not in their respective dogmas but in the degree to which each contributed to a moral, civilized, educated, antisectarian community made up of truly pious individuals who collectively transcended religious difference.

Bustani said that rather than being a source of consternation or a problem that had to be pacified, the diversity of religions ought to promote tolerance, healthy competition, and individual conscientiousness. Bustani's usage of the plural form *religions* was crucial. It adapted the strident evangelical Protestant missionary refrain that *other* religions needed to be revivified into an explicit plea for ecumenical diversity in which no single religion was superior to any other in the common nation:

> [We need] living and attractive religions to teach their children to view those who hold different beliefs neither with contempt nor scorn as is now often the case, but with care and affection as among members of one family whose father is the homeland, its mother the earth, and God the single creator, with all members created out of the same substance, sharing the same destiny. God does not favor one individual over another for their title or group association, but for their knowledge, piety, reason, virtue, neighborliness, and the upholding of human rights and the [common] good.[47]

Bustani translated a theological realization into a social and reformist framework in the immediate aftermath of the events of 1860. Bustani's eleven pamphlets outlined his vision of a new society sheltered within an ecumenical frame. His was a project still very much on the drawing boards: as he admitted in his second pamphlet on October 8, 1860, "to build is more difficult than to destroy."[48]

Bustani's sketch of an *antisectarian* community contained several distinctive ideas about religion, citizenship, and equality that would define the ecumenical century ahead. The most important of these was the call for an explicitly antisectarian, rather than dogmatically secular, consciousness. For Bustani, as for so many others after him, this was a crucial first step for the creation of a viable social polity that could transcend the very real problem of the politicization and militarization—the *sectarianization*—of religious difference in the modern era.[49] Bustani also reversed the negative imperative of the Tanzimat to *not discriminate* into a positive injunction to *respect* diversity, and to cohere an active, committed, and conscious citizenship. Agency, in other words, was not simply the preserve of the sovereign who issued decrees, but also the obligation of the subjects who inhabited the imperial domains. In his eyes, therefore, the sectarian strife that had devastated Mount Lebanon—which Bustani estimated to have destroyed thirty thousand houses and left twenty thousand dead—was a black stain on Syria that Syrians themselves were responsible for and had the capacity to overcome.

Throughout the *Nafir*, Bustani emphasized the stark contrast between "sectarian fanaticism" and "patriotism."[50] He anticipated how tightly the modern trope of sectarianism was tied to a political vocabulary of citizenship and nationalism. More consistently than any other Ottoman Arab figure, Bustani invoked the modern Arabic refrain that categorized religious fanaticism as the corruption of true faith, as an insidious mark of barbarism, as a descent into irrational passion, as an emanation of madness, and—above all else—as a moral and religious failure in an age of putative compatriotship and civilization. Bustani thus referred to the "wicked" partisanship and prejudice that could take on "different colors at every stage." For Bustani, sectarianism was not fixed like pure faith, but variable according to political conditions and the human capacity to interpret these conditions—hence the need for civilized Syrians themselves to develop an antisectarian, ecumenical awareness that had to be inculcated among the "sons of the nation."[51]

Bustani suggested that the *Nafir* was a clarion call that could either be drowned out by the "crude drumbeat of prejudice" or an inspiration for his countrymen to "read and reflect" on their condition.[52] The choice was ultimately theirs. Bustani regarded the problem of 1860 as, first and foremost, a pedagogical problem of the self, of "ignorant" and "uncivilized" compatriots, not a political problem involving the pacification of distant and allegedly savage tribes. He refused, therefore, to judge any Syrian community as a whole on the basis of the individual actions of its members, just as he rejected either blind native chauvinism or slavish imitation of the West.

Indeed, as terrible as the sanguinary events of 1860 were, they represented for Bustani not the final and irrevocable negation of coexistence but an opportunity for its reconstitution on a firmer basis. Because they were anomalous events—and not the deliberate, cold calculus of statesmen exchanging or ridding themselves of unwanted and undesirable populations—they left open the possibility of interpreting sectarian violence as exceptions to the rule, rather than the rule itself. This is what Bustani did, and in his interpretation lay the crucial difference between understanding events contextually and understanding them as the inevitable expression of a uniquely deficient culture. Bustani was adamant that any society, any country, and any age could be afflicted by corruption and evil. There was nothing inherently "oriental" or "Muslim" or "native" about what had occurred in 1860, although Bustani lamented the state of civilization and "blind partisanship" that had long afflicted his homeland.[53]

The specific contrast between fanaticism and civilization, to be sure, echoed Ottoman and European statesmen who converged upon Beirut. But unlike the Ottomans and Europeans who viewed the different communities of Syria as pieces on the diplomatic chessboard, Bustani was not ultimately interested in the specific form of the Mutasarrifiyya over which he, like all his compatriots, had no actual say. As we have seen, the Mutasarrifiyya consecrated the specific geography of European intervention on behalf of certain Ottoman Christian subjects; it also indirectly legitimated draconian Ottoman state violence in other presumptively Muslim parts of the empire. Bustani's "Syria," however, described the events of 1860 as a "civil war"— *harb ahliyya*—which, in turn, raised for him a series of questions about meaningful, conscious citizenship elided by the great powers and the Ottoman state. What does conscious and ethical citizenship entail? And what ought to be the relationship between religious difference and national belonging? What is the relationship of the individual subject with group association? And, above all, what is the relationship between the abjuration of sectarian "fanaticism" and the promotion of "brotherhood" in a nation made up of communities and people of different faiths?

These were not questions that interested the great powers to any great degree, but they were questions that Bustani insisted went to the heart of a meaningful coexistence between Muslim and non-Muslim in the post-1860 age. To answer these questions one needed, in Bustani's estimation, a basic ecumenical awareness, which he hoped his pamphlets would instill among their readers. Syrians, in turn, had to understand how their "personal well-being" requires that "virtuous ties of unity and concord exist between the different communities and among themselves individually."[54] The idea of coexistence that Bustani turned to repeatedly was *ulfa*—which suggested unity and meant concord, familiarity, love, and intimacy.

Ulfa evoked a far more powerful form of neighborliness than the modern Arabic neologism for coexistence, *al-ta'yush*, which had not yet been coined at the time. For Bustani, communal awareness without critical individual piety and consciousness encouraged blind fanaticism. More immediately and within the scope of his own agency, however, Bustani realized that a new kind of education was required in order to inculcate ecumenical values in individual subjects: to explicitly respect different religious traditions and to work toward a new society that belonged equally to non-Muslim and Muslim alike.

Bustani thus founded his Al-Madrasa al-Wataniyya (National School) in Beirut in 1863 as the first explicitly ecumenical school in the Ottoman Empire. The school had no foreign missionary or Ottoman equivalent—the modern Ottoman educational system had not yet even been established at this point. The teachers were drawn from different communities—Muslim and Maronite, Protestant and Orthodox—and included Bustani's daughter Sarah. The school initially admitted 115 fee-paying boarders from various sects, including Muslim, Druze, and Maronite Christian boys. Remarkably for the period, an American missionary couple enrolled their two sons in the "native" school. In 1870, the Ottoman governor of Beirut praised Bustani's enterprise. The school's politically quietist antisectarian pedagogy, in which different religious traditions constituted the pillars of a common belonging, fit in well with the Tanzimat ethos, for by "national" Bustani meant not "nationalist" in any political or ideological sense, but specifically the coming together of men and women of different faiths in schools across Syria, Palestine, and Mount Lebanon under an Ottomanist rubric.[55]

But far more deliberately than any Ottoman imperial official, Bustani sought to provide a common education for students of different faiths that affirmed the particularity of each of their religious traditions in order to build a common national structure; he was adamant that no attempt should be made to convert students or indoctrinate them in religious teachings of any religious faith other than their own. This form of ecumenism clarified how far Bustani had traveled from the proselytizing ethos of American missionary schools with which he was intimately familiar, for he had served in them as a teacher and translator. His pedagogy also differed from that of the religious or parochial communal schools that proliferated across the Levant.

As much as Bustani's school constituted a radical break with convention, it was *not* radical in the sense of being antireligious or subversive of authority. Far from it. Bustani's desire to affirm comity also suggested that religious traditions themselves were the unshakeable foundation of cultural, moral, and social life. His advocacy of the separation of church and state was derived not from any commitment to secularism, but rather from a desire to protect freedom of conscience and national harmony—a desire that appeared to paradoxically entrench religious difference at the same time that it sought to transcend it. Like virtually every other reformer of his era, moreover, Bustani was a man who privileged the civilized and educated elites, whom he described as "intelligent, honorable and wealthy compatriots," over the allegedly "ignorant" masses.[56] The *Nafir*, tellingly, emphasized concord (ulfa) far more than it did "equality"—a word that does not appear across its eleven pamphlets. Bustani's pedagogy of anti-sectarianism drew heavily on an older, established differentiation between the knowledgeable, and hence ultimately responsible, elites and the mass of "ignorant" commoners who were "mere instruments in the hands of those in power." For Bustani, the figure of the shadowy, "sly conniver" who promoted unrest for personal gain exemplified moral depravity among men who ought to have known and acted better.[57]

Moreover, Bustani's pedagogy consecrated a new kind of nineteenth-century citizen-reformer who worked to elevate society up the ladder of global civilization. The great commission was no longer an evangelical one in a narrow religious sense, yet it drew directly on an evangelical vocabulary. The reformer had urgently to mold his ostensible compatriots, much as a potter shapes lifeless clay. The ostensibly refined, literate, and educated reformer had to enlighten and *lead* his ignorant, and potentially fanatical, ordinary countrymen. The events of 1860 constituted a glimpse of the apocalypse that men had it in their power to avert; but they just as obviously represented a glorious opportunity for spiritual redemption and material progress toward a liberated and civilized state.

"Awake! Awake! Oh Shepherds of Israel and leaders of the people," Bustani exhorted his readers in the *Nafir*. "Why are you asleep and pretending ignorance? Behold the ferocious lions who come to devour flock and shepherd alike." Here were words inspired by Ezekiel 34:2, addressed not to the general population of Syria but specifically to its leaders, kings, priests, and false prophets. They led their flocks astray for their own personal gain. Instead of feeding them, and guiding them to righteousness, the shepherds had fed themselves and thus brought disaster to their people.[58]

Bustani's criticism of the dereliction of duty among the supposedly knowledgeable leaders, however, also anticipated another great conceit within the modern understanding of sectarianism: that it was ultimately the disease of the lower classes, the uneducated masses, and that it reflected their unruly intrusion into the affairs of the civilized state. Members of the inherently sectarian classes had no agency and no will-power of their own. Anything they did that opposed Bustani's didactic vision of a civilized, bourgeois, obedient Ottoman subject was, ipso facto, "uncivilized." Bustani's antisectarianism, in short, was utterly and obvi-ously hierarchical. It was deferential to power; it was about harmony not equality, obedience not revolution. The intent here was not to mobilize the people for revolution; it was certainly not anti-Ottoman; rather, the goal was to instruct them into individual moral change that ultimately, through the peaceful aggregation of myriad individuals of different religions, would embody a civilized society greater than the sum of its communal parts. Bustani personified the one strand of the Ottoman Tanzimat that upheld nondiscrimination. He did not perceive or recognize its other strands that were intimately and obviously tied to statecraft, to centraliza-tion, to power, and to violence.

Yet within Bustani's pedagogy was something that was indeed poten-tially revolutionary. Bustani declared that the only effective form of mod-ern politics in a multireligious society was the separation of religion from politics—a secularism of the American kind that rejected the idea of an established church without rejecting religion itself. One of the great les-sons that Bustani drew from the violence of 1860 was the need to build a "barrier" between the secular affiliation of citizens to their common state and their pietistic belonging to different and exclusive religious communi-ties. "This mixing [between religious and civil matters] should not be allowed on religious and political grounds," he wrote.[59] To be properly religious, one needed a secular state that enforced freedom of conscience; for the state to become the equal patrimony of all its pious citizens, how-ever, it also needed first to be available to them on equal grounds. In other words, Bustani came to precisely the opposite conclusion about how and why religion mattered in the East than that reached by the imperial architects of the Mutasarrifiyya, who made religious affiliation central to the confessional politics of compromise and equity heavily mediated and inevitably distorted by European power.

Bustani's antisectarian consciousness was not necessarily commensurate with the political or economic imperatives of the Istanbul-centric Ottoman state. Yet, by the same token, it was by no means immediately antithetical to them. Akin to Jewish intellectuals in fin-de-siècle Vienna, or Arab-American ones in contemporary America, being decidedly outside of political power sharpened a critical disposition toward the whole of which Bustani believed himself to be a part. His being a Protestant Christian was central to his way of thinking; the lessons about and allusions to critical piety that he emphasized, the language of awakening and salvation, the printing press where he worked, and his own evident piety all affirmed this aspect of the *Nafir*. But Bustani did not devote himself to elaborating a new culture of coexistence because he was a Christian. He never described himself in the *Nafir* as a Christian, but rather as a "lover of the nation," or a "patriot." This distinction is key.

As much as his call for a separation of religion from politics fell on deaf ears, his belief in the "public welfare" that included Muslim and non-Muslim citizens became pervasive in virtually every imagining of politics in the decades to come across much of the Ottoman and post-Ottoman Mashriq.[60] The validity and possibility of brotherhood among "sons of the nation" would, soon enough, lie at the core of various other, more explicitly political, philosophies that Bustani did not actually contemplate. Although the secular nationalist, the anticolonial revolutionary, and the Marxist were a universe away from the quietist, civilized, and bourgeois Ottoman Bustani, he nevertheless became entangled in their respective genealogies. This occurred not because Bustani ventriloquized Western secularism but because, in a moment of acute crisis that witnessed terrible episodes of intercommunal violence, he pieced together, in Arabic, aspects of different religious traditions and different elements of Ottoman and European civilizations. He saw no other way to build an *antisectarian* political community that both preserved meaningful diversity and upheld substantive equality.

By the turn of the twentieth century, the idea of being a cultivated adherent of one religious community no longer necessitated, or even necessarily implied, defining oneself against other infidel religions or heresies, but rather against "ignorant" compatriots in a multireligious national community. The tragedy, however, lay in the fact that the same trauma of 1860, and the late Ottoman age it anticipated, also encouraged the no-less-contemporary consciousness of being a beleaguered "Christian" minority in need of European protection, or of being a defensive "Muslim" threatened by a European-dominated world. The dichotomy Bustani drew between an insidious sectarian passion on the one hand, and true national piety on the other, was reformulated in different ways across the final decades in the Ottoman Empire. Bustani's particular way of thinking about coexistence was one of many different interpretations of the ecumenical frame. None were inevitable, and all were deeply contested.

3 Coexistence in an Age of Genocide

I am an Arab, an Easterner, a Revolutionary.

— Amin Rihani, *Al-Qawmiyyat,* 1911

Donald Bloxham describes the history of the late Ottoman Empire as the setting for a "great game of genocide."[1] The great game to which Bloxham refers was complex. It involved a European pretense to intervene on behalf of the Armenians, the extraordinarily harsh reaction of the Ottoman state to this pretense, and, most of all, the genocidal actions of the Committee of Union and Progress that seized control of the empire in its final years. The specter of European intervention, which Bloxham insists was never as serious as the Ottomans thought it was, hastened the destruction of the Armenians. In its main outlines, the Armenian tragedy is fairly well known, although it remains until our own day the subject of intense recrimination.[2]

The recent scholarship on the Armenian Genocide has ignored what seems to me a different but still fundamentally important question, namely what to make of the different fates endured by different groups in the empire in what, after all, had promised initially to be an age of political equality. To put it simply, Bloxham's "great game of genocide" bedeviled the Armenian Christians. It also haunted the Greek Orthodox, and to a lesser extent the Kurdish populations of Anatolia. However, it largely bypassed the Christian Arabs, who enjoyed a belle époque at more or less the same time that Armenian Christians had to endure systematic violence culminating in genocide. Neither Arabic-speaking Christians nor Jews in cities such as Baghdad faced an existential threat in any way comparable to the upheavals endured by Muslim populations in the Balkans and Christians in Anatolia.[3] Ethnic cleansing and nationalism were prominent in Anatolia and the Balkans, while in the Levant coexistence flourished in a manner scarcely conceivable a century earlier in Syria or Egypt.

The late Ottoman Empire effectively split into two. The Balkans and parts of Anatolia were deeply contested by Turks, Kurds, Greeks, and Armenians. There, the nondiscriminatory aspects of the Tanzimat, which I alluded to in the previous chapter, were abruptly abandoned and overwhelmed by the reform project's draconian, modernist statist aspect. The other part of the empire in the Mashriq inhabited primarily by Arabic-speaking Muslims, Christians, and Jews was largely peripheral to the machinery of state and to the militant and mutually antagonistic nationalisms that the Ottomans alternatively feared and professed. Before World War I, the vast majority of Arab inhabitants accepted an Ottoman framework; Arab nationalism in the sense of a national liberation movement did not then exist.[4] This great divergence is central to understanding the nature of coexistence in the late Ottoman Empire and the post-Ottoman era.

Unlike the sectarian outbursts in cities such as Aleppo and Damascus of the Tanzimat era, which were directed as much against state authority as against non-Muslims, the nationalist violence perpetrated by Balkan Christian and Ottoman Turkish states was not the product of circumstance or prejudice alone, but of deliberate state policy. The counterpoint to the new ecumenical ethos that began to emerge in the Mashriq after 1860 was not therefore to be found only in the sectarian violence that had plagued Mount Lebanon and Syria between 1840 and 1860. Rather, it lay in the nationalist politics and the ethno-religious nationalist mobilizations in the Balkans, Istanbul, and Anatolia.[5] In the northern parts of the empire, religion increasingly stigmatized specific minorities within the emerging nationalist body politic; in the Mashriq, religion stigmatized the uncivilized "ignorants" of all faiths who needed education and enlightenment under the distant eye of a beleaguered sultanate.

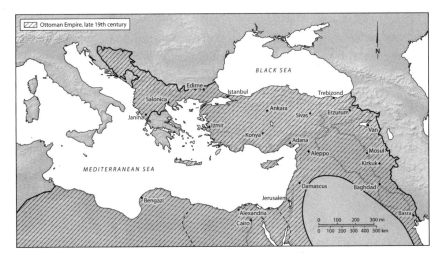

Map 2. The Ottoman Empire in the late nineteenth century. (Bill Nelson Cartography).

THE FATE OF THE TANZIMAT IN THE OTTOMAN NORTH

Hard on the heels of uprisings by Christians in Crete in 1866 and in Bosnia in 1875, the Bulgarian uprising of 1876 recalled the events of the Greek revolution that had so dramatically shaken the assumptions of Ottoman Muslim supremacy. As had been the case during the Greek revolt of the 1820s, both the Bulgarian uprising and the Ottoman response singled out victims on the basis of their religion.[6] The bankruptcy of the sultanate in 1875, the creation of a European-controlled Public Debt Administration that privileged European creditors, the British occupation of Egypt in 1882, and the flow of Muslim migrants and refugees from the Balkans and Caucasus into Istanbul and Anatolia beginning in the 1860s further strained the Tanzimat credo of nondiscrimination. Moreover, the secessionism inherent in Balkan nationalisms, the pervasive association of Christianity with European imperialism, and the prominence of the remaining Ottoman Christian commercial bourgeoisie, whose members were often protected by European consulates or embassies, conspired to neutralize, if not nullify, the potential of ecumenical thought in Istanbul, in the Balkans, and in Anatolia.[7]

Some caveats, however, are in order. Like the Arab provinces, the Balkan and Anatolian provinces of the Ottoman Empire were not uniform. Albanians and Bosnians, for example, witnessed examples of ecumenical solidarity that paralleled the efforts of Arabs in the Mashriq; they were not torn apart by sectarian nationalist pressures as Armenian or Greek Orthodox Christians would be from their Turkish and Kurdish Muslim neighbors.[8] Late nineteenth-century Arabic writers and editors had Armenian, Greek, Turkish, Bulgarian, and Albanian analogues who were not necessarily or directly implicated in state power. The developing ecumenical frame, after all, depended on the Tanzimat precept of nondiscrimination, which was not specific to the Mashriq. The secularization of Ottoman law during the Tanzimat was the rule across the empire. The 1869 Law of Nationality created a territorial definition of Ottoman citizenry, the 1876 Ottoman Constitution promulgated the equality of all citizens irrespective of religious affiliation, and the great Ottoman civil code known as the Mecelle was codified between 1869 and 1876. These established the crucial legal space for a new form of modern Ottomanism that superseded the historical emphasis on discrimination between Muslim and non-Muslim without denying or even abandoning the empire's Islamic heritage.[9]

A new Ottoman worldliness—that is to say, the deliberate positioning of the empire in its final decades as part of the "civilized" world—was evident across the major cities of the empire and especially in Istanbul. This worldliness was expressed through visual and architectural propaganda; through increased rail, telegraph, and steamship links with Europe and America; and through participation in universal expositions. The modern architecture and urban reconfigurations of Beirut, Cairo, Alexandria, and Jaffa were not radically different from those of Izmir and Istanbul.[10] The emergence of journalism and new technologies of print capitalism; a new professional class of doctors, engineers, and school teachers; the facilitation of travel; and the development of transnational migrant networks were pronounced in the European, Anatolian, and Arab provinces of the empire. New literary societies, theater troupes, and masculinist sports clubs arose in this period in all parts of the empire in which religious minorities played a prominent part.[11] New civil and military schools appealed mostly to Muslim subjects in the Arab provinces, as in Istanbul, Anatolia, and Salonika. The rise of the "middle class" in the Arabic-speaking parts of the empire was also not dissimilar from that in its Turkish-speaking parts: both represented urban minorities in what remained largely rural and illiterate societies.

Late nineteenth-century Istanbul, Ottoman architecture, cultural life, diplomacy, and statecraft all reflected the still obvious religious and ethnic diversity of the empire. The Ottoman census of 1881–93 underscored the heterogeneity of the roughly seventeen million inhabitants of the empire that it counted, split between the demographically dominant Muslim millet (regardless of ethnicity) and the more than four million non-Muslim—Greek Orthodox, Armenian, Bulgarian, Catholic, Jewish, Protestant, Latin, Syriac, and Gypsy—communities of the empire.[12] In the face of such diversity, Sultan Abdülhamid II famously cast himself as a sovereign committed to building a modern state of Ottoman citizens and also as a caliph who could appeal to Muslims around the world.[13] Despite the imperial rivalry with Iran, the late Ottoman Empire sought to co-opt its Shi'i subjects as part of an aggressive project of Ottomanization. Although the empire promulgated laws in 1874 that specifically prohibited its citizens from marrying "Iranian" citizens, the sultan nevertheless repaired Shi'i mosques in the 1880s and sought to enroll Shi'i students in Sunni seminaries and to co-opt Shi'i clerics in Iraq by outlining the urgency of Muslim unity in the face of Western imperialism.[14] Abdülhamid II invited the famous modernist thinker Jamal al-Din al-Afghani to Istanbul in 1892 to consolidate his reputation as a Muslim leader.

Ottoman Christians still occupied high places in the Ottoman world. The chief Ottoman negotiator at the Congress of Berlin, for example, was an Orthodox Christian by the name of Caratheodory Pasha. Ottoman Armenians continued to be appointed to the governorship of Mount Lebanon, and Christians and Jews were overrepresented in the first, short-lived Ottoman parliament that was suspended by Abdülhamid II in 1878. The Ottoman statesman Midhat Pasha, who had played such a major role in the writing of the Ottoman Constitution of 1876 and who had used Bulgaria in the mid-1860s to showcase Ottoman reform, published a memorable modern apologia for the Ottoman Empire in 1878.

Since "our enemies," Midhat Pasha asserted, "have not ceased to speak of the alleged servitude of the Christians, as well as the duty incumbent upon Europe to deliver them from the yoke under which they groan," he now felt compelled to lay out a history of "essentially democratic" principles of Muslim rule, and of Ottoman and Muslim tolerance that "have always guided the Government in its mode of action towards its non-Mussulman subjects." The Ottoman Empire had never forced non-Muslims in its domains to convert, "so that our tolerance in the matter of religious belief has become proverbial."[15] In turn, Midhat Pasha's son and biographer admitted in 1903 that some "excesses" had been committed by irregular Ottoman soldiers in Bulgaria but claimed that most of the stories produced about the situation there were "fictions."[16]

But behind such equivocations—for the empire had never been democratic, nor had its toleration been any more an imperial norm than its violence—was a basic reality that had become abundantly clear by 1878. As important and revolutionary a shift as it was in the mid-nineteenth century, nondiscrimination had been primarily a policy imposed from above, and very much at the point of a bayonet (think Aleppo 1850 and Damascus 1860) amid incessant European economic, political, and cultural encroachment. It had never reflected any deep repudiation of Muslim primacy on the part of Ottoman thinkers, writers, and educators. To be sure, the Tanzimat refrain of nondiscrimination was ubiquitous in official communications, and after 1856 it became a set of solemn edicts backed by international commitments. It constituted a vital point of dialogue between Ottoman and European officials, but not within Ottoman Muslim society or between rulers and ruled. Tellingly, I think, Midhat Pasha addressed his 1878 essay on Ottoman tolerance not to Ottoman readers but to European ones. Because the emphasis on nondiscrimination had been meant to consolidate the empire, when the conditions on the ground in the Balkans and Anatolia changed to make this mantra less urgent (or, more accurately, to make other ways of mobilizing a population more urgent), it fell by the wayside. From the vantage point of the political leaders in Istanbul, what mattered far more than coexistence was a rejuvenated sovereignty of the state.

NATIONALIST STRUGGLES IN THE OTTOMAN NORTH

The fate of the Armenians in Eastern Anatolia in the 1890s reflected the degradation of diversity in the Ottoman Empire. The Armenians of

Anatolia had long constituted a substantial minority—some 17 percent of the total population in six provinces in Eastern Anatolia that had been singled out for protection in the Treaty of Berlin.[17] But it was this ostensible protection, and the concomitant rise of Armenian nationalism, that made the Armenians objects of Ottoman imperial suspicion. The Hamidian sultanate viewed any sign of Armenian irredentism as a major threat to Ottoman sovereignty. When Armenians associated with the Armenian Revolutionary Federation rebelled against onerous taxation and Kurdish tribal deprivations in Sassoun in 1894, they were crushed. State-backed Kurdish militias known as the Hamidiye Regiments then wreaked havoc on Armenian villages and towns in Eastern Anatolia.[18]

These sanguinary events, in turn, encouraged Armenian ecclesiastic and nationalist pleas for European intervention. They also provoked European-led calls for sectarian administration in Eastern Anatolia. When Armenian nationalists seized the Ottoman Bank in Istanbul in August 1896 to publicize the fate of their compatriots, their actions precipitated a slaughter of Armenians in Istanbul carried out by soldiers and students in Muslim seminaries, and by Muslim clerics and ordinary folk, that lasted several days and left hundreds of Armenians dead.[19] In the meantime, fearful of what they felt were too many concessions on the part of their sultan to the Armenians and to European pressure, Kurdish and Turkish villagers and irregulars again overran Armenian villagers, and destroyed American missionary schools associated with the Armenians, in different locales across Eastern Anatolia. Tens of thousands of Armenians, and perhaps as many as a hundred thousand, were killed over two years.[20]

What was most novel about the violence of the 1890s was that it indicated not a temporary, partial breakdown of coexistence, as was the case in Damascus 1860, but the beginning of a deliberate and systematic unraveling—as a desired end in itself—that would culminate in outright genocide in 1915.[21] The Ottoman state acted as if the Armenian inhabitants of the empire were fundamentally not its concern. The bitter struggle over Macedonia in 1902, which saw Greeks, Serbians, Ottomans, Bulgarians, and Macedonians fight to control an agriculturally rich Balkan province, deepened the nationalist shadow over fin de siècle Istanbul of the Hamidian period. In this context, the sentiment expressed in 1904 by Yusuf Akçura, a Young Turk of Tartar descent, that the best alternative to a diffuse

Ottomanism or to Hamidian pan-Islamism was "to pursue a Turkish nationalism based on race," and his notion of Turkish unity (*tevhid-i etrak*), was striking not because it evoked age-old animosities, but because it expressed a new and still inchoate Turkish identity that would flourish amid the crisis of nationalism that plagued the late Ottoman Empire's northern part.[22] This late-Ottoman Turkish nationalism's ability to assimilate Circassians, Albanians, Alevis, and Kurds would prove to be fraught, but its exclusion of Christian Armenians and Orthodox was far less ambiguous. Nondiscrimination was not abolished in Istanbul or in Anatolia; it was rendered irrelevant by events on the ground.

THE ARMENIAN GENOCIDE

Despite the brief window of optimism opened by the Young Turk Revolution of 1908, the leaders of the Committee of Union and Progress (CUP) fused religion and citizenship far more tightly and coercively than had been the case during the "pan-Islamist" Hamidian era. Although it cast itself as the legitimate, inclusive, and democratic opposition to the absolutism and tyranny of Sultan Abdülhamid II, the CUP contained no non-Muslims in its most senior ranks.[23] When massive anti-Armenian riots broke out in Adana in April 1909 amid rumors of an Armenian separatist uprising, they revealed the precarious state of post-revolution Ottomanism. The riots led to the total destruction of the Armenian quarter of the city and the massacre of thousands of Armenian subjects. Although the CUP blamed the old regime for the "regrettable" violence, it was the CUP-directed army that had participated in some of the most gruesome episodes of the massacre and in the looting that followed.[24]

The Italian conquest of Libya in 1911; the bitter Balkan Wars of 1912–13, which witnessed ethnic cleansing precipitated by the competing national armies; and the outbreak of World War I delivered the final blows to the Tanzimat-era refrain of a nondiscriminatory Ottomanism. "Before they do away with us, we will get rid of them," confessed Mehmed Reşid, the Ottoman governor of Diyarbakır and a medical doctor, about the Armenians in 1915.[25] In Eastern Anatolia, Armenians were marked for elimination in what has become known as the Armenian Genocide. The wartime Ottoman state emptied Eastern Anatolia of the bulk of its Armenian population in 1915 and 1916. Several hundred thousand men, women, and children were deported to Syria and were subjected along the way to extreme and system-atic violence, including rape, starvation, and murder. They were also ravaged by disease. They became victims of "necropolitics"—the term coined by philosopher Achille Mbembe to describe the way in which sovereign states classify certain populations as disposable and then subject them to conditions that amount to living death.[26] These erstwhile citizens, however, were not living in a colonial realm in which Western conquerors dominated "natives" absolutely, but rather in a part of the world in which Armenians had for centuries constituted a recognized community in a religiously and ethnically diverse empire.

The state violence was not limited to the Armenians—it was part of a war against any potentially hostile "minority." The Greek Orthodox popu-lation of Anatolia suffered enormously, first through deportations along the Aegean coast in 1913, then by being subject to a "national" boycott of Greek goods in 1914 directed by the CUP, and eventually by being uprooted and "repatriated" en masse to Greece after the war. Hundreds of thou-sands of Assyrians and Kurdish Muslims were also deported in April 1916 from what the Ottoman government considered to be strategic areas of Eastern Anatolia. Circassian, Albanian, and Kurdish Muslims in the South Marmara region were caught up in the maelstrom of violence during and immediately following World War I. Kurds *as Muslims* were not, however, excluded totally; they could still be potentially incorporated into the emerging Turkish body politic by invoking their Islam, by adopting the Turkish language, and by assimilating—or, rather, being forcibly assimi-lated into the ethos of an anti-Christian modern Turkish nationalism. Armenians, Syrian Orthdox, and Greeks were not afforded any such opportunity.[27]

The CUP's struggle for sovereignty became a war against meaningful coexistence in Istanbul, the South Marmara region, and Eastern Anatolia. It is not a coincidence that Mount Lebanon's autonomy was abolished during World War I, nor that the hated Capitulations were also eliminated in September 1914. Nor that one of the main precipitants of anti-Armenian fury was yet another version of pro-Armenian "reform" forced upon the Ottoman government in February 1914 and supervised by a Dutch colonial administrator and a Norwegian officer. The British landings at Gallipoli and the Russian invasion of Eastern Anatolia in 1915, and the Allied-backed Greek conquest of Izmir in 1919, fueled this generalized Turkish Muslim antipathy toward Christians. The wartime Ottoman state, and even more so the Turkish republic that emerged from its ruins, conflated "Turk" with "Muslim" and conflated the state with the *nation* of Turkish-speaking Muslims fighting a war of survival in which religion played a key role in mass nationalist mobilizations that destroyed, once and for all, the idea of an ecumenical Ottomanism.[28]

When Turkish nationalist forces recaptured Izmir and oversaw the pillaging and burning of the Christian quarters of the city in 1922, the Greek Orthodox Bishop Chrysostomos, who had blessed the initial Greek invasion, was killed. A mob tore out his beard, gouged out his eyes, and cut off his nose, ears, and hands.[29] Unlike the hanging of the Greek Orthodox patriarch in 1821, the violence here was no longer meant to be salutary. It was no longer a warning for a non-Muslim to heed his limit, or for an elite to remember its station within the hierarchy of the Ottoman Empire, but an act of extirpation within a campaign of nationalist mobilization. Both instances involved Muslims killing Greek Orthodox clerics, but in circumstances utterly different. The former intended to terrorize the Greek community back into the Ottoman fold, the latter to eliminate the Greek presence from Anatolia. Turkish nationalism apotheosized one strand of the nineteenth-century Ottoman reformation. It centralized power against Armenians, Greeks, and, to a lesser extent, Kurds. At the same time, Turkish nationalism represented the total repudiation of the Ottoman reformation's other major strand—that is, its avowal of nondiscrimination, and thus of a political equality between Muslim and non-Muslim that depended, in reality, on a diluted Ottoman sovereignty.

RELATIVE TRANQUILITY IN THE OTTOMAN SOUTH

There was no similar existential crisis in the part of the empire that had witnessed the infamous violence of 1860, namely Ottoman Syria and Mount Lebanon. Nor was there any similar crisis in Ottoman Baghdad and Palestine or in British-occupied Egypt, all of which remained relatively tranquil in the last decades of the Ottoman period. This divergence between the Ottoman North of the Balkans and the Ottoman South of the Arab Mashriq has several possible explanations, some of which I have already alluded to: the political and military center of the empire, and the elements that mobilized the coercive machinery of state, including the army, were located in Istanbul and Salonika, not in Beirut, Baghdad, Damascus, or Cairo.

Not a single leading member of the CUP was Arab. The minority of Arab officers in the Ottoman army, in late Ottoman schools, and in the ranks of the CUP may have come close to actual state power, and may well have faced the same imperative to save "their" state that vexed their Ottoman Turkish contemporaries.[30] Yet there was no separatist Christian nationalism to speak of in Egypt or Syria, nor were the political, economic, and demographic conditions conducive for any nationalist fragmentation along sectarian lines. The British occupation of Egypt of 1882, for example, did not actively encourage Arab separatism from the Ottomans and was thus different from the Russian and Austrian onslaught in the Balkans and Caucasus. The Arab Christian subjects of the empire, therefore, were largely insulated from the Ottoman Empire's transformation into a Muslim-majority state with unwanted Armenian and Greek minorities. Far more than was the case with the inhabitants of the Balkans or Anatolia, the Ottoman subjects in the Mashriq were able to take advantage of Ottomanism because they were sheltered from its most draconian centralizing imperatives.

Paradoxically perhaps, but not at all surprisingly, late Ottoman modernity in the Arab Mashriq allowed for the emergence of a new ecumenical Arab subjectivity long before the creation of a politically independent Arab world. Unlike the war-induced influx of Ottoman Muslim refugees from wars in the Balkans and Caucasus into Istanbul and Anatolia between 1878 and 1914, which produced some of the most embittered anti-Christian Ottoman and Turkish nationalist figures, the movement of nearly twenty thousand Syrian Christians to Egypt, and of nearly three hundred thousand mostly Ottoman Christian subjects to the New World, between 1860 and 1914 inadvertently bolstered the ecumenical frame. The motives for the latter migration were, to be sure, overwhelmingly economic: they followed the collapse of the silk industry in Mount Lebanon in the 1880s. But in and from New York and Boston, some migrants such as Amin Rihani and Khalil Gibran conjured up a new "Eastern" spiritual identity in contrast to alleged Western materialism.[31] Meanwhile, and far closer to home, the various urban locales in the Ottoman Empire itself witnessed sustained interaction between Arab Muslim and Arab non-Muslim compatriots as the Ottomans transitioned from being a Muslim empire to being an empire of nominally equal citizens.

Inevitably, the intensity and quality of ecumenical thought varied enormously from neighborhood to neighborhood, city to city, and region to region. Inevitably as well, sectarian tensions and incidents occasionally shattered the long Ottoman peace. Many of the Christian survivors of 1860 and their descendants undoubtedly harbored fears about further depredations at the hands of their Muslim and Druze neighbors. Clashes such as those between Muslim stevedores and Christian quarrymen in Beirut in September 1903, or the meeting of the so-called Coptic Congress held in Asyut in 1911, enflamed sectarian tensions but also heightened a new consciousness of sectarianism as a problem that had to be resolved by self-described civilized compatriots of the late Ottoman era.[32]

The two major and cosmopolitan cities of Beirut and Cairo, where many Syrian Christian migrants established themselves, became central nodes of the ecumenical frame. Beirut, a booming Mediterranean port city that quadrupled in size between 1820 and 1880, had a large native and foreign Christian population that constituted the majority of its inhabitants by the turn of the century. It boasted many major mission schools and universities as well as a number of foreign consulates. Its religiously mixed municipality was one of the first established in the Ottoman Empire, and it became the seat of the newly created Ottoman province of Beirut in 1888.[33] Cairo was the seat of British-occupied Egypt and the center of the Khedival state, which became increasingly Arabized even as it existed under nominal Ottoman sovereignty.

In both cities the influx of foreign Western capital and missions elevated the position of Christian and Jewish entrepreneurs associated with them at exactly the moment when the Ottoman state itself expanded its presence in the region and thus provided mostly Muslim Arab subjects with hitherto unparalleled access to imperial education and bureaucracy.

Ottoman Arab Christian merchants and bankers enjoyed access to European firms and capital, benefited from European consular protection, dominated the export trade, and figured prominently in the imperial concessions to build railways and ports in Syria. But many of them were perfectly capable of working with their Ottoman Arab Muslim merchant compatriots who controlled inland trade—and so, too, were workers who protested against foreign concessions that deprived them of a living wage.[34] What was made into a zero-sum game in the Balkans that sundered Muslim from non-Muslim was experienced as a far more cohesive late-Ottoman modernity in the Mashriq.

But these contingent, contextual, and material factors, in and of themselves, by no means tell the whole story. What Ottoman statesmen changed from above during the Tanzimat, Arab subjects changed on the living ground of culture. Despite censorship, the modern Arabic press flourished in this late Ottoman era—especially in Egypt. The press often consisted of short-staffed family operations and often produced only limited runs in societies that remained overwhelmingly illiterate (in Egypt only 6.8 percent of the population could read or write by 1917; in Palestine the rate even as late as 1931 was merely 20 percent for the Arab population, with urban male Christians being far more literate than their Muslim counterparts). Even so, the press offered a profusion of didactic prescriptions for civilized knowledge, manners, science, hygiene, and piety.[35] The educated minority of Arab men and women founded, taught, or enrolled in so-called national institutions in Syria, Palestine, and Egypt—such as Butrus al-Bustani's National School, Christine Qardahi's Madrasat al-Banat al-Wataniyya (National School for Girls) in Alexandria, Khalil Sakakini's Al-Madrasa al-Dusturiyya (Constitutional School) in Jerusalem, and Marie Kassab's "nonsectarian" Ahliyya (National Civic) school in Beirut.[36] These schools competed with modern Islamic schools such as the Islamic Al-Maqasid school, which was set up in Beirut in 1878, or Shaykh Husayn Jisr's Al-Madrasa al-Wataniyya al-Islamiyya (National Islamic School), which was established in Tripoli in 1879, as well as a plethora of parochial Christian, foreign missionary, and Ottoman state secondary schools, such as Maktab 'Anbar in Damascus, which was named after a wealthy Jewish merchant whose home became the school.[37]

THE ECUMENICAL NAHDA

The men and women who plied their trade in journalism or writing, or who made money as merchants and supported schools, literary societies, charities, and journals, possessed no single cultural agenda—some were more pious, others more communal, still others secular in outlook, while others were vehemently antisecular. Many journal publishers and actors courted and depended on the financial support of the Egyptian khedives or Ottoman sultans; others were self-financed.[38] But they did collectively believe that they were at the beginnings of what they themselves described as a nahda, or renaissance. The Arabic term *nahda,* in the sense of an Arab cultural awakening, action, and movement, was most famously defined by Jurji Zaydan, the self-made and largely self-taught Syrian Christian émigré in Cairo whose father worked as a baker in Beirut.

Zaydan was born in Beirut in 1861 and moved to Cairo in search of work in 1883. In Cairo, he established his press and the literary and historical journal *Al-Hilal* (The Crescent, redolent with Muslim symbolism) with the assistance of his family, fellow Syrian émigrés, and Freemasons (of whom Zaydan was one).[39] He made a name for himself as the author of numerous novels about Arab and Islamic history. In 1912, Zaydan published his landmark *Tarikh al-tamaddun al-islami* (History of Islamic Civilization), the first such desacralized account written by an Arab author in the modern era. Zaydan described the nahda in 1914 in the fourth volume of his history of Arabic literature, *Tarikh adab al-lugha al-'arabiyya.*[40]

Although the nahda never constituted a single political or cultural project, Zaydan's interpretation of the nahda remains influential: he regarded his age as a contemporary revival of Arabic literature and culture in the shadow of Western civilization, a renaissance of Arab thought that shook the Arabs out of the torpor of stagnation and "backwardness." He referred to his generation as living during "the latest nahda," seeing it as the culmination of a series of earlier Arab nahdas that began before the rise of Islam but expanded dramatically with Islam. Zaydan insisted that the contemporary nahda was characterized by nine distinguishing features: the establishment of modern schools, printing, journalism, the spirit of individual freedom, literary and scientific societies, public libraries, museums, theater, and the interest of orientalists in Arabic culture.[41]

The great paradox of all these signposts of a demilitarized modernity across the Mashriq was that they provided the impetus both to transcend and to consolidate communal identifications. Ottomanism was not predicated on an embrace of secularism, or even on abolishing Islam's very public role in the state and society. Rather, it sought to recraft the relationship between religious communities into an allegedly national relationship, making each religious or ethnic community a central component of a national whole in which Islamic symbolism and motifs, and indeed Ottoman Muslims politically speaking, consistently remained paramount. The Mecelle, the massive Ottoman civil code that appeared between 1870 and 1877 in 1,851 articles, codified Hanafi Muslim jurisprudence and was specifically *not* an emulation of the French Civil Code.[42] The era that produced the first modern "national" school also produced the first modern "Islamic" school. If one major strain of *nahdawi* thought explicitly rationalized the cultural unity of Arabic-speaking Muslims and non-Muslims, another strain fought strenuously for communal or religious unity. The former was expressed through an Arabic discourse of progress, civilization, civilized religion, education, and modern science that sought to instruct and "awaken" an imagined secular community of Arabic readers irrespective of religious affiliation.[43] The latter was a range of religious, pietistic, or communal writings and activism that were concerned with a single community but that, crucially, assumed and took for granted the existence of other communities against which one had to compete and with which one had to coexist.

These competing secular and communal spheres were shaped by the state-approved ecumenism, or what Suleyman al-Bustani, a Christian from Mount Lebanon who served as Ottoman minister of commerce and agriculture, specifically hailed as the idea of Ottoman "brotherhood" following the Young Turk Revolution of 1908.[44] Bustani insisted that the late Ottoman era constituted an opportunity to turn away at last from what he considered the "reprehensible fanaticism that makes you hate those not of your race or religion," a fanaticism often stoked by foreign powers. In his eyes, Ottomanism promised "harmony" and "equality."[45]

Far more than harmony and equality, this late Ottomanism legitimated inharmonious and often discordant notes of antisectarianism. These notes revealed the struggle to create a new, I think vitally significant, normative public code of antisectarian behavior and expectations embraced by "civilized" Muslim and non-Muslim alike. When the Maronite archbishop of Beirut, Yusuf Dibs, published his multivolume *Tarikh Suriyya* (History of Syria) between 1903 and 1905, he alluded repeatedly to the intimate intellectual community made up of men of different faiths in Syria who served "knowledge" and were part of the nahda. He made his own acute consciousness of being a Maronite fit in seamlessly within a wider, culturally pluralist nineteenth-century renaissance of knowledge.

In the final volume of *Tarikh Suriyya,* which addressed the contemporary period, Archbishop Dibs balked at delving into the massacres of 1860. "We stop our pen," he admitted, "from writing down the details [of these massacres] lest they awaken buried hatreds and recall events that neither side wishes to recall and that both wish had not occurred."[46] Tellingly, he understood that a kind of self-censorship was an integral part of a renascent knowledge of the religious self and other. This knowledge required the continual suppression of bitter sectarian memories and smoldering resentments. In other words, a crucial part of the ecumenical nahda worked not only to uncover the past, but also, at crucial junctures, to bury it more deeply and to create powerful and enduring taboos about the alleged sectarian.

As anywhere else in the world, classes of people were generally excluded from having a voice heard in the nahda's secular and communal public spheres: the poor and the indigent, marginalized rural communities or tribes, peasants, women more than men, and the many factory workers who had yet to organize and unionize—that is to say, a whole raft of nominally equal citizens of the late Ottoman state. Most of the famous nahda thinkers were indeed men who took for granted their religious, pedagogical, and civic leadership. They imagined a nation without mass politics, a nation of passive and "ignorant" coreligionists and citizens (and wives and daughters) who had to be educated and enlightened, not mobilized for a great struggle of "national" survival. They *reflected* an aspect of their age far more than they were *representative* in any democratic sense. The modern schoolteacher, printer, actor, painter, municipal council member, doctor, writer, and reformer were the nahda's quintessentially "civilized" figures who inculcated an antisectarian Arab, Eastern, and Islamic sensibility in their students, audiences, and constituencies, like spoonfuls of medicine administered to hapless patients. The nahda was an affair of the actual or aspiring intellectual elites defined by the figure of the reformer (*al-muslih*) who thrived in the space opened up by Ottoman reformation and European interventionism.

This top-down view informed an entire panoply of nahda thinkers. What brought pietists and secularists together was their shared obsession with the problem of religious difference and their taking social difference for granted. The significant property and gender qualifications to vote in new municipal and parliamentary elections after 1877, the reality of mass illiteracy across the empire, and the high cost of a journal subscription compared to the average silk-factory worker's or tobacco grower's earnings meant that the ecumenical nahda was never socially egalitarian.[47] Then again, it was never imagined to be. The pen and print, not populism, was its principal medium. There were, to be sure, many aspects to the nahda, and arguably many "other" nahdas, as Ilham Khuri-Makdisi reminds us in her work on transnational radicalism, that were far more invested in labor rights and anarchism than in the didacticism of the elitist nahda thinkers in the seminal half century between the massacres of 1860 and the outbreak of World War I.[48]

DISSONANCE WITHIN THE ECUMENICAL FRAME

The ecumenical frame was fundamentally imbalanced from the outset. Its design was haphazard rather than methodical, and the rules that emerged to define the point and counterpoint of coexistence were the fruits of an unstated consensus rather than the explicit embrace of secular principles. The new culture of coexistence was riddled with caveats that diminished the quality of the ecumenical frame and muted the most radical implications of secular equality in the name of national harmony. Whereas the post-1860 Ottoman context cumulatively legitimated the principle of secular constitutional equality between Muslim and non-Muslim Arabic-speaking subjects and citizens, the question of where and how to distinguish between unity and equality was never clear. There was a world of difference between being antisectarian and advocating secular equality, and between advocating secular equality and actually implementing it in tangible ways. These ambiguities reinforced religious difference as much as they promised to supersede it.

The indisputable fact is that the most unambiguous calls for equality between Muslim and non-Muslim in the Mashriq, as well as the earliest calls to separate religion from the state in order to promote this equality, were mostly voiced by individual Christian Arabs—though these men and women did not necessarily identify themselves as Christian.[49] These calls by figures such as Butrus al-Bustani were made not only to advocate for solidarity with Muslim Arabs. They were also made to fight against the siren song of modern minoritarianism, that inability or refusal of non-Muslims to imagine the possibility of solidarity with Muslim compatriots in a European-dominated age. So long as Ottomanism was sustained in the Mashriq, as it was in fact, and so long as this Ottomanism was able to restrain the worst impulses of European colonialism, the ecumenical strand of Arab thought held a clear structural, political, economic, and moral advantage over its sectarian and separatist cousins. Bustani's compatriot Jurji Zaydan anticipated the ecumenical potential of the post-1860 age when he advocated from Cairo what he described as the community of shared interest, or *jami'at al-manfa'a*—that is to say, the set of affiliations that promoted the actual self-interest of individuals as opposed to the illusory affiliations of abstract loyalties, particularly religious ones, that appeared to motivate people to act irrationally for the benefit of self-serving leaders.[50]

Ottoman Arab non-Muslims worked in the moment after the visible waning of Ottoman Islamic primacy had commenced, but before the shock of the European destruction of the Ottoman Empire. Their styles differed, but their core message of ecumenical solidarity with Muslim Arabs through the medium of the Arabic language was remarkably consistent. Some, like Bustani, were careful to avoid any subject that might provoke sectarian sentiment. His journal, *Al-Jinan*, which was supported by the khedive of Egypt and was emblazoned with the apocryphal prophetic saying "Hubb al-watan min al-iman" (Love of the nation stems from faith), and his lectures on the need to educate women and on Arab civilization consistently struck a cautious, almost anodyne ecumenical note that real piety and religion were the bedrock of national harmony.

Others, such as Farah Antun, a *nahdawist* publisher, essayist, playwright, and early socialist whose self-financed journal *Al-Jami'a* was struggling for readership in Egypt, were far more provocative in pushing the limits of ecumenical thought. Antun asserted that Islam and Christianity were "conjoined twins" and essentially similar. He called, on principle, for the right of members of any faith, including atheists, to occupy every state position—a public call almost no other individual was willing to make so stridently in this period, and certainly a call that no significant Muslim Arab intellectual of his era made.[51] Still other Christian Arabs were almost poetic in their ecumenism. When the socialist thinker and proponent of Darwinism Shibli Shummayil, a Syrian Greek Catholic living in Egypt, wrote to Rashid Rida, the Muslim founder of the journal *Al-Manar,* to express his admiration for the Prophet Muhammad, he anticipated a trope that would become a commonplace in the twentieth century: that Islam was an integral part of a broad multireligious Arabic culture. "You look at Muhammad as a prophet and make him great," he confided to Rida, "while I look at him as a man and make him greater." Shummayil's point may seem hackneyed today, but that he could write explicitly and confidently about Islam's prophet as a secular and ethical figure for non-Muslims emphasized the promise of the Arab multireligious culture in the late Ottoman Mashriq.[52] The populist Coptic clergyman Qommus Sergius, in turn, dramatically preached anticolonial national unity in 1919 from Al-Azhar, the great citadel of Islamic learning in Cairo. He was the first Christian priest to preach there—and his message was emphatically one of national solidarity across religious lines.[53]

This prominence of Christian Arabs in the ecumenical nahda is often noted and yet passed over far too quickly in the existing scholarship, as if voicing secular criticism was either "proto-nationalist" (without ambiguity, ventriloquizing a notionally original Western secularism) or a mere tactical maneuver by so-called minority thinkers in the Muslim world—and as if what counted more was their passive filial communal identity and not their active will to affiliate with and participate in the creation of a dynamic, variegated, and, as we shall see, deeply ambivalent ecumenical culture.[54] The vast majority of their coreligionists did not think like Bustani, Zaydan, Shummayil, Sergius, or Antun, any more than the vast majority of European Jews thought like Walter Benjamin or most African Americans thought like like W. E. B. Du Bois. Similar to Bustani before them, Zaydan and Antun rarely concealed their debt to European orientalists or to American missionaries. Antun, in fact, openly admired the anti-Semitic and anti-Muslim French philologist and orientalist Ernest Renan, who in 1852 had juxtaposed the critical and free-thinking medieval Arab Muslim philosopher Ibn Rushd with the dogmatic literalists of Islam who allegedly shut down the possibility of scientific thought. Renan's work provided Antun (and indeed many Arabs after him) with a template for thinking about the place and meaning of religion in modern society. Yet he also disavowed totally Renan's racial supremacy. In this regard, the so-called "master" Renan had nothing to teach his Christian Arab disciple.[55]

Nevertheless, in their emphasis on agency, self-improvement, and individual ethical and moral choice, many of the most prominent Christian Arabs of the nahda consistently privileged a rationalist antisectarian sensibility over an overtly anticolonial one. Qommus Sergius's actions in 1919, in other words, were the culmination of a formative ecumenical era that cannot be taken for granted. During the late Ottoman era, Syrian and Coptic Christians, generally speaking, appeared to be less troubled than their Muslim Arab peers by the looming military, cultural, and economic presence of Europe in the Ottoman Empire. Zaydan briefly worked as a translator for the British army in the Sudan. Literate émigré Syrian Christians played a leading role in the booming press in Egypt under British rule (including moving the most important nahda journal, *Al-Muqtataf*, from Beirut; founding the country's major newspaper, *Al-Ahram*; and both Zaydan's *Al-Hilal* and Antun's *Al-Jami'a*). Foreign and Syrian Christians were disproportionately employed by the British colonial administration in Egypt (as indeed were Coptic Christians), and several of their leading lights openly ingratiated themselves with British colonial rulers. Several Coptic Christians took advantage of the British occupation to advocate and organize along avowedly communal lines.[56]

Christian Arabs of the ecumenical nahda were acutely aware of the problem of religious "fanaticism" that haunted the quality of contemporary coexistence with their Muslim compatriots. Yet for them, while the allegedly ignorant, uneducated, and fanatical populace and the shadowy elites who allegedly manipulated them represented either the absence or corruption of religion, "true" religion was invariably embodied in the actions and words of men of social standing, whether the medieval Arab caliph in

Baghdad who tolerated non-Muslims or the iconic Muslim Algerian prince in exile in Damascus, Abdelkader, who saved many Christians in July 1860.[57]

This affirmation of "true" piety revealed the priorities of the ecumenical nahda: the impetus to discourage sectarianism preceded, but also paved the way for, calls for national unity; the promotion of national unity between adherents of different faiths, in turn, became far more evident than the advocacy of secularism, let alone of a radical, dissenting secular consciousness. The brilliant Arab émigré Amin Rihani, who said in 1910 that the great struggle of the age was "between those who do not belong to any clan and the clans themselves," was emblematic of the secular potential of the ecumenical nahda. But in expressing this potential so boldly, he was also a minority of a minority.[58]

Many leading nahda figures who specifically identified as Christian were, if anything, hostile to secularism. Louis Cheikho, the Chaldean-born Jesuit theologian and Arabist, was a case in point, but hardly the only one. Unlike the largely self-taught and dilettantish Zaydan or Rihani, Cheikho imbibed his Catholic education, first in Ghazir, Mount Lebanon, and then in France. He settled in Beirut, where he founded in 1898 the Arabic Catholic journal *Al-Machriq* (Mashriq) and aggressively defended Catholic dogma in the face of what he perceived to be the heretical (especially secular and Protestant) enemies of the Catholic Church.

The heretics that consumed Cheikho's attention were not the Muslims, but the materialists and the secularists: in a word, so-called atheists like Rihani. Cheikho published an essay in 1901 on "Religious Tolerance" in *Al-Machriq* in which he fretted about the "new civilization" that threatened to undermine the foundations of piety in the East. He cited approvingly none other than the itinerant Muslim luminary Jamal al-Din al-Afghani to bolster his case against atheism. Yet he also admitted that there were some basic principles of modern social organization by which everyone had to abide: the acceptance of religious pluralism and difference, and the duty of the government to ensure freedom of religion to each subject so long as religion was not used to "sow discord."[59] In other words, for Cheikho, the ecumenical nahda, while real, had also to be limited and conditional. Far more important than absolute freedom was the absolute commitment to not transgress the religious beliefs and dogmas of each

religious community. To be Christian in the Ottoman Empire did not pre-
dispose one to secularism, just as it did not necessarily impel one to
embrace minoritarian consciousness.

ISLAM AND ECUMENICAL NAHDA

In the shadow of the late Ottoman state, Muslim Arab figures also played
their own vital role in legitimating the ecumenical frame. Unlike most
Christian proponents of the ecumenical nahda, educated Muslim Arabs
had far more to salvage from the ideological and legal structures of the
dying Islamic imperial system. Like their Christian peers, Muslim Arabs
were divided and diverse in their recognition and understanding of the
implications of the new ecumenical frame. Landowners, government
functionaries, traders and merchants, scions of important families, and
religious reformers and pietists hardly shared a common religious or
political outlook. Consistently, however, most of them conflated a sense of
being Arab with being Muslim, without necessarily excluding their fellow
Arabic-speaking Christian and Jewish Ottoman citizens from a new sense
of public community. While some were pulled into the new orbit of pan-
Islamic cosmopolitanism that connected the Arab world to South and
Southeast Asia, in which Arab Muslims could take pride of place, they
were also, and even mostly, grounded in the distinctive Ottoman Arab
political and social environment of the Mashriq. For Muslim Arabs such
as Rashid Rida, founder of the Islamic journal *Al-Manar,* there was little
contradiction between being part of a global community of Muslims and
participating in the ecumenical nahda that perforce included significant
Christian and Jewish Arabs.[60]

Rida's correspondence with various well-known Egyptian and Syrian
Christian Arab essayists and publishers underscored a depth of social intimacy that cut across religious lines and a sharpened religious consciousness that were both hallmarks of the Arabic ecumenical frame. Rida had
first traveled to Egypt in 1897 from Tripoli in the company of his Christian
friend Farah Antun. Although Rida himself rejected the legitimacy and
applicability of new currents of socialism, secularism, and separatism, he
did not question the legitimacy of the presence of the religious other. Rida

informed fellow Syrian émigré writers and journal founders in 1898 that he wanted to establish a journal, *Al-Manar*, in Cairo to promote both Muslim religious reform and "reconciliation" between Islam and Christianity.[61]

Rida also crafted a deliberately ecumenical portrait of his mentor, Muhammad Abduh, who openly accepted Coptic Christian students to his weekly study circle in Egypt. Abduh also attended the inauguration of a Coptic charity association in 1881 and reassured Copts in 1882 of their role in the unsuccessful 'Urabi revolution against the British-appointed khedive that precipitated the British invasion of Egypt and Abduh's exile from his homeland. Rida boasted how Abduh held councils during his exile in Beirut in the 1880s with religious dignitaries from among "the Sunni, the Shi'i, the Druze, the Christian and the Jew" and insisted that all had to be treated with respect.[62] Indeed, although he objected to Jurji Zaydan's secular history of Islam, Rida praised Zaydan for being a "pillar" of the nahda shortly after the latter's death in 1914. Rida also insisted on delivering the eulogy for Farah Antun in 1922, for which the latter's sister Rose wrote him a note of heartfelt gratitude.[63]

For his part, the founder of the Beirut journal *Thamarat al-Funun*, Abd al-Qadir al-Qabbani, who had been a student of Bustani's National School, imbibed his outlook of proper religion in the service of "equality in rights and responsibilities" in a multireligious nation. The exiled Damascus-based Algerian Emir Abdelkader likened the prophets of monotheism to people who "have one father and different mothers."[64] And in Egypt, the khedive and other Muslim Egyptian notables patronized a variety of publications written by Christian Arabs, supported and viewed theater troupes, attended an Arab opera that included Christian Arabs, and participated in Arabic language societies, such as the Academy of Arabic Language in 1892, that reinforced a sense of commonality that bridged a religious divide.[65]

These various expressions of ecumenism—whether in writings, eulogies, or dignified comportment—by leading Muslim Arab figures marked and dogged the transition from an ideology of Ottoman rule that had clearly privileged Islam over all other religions to one of Western colonial supremacy—a shift that had occurred in what appeared to be a blink of an eye. With a few notable exceptions, there was little indication in the prodigious nahda literature produced by Muslim Arabs of the simmering racial or nationalist animosity evident either in the post-emancipation United States or in the post-1878 Balkans. If anything, the remarkable fact was how quickly many leading Arab Muslims in the Mashriq acquiesced to the idea of constitutional equality with their non-Muslim male compatriots. This veritable revolution has never been properly appreciated, especially in contrast to how the Young Turks acted against the Armenians and Greeks, or the white American backlash against black emancipation, or the emergence of anti-Semitism in Europe, or the unfathomable notion for most Europeans of the principle of equality with their colonized subjects.

The sting, however, was in the tail. The acceptance by Muslim thinkers and writers such as Abduh and Rida of a pluralist nation defined by constitutional equality of (male) citizens irrespective of their religious affiliation was coupled with a pervasive assumption that the essential sovereign core of this nation had to remain Muslim—just as Ottoman Turks assumed that the ruling core of the reforming multinational Ottoman Empire had to be Turkish. New nineteenth-century private Islamic schools established in Syria and Egypt, for example, as well as the bulk of the Ottoman state civil and military schools that opened across the empire by the turn of the century, catered either exclusively or primarily to Muslim students. They were premised on the understanding that non-Muslims had their own well-funded network of local and foreign missionary schools and so what was urgently needed were Muslim or Ottoman equivalents to these schools. When Rida asked Abduh in 1898 about the dangers of foreign and missionary influence, Abduh allegedly responded by saying that proper religious education was the "barrier" that protected Muslims. If this "feeble barrier" were to fall, wrote Rida, paraphrasing Abduh, the condition of the Muslims would become "worse than that of the Jews," who at least had been recompensed with "great wealth" for their "loss of sovereignty and power." [66]

Muslim Arabs such as Rida and Abduh shared with the Christian Arabs of the nahda the understanding that the best antidote to sectarian thinking was sustained pedagogical intervention; they too called for schools, though not so much to create a national community of the kind that Bustani had envisioned, but rather to achieve Muslim unity. Abduh deplored "ignorance" among his Muslim brethren in much the same way as Bustani lamented it among his Syrian compatriots. In his most famous work, *Risalat al-Tawhid* (Theology of Unity), Abduh discouraged "foolish disquisitions" that caused an otherwise united band of brothers traveling toward a common destination to take different routes. Abduh warned that when darkness set in, the erstwhile brothers in faith mistook each other for enemies though they all shared the same ultimate goal.[67] Elsewhere, Abduh noted that where there were sectarian wars in Islam, the motivation was not faith, but politics, greed, and "ignorance."[68] Almost all of the Islamically minded reformers advocated an Islam that could steer the Muslim community away from what they regarded as moribund traditions, and against what Abduh's disciple, Shakib Arslan, himself from a feudal family, would describe as the superficial Islam of the "ignorant commoner and the ossified shaykh."[69]

But Muslim Arabs such as Rida, Abduh, and Arslan were also preoccupied with the alleged sectarian fanaticism of the Western "Christian" colonial powers and missionaries. With good reason, they believed that Islam, and the Ottoman domains, were under serious and sustained attack. In the name of defending a rational Islam from ignorant Muslims and devious Western Christians alike, they viewed the Christians of the Mashriq in two distinct ways; on the one hand, as communities whose protection was a pretext for anti-Muslim Western colonialism; on the other hand, as individuals whose love of Arabic marked them as brethren, potential converts, or compatriots in Islamic societies. The defense of Muslim sovereignty nevertheless precluded empathy with the anxieties of non-Muslims of the Mashriq who had long lived under discriminatory Islamic rule; the rhetoric of Islam's tolerance of non-Muslims, in fact, consistently obscured the inequality of Islamic empires; it elided the obvious fact that the secular equality that underpinned modern coexistence did not emerge from, and was not easily reconcilable with, any religious tradition, including Islam.[70]

In the reformist secular and pietistic Islamic imagination, for the ecumenical frame to be viable it had to reflect the fact that Egypt and the rest of the Mashriq were "Muslim," as opposed to multireligious, societies. Virtually all of Abduh's and Rida's work had this as an unquestionable premise. And it was not just they. Like Abduh and Rida, the well-off Egyptian lawyer and nationalist Mustafa Kamil, who would found the anticolonial National Party in Egypt in 1907, reiterated this conviction.

For Kamil, Egypt's Islam constituted a counterpoint to Europe's Christianity. In Kamil's view, Eastern Christians (especially the native Copts) and Jews could be, and ideally had to be, included in nationalist Egypt, but they had *collectively* to know their place, just as "ignorant," lower-class Muslims had also to understand the need to reformulate their allegedly vulgar form of Islam.[71] This hierarchy of belonging reflected one of the chief ambiguities of the ecumenical frame: Muslims and non-Muslims belonged "fully" to the modernizing states of Khedival Egypt and the Ottoman Empire, but also differently. It was out of the question for a non-Muslim, by definition, to think about being head of state, governor of a province, or a general in the army. Yet, by the same token, it was also impossible to ignore the fact that under the British occupation, the Syrian Christian community thrived in Alexandria and Cairo, foreign missionary societies flourished, and Copts in Egypt were overrepresented as graduates from the newly established state, law, and medical schools, and hence in the Egyptian bureaucracy. Britain even appointed a Coptic Christian, Butrus Ghali, as prime minister of Egypt in 1908, although he was assassinated two years later by an Egyptian nationalist.[72]

Rida's scathing response to the so-called Coptic Congress, which was held in Asyut, Egypt, in 1911, captures precisely this hierarchy of national belonging. The controversial congress was convened in defiance of the Coptic patriarch by several Coptic journalists, Protestant converts, and activists, some of whom were based in England. They demanded equal rights with Muslim Egyptians and, more specifically, a sectarian electoral system and the exemption of Copts from official work on Sunday. Outraged, Rida declared that Coptic Christians should realize that their Christian Coptism was a religious identity protected by the historical norms of Islamic toleration. He dismissed the claims for equal religious education as a violation of modern statecraft: the religion of the majority had to be respected and taught and it was incumbent upon the minority to heed its place. He insisted, therefore, that politically Copts had to identify as "Arab Egyptians," which he maintained was inseparable from Islam.[73] Rida, like Kamil, trod the very fine line between a defensive articulation of proper, historically tolerant, inclusive, "true," and civilized Islam and a chauvinistic reaffirmation of Islamic primacy in what remained, after all, a multireligious empire.

THE CHOREOGRAPHY OF COEXISTENCE

The irony of modern coexistence was that it reinforced the immanence of religious communities just when their transcendence first became imaginable. The constitutional state that Sultan Abdülhamid II had conceded in 1876 had never suggested a "melting pot" where various ethnic and religious identities would be dissolved into a single secular (and racial) commonality. Instead, Ottoman unity was premised on the national concordance of different religious and ethnic elements, each of which preserved its distinctive and allegedly "age-old" character under a sovereign centralizing state. No matter how secular any Ottoman subject might have been in outlook, he or she remained forcibly tethered to an established religious community, since secular marriage, divorce, and inheritance were not possible in the empire. Islam remained symbolically and constitutionally ascendant over all other religions in the empire, for it was *the* religion of state according to the 1876 constitution. Equality was therefore a matter of degree even at the level of theory and law.

To push too hard in one direction or the other—to appear to be too discordantly secular or stridently sectarian—was to court trouble. When Farah Antun appeared to suggest that Islam was inherently less tolerant than Christianity in 1902, or when Jurji Zaydan described in his 1912 history of Islamic civilization that the early Muslim Umayyad dynasty in Damascus was capricious and chauvinistic, both men were met with a backlash that centered on their unfittedness to write about Islamic history and their alleged anti-Muslim fanaticism. Zaydan was severely criticized in the pages of *Al-Manar* by the Lucknow-based Indian Muslim reformer Shibli Nu'mani. He was also prevented from taking up a post teaching Islamic history at the newly established Cairo University.[74] Antun was severely condemned by none other than Muhammad Abduh, whose rebuttal was eventually published under the title *Al-Islam wa al-nasraniyya* (Islam and Christianity) in 1904. The tone of Abduh's riposte to Antun certainly had little resemblance to the forbearance he was remembered to have displayed and embodied in Beirut in the 1880s. Abduh drew attention to the Iberian expulsion of the Jews from Spain in 1492 and the St. Bartholomew's Day massacre in France in 1572 as evidence of Christian fanaticism, yet he ignored the more recent Damascus massacre of 1860 and the bloody Ottoman campaigns against the Armenians of the 1890s. Far more aggressively than anything Antun had done with respect to the Quran, Abduh also engaged in a vulgar reading of a verse from the Gospel of Matthew in which Jesus says, "I have not come to bring peace, but a sword" (10:34–36), to insist that whereas Christianity was inherently violent, Islam was fundamentally tolerant. Nowhere was the ambivalence of the ecumenical frame more evident than in the outburst of a religious scholar famed for his antisectarianism. In the eyes of Abduh, the secular Antun was sectarian.

The issue at work here was more complex than mere chauvinism. Fundamentally, it had to do with a sense of propriety calibrated to fit the requirements of the age: neither Abduh nor Nu'mani criticized their Christian Arab contemporaries because they were dhimmis, but rather because Antun and Zaydan had engaged in what their Muslim critics considered to be demonstrably injurious and tendentious anti-Muslim narratives. Zaydan and Antun had drawn, in part, on the authority of European orientalists to make a secular argument about the stagnation of Islamic civilization. They had suggested that they were more objective than traditional Muslim chroniclers. Both nahda writers had infringed upon what Nu'mani, Rida, and Abduh—themselves, of course, also men of the nahda—presumably felt strongly was the right of Muslims to narrate their own history on their own communal and pietistic terms.[75]

By the same token, when Antun responded to Abduh's criticisms in print in his journal *Al-Jami'a*, he clarified just how conservative was Abduh's antisectarian reformism and its underlying rhetoric of Muslim toleration. Antun held that different religions were ultimately divergent expressions of the same basic spiritual truth that men of religion had systematically misconstrued into particular rigid and compulsory edifices. He claimed, therefore, that the universal and underlying humanistic principles of religious laws, not their formal proscriptions, were what ultimately mattered. For this reason, he claimed to be "astonished" that Abduh would present a biblical verse so out of context that it flagrantly violated "Christian feelings." Antun presented a pedagogy of ecumenism that would see "religious books purified from every word that oppresses or causes harm" by the deliberate and judicious interpretation of enlightened men of good will from all religious communities. To do this was to squeeze from otherwise dangerously ambiguous verses from the Quran or the Bible "the good of tolerance [*tasahul/tasamuh*] to the greatest degree possible rather than the evil of fanaticism [*ta'assub*] that [Abduh] has extracted from them."[76]

Antun pointedly insisted that "tolerance" (*al-tasahul*) was a neologism that belonged neither to an exclusively Islamic nor Christian tradition, but to a modern condition that had opened new cultural, social, and political horizons of coexistence based on secular equality.[77] Antun went further: "true tolerance" in a multireligious society meant fellowship with those who are fundamentally different in a world defined by pluralism and diversity (*tanawu'*). According to Antun, Islamic brotherhood was neither universalist, for by definition it excluded non-Muslims, nor truly tolerant, because it judged things from within an Islamic tradition. "Truth be told," wrote Antun, "the Ottoman Christians and all the Christians of the East do not want to hear about religious reform in this era, neither in relation to Christianity nor Islam."[78] Antun was adamant: there could be no equality outside a secular state.[79]

More than anything else, the exchange between Abduh and Antun brought to the fore a central ambiguity at the heart of modern coexistence in the Mashriq. For Abduh and his hagiographer Rida, to be acceptable, secular equality—and virtually every other modern constitutional principle introduced in this era—had to be reconciled with a rejuvenated Islamic tradition. Where they felt there was no way to reconcile secular equality and Islam, it was secular equality, not Islam, that had to give way. Antun saw things quite differently. For him, the principle of secular equality, and not religious dogma or laws, was sacrosanct. Far more openly than anything Butrus al-Bustani had written decades before, Antun desired not merely a lack of persecution, but full political rights and unconstrained freedom of thought and expression within a secular constitutional state.[80]

DUALISM WITHIN THE ECUMENICAL FRAME

The problem with the ecumenical frame was that it was not inherently emancipatory in the secular sense that Antun envisioned. Rather, contradictory emancipatory impulses proliferated within it—reformers from all sects desired freedom from suffocating communal traditions, secularists desired freedom from religious obscurantism, anxious non-Muslims wanted freedom from fear of the Muslim majority, Muslims wanted freedom from fear of domination of Islamic lands by Christian Europe, many Muslims desired freedom from the tyranny of "despotism," and women of all faiths desired better education. To be free was not necessarily to want to be secular. Despite Antun's debate with Abduh, in fact, the most *sustained* intellectual battles in the Mashriq were often fought within the confines of each religious community—or at least among members of the same recognized community. There were, after all, legal, financial, and political stakes, not simply aspirational ones, involved in being able to represent a religious community—or, more precisely, to represent what it meant to be a Muslim, a Christian, or a Jew—before Ottoman or European colonial authorities in local politics, courts, and administration.

The acute awareness of religious difference and its social reproduction through the establishment of late nineteenth-century communal schools, philanthropic associations, printing presses, newspapers, and women's societies that catered to specific communities were integral aspects of the ecumenical nahda. Organizations such as the Syrian Orthodox society, the Armenian Orthodox Society, the Islamic Benevolent (Maqasid) Society, and the Great Coptic Benevolent Society were all set up in rapid succession in Egypt, Palestine, Mount Lebanon, and Syria. But this proliferation of communal groups masked a fundamental conflict within each group over where to draw the proper boundary between natal filiation and affiliation with Ottoman or Egyptian compatriots belonging to different communities, between faith and society, and between church and state.

Each community was divided into myriad factions, classes, regions, and outlooks that belied a singular sectarian identity. At the same time, members of each community assumed that members of other communities were not their responsibility to educate or discipline. The constant interplay between communal and national belonging was one of the hallmarks of the modern ecumenical frame—not so much (or not always) a clash between old and new, or traditional and modern, but instead the inevitable dualism of modern identity in the region, a dualism structured and sustained by the history and transformation of imperial politics, law, and culture. This dualism demanded a careful choreography to know when to

emphasize the communal, when to mute it, and when to sublimate it genuinely or cynically within an ostensibly cohesive national whole. Occasionally,
this choreography faltered, such as in the staging of the Coptic Congress of
1911, but it rarely failed outright.[81]

Constant thought, activity, and energy were poured into defining the
communal side of identity. The battles to reform the conditions of the
Coptic Church and clergy were constant after 1860. The creation of a lay-
dominated Coptic Communal Council in 1874 and the 1891 *jami'at al-
tawfiq* sought to limit the power of the church in organizing the civil
affairs of the community; run its pious endowments (and demand financial disclosure); establish schools, student associations, and charities for
Copts; and provide regular salary and education for the clergy. These
struggles underscored the fact that the battles that raged most intensely
were communal, not separatist, ones. They involved Coptic notables, merchants, landowners, intellectuals, and church figures far more than they
did Muslim Egyptians. They were about identifying the proper location
and face of the community within the ecumenical frame in which the
Coptic Church continued to dominate the social meaning of the Coptic
community, especially as the rules governing marriage, inheritance, and
divorce were adjudicated by Coptic judges drawn from the priesthood.[82]

The powerful, landowning Maronite Church in Mount Lebanon waged
its most bitter battles not with Muslims or Muslim thought, but with a
significant strain of anticlericalism espoused by émigré writers such as
Amin Rihani, whom the Maronite Church excommunicated in 1903. This
dissenting thought was of far greater concern to the Maronite Church
than the intense debates raging among Muslim intellectuals in nearby
Damascus.[83] Yet almost all overtly anticlerical writers who came from
Christian backgrounds, such as Rihani or Khalil Gibran, left the task of
criticizing Islam, which after all was the religion of the state, to Muslims
themselves. In turn, Qasim Amin's *The Liberation of Women* (1899) called
for the education and emancipation of upper-class *Muslim* women from
the yoke of what Amin described as capricious, despotic, and un-Islamic
traditions that kept Egyptian Muslims mired in "backwardness" and
"ignorance." Amin was a prominent Muslim Cairene lawyer and a student
of Abduh's. His book provoked massive controversy within Egypt about
the rights and responsibilities of Muslim women. Amin and his many

critics assumed that Coptic women answered to their own separate "woman's question."[84]

The emergence of the women's movement at the turn of the century itself reflected the ecumenical age of which it was a part, reproducing its class and communal bias and its overwhelming preference for reformed religiosity over unadulterated secularism as the means of transforming the status and role of women in society. Virtually every prominent female nahda writer—from Zainab Fawaz to May Ziadeh to Huda Sharaawi to Nazira Zeinnedine—shared this outlook and expressed it in her individual writings and in salons, communal ladies' societies, and nascent national women's organizations. An acute awareness of religious difference was coupled with a commonality of prescriptions for "oriental," "Syrian," and "Egyptian" women about motherhood, child rearing, and furnishing a home.[85] Labiba Ahmad's late nineteenth-century journal *Al-nahda al-nisa'iyya* (The Women's Awakening) emphasized the urgent role that pietistic Muslim women had to play in elevating their society—by being better Muslim mothers, raising properly pious Muslim children, and promoting a virtuous and Islamic society.

Esther Azhari Moyal, who was a Jewish correspondent for the first Arab women's journal, *Al-Fatat* (Young Girl), was also a cofounder of the Beirut-based association Nahdat al-nisa' (The Awakening of Women) in 1896. Whereas Labiba Ahmad emphasized the role of women within an Islamic environment, Moyal spoke about women's rights in the context of a more capacious and secular "Eastern Arab civilization" that included Muslims, Christians, and Jews.[86] The almost identical names given to an Islamically oriented women's journal in Cairo and to a more secular women's society in Beirut mirrored the debate about what it meant to be an Arab, an Egyptian, or a Syrian in the late Ottoman era, and about how to reconcile the rights and responsibilities of being a Muslim, Christian, or Jewish woman with the reality of religious diversity.

Their roles as mothers, wives, and daughters ensured that women across the Mashriq embodied the dualism of distinct communal and multireligious national belonging. They contended with its inequalities more than men of similar social status did: they had to make a case to be educated, to raise the age of consent for marriage, to have better access to divorce, to claim a share of inheritance, and to control the custody of children. But they could only do so as separate Muslim, Christian, or Jewish mothers, daughters, or wives and never as secular Ottomans. Yet most female proponents of the nahda, as far as I can tell, fundamentally accepted the principle (but crucially not the content or implications) of new, religiously segregated communal and legal structures known as "personal status" laws (*ahwal shakhsiyya*) that governed marriage, divorce, and inheritance across the region, drawn up by male jurists and reformers.[87] These laws were not generally identified as sectarian, although their effect was precisely to distinguish between Muslim and non-Muslim in the most intimate areas of social life.

The Ottoman Family Law of 1917, which was drawn up by a committee of Muslim, Christian, and Jewish experts, drew on multiple schools of Islamic thought to produce a single, codified, "rational" law of personal status for all Muslim citizens, but also included separate statutes for Christian and Jewish citizens. The marriage of a Muslim woman to a non-Muslim man was expressly forbidden.[88] As members of one family living in a new national house, Arabic-speaking brothers and sisters ostentatiously shared one living room, only to retreat each evening to carefully guarded bedrooms. In Syria and Egypt, the acknowledgment of seemingly irreconcilable religious difference in one sphere was crucial for its deemphasis in another. The codified, gendered, religiously segregated realm constituted a buttress for a notion of public secular harmony of ostensibly politically equal religious citizens *and* communities.

AVOIDING FANATICISM

By the end of a half century of Ottoman peace across the Mashriq, an "overlapping consensus" (to borrow a term from philosopher John Rawls) developed within the ecumenical frame.[89] The main elements of this consensus were loyalty to the diminished sovereignty of the Ottoman state that ostensibly treated its constituent elements equitably; the avoidance of sectarian "fanaticism" in a multireligious society, and the understanding that harsh and infelicitous sectarian language would be eschewed and religious controversies avoided; the notion that the sectarian was fundamentally a problem of "ignorance" and especially of the lower, uneducated, and allegedly uncivilized class of Muslims and non-Muslims; and finally, the enduring and categorical differentiation between the promulgation of secular citizenship and the parallel development of inegalitarian, gendered, and religiously informed laws of personal status. For all its contradictions and paradoxes and elisions, indeed because of them, in the half century after 1860, the ecumenical trajectory was far more pronounced in the Ottoman Mashriq than anywhere else in the late Ottoman Empire.

Following the 1908 Young Turk Revolution, many Arabs favored decentralization while others were firmly committed to strengthening and serving the cause of Ottoman unity. The main Ottoman Arab opposition party to the CUP, which was established in Cairo in 1912 under the name the Ottoman Decentralization Party, and which included figures such as Rashid Rida, was explicit in its embrace of religious pluralism. Its slogan was "Religion is for God; [the] homeland is for all."[90] Even the Arab National Congress that convened in Paris in 1913 to call for more Arab representation in the Ottoman parliament, and for equal treatment of Arabic and Turkish, premised its "national" cause on the commonality of Muslim and non-Muslim Arabs. The upshot was that Arabs had varying social positions and relationships to political authority and often held diametrically opposed conceptions of the role of religion in statecraft. To the extent that a sectarian problem in the Levant in this period was recognized, it was construed largely as an internal, pedagogical one, and not, as was the case with the Young Turks especially after 1912, projected onto specific and now alien and alienated communities, minorities, and "cancers" within the nation that had to be removed or destroyed.

The publication in 1913 of Yusuf al-Bustani's *Tarikh harb al-Balqan al-ula* (History of the First Balkan War) epitomized this differentiation between the ethno-religious nationalisms of the northern empire and the ecumenical Arabism of the Ottoman Mashriq. In the book, Bustani, a Cairo-based Christian journal editor, offered a diagnosis of the problem of the late Ottoman Empire, which had stymied its "revival" and led to its defeat in the First Balkan War. For him, the main problem was not the diversity of communities, but the reality of corruption and backwardness that had rotted the empire to its core. Bustani collected testimonies from major Christian and Muslim Arab figures, Syrian and Egyptian—

including Rashid Rida and Farah Antun, politicians, teachers, reformers, journalists, and jurists—to analyze the war and suggest the best way to resurrect the Ottoman Empire.[91]

What is remarkable about the tone of these testimonies, as well as Bustani's own narrative about the war, is how different it was from the pessimistic tones struck by both Ottoman officials and European observers—a function as much of their continuing investment in the idea of a viable multireligious Ottoman dominion as of their distance from the horrors of the battlefields.[92] The Muslim and Christian Arabs collectively echoed typical *nahdawist* refrains: to be saved, the empire had to embrace constitutionalism, end corruption, and strengthen the bonds of unity of its diverse religious and racial elements. The single note of skepticism among Bustani's contributors was sounded by Farah Antun. He insisted that "we do not lack declarations [about equality, progress, and unity]; we lack putting these declarations into practice."[93] He was right. Official proclamations, laws, and aspirations to unity and reform were one thing; the implementation of them was quite something else. Yet Bustani's staunchly Ottomanist and modernist position was not simply a theoretical exercise; it was a reflection of a fundamentally changed late nineteenth-century Ottoman Empire that had produced two irreconcilable cultures: a militant nationalist one that violently repudiated religious difference in the name of ethno-nationalist coherence and an ecumenical Arabic one that embraced this difference under a diminished, but still capable, Ottoman sovereignty.

By taking hard politics off the table—or, rather, by being absent from the table where great diplomatic and military decisions were decided—Arab subjects could, in the relative security of the late Ottoman age, posit and debate any number of variations on a single theme: how best to assure the bonds of unity, how to "catch up" to the standard of Western scientific development, and where and how to best draw the lines between secular and religious, as well as individual, communal, and national, identifications. The Arabic ecumenical frame, in short, was a creation of the late Ottoman age. The fact of the Ottoman reformation was the umbilical cord that nourished and sustained an embryonic project. When the Ottoman state was brought to its knees during World War I, the Arabs of the

Mashriq were confronted by a new and abrupt reality of direct European rule. They who had thrived in the space between diminishing, yet reforming, Ottoman and expanding Western sovereignties in the late nineteenth century had now to recalibrate the ecumenical nahda within a new, European-dominated Arab world.

PART II

4 Colonial Pluralism

Colonial pluralism was basically dual: on one side was a
patchwork of customs and practices considered customary,
their single shared feature being some association with the
colonized; on the other side was the modern, the imported
law of the colonizer.

— Mahmood Mamdani, *Citizen and Subject* (1996)

When Sharif Husayn bin Ali of Mecca declared the Arab revolt against
Ottoman rule in 1916, he opened a canonical chapter in modern Arab history. The sharif threw in his lot with the British agent T. E. Lawrence
("Lawrence of Arabia") in an effort to secure for himself a vaguely defined,
independent Arab kingdom. Although the Hashemite leader later realized
that he had been deceived by his British handlers, who had drawn up a
separate, secret plan with their French allies to partition the region
between their respective empires, he and his sons nevertheless continued
down the path of collaboration. Their dreams of a vast and unified Arab
kingdom never materialized.

This tragic and sordid story is well known in its broad outlines. Less
appreciated, I think, is the degree to which the Hashemite attempt to create Arab kingdoms in the Hijaz and in Syria reflected one of the earliest
efforts to nationalize the ecumenical nahda. These efforts were beset by
the immense difficulties and ambiguities inherent in transforming ideals
of unity into projects of effective sovereignty. The masthead of Sharif
Husayn's short-lived newspaper *Al-Qibla* declared the scope of its mission: "to serve Islam and the Arabs." Its first editorial stated that the Arab
rebellion against the Turks was a struggle of the "Arab nation" against

what the newspaper characterized as the anti-Islamic and anti-Arab tyranny of the "Turkish" Committee of Union and Progress. It maintained that the Arabs fought for the "unity of Islam" that had been defiled by the "secularism" and the military incompetence of illegitimate "atheist" Turkish rulers. Another column in the first issue of *Al-Qibla* described the revolt as "the Arab nahda," which in this instance meant specifically the beginnings of the military uprising against allegedly intolerable and barbaric "Turkish" oppression.[1]

As was the case in the wartime Ottoman state against which the sharif rebelled, the recourse to Islamic symbolism was not inconsistent with his plainly secular ambitions to become a member of the "civilized" world. The revolt may have begun in the heart of Arabia and in the cradle of Islam, but Hashemite ambitions stretched across the Mashriq. Sharif Husayn understood that he would have to contend with a multireligious citizenry. Indeed, during the secret correspondence between the sharif and Henry McMahon (the British High Commissioner in Egypt) that had paved the way for the Arab revolt, the latter had countered Husayn's expansive territorial claims by falling back on a sectarian reading of the Orient. For McMahon, to be "Arab" was to be Muslim. He therefore challenged Husayn's desire that all of Syria—including what is today Lebanon—should fall under his sovereignty because not all of its inhabitants, he said, were "purely Arab." Husayn replied that these provinces were indeed "purely Arab" because "the Moslem is indistinguishable from the Christian, for they are both descendants of one forefather."[2] Husayn's claim for political independence thus encompassed an overtly Arab Muslim discourse evident in *Al-Qibla* and centered specifically on the caliphate and Mecca; but his ecumenical discourse emphasized the fraternity of Arabs of different faiths. For Husayn, religious difference was not an impediment to an independent Arab world ruled by the Hashemites; for the British and French officials who contemplated their newly acquired Middle Eastern dominions, it was one of its most important foundations.

Following the end of Ottoman rule in the Arab provinces, Sharif Husayn's son Faysal briefly became king of an independent "Arab kingdom" based in Damascus. The constitution drafted in March 1920 by a hastily convened congress made up of Muslim and Christian men, including Rashid Rida, stressed the equality of all Syrians before the law, guaranteed freedom of religious thought and religious practices for "all sects," and maintained that each community had the authority to administer autonomously its own personal-status laws, pious endowments, and communal councils.[3] In 1919, meanwhile, when Egyptians demonstrated against the British occupation of their country, the Coptic priest Qommus Sergius famously preached unity from inside Al-Azhar. This was unquestionably a radical gesture by one of the most traditional of Ottoman-era figures—the cleric—in the most venerable of religious institutions. The value of the priest's gesture lay in its embodiment of an ecumenical national imagination that appeared to put both Islam and Christianity at the service of a unified Egypt. At a time when the Greeks were preparing to launch their disastrous invasion of Izmir and Ottoman Turkish nationalists had already emptied Anatolia of much of its Armenian population, a different kind of nationalism was being elaborated in the Mashriq for the first time.

The Egyptian revolution was crushed by British soldiers. In Syria, Faysal was himself unceremoniously deposed by a French army in July 1920. Britain and France then parceled out what had been interconnected provinces of the Ottoman Empire into new and separate states. They established mandates in Lebanon, Syria, Palestine, and Iraq under Article 22 of the League of Nations charter. Article 22 described mandates as "a sacred trust of civilization." It entrusted to Western powers the allegedly lesser nations—in this case the populations of Syria, Lebanon, and Iraq—in order to prepare them to fulfill their "provisional" independence. The Palestine mandate was exempted from this notional independence, because it was created explicitly in order to fulfill the terms of the 1917 Balfour Declaration that had pledged British imperial support for the establishment of a "national home for the Jewish people" there.

European colonial powers solemnly vowed to protect religious freedoms and uphold religious diversity in the Arab world. Article 8 of the League of Nations Mandate for Syria and Lebanon stipulated that the "Mandatory [i.e., colonial power] shall ensure to all complete freedom of conscience and the free exercise of all forms of worship which are consonant with public order and morality. No discrimination of any kind shall be made between the inhabitants of Syria and the Lebanon on the ground of differences in race, religion or language."[4] The mandatory authority, however, was not

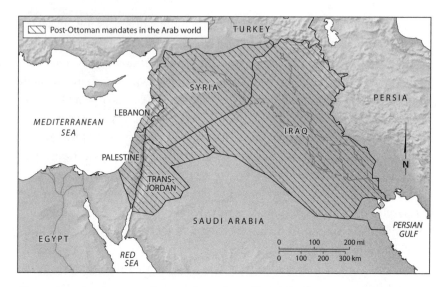

Map 3. Post-Ottoman mandates in the Arab world. (Bill Nelson Cartography).

freely chosen. European empires put down any significant violent protest against their rule. Major anticolonial uprisings were bloodily suppressed in Iraq in 1920, Syria in 1925, and Palestine in 1936.

Religious freedom, in a word, became a metaphor for colonial domination. Upholding religious diversity became its explicit rationale. The irony is that neither France nor Britain accepted the applicability within their mandates of formal protections or rights for "minorities" that they imposed harshly on the defeated Ottoman Empire and that they required of newly independent Poland.[5] The Treaty of Sèvres of 1920 forced what was left of the Ottoman state to give up its Arab provinces, consent to a foreign occupation of Istanbul, and subsidize the linguistic, religious, and educational autonomy of so-called racial minorities in what was left of its domains, all of whom could appeal to Britain and France to intervene on their behalf. At the same time, the guarantee of the right to religious freedom in the Mashriq went hand in hand with a system of coercive colonial rule implemented through martial law, secrecy, and government decree, and the constant threat and use of state violence stifled opposition to British and French colonialism. Historian Michael Provence succinctly describes the powerful effect of a "liberal language [that] shrouded illiberal practice" during the mandate years.[6] The possibility of an overarching secular anti-colonial Arab unity became Western colonialism's great anxiety, not so much because this unity was evident or inevitable, but because the possibility of its existence would have demanded an end to the colonial tutelage that neither Britain nor France was willing to concede.

An iconic photograph of General Henri Gouraud during the proclamation of the state of Grand Liban, or Greater Lebanon, in September 1920 encapsulates the moment when Ottoman-era ecumenism was transformed by European colonialism. Gouraud, fresh from his destruction of Emir Faysal's nascent Arab kingdom in Syria in July of that same year, is flanked by the Maronite patriarch, Elias Hoyek, and by the mufti of Beirut, Mustafa Naja. The inclusion of both religious figures recalls the historical diversity of the Ottoman Levant. But far more obviously, it suggests as well the deliberate manipulation of this diversity by French colonialism. The Christian patriarch, for instance, helped legitimate French rule, at least among the Maronite Christians of the country. Likewise, by promoting the hitherto local mufti of Beirut to appear on the new national stage of Lebanon, he was made to appear the equal of the Maronite patriarch. The centrality of Gouraud in the photograph, above all, underscores the indispensable role France believed itself to be playing in the emerging Arab world as protector of Christians and mediator between various, supposedly antagonistic, communities.

The impulse of Western colonial rule was thus to segregate, disarticulate, and deconstruct an Ottoman whole into various sectarian and regional parts but also to commit to building up new separate, pluralist, dependent national polities. Mahmood Mamdani describes the European colonial partition of Africa as a selective recasting of the societies they encountered there. "The customary," Mamdani writes, "was neither arbitrarily invented . . . nor faithfully reproduced."[7] The same words could be used to describe the European colonial pluralism that manipulated religious diversity in the post-Ottoman Arab world.

Britain, in particular, drew on its vast colonial experience in Egypt and India. From the outset, British rule in Iraq was not interested in transcending religious, tribal, communal, or ethnic differences in the country. Instead, it had reinforced these differences to deflect, undermine, and expose anticolonial sentiment. Initially, at least, the French colonialists in

the Levant adopted an even more divisive strategy than their British counterparts. The enthusiastic champion of "French Asia" Robert de Caix, who
would become France's representative at the Permanent Mandates
Commission in Geneva, wrote in April 1920 that "world peace" would be
better served if there were in the "Orient a certain number of small states"
controlled by European powers that could stifle the "aggressive tendencies
of large unitary national states."[8] France detached Lebanon from Syria to
create a Christian-dominated republic. It separated Druze and Alawite
territories from the rest of Syria. French officials assiduously cultivated
Uniate and Armenian Christian sympathies in order to undermine resistance to French colonialism.

The French mandate in Syria, moreover, established auxiliary military
units that deliberately drew on Alawites, Kurds, Circassians, Armenians,
and Druzes in order to divide and rule.[9] In this way, taking advantage of
the marginalization or the poverty of these groups, and offering some of
them an avenue for social advancement, the mandate willfully cultivated
communal consciousness among Syria's diverse population. In the words
of historian Philip Khoury, the Armenians became a "client community of
the [French mandatory] state."[10] Armenians in Aleppo, for example, were
encouraged by French authorities to suppress the largest anticolonial
revolt of the interwar era, which erupted in Syria in 1925. The French
mandate therefore privileged Christians over Muslims, and heterodox
rural minorities such as Alawis and Druzes over the majority Sunni inhabitants of the cities. Similarly, British officials created and deployed the so-
called Assyrian Levies in their mandate in Iraq as part of their own deliberate strategy to divide and rule.

The upshot was that the post-Ottoman mandatory states reflected a
European imperial will that read the Orient as a mosaic of irreconcilable,
antagonistic religious and ethnic communities. The important point here
is not that colonial authorities were always insidious or ill-intentioned.
Rather, it is to stress how often they drew on the logic of the previous
Ottoman millet system at the same time as they dismantled the unified
structure of Ottoman sovereignty. The aggressive sectarianization inherent in the mandate system was not a concession to European power (as it
had been under Ottoman rule in places like Samos and Mount Lebanon),
but a reflection of this power. To the extent that European colonial powers

made concessions, they did so toward the principle of national unity. Colonial authorities irritably and often, in the face of outright rebellion, relented before the idea of self-determination that their mandates were meant to fulfill. Only following the Great Revolt of 1925 in Syria, for instance, did mandatory authorities finally promulgate Lebanese and Syrian constitutions and establish elected parliaments. Three years after crushing anticolonial demonstrations in its "protectorate," Britain, in turn, granted Egypt a nominal independence in 1922, reserving for itself the right to control the Suez Canal and the Sudan, to protect minorities and foreigners, and to oversee foreign policy. Britain also retreated from its plan to partition Palestine following the rekindling of the massive revolt, which began in 1936 and had widespread sympathy in the Arab world.

THE STRUGGLES FOR ARAB SOVEREIGNTY

Although the map of the modern Arab world, like that of modern Africa, was largely drawn by Britain and France to serve their own colonial interests, my concern in the rest of this book lies primarily in tracing how Arabs adapted to their post-Ottoman world. Unlike the nationalist Turkish republic, which mobilized every ounce of its coercive capacity to make an ostensibly homogeneous Turkish people, and in the process waged a ferocious anticolonial war that took aim at the legacies of Ottoman religious and ethnic diversity, nationalists in the Mashriq neither had military power nor waged outright war on diversity.[11]

Arabs had to negotiate, not fight, their way to independence. The projects of national unity in Syria, Lebanon, Palestine, Iraq, and Egypt inevitably had to rely far more on persuasion than on the raw calculus of power. The great colonial question in the post-Ottoman Arab world, therefore, was not how many guns anticolonialists could gather, but how credibly, and on what terms, they could appear to unify their own people in the face of colonial overlords who typically insisted there was no such people. These questions never suggested an easy answer. The relationship between anticolonial nationalism, national culture, and religion was a fiercely debated question across the region. Many Syrians, Lebanese,

Palestinians, Iraqis, and Egyptians advocated a more religious state; others, a more secular one.

Ironically, despite their military supremacy and their aggressive sectarian politics, Britain and France nationalized what I have called the ecumenical frame even as they assiduously worked to de-Ottomanize Arab political culture. The European abolition of Ottoman sovereignty axiomatically created a new geopolitical context and new economic, political, and cultural borders.[12] Inevitably, separate national discourses were inculcated in Syria, Lebanon, Palestine, and Iraq, but so too were dissenting pan-Islamist and pan-Arabist visions of the political future of the region that rejected these arbitrary borders. The population of the mandate states remained largely illiterate, but as the cities of Damascus, Beirut, Jerusalem, and Baghdad replaced Istanbul as the capitals of new states, they became loci for anticolonial political, labor, and social organization. They also became nodes for invigorated nationalist, pan-Arabist, and pan-Islamist thought; centers for multireligious national bourgeoisies; and locations of separate national print cultures that appealed to, and thus helped create, new national reading publics. Although colonial officials made only meager investments in public education, health, and economic infrastructure, they did increase rail and road development across the mandates. During the mandates, national maps of Syria, Palestine, Iraq, and Lebanon were created for the first time. In Syria and Iraq, new military academies incorporated rural, hitherto marginalized peasants and townsmen from the less affluent classes into the officer corps.

All these structural factors accelerated the nationalization of the ecumenical frame in different ways. Western colonialism lacked the basic legitimacy among most Muslim Arabs that the Ottomans had enjoyed until the very end of their rule.[13] In an age in which self-determination was the catchphrase, imperialism demanded a hard sell. Even those Arab rulers directly set on their thrones by European power—the Hashemite King Faysal of Iraq for instance—recognized the need to encourage a unifying nationalist sentiment, which often set them at cross-purposes with their European overlords.

Because European colonialism was not omnipotent, it could neither fully contain nor control vibrant public national spheres. In the intellectual, ideological, and political ferment of the interwar colonial age, intense culture wars unfolded in Iraq, Lebanon, Palestine, Egypt, and Syria that often revolved around the question of religion in public and political life. At stake was the nature of post-Ottoman states and societies. Pharaonism, Phoenicianism, Salafism, Wahabism, Syrianism, Mediterraneanism, Arabism, communism, and socialism were all proposed in this period as panaceas for educating and unifying populations. The astonishing ubiquity of elitist political, civic, nationalist, feminist, and Islamist organizations and societies that adopted the *nahda* moniker testifies to how widespread the desire for self-improvement was in the Arab world, and to how multiple and often incommensurable its prescriptions were. Yet it is striking how almost all these different political and ideological outlooks fought wars of position within the ecumenical frame, not against it.

CHALLENGING COLONIAL PLURALISM

Citizens of the new European-dominated, post-Ottoman Arab states had to make fundamental decisions about how to relate religion to national affiliation in what were deeply multireligious societies. There was, after all, a crucial distinction between thinking of oneself as a Christian Arab and describing oneself as a Christian *in*, but not *of*, the Arab world; between being a Muslim Arab with Christian and Jewish Arab compatriots and being primarily a Muslim in the Islamic world, surrounded by *dhimmis;* between being an Arab Jew and being a Zionist. The modern idea of *being Arab*, in other words, encompassed more than a secular emphasis on material progress and national unity, and more than a religious identification with Islam's manifest relationship to Arab language, history, and culture. Just as obviously, being Arab was an ecumenical position in the face of a Western colonial discourse that aggressively sought to sectarianize the landscape of the post-Ottoman Middle East.

Whether religious or not, virtually all Arabic-speaking Christians and Jews recognized that they lived in a predominantly Arab Islamic environment. Some processed this fact intellectually, others politically, and still others spiritually. Some embraced Islam and others rejected it—but all had to locate themselves within a new era that threw up the question of how precisely to relate the reality of religious difference with the aspiration for a meaningful, independent sovereignty. The visibility of Arab Christians in the post-Ottoman Mashriq, and specifically in the new state of Lebanon, but also in Palestine and Syria, was hardly coincidental. Diverse Christian communities in these countries had never historically been confined to ghettos. Their elites had benefited from the late Ottoman educational, print, and commercial renaissance. Far more overtly than in the Ottoman era, the mandate period inculcated in Christian and Jewish Arabs a *political* consciousness, and a realization on their part—as well as on the part of their Muslim compatriots and of the colonial powers that ruled them both—of their unique role in making or breaking the ecumenical frame. With them, there was the possibility of a vibrant challenge to the logic of colonial pluralism. Without them, there was essentially its confirmation.

In different ways and with different emphases, many Christian Arabs of the mandate period, men and women, personified the nationalization of the nahda. They followed, in this sense, the same ecumenical trajectory that had begun with Butrus al-Bustani's explicit embrace of coexistence after 1860. Just as with certain critical Jewish intellectuals in Europe, or African Americans in the United States, not belonging to the historically privileged community heightened their critical consciousness of pluralism. It made these individuals all the more aware of the ecumenical moment they lived in, and of the possibility and urgent necessity of building a new community of equal citizens. They were also, however, keenly aware of the major imperialist and communalist currents that pulled them away from a common Arab shore.

The same era that produced nationalist responses to the unfolding post-Ottoman age also inspired the strident communalist Christian and Jewish responses.[14] Minoritarian discourse was as diverse as the minorities themselves. It ran the gamut from being a testament to the long history of jealously cloistered religious communities, to corrosive chauvinism and racism fueled by anti-Muslim sentiment, to a more tempered disquiet at the prospect of losing the alleged protection of Western powers, to active thinking about how best non-Muslims could reconcile politically and culturally with the Muslim-majority Arab world outside of a secular nationalist framework. The common core of a minoritarian outlook was the unmitigated skepticism of the possibility of being both a member of a religious minority and an Arab, and a rejection of the sincerity, let alone viability, of secular Arab nationalism.

During the mandate era, Muslim Arabs also had to contend with the presence of Christian and other non-Muslim Arabs as well as Kurds and others as constitutionally equal citizens. This they did in a variety of ways: politically, poetically, individually, collectively, with profound acceptance or basic insecurity. With the Ottoman Empire dead, Islam was no longer an imperial religion. And yet, because Islam remained the religion of the overwhelming majority of the population of the Arab Mashriq, the question of formulating a new relationship between Islam and sovereign post-Ottoman states became a far more vexed one than that of the states' relationship to Christianity or Judaism.

Just as Christians and Jews had to choose between being a cloistered, dependent "minority" and belonging to the anticolonial nationalist majority, so too did Sunni and Shi'i Muslim individuals have to decide where and how to draw the line between belonging to an imagined community that transcended their faith—the very essence of a modern political community, whether Iraqi, Syrian, Egyptian, or pan-Arab—or belonging to an imagined community defined principally by their faith. Inevitably, Muslim Arabs such as the Hashemite king of Iraq, Faysal; the Syrian prime minister, Jamil Mardam Bey; the pan-Islamist Shakib Arslan; the Egyptian feminist Huda Sharaawi; the great nationalist pedagogue Sati' al-Husri; the cofounder of the pan-Arabist Baath party, Salah al-Din Bitar; and the founder of the Muslim Brotherhood, Hassan al-Banna—each affiliated with the idea of an ecumenical nation in different ways. The same interwar era that produced new secular nationalist parties such as the Baath, whose very first principle insisted that "all differences among the sons [of the nation] are incidental and false,"[15] also produced the new, antisecular Muslim Brotherhood, which took root in Egypt in 1928 and spread across the region.

NATIONALIZING THE NAHDA

The major nationalist interwar parties in Syria, Palestine, Iraq, and Egypt were all led by men born in the late Ottoman era. Despite their factions, many were graduates of Ottoman military and civil academies. Not a few came from families of wealth and property whose ancestors had served Ottoman masters for centuries. They desired not a major social revolution, and still less mass mobilization, but to sit across the "green baize table" from their European overlords in order to be granted independence. They were, in any case, in no position to seize independence. It was these men whom Amin Rihani caustically referred to in 1927 as "spurious nationalist[s]."[16] They offered a simulacrum of the nahda rather than the real thing itself. Rihani insisted that the true nahda encompassed a revolution of substance, not the mere outward form of change: it was not the new buildings or new clothes or new appearances that counted for him. Rather, the nahda signified the overturning of moribund structures and traditions in law, beliefs, literature, and science. Above all, it required acknowledging the reality of Western influence without internalizing a sense of inferiority in relation to it.

Rihani noted that the great problem of the mandate era—what with its nominal parliaments, sovereigns, and constitutions—was that it produced glorious signs of the nahda emptied of any significant political or moral strength. "Kings, parliaments, and constitutions: they were all shackled" by colonialism.[17] Rihani was undoubtedly right, but his criticism of the deep flaws in the "contemporary Eastern nahda" overlooked one vitally important aspect of the burgeoning ecumenical frame personified in Rihani himself. Almost all the dissonant political perspectives of the interwar period were actively committed to, or at the very least felt compelled to profess, an antisectarianism.

And of all these perspectives, the so-called secular nationalist eventually captured the hearts and minds of the greatest proportion of Muslim and non-Muslim Arabs alike, precisely because it promised to turn the aspirational nahda into a modern sovereign reality, much as Mustafa Kemal appeared to have achieved in Turkey. Insofar as this perspective generally downplayed sectarian affiliation, emphasized anticolonial solidarity, and focused on securing independence and on building modern states, it drew adherents from all religious communities and, as best as we can tell, from all social classes. Unlike either minoritarian or Islamist perspectives, the "secular nationalist" one was resolutely focused on consolidating something greater than the sum of the nation's religious or communal parts, rather than reifying those separate parts. Nationalists during the immediate post-Ottoman era were also more ecumenical than they were secular in any dogmatic sense. They repeatedly emphasized the place of religion, and of men of religion, at the heart of their bids for independence.

Nationalism did not invent the ecumenical frame. Instead, it inherited this frame from the Ottoman era, politicized it, and reconfigured it within new territorial domains. In Syria, Iraq, and Egypt, anticolonialism was predicated on making nationalists out of so-called minorities, traditional notables, feudal lords, and tribal leaders.[18] In Lebanon, as we shall see, a quite different trajectory was followed, owing to the country's strong and assertive Christian political presence empowered by French colonialism. Rather than making nationalists out of minorities, as was the case in neighboring Syria, Lebanese elites consecrated a sectarian state, whereby political power was parceled out along communal lines. In Palestine, Muslim, Jewish, and Christian Arabs had to respond to the British-backed European Zionist settler-colonial project intent upon establishing a Jewish state there. These contradictory politicizations of diversity grew out of a broad and common ecumenical trajectory that began after 1860 and in which Arabs of all classes and religions continually invested in different ways and with different agendas.

I do not, therefore, suggest that we obscure the contradictions, assumptions, inequalities, or elitism of these forms of nationalism.[19] There is, if anything, a need to explicitly demystify Sergius's ecumenical gesture at Al-Azhar in 1919, or Faysal's in 1920, and to understand how they begged major questions about the nature of power and political economy, secular equality, the meaning of gendered citizenship rights, the salience of religious and ethnic diversity, separation of powers, elitist representation on the cusp of a new era of mass politics, and, above all, the relationship of religion to postcolonial sovereignty. These questions could not possibly be resolved by a cleric's gesture or by the rhetoric of national unity. They were, instead, postponed for a later reckoning.

Yet the fact that Sergius would preach national unity from Al-Azhar— or that Shi'i and Sunni clergymen and laymen collaborated during the great anti-British uprising of 1920, or that Christian Arabs invoked the figure of the Prophet Muhammad as a common Arab icon—was not merely a nationalist conceit or a fantasy peddled by the prophets of messianic nationalism. Rather, these gestures were *historic* ones precisely because they were *not* inevitable, and nor were they uncontested. In the second part of this book, therefore, I present an empathetic reading of contending political secular nationalist and sectarian models of meaningful sovereignty in Lebanon and Iraq.

For all their notable differences, these models reflected rival interpretations of a common ecumenical frame that outlasted its Ottoman environment. They also reflected how the inhabitants of the region were used to living as part of a much larger and diverse whole over which they had had little actual sovereign control. Although these models were, from the outset, discriminatory and saturated by considerations of power, they shared far more than the fundamentally different Zionist politics that emerged on the Middle Eastern scene at the same time. Transplanted from Europe and bearing almost no affinity to the Ottoman past, the Zionist project urgently sought to remake Palestine into an idealized and exclusively Jewish state. Inevitably, such a radical project posed a massive, and ultimately tragic, challenge to the tentative ecumenical frame in the Mashriq.

5 Sectarianism and Antisectarianism in the Post-Ottoman Arab World

Nobody would speak of minorities if he did not himself fear
a majority. But there comes a point, in certain domains,
where the fear becomes excessive and delusory.

—Michel Chiha, *Liban d'aujourd'hui* (1942)

Do you think that 'political stability' (whatever its form) is
always in the interest of a country? And can you honestly
say to us that any Eastern nation has suffered political and
social problems by having too many of its citizens educated? Some nations need 'stability' in certain cases, but
require 'revolution' in others.

— Sati' al-Husri, *Naqd taqrir munru* (1932)

It is not clear whether Michel Chiha and Sati' al-Husri ever met. Both men
were born in the late Ottoman era. Chiha was a wealthy cosmopolitan
francophone, a Catholic who had lived in Lebanon, Egypt, France, and
England. His family originated in Iraq but had long since settled in
Lebanon and married into Maronite Christian notability. Chiha was first
and foremost a banker, but, by reason of circumstance and self-interest,
he played a leading role in designing the sectarian architecture of the
philo-colonial state of Lebanon established by France in 1920. Husri was
a different kind of cosmopolitan. His Syrian family was originally from
Aleppo, though Husri was born in Ottoman Yemen, where his father
worked as a judge. Educated at the leading civil state school in Istanbul,
he was fluent in Ottoman and French. Husri worked as a teacher and pedagogue in the Balkans for eight years, after which he directed the Ottoman

Teachers' Training College in Istanbul and traveled to Europe to study its educational systems. He was a secular Ottoman until the empire's demise, after which he embraced the cause of Arab unity. Husri dedicated his life to laying the pedagogical foundations for what he hoped would become a strong postcolonial state. Whereas Chiha made religious difference the cornerstone of post-Ottoman politics, Husri aimed to transcend this difference. Husri's expansive anticolonial Arabism was a foil to Chiha's narrower pro-colonial Lebanism within a new and still fragile Arab world.

Clearly, an ideological and political chasm separated Chiha and Husri—a chasm that would be widened and deepened by lesser partisans of both men long after they departed the political scene. Both men inherited the same ecumenical frame. Their contending visions of the region reflected the massive transformation of what had once been a unified Ottoman sovereignty into fragmented polities dominated by Britain and France. Chiha and Husri belonged to a generation of Arab political elites who emerged from the wreckage of the empire having to confront the meaning and implications of national unity in mandate states that were not, in the first instance, created by them. This generation had to grapple with questions about the territorial integrity and sovereignty of their countries; for the first time, Arabs had to make—under different colonial constraints—substantial choices about where and how to draw the line between recognizing or effacing the ethnic and religious diversity of their citizenry. They had to choose how to engage with British and French power, omnipresent in the European military garrisons, airfields, exclusive clubs, embassies, and high commissions across the post-Ottoman landscape of the Arab world. In this chapter, I trace how the ecumenical frame, whose foundations were laid in the late Ottoman era, was politicized during the mandate era in fundamentally divergent ways.

I see Chiha and Husri as embodiments of competing models for reconstituting the post-Ottoman ecumenical frame. One model advocated an overtly communalist political culture that arose in Lebanon; the other anticipated the secular nationalist culture that became evident in Iraq, Syria, and Egypt. Both claimed to hold the keys to a viable future. Alone among all post-Ottoman states, Lebanon instituted a formal communal power-sharing formula among the ruling elites of the country. Often described as "political sectarianism," this formula made religious affiliation central to formal politics and administration, both of which were weighted in favor of the country's French-backed Maronite community. If the Lebanese state mirrored the decentralized Ottoman-era Mutasarrifiyya in its confessional politics, the other mandates reflected the former Ottoman Empire's centralizing drive in the name of national unity, but now on a substantially circumscribed scale. Iraq, Syria, and Egypt, all Muslim-majority states, denied political significance to the ethnic and religious diversity of their citizens.

For all the noteworthy differences that distinguished Lebanon from Syria and Iraq, and that separated Chiha from Husri, all these states and their respective political elites participated in the consolidation of the ecumenical frame, and of what historian Albert Hourani has described as "the culture of nationalism" that took root in the interwar Middle East. In Hourani's empathetic view, this culture was "secularist, believing in a bond which could embrace people of different schools or faiths," and it was also constitutionalist. New parliaments and political parties, modern water and drainage and sewage systems, electricity, telephones, radio, tramways, and road, rail, and bridge construction helped to transform the landscape of European-created mandates. The population of the entire Arab world (including the Maghreb and the Gulf, which are beyond the scope of this narrative) grew from roughly thirty-five million to fifty-five million between 1914 and 1939—this despite the catastrophes of emigration, famine, and fighting during World War I that took a significant toll on the Levant. Migration to growing cities drew people together in new quarters and new buildings. The journey from Baghdad to Damascus, which had taken a month before the war, took less than a day by the end of the mandate era. New media, cinema, publishing houses, flags, maps, and schools helped concretize new national reading publics, national questions, and national identities.[1]

The majority of the inhabitants of this Arab region still lived in villages and smaller towns. As elsewhere in the world, a small circle of dominant political, cultural, commercial, financial, and landowning elites were quite removed from the agonies and aspirations of the vast majority of their fellow citizens. Yet they were the ones in charge of defining sovereignty in the post-Ottoman era in varying degrees of collaboration and confrontation with European colonial rulers. Workers, meanwhile, toiled in largely unregulated factories, and emerging communist parties and trade unions aspired to mobilize them. At the same time, students, petty shopkeepers, small tradesmen, bureaucrats, and professional men and women of the middle classes made up the basic constituency of new nationalist parties as well as of equally new, deeply conservative organizations like the Muslim Brotherhood in Egypt or the Phalangists in Lebanon. And peasants, who harvested agricultural produce and cash crops, became objects of mobilization by modernizing state officials and nascent socialist movements.

This gulf between ruler and ruled did not make political elites in the Arab world substantially different from their Turkish counterparts. But quite unlike their former compatriots who built the overtly secularist Turkish republic, the post-Ottoman Arab political elites were not yet, generally speaking, military men. They were not haunted by the experience and memory of the Balkan Wars, nor were they anywhere near as radical or draconian in their nationalism. In this sense, the Arab states were far more faithful to their ecumenical Ottoman heritage than was Mustafa Kemal's Turkey. Although they were tailored differently by Western colonial rulers and their local nationalist apprentices, the countries of the Mashriq were all cut from the same colorful patterns of the Ottoman-era political fabric. Too much, in short, has been made of Lebanon's "sectarian" exceptionalism, and not enough has been made of how it and the nationalist Arab states contributed in different ways to the consolidation of the conservative ecumenical frame begun during the Ottoman period.

Lebanese, Syrian, Iraqi, and Egyptian political elites normalized the idea of political equality between Muslim and non-Muslim citizens—but with caveats that hollowed out its meaning. They embraced national unity and ubiquitously, and often ostentatiously, eschewed a divisive sectarianism (al-ta'ifiyya), which was named as a political problem for the first time during the mandate era. No political party, faction, or individual—in Lebanon or anywhere else in the Mashriq—would or could claim to be sectarian. At the same time, the mandate states upheld, while also reforming and elaborating, segregated religious personal-status spheres. This dualism was *not* a contradiction. It was, in the language of theory, a condition of possibility. It defined the conservative and gendered underpinnings of the modern ecumenical frame in the Arab East. This reality was as evident in "secular" nationalist Arab states as it was in "sectarian" Lebanon.

The parallel discourses of coexistence and national unity co-opted conservative communal and religious pieties in the name of building sovereign states. From the outset, they delimited the potentially emancipatory aspects of secular citizenship that Husri desired and of which Chiha remained profoundly skeptical. They also embedded the communalist logic embraced by Chiha and detested by Husri. In Lebanon, political elites dexterously marshaled an explicit language of the coexistence of "communities" that elided the rights of secular individuals and ignored the brute reality of disparate geographic, class, and gender inequalities within and across communities. They thus justified their domination of a state whose leading architect appeared to be uninterested in building a cohesive national ethos. Secular Arab nationalists in Iraq, Syria, and Egypt, in turn, glorified the "nation" rather than the "community." They invoked the powerful language of "national unity" to justify sovereign projects that could be tone-deaf, and sometimes utterly callous, to the concerns of non-Muslim and non-Arab communities in their midst.

A COMMUNALIST FORMULA FOR COEXISTENCE

The Ottoman-era Mutasarrifiyya in Mount Lebanon had established a basic template, albeit under Ottoman sovereignty and European supervision, for dividing local administration along sectarian lines. But it was French colonialism, which separated Lebanon from Syria, and which made Beirut the center of its mandate, that transformed the provincial administrative structure into a nominally sovereign entity.[2] What was exceptional in the Ottoman era became paradigmatic in the European colonial one. Absent French will, there would not have been an independent sectarian polity: the Maronite-dominated Lebanon thus became a sign of the deliberate European division of the Mashriq into several states. Why Lebanon existed to begin with, and where its precise borders lay, was not, in the first instance, a Lebanese decision.

The declaration of the state of "Grand Liban," or greater Lebanon, in September 1920 emphasized this fact: representatives of the French Republic were the men in charge of this new country. During his proclamation of the new state before local dignitaries and colonial officials,

General Henri Gouraud, vanquisher of the short-lived Arab kingdom of Faysal centered in Damascus, referred to Lebanon's ancient history and to France's benevolence toward the Lebanese. He ignored over a millennium of Islamic history—and the reality of extensive and obvious Muslim as well as secular Arabist opposition to separating Lebanon from Syria.[3]

Yet if there was ever a case where native elites collaborated openly with European power it was in Lebanon. And nowhere was this more apparent than among Lebanese Maronite Christians, who predominated politically and whose ambitions and anxieties inevitably shaped the country's political orientation. No matter that their community had thrived demographically and that the Maronite Church had massively expanded its land holdings in the Ottoman era, Maronite elites were quick to celebrate the end of the Ottoman Empire. They seized on the fact of a famine and locust plague during World War I that had hit Mount Lebanon hard, since the Ottoman military had requisitioned harvests and animals and had drafted able-bodied men (at the same time that local merchants hoarded stores of grain, and Britain and France imposed a naval blockade of coastal Syria).[4] The swings in the fortunes of the silk and tobacco cultivation upon which many Lebanese villagers and farmers depended had encouraged mass emigration by mostly Ottoman Christian subjects to the New World during the late Ottoman era. The often enthusiastic, and occasionally sugary, acceptance of the tenets of a French civilizing mission by significant sectors of the Arabic-speaking inhabitants of the new country had no parallel in any other Arab state. Neither the Copts in Egypt nor the Greek Orthodox Christians in Syria or Palestine, nor the Chaldeans or Jews in Iraq, had nearly as dominant a hand as Maronite Christians enjoyed in national politics.

The earliest years of the French mandate, in fact, witnessed several mostly Maronite Lebanese Christian writers exhibit open chauvinism toward Muslim Arabs. The notion of Christian Lebanese civilizational exceptionalism pervaded the outlook of several proponents of Lebanese separatism, including Charles Corm, a friend of Michel Chiha's who would make his wealth as sole agent and distributer of Ford vehicles in Syria and Lebanon, and who was the founder of the short-lived *La Revue Phénicienne*. Like French and Jesuit colonialists whose prejudice he imbibed, Corm feared that Arab nationalism was a cipher for Muslim domination. "We have always been . . . a rampart of civilization set against the darkness of Asia," he wrote in 1919.[5] Such beliefs in Lebanese suprem-acy were paradoxically reinforced by a legend of Lebanese Christian vic-timization. Together, they justified the existence of a separate state of Lebanon by claiming that the country had an ancient Phoenician past and that "Christians" had suffered from "Turkish" or "Muslim" persecution.[6]

Maronite Christians were, however, never of one voice. There was no single political agency that guided their secular ambitions. Far more con-sequential than the few fantasists like Corm were men like Chiha who shared Corm's francophone philo-colonialism and yet also understood the urgent need to co-opt Muslim and Druze political elites into his vision for an independent Lebanon. The new country was made up of six hundred thousand inhabitants, nearly half of whom were Muslims who predomi-nated in the coastal cities of Tripoli and Sidon, in the fertile Bekaa Valley and in the tobacco-, citrus-, and olive-rich regions in the south of the coun-try. This basic reality suggested to Chiha the necessity of a more pragmatic approach. But it did not for a moment sway Chiha from actively collaborat-ing ("without servility," he insisted) with French colonial officials, especially the colonial ideologue Robert de Caix, and with the high commissioners in Beirut, several of whom he considered among his friends.[7]

Chiha was not merely a cipher for a reactionary French worldview exported overseas. He did read and admire conservative, monarchical, and anti-Semitic French authors and politicians such as Charles Maurras and Maurice Barrès. But his importance lay in his ability to justify a mod-ern sectarian political system that was as much locally rooted as it was an extension of French colonial will. Therein lay both its continuing allure, long after the end of formal French colonialism in the Middle East, and the horror it provoked in those many Lebanese and Arabs deeply opposed to political sectarianism. Chiha was dangerous because he was, first and foremost, indigenous. His embrace of the idea of Lebanon was romantic and self-serving; yet his francophone advocacy of sectarian politics belonged as much to the logic of the late Ottoman age as the anticolonial politics of any secular nationalist. Just as importantly, he translated—or, rather, was encouraged and allowed by French colonialism to translate— this politics into practice in Lebanon. From his work as an elected repre-sentative in the 1920s, to his work on the French-created constitutional commission of 1925, to his range of writings on Lebanon published mostly between the 1930s and '50s in pamphlets, books, and newspaper editorials for the French-language daily *Le Jour*, which he owned, Chiha held fast to a basic position from which he would not waver. Chiha insisted that the sectarian state was far more ecumenical, rational, and faithful to the history of the Levant than the stridently anticolonial secular Arab nationalism that was beginning to take shape in Lebanon and in neighboring Arab countries.

Chiha believed that being a "minority" reflected an immutable identity that was rooted in the history, geography, spirituality, and humanity of the small Mediterranean country of Lebanon. For Chiha, being a "minority" did not stem from a political faction, as in Thomas Jefferson's 1801 exhortation on the need for equal laws to protect the equal rights of a (white) minority. Nor did Chiha's conception of minority necessarily suggest a series of antagonistic, racially defined groupings, or "national minorities," that were the concern of that era's League of Nations.[8] Rather, for Chiha, the raison d'être of Lebanon was that it had historically constituted a mountain refuge and had thus become, over time, a land of multiple, coexisting religious communities, none of which should be able to dominate the others. These communities required a particular political "balance" or "equilibrium" between them to ensure equity and stability. Hence Chiha's insistence on a parliamentary body organized along sectarian lines that inaugurated what he labeled a "novel" form of federalism. "Just as Switzerland has its cantons," he would write in 1942, "here there are confessional communities."[9]

Chiha's views prevailed decisively in the Lebanese constitutional committee created in 1925, which included members selected by the French rulers of Lebanon from all the major communities of the country, including the Druze, Sunni, Shi'i, Greek Orthodox, Greek Catholic, and, of course, Maronite sects. Among the commissioners were feudal lords, men of property, politicians, lawyers, and an engineer. Most were fluent in French, an official language in the mandate alongside Arabic. The thirteen-man committee traveled across the country seeking the views of notables, religious leaders, politicians, senior civil servants and judges, heads of municipal councils and chambers of commerce: all men of social, economic, and political standing. They asked, in writing, the same set of twelve questions—including whether the government should be a republic or a monarchy. The sixth question asked whether parliamentary representation should rest on a confessional basis. The twelfth question inquired whether sectarianism (*al-ta'ifiyya*) should be taken into account when allocating state positions and cabinet posts.[10] What was not asked, because the Lebanese had no say in its answer, was whether Lebanon should remain subordinate to France.

This was the colonial moment when the term "sectarianism" entered the modern Arabic political lexicon.[11] The irony lay in the fact that within France the term had no political significance, since the French Republic was overtly secular, or *laïc*. Thus, despite France's long history of Catholic-Protestant violence, its colonial racism and prejudice toward Islam, and its problem of anti-Semitism, French citizens of different faiths were presumed to be capable of secular national unity. In French-dominated Lebanon, however, neither the French colonial officials nor Michel Chiha and most of his fellow commissioners could envision a sustainable secular political system.

Although the commission received only a fraction of the written responses it had sought, its final report insisted that sectarian representation was the only viable form of government in a religiously diverse society—even though several of the responses it received noted the inherent problem of a system of confessional representation on the grounds that it was divisive. It justified its decision by alleging the atavistic pull of the country's different religious communities: "The Lebanese people are made up of a mass of communities, each with its own religious convictions, mentality, and its own customs and traditions. The rejection of a system of sectarian representation would disrupt equilibrium and give a preponderance to certain communities over others. This would result in jealousies, resentments and perhaps even, continual troubles." This same report noted that parliamentary representation had to "reflect" the "physiognomy of the country," which in Lebanon's case was a number of communities, each of which had to be represented in order to ensure the most "faithful" parliamentary representation. The country was "still imbued with a confessional spirit. The moment has not yet arrived to sacrifice these prejudices, for a mentality that has endured for centuries cannot be renounced in a single day." The report claimed that a sectarian system was also key to "safeguarding minority rights" because the "communities of Lebanon took the place of political parties."[12]

From its beginnings, however, "sectarianism" was a tainted term. For its proponents, sectarian representation was a necessary evil; at best, it constituted a transitional mechanism allegedly paving the way, in a multireligious society, to a common "national" post-sectarian future; for its detractors, sectarian representation represented a dangerous and formidable obstacle to this future. A minority of deputies who debated the report condemned political sectarianism outright. They pointed out that the "confessional spirit was a dangerous malady for our national life" and that it was "incorrect to view communities as if they were political parties, because one voluntarily chooses a political party, whereas one has no choice to be born into this or that community." The dissenters noted that "the confessional spirit is a basis for social ills; it creates an abnormal mentality among the different elements of the population."[13] Outside of parliament, the nascent communist party of Lebanon called for free and democratic elections for a parliament on the basis of *al-la ta'ifiyya,* or "nonsectarianism." On June 11, 1925, it identified sectarianism as "the greatest obstacle in the path of the unity of the people and true independence."[14]

Drafted by Chiha, the constitution of 1926 enshrined the ambivalence in modern political sectarianism. It upheld its overtly communal logic—that different communities had to be represented formally in public office in the name of harmony and tradition. It also provided an explicitly secular, not religious, rationale for this communalism: that this representation was linked to equality and merit, not religious dogma. Article 9 of the constitution guaranteed each religious community control over its personal-status affairs. Article 10 protected "freedom of conscience," the "dignity of all of the religions or sects," and the right of each community to oversee the education of its students so long as this pedagogy followed state guidelines. The same constitution also categorically declared all Lebanese equal before the law, irrespective of religious affiliation, and affirmed that "they shall enjoy civil and political rights and shall equally be bound by public obligations and duties without any distinction." Article 12 reinforced this by stating that "every Lebanese [citizen] shall have the right to hold public office, no preference shall be made except on the basis of merit and competence, according to the conditions established by law." And yet Article 95 specified that as "a provisional measure," and in the interest of "justice and harmony," the Lebanese "communities will be equitably represented in public employment and in the composition of ministries" so long as such representation did not prejudice the cause of the state.[15] Sectarian representation was meant, in theory at least, to diffuse and to neutralize an inherent sectarianism: to give rational, inclusive form to the ostensibly irreducible religious essence of the country without giving in to its segregating impulse.

It was this last point that Chiha hammered home repeatedly for nearly three decades until his death in 1954: that the primary task of government in Lebanon was to harmonize relations between communities, not democratize relations between individual secular citizens. He was acutely aware of the opposition that existed to political sectarianism from across the confessional spectrum. In response, Chiha echoed arguments that antisecularist Catholic and Islamic fundamentalists had marshaled for decades. He insisted that secular democracy was an abstraction with no relation to the history of the region, and that monotheistic communities were the epitome of that history. To call for a nonsectarian parliament was, he claimed, to privilege an illusory Western notion of a purely secular nationalist subjectivity over actual people and communities. Indeed, it was to invite chaos, for to deny elitist sectarian political representation was to force Lebanese identity back to its more "vulgar" and chaotic forms and, inevitably, to return political discourse to "the church, the mosque and the synagogue."[16] According to Chiha, this reversion to an archaic sectarianism was as dangerous as it was absurd. From his perspective, the modern confessional politics of the country had organically developed from "the direct proximity between faiths and rituals . . . the long history of living together . . . the intermingling, and mutual respect and friendship and the deep knowledge of one another [which] is what brought us to the point of equilibrium."[17]

To legitimate this notion of communal equilibrium, Chiha, and the French colonial authorities upon whom he depended, urgently needed to co-opt the leaders of the Muslim Arabs of Lebanon into the Lebanese sectarian republic that had been created despite their manifest wishes. To gain cooperation, Chiha and his fellow Maronite Christian political elites offered their Muslim counterparts—mostly urban and feudal Sunni and Shi'i Muslim notables—a significant communal, political, and financial stake in the new country's official institutions. Chiha had wanted to limit sectarian representation to the national parliament, and not extend it to the executive, administrative, or judicial branches of government for which he advocated secular meritocracy.

According to the constitutional scholar Edmond Rabbath, it was the prominent Sunni and Shi'i Muslim deputies who were very much in favor of the sectarian Article 95 of the constitution. They feared that Muslims lagged behind Christians in state employment and sought guarantees for an "equitable" share of lucrative government posts.[18] Although Sunni Muslim Arab opposition to the Lebanese mandate continued well into the 1930s, a well-known Sunni Muslim notable from Tripoli, Muhammad Jisr, was made president of the short-lived Senate in 1926; another prominent Sunni Muslim from Beirut, Omar Daouk, was made vice president of the Chamber of Deputies a year later. These and other Muslim and Druze deputies and state officials helped create new patronage and employment networks in the nascent Lebanese public sector that saw approximately 75 percent of the national budget consumed by state bureaucracy by 1927.[19] Co-opting the Shi'i community proved no less important. Shi'i Ja'fari courts were officially established in Lebanon with French colonial support for the first time during the mandate era.

Rather than diminishing sectarian sentiments, the Lebanese political structure made them central to claims of justice, equity, and democracy. The sectarian state apotheosized what had historically been antidemocratic, hierarchical, and exclusive religious communities into sacrosanct political ones—citizens could vote for or occupy a parliamentary seat designated for one of the seventeen officially recognized communities in the country, but never as a secular citizen. The formalization of sectarian politics legitimated the birth of a new language of so-called Muslim or Maronite or Shi'i or other sects' rights, and tied these to each other in the new state. Each community felt that it had to cohere its own representation lest its alleged "rights" be subordinated or cannibalized by others. For example, a three-minister cabinet, formed in 1928 to tackle a serious budgetary crisis, did not include Shi'i or Druze members. The Shi'i member of Parliament, Yusuf al-Zayn, complained that "his sect" was not represented in most branches of government. He said that the Shi'i community was "deprived of rights." Zayn insisted that he was not "fanatical," claiming not to ask for "sectarianism" or to advocate "sectarian rights." He said he demanded only "equality," given that the Lebanese state was organized along sectarian lines.[20]

The same general line of argument was advanced, in turn, by Armenian and Druze members of parliament. In 1930, a new association of Shiʿi religious scholars petitioned the Lebanese president demanding redress for a disappointed community following administrative appointments that did not, in their view, include enough Shiʿi individuals.[21] Far from a delicate equilibrium between communities, then, the sectarian state of Lebanon witnessed constant friction between the imperative to create a secular "national" Lebanese identity and the equally strong imperative to create coherent, separate, and contending communal identifications around which formal politics was organized. The former outlined the common good that citizens and lawmakers claimed to cherish; the latter was the sanctioned method for gaining political representation and access to the country's scant resources.

The culmination of this notionally integrative national communalism was the National Pact of 1943, cobbled together on the eve of Lebanese independence. The unwritten pact was negotiated by Michel Chiha's brother-in-law, the Maronite Bishara al-Khuri, who would become the first president of the independent republic, and the Sunni Muslim Riyad al-Sulh, from a notable family from Sidon, who would become Lebanon's first prime minister of the postcolonial era. The National Pact epitomized the fundamentally undemocratic nature of communal politics, but also its capacity to appeal to the secular political elites of each of the so-called major communities of the country. The National Pact was not recorded in any official government decree, nor was it subject to any referendum or democratic vote, but it did require foreign Arab and Western backing. The pact reserved the powerful post of the presidency for a Maronite Christian; prime minister for a Sunni Muslim; and speaker of parliament for a Shiʿi Muslim—although, in theory at least, none of these figures represented only their sect. The ratio of parliamentarians was also fixed at six to five in favor of Christians, ostensibly because the Christians formed a slight majority of the overall population.[22]

The National Pact was an undemocratic expression of pluralism. It confirmed both the secular basis of communal politics and the communal basis of secular national unity. The pact guaranteed that no single community had a right to monopolize the government or resources of the state. It also upheld Maronite political preeminence as part of the "equilibrium" that granted Sunni and Shiʻi (and Druze) elites a far larger share of the political spoils than was the case in the 1920s. In Edmond Rabbath's classic formulation, the pact sought to make Lebanese out of Muslims and Arabs of Christians.[23] The pact paved the way for Lebanon's formal independence the same year—aided by British support and quick Egyptian recognition.

The prominent role played by Sulh confirmed the degree to which Muslim Lebanese politicians had become indispensable figures in legitimating the sectarian state of Lebanon. Their initial overwhelming rejection of the French-Maronite country in favor of Arab unity with Syria had softened gradually over two decades. They were granted a large share of power, cultivated their own communal patronage networks, and compelled the abandonment of any French and Maronite fantasy of an overtly philo-colonial, anti-Arab, Christian-dominated state. Sulh's inaugural cabinet declaration in 1943 described Lebanon as a "country with an Arab face that appreciates what is good and beneficial from Western civilization"—a compromise formulation underscoring Lebanon's independence and sovereignty while acknowledging that the country was part of the Arab world.[24] This compromise upheld Lebanon's basic pro-Western and free-market orientation, maintained economic relations with Syria, and opened other potentially lucrative Arab markets to a multiconfessional—but predominantly Christian—Lebanese bourgeoisie. The constitution was duly amended to remove references to the French mandatory; Arabic alone was made the official language of the country, and the new national flag erased France's *tricolore* upon which the Lebanese cedar had been superimposed during the mandate.

The sectarian system, however, was entrenched. The first independent Lebanese government was made up of ministers drawn from each of the prominent communities of the country—that, in fact, was their principal qualification to hold office. Yet even as they made sectarianism a political norm, successive Lebanese governments also, ironically, claimed to be working toward a post-sectarian future. Sulh pledged in 1943 to move toward the abolition of "sectarianism"—whose "ills," he said, "hinder national progress" and "poison the spirit of relations between the diverse religious communities which make up the Lebanese people."[25] No other political system embraced communalism so tightly and yet insisted time and again that it was working toward a post-sectarian future. No other political system in the region so consistently proclaimed its own obsolescence.

THE INEQUALITIES OF COEXISTENCE

Behind this façade of the harmony of communities and of coexistence, connoted by the Arabic word *ulfa* and the mid-century neologism *al-'aysh al-mushtarak*, lay obvious inequalities that the proponents of the sectarian state, including the eloquent Michel Chiha, consistently refused to acknowledge or simply took for granted. The most obvious elision in Chiha's idea of Lebanon as a country of multiple, associated communities, for example, was the fact that this country was stitched together by colonial violence—French soldiers and officials determined the destiny of the area's inhabitants far more than their allegedly ancient and deeply felt communal aspirations. Chiha surely understood the fact that the destruction of Faysal's Arab kingdom and the creation of Grand Liban in 1920 had forcibly incorporated hundreds of thousands of unwilling Muslim inhabitants into the new state to make it economically viable. Left unsaid by him was that Bishara Khoury and other "moderate" Lebanese politicians were willing to reach out to Lebanese Muslims only under certain conditions. Their rapprochement with Lebanese Muslims needed France first to snuff out any hope that the small country would be absorbed into a larger Syrian state.

Chiha thus did not draw attention to the French bombardment of Damascus in 1925 during the suppression of the major anticolonial Syrian revolt of 1925, which was the largest of the interwar era anywhere in the world. Nor did Chiha dwell on how the Syrian revolt had forced the French authorities to concede limited parliamentary life in Syria. For all the talk about the "essence" of Lebanon, Chiha did not acknowledge publicly how his ability to design the sectarian state depended entirely on the authoritarian will of the French high commissioner and on a dominant foreign colonial empire. Most of all, Chiha's invocation of communal equilibrium presumed that the Maronite community, or at least its leaders, and the

Christians of Lebanon more generally, would routinely be favored over the country's Muslims. Chiha was nonplussed. He accepted that the sectarian harmony in Lebanon necessarily privileged some communities—mainly the one he was married into—over others. Such was the price of an equilibrium manufactured under colonial conditions.

This disingenuousness was accompanied by a refusal to see what was glaringly obvious in the communal system Chiha had a large hand in designing. Rather than being temporary as Lebanon's constitution had called for, political sectarianism became a permanent feature of national politics. The constant references to "communities" by Sulh, Chiha, Khoury, and other mid-century Lebanese elites obscured the ideological feint of hand that sustained political sectarianism.[26] The active embrace of sectarian politics was hardly an immutable or inevitable reflection of the country's diversity. Neighboring Syria and Iraq further afield were, after all, equally diverse. Still less was any community politically monolithic; secular opposition to political sectarianism emerged from within every religious or ethnic community. The predominantly Maronite Christian mountain town of Bikfayya is most famous today for being the seat of the deeply conservative Phalangist party that was founded in 1936 and directly inspired by European fascism. But this same town, in which a number of tobacco factories were located, was also the setting in 1925 for the precursor to the anticolonial Communist Party of Lebanon. The communists recognized what Chiha, Sulh, and Khoury would not—that beneath the ubiquitous invocation of "community" lay the reality of enormous social, class, and gender disparities within and across communities.

Affluent, propertied, and landowning men, not nature or age-old communities, methodically sectarianized the workings of the state of Lebanon—through electoral lists organized along communal lines; through the formal distribution of parliamentary seats according to fixed sectarian ratios in each district; through polling stations that directed citizens into sect- and gender-segregated voting booths; and, perhaps most importantly, through the promulgation of distinctly Lebanese personal-status laws for each recognized community that denied secular citizens the possibility of civil marriage in the country and denied women equality in the name of the sanctity of coexistence. Whereas Sulh openly admitted in 1943 that his first independent government "could not" promise suffrage (women were granted the right to vote in 1951), Chiha conceded in 1953 that religiously segregated personal-status laws constituted a safety valve for the overarching modern, communally organized national politics. This was the one domain where religious difference was not expected to be in harmony with the imperative of equality, but rather with that of alleged tradition and custom.[27]

Justified as the necessary and unavoidable pathway to a common Lebanese national identity, communal considerations paralyzed the nominally secular state from the outset, no matter how sincerely a politician like Sulh believed himself to stand against "sectarianism." The sectarian turn exacerbated what Rabbath described astutely as the "pathological development of a political sectarianism into a metastasis that has invaded mentalities and institutions."[28] The only official population count of the country was the much-disputed census held under French colonial auspices in 1932. The census found that Christians had a slight majority in the country, and that Maronite Christians enjoyed a plurality among Lebanon's communities.[29] Although Sulh pledged to conduct a new census in 1943 in the name of "true" independence and real sovereignty, his government, and every successive government, was unable to do so. To carry out an updated, accurate population count in the country would upset the notion of an equitable sectarian distribution of posts and privileges calibrated, in theory, to the respective demographic weight of each community. A new census would strip the Maronite-dominated establishment of the country of its major justification for acquiring and clutching onto the lion's share of political power.

And what occurred in relation to a national census was repeated in the failed attempt to establish a coherent national pedagogy.[30] The new country was gripped by an educational communalism enshrined by Article 10 of Chiha's constitution—education was free but it could not detract from the public order or "contradict morality or contravene the dignity of any religion or sect." Every community was guaranteed, moreover, "the right" to educate its children in its own parochial institutions, subject to as-yet-undefined state educational guidelines. The mandate thus contained a poorly funded official public school system that catered primarily to middle-class and lower-middle-class Muslim students. But in terms of prestige, numbers, and resources, these schools lagged far behind the private, parochial, and often francophone and foreign missionary schools in the country in which Christian and many affluent Muslim students typically enrolled. Until 1954, there was no university or college not in the hands of foreigners.[31]

Despite Riyad al-Sulh's ministerial pledge in 1943 to encourage the Arabic study of history to inculcate a common Lebanese national identity, it was Chiha's idea of Lebanon as "a nursery for ideas, languages, and culture" that prevailed.[32] The state-commissioned *Tarikh Lubnan al-mujaz* (The Concise History of Lebanon, 1937) was written by Lebanese Christians Asad Rustum and Fouad Afram al-Bustani. This textbook celebrated the ancient Phoenician past, presented Muslim Arabs as outsiders, and accepted the French mandatory's paternalism; another textbook, *Tarikh Suriyya wa Lubnan al-musawwar* (The Illustrated History of Syria and Lebanon), written by a Lebanese Muslim, 'Umar Farrukh, emphasized Lebanon's Arab and Islamic character and its belonging within a broader Arab Syrian framework.[33]

These competing narratives converged, however, in their fundamental acceptance of the need to preserve the comity of the different religious communities in Lebanon. This was especially apparent in how the books glossed the controversial 1860 events. Rustum and Bustani's account emphasized the perfidious, foreign "Turkish" divide-and-rule policy that allegedly split the Druze from the Christians of Lebanon. It blamed Maronite peasant insurgents for turning on their Maronite lords, disturbing the social order, and thus bringing catastrophe on Lebanon. And it described how the events of 1860 began as innocuous child's play that escalated out of control—so that a quarrel over a "marble game" between two Druze and Maronite boys allegedly led to the sectarian catastrophe of 1860.[34]

'Umar Farrukh's *Tarikh,* by contrast, referred obliquely to the "inauspicious *fitna* (discord)" of 1860 caused by the "ignorants" among the Druze and Christians, which "led to massacres that spread across Lebanon and reached into Syria." Farrukh could not bring himself to acknowledge that Muslims had massacred Christians in Syria in July. He instead noted that "the intelligent [elite] men among Muslims and Christians tried to avert the bloodshed and restore order," leaving unsaid what actually transpired.[35] It was as if to acknowledge the massacre of Christians in Damascus was tantamount to conceding the need for a separate Lebanese state.

The different stories about 1860 produced vacuous narratives of coexistence. They also tellingly located a dangerous sectarianism at precisely the point where Chiha, and before him Butrus al-Bustani, Jurji Zaydan, and Muhammad Abduh, had collectively suggested it lay: at the point of breakdown between the will of discerning elites and the irrational, violent, and uncontrolled fanaticism of the "ignorant" populace who needed always to be managed and directed. But unlike Bustani's nineteenth-century plea for a just and antisectarian civil society, the modern sectarian state transformed coexistence into a buttress for a manifestly unequal hierarchy. Muslim, Christian, and Druze political elites competed and socialized with each other, knowing that "coexistence" for them never meant the equality of individual Sunni or Maronite or Druze or Shi'i or Orthodox citizens. Instead, it referred to their presumed right to negotiate, gain, distribute, or defend a share of the state's jobs, revenues, seats, resources, and privileges for their respective communal constituencies.

Whenever Chiha spoke about religion, ritual, harmony, and coexistence, he had in mind a very narrow intersection of men of a similar social background—and never the potential camaraderie of workers or peasants or any social class other than his own. From his vantage point as a privileged banker, at ease with French culture, Chiha repeatedly deplored the ignorance of what he regarded as the vulgar mass of Arabic-speaking Muslim and Christian compatriots. Because he believed that the differentiation among sects was thoroughly entrenched in Lebanon, Chiha rejected out of hand the notion that government might alter what he saw as inherent sectarian, social, or class differences. Chiha balked at grand nationalist projects, investment in industry, or significant development of the country's agricultural sector. Instead, he supported financial policies that privileged import trade, the deregulation of exchange markets, and balanced budgets. He believed that social spending should be limited as much as possible, and accepted as natural the tremendous inequalities in a society in which he was a prominent member of what historian Fawwaz Traboulsi describes as the "commercial/financial oligarchy."[36]

Such, then, was the nominally independent state that attempted to reconcile communalism and nationalism: it was hollowed out from the inside by a relentless stream of communal considerations. At the same time, it was exposed to an uninterrupted stream of foreign influences. The result was an open cultural field, and an arena of contentious politics in which no single political party or intellectual current was able to predominate. As much as Chiha celebrated Lebanon as the most astute and authentic example of coexistence, it was a country that produced both the most overt sectarian politics and, paradoxically, the most eloquent antisectarian opposition to the sectarian state.

On the one hand, a panoply of social movements, religious associations, publishing houses, journals, and political parties made no secret of the fact that they indeed had the interests of the "Christians" or "Muslims" or "Druze" at heart. They thrived on the logic of a sectarian state but often criticized it for not being equitable enough to their particular sect, or to Muslims or Christians more generally. But these same organizations were also acutely aware of the stigma of being labeled sectarian. Thus, the overwhelmingly Maronite Christian Phalangists, who fought vigorously to uphold the pro-Maronite status quo in the country, methodically mobilizing Christians, never did so in the name of sectarianism but in that of "Lebanese" nationalism.[37] What the Maronites could do, so too the Druze, Sunnis, and Shi'is could learn to do. Claiming to be antisectarian by the mid-century had become an indispensable way to advance sectarian claims, a kind of double-talk akin to how xenophobic Americans and Europeans claim not to be racist.

At the same time, the fact that sectarianism had become a taboo by mid-century was itself crucially important. It underlined the enduring legitimacy of the ecumenical frame, if not the means and method of politicizing it. The same weak sectarian state that provided fertile ground for the Phalangists provoked numerous genuinely antisectarian individuals, social movements, and political parties to fill their ranks with men and women who felt imprisoned within the sectarian state's unimaginative and ultimately paralyzing structures of pessimistic communal thought and politics. They rejected the pieties of Chiha's coexistence—that communities trumped individual or nonreligious collective rights; that sectarian balance trumped secular democracy; and that Maronite Christians had, implicitly if not by the letter of the law, always to remain at the top of the political totem pole. This antisectarian opposition included the communists and internationalists; the Syrian Social National Party, which was founded in the 1930s by the Lebanese émigré Antun Saadeh, who was executed by the

Lebanese state in 1949; the Progressive Socialist Party, created in that same year; and secular Arab nationalists drawn from all faiths who mobilized university students well into the 1950s, like Constantine Zurayk and Abdullah al-'Alayli.[38]

These movements hardly all advocated identical post-sectarian futures. To support the Lebanese state project did not make one anti-ecumenical; to oppose its sectarian political culture did not make one secular. But the emergence of these movements, as well as of trade unions and teachers' associations in the 1940s, signified the increasing visibility and viability of an alternative language of secular rights in place of sectarian ones.[39] Indeed, as Chiha approached his death in 1954, both he and the pro-Western sectarian state that he had helped establish swam against the increasingly noticeable anticolonial nationalist currents across the post-Ottoman Arab region in which Lebanon was adrift.

NATIONAL UNITY AGAINST DIVERSITY

If Michel Chiha indefinitely put off answering the question of how an explicitly communalist system was meant to arrive at an antisectarian future, anticolonial nationalists in neighboring Syria, Iraq, and Egypt claimed to already be antisectarian in their quest for national unity. Yet they too were confronted by the central question upon which Chiha had staked his defense of a modern sectarian system: How was a viable sovereignty to be secularized and reconciled with the secular equality of a religiously diverse citizenry? Instead of Chiha's political sectarianism, they opted for antisectarian nationalism. The tensions in the ideology and practice of this nationalism became especially evident in the work of Sati' al-Husri, the first director general of the Ministry of Education in the British-created Hashemite Iraq, who, in that capacity, attempted to create a unified, state-controlled public education system. Husri was one of the greatest interwar proponents of a secular anticolonial Arab unity.[40]

Read one way, Husri's unapologetic inculcation of secular modernist Arabism has been understood—entirely wrongly I think—as an expression of an intolerant interwar "fanatical" ultranationalism, and as a veneer for sectarian "Sunni" hegemony.[41] Husri's contemporary Amin Rihani struck far closer to the mark when he noted that Husri was convinced, to the point of obdurateness, of the righteousness of his path. More than any other figure, Husri personified the transformation of an Ottoman to a post-Ottoman Arab *nationalist* ecumenical frame. Rihani said of him that "his love for the Arabs was in his heart, not his tongue."[42]

The common thread in Husri's distinguished professional life was his commitment to secularizing anticolonial national pedagogy. Husri understood what Chiha papered over: that diversity in the modern Arab world constituted a centrifugal force that might tear apart its fragile states as comprehensively as the Mashriq had been ripped away from its centuries-old Ottoman environment. Husri also fundamentally believed what Chiha would not: that the antisectarian secular nationalist state was not so much artificial as it was a pedagogical and political project that had to be built from the ground up. As the case of Lebanon illustrated, diversity had no inherent meaning. It had to be interpreted and politicized. In the case of Iraq, Husri was adamant that this diversity had to be depoliticized.

Just as France played the crucial role in enabling Chiha's sectarian state in Lebanon, Britain played an equally obvious role in setting on the throne of their mandate of Iraq the Hashemite King Faysal, whom Husri had joined in Syria in 1919 before following him to Baghdad in 1921. Britain propped up the Hashemite monarch enough to make him a viable ruler, but they consistently reminded him of his dependence on Britain. This subordination was formalized by the 1922 Anglo-Iraqi treaty that gave Britain, not the king, full control over the country's military and foreign affairs. Faysal's kingdom was also saddled with the Ottoman-era debt burden. By 1923, the new Iraqi state still had no defined borders and was confronted by Turkish and Iranian claims to much of its territory and many of its would-be citizens. In the north of the country, Kurds and Assyrians, many of whom had fled Ottoman persecution during the war, often resisted the still inchoate idea of secular Iraqi nationality tied to a tenuous Hashemite sovereignty. Much the same could be said about several Shi'i Arab tribal leaders, religious figures, and urban notables in the overwhelmingly Shi'i south. Some Shi'i notables in the 1920s aspired to decentralized rule or an independent Shi'i state under British protection—despite the massive anti-British rebellion in 1920 that had severely challenged British rule in Iraq at its outset.[43]

Colonialism was no figment of Arab imagination. Britain was crucial in ensuring that the oil-rich region of Mosul became part of Iraq in 1926 in spite of Turkish claims. In return, Faysal accepted the unfavorable terms that Iraq's oil be dominated by foreign interests. Britain relied on what it called the Tribal Criminal and Civil Disputes Regulations, which placed Iraqi tribes outside of the sovereign power of the king and modern Iraqi law. It packed the Iraqi Constituent Assembly with nearly forty pliant, pro-British tribal shaykhs and ensured that Christians and Jews were each guaranteed four seats. British policy in Iraq was driven by the premise that educated, urban, anticolonial nationalists were unrepresentative and untrustworthy. It also refused to invest significantly in educating natives, following the colonial notion that higher education among Iraqis was both unnecessary and potentially dangerous.[44]

Within the broad parameters of dependency on Britain, the Hashemite king was nevertheless granted significant autonomy to forge a new national Iraqi identity. The "social meaning"—the phrase is historian Hana Batatu's—of the Hashemite monarchy in Iraq was a unifying one, and the king brought far more Iraqi Shi'is into governance than had been the case in the Ottoman era.[45] In this context, Husri was able to insulate himself sufficiently from British supervision. In his early years in Iraq he was still, after all, Faysal's man, and the British had far more urgent political and military concerns in Iraq in the 1920s than the meagerly funded educational policy. Husri thus had a relatively free hand to lay the foundations for an antisectarian educated national citizenry.

The stakes, in Husri's view, could not have been higher. Chiha's communalist Lebanon was an urgent reminder of that. So too were parochial nationalisms that were taking root across the Mashriq, the Shi'i religious establishment in Iraq, Kurdish and Assyrian desires for autonomy and independence, new communist parties that rejected Arab nationalism, the Muslim Brotherhood in Egypt, and the anticolonial pan-Islamism of the great interwar exile in Geneva Shakib Arslan—all of which offered serious alternative political visions for how to rebuild the ecumenical frame in the post-Ottoman era. From his urban perch in Baghdad, Husri was confronted by a largely illiterate, impoverished, and heterogeneous population in thrall to a foreign power.

Husri understood from the outset that formal decolonization from French or British rule would never suffice to liberate the Arab world.[46] For him, the struggle for "cultural independence" was just as important as political independence. The key to this cultural independence was a unified but centrally directed system of public education that could create, teach, inspire, and embody in material structures (new school buildings), form (newly trained teachers), and content (a new curriculum) what was a manifestly new antisectarian national identity. He believed firmly that "every nation" needed "an enlightened elite" to educate and lead the mass of otherwise "backward" citizens toward progress and real independence.[47] Because this educational system aimed to uplift "all the citizens" of Iraq, it necessarily broke with the traditional Quranic and foreign missionary schools that had hitherto dominated Iraq's educational landscape. For Husri, these schools were two sides of the same sectarian coin. They were also, he insisted, totally unregulated and entirely out of keeping with modern educational standards.[48]

To Husri the point of the Arabic-language national curriculum (*al manhaj al watani*) that he introduced in 1923 was to overcome what he described as the divisive sectarian passions (*al-niza'at al-ta'ifiyya*) of Iraq—precisely the opposite of Chiha's celebration of the polyphony of Lebanon and its educational communalism. Husri was determined to inculcate an identification with a common Arab past in Iraqis of all religious backgrounds. He put his faith not in the prophets of old but in the secularized *Arab* children of the future. Having witnessed the destruction of both the Ottoman Empire and Faysal's kingdom in Syria in 1920, it was nationalist educational practice that consumed him in colonized Iraq.[49]

Despite perennial problems of staffing, budgets, and disagreements over the appropriate curriculum for Iraqis, Hashemite Iraqi educational policies massively increased both male and female enrollment at both primary and secondary levels.[50] Under Husri's watch, a far greater percentage of the national budget was funneled to education than the British had thought necessary.[51] Husri reduced both religious and foreign-language instruction in schools, introduced a secular Arabic primer, worked to secularize Iraq's Islamic heritage, and rejected (to the dismay of British colonial officials) corporal punishment in secondary schools.[52] He hired teachers from across the Mashriq to indoctrinate students in the belief that they were simultaneously *modern* citizens of Iraq and members of the greater Arab "homeland" of which Iraq was a part. The Higher Teachers College, which was established in Baghdad in 1923, eventually set the tone by offering students drawn from across Iraq a free education, housing, books, medical care, and a small stipend.[53]

For Husri, national education of girls and boys of all socioeconomic classes and sects, as well as the establishment of institutions of secondary and higher education, were meant to lead to a revolution (*inqilab*), not confirm the stability (*istiqrar*) of the colonial status quo.[54] He advocated a carefully managed nationalism anchored in an enlightened but elitist (in the sense of an educated vanguard exemplifying and embodying proper nationalist principles and dogma) antisectarian Arabism: the king of Iraq, after all, was a Hashemite Arab; the majority of Iraq's population were Arab; and the predominant language of the country was Arabic, which, in Husri's view, constituted the key component of nationalism along with history. Husri was adamant, however, that Arabism was defined not by ethnicity, blood, or race (he had always rejected racial nationalism) but by a common culture.[55] For him, therefore, an Arabic nationalist pedagogy was the only glue that could bind together an otherwise extraordinarily diverse Iraq. Kurds in Iraq presumably could be Arabized, but the past that mattered for Husri, and for the pan-Arabists he encouraged in Iraq's schools, was the nationalist Iraqi *Arab* nation. This outlook axiomatically rendered Kurdish history, for example, both invisible and potentially dangerous given the fragility of Iraqi sovereignty and the strong Kurdish claims to autonomy in the oil-rich northern regions of Iraq.[56]

Unlike Chiha's communalist outlook in Lebanon that celebrated religious diversity but obscured the violence of French colonialism, Husri's Arabism consistently obscured diversity in the name of antisectarian and anticolonial national unity. Rather than deny it outright, he sought to sublimate this diversity within a general, often one-dimensional, identification of Arabness. This entailed valorizing non-Muslim (far more than non-Arab) difference insofar as members or churches of minority communities contributed to, or deferred to, an ideology of Arab nationalism. Husri acknowledged the important role that Arab Orthodox and Protestant Christians had played in the nahda to underscore his belief that nationalism and religion were not synonymous. Yet he also worried that too strong a concentration of Christian or Shi'i students in any single location in Iraq might lead to a consolidation of the "spirit of sectarianism" and a threat to the integrative power of secular patriotism. The door to Husri's capacious Arabism was a wide one indeed, though there would have been little choice not to walk through it had matters been left to him.[57]

Like many educated Arabs, Husri accepted the formative historical role of Islam and the Quran in the preservation of a vital Arabic language. He understood that the secularity of modern Arabism depended on the nationalization of Islamic symbols and motifs. A commissioned history textbook written by the Palestinian historian Darwish al-Miqdadi, recruited by Husri, exemplifies this dependency. It opens with the invocation "in the name of God and in the name of *our* prophet and national hero Muhammad, and in the name of Arabism and on its behalf" to emphasize its overarching Arabist intent.[58] The nationalist sensitivity toward sectarianism and colonialism was mirrored by a continuous privileging of Islam and Muslims in political discourse. In Husri's case, the impetus was unquestionably toward desacralizing the rich, already available, and hugely salient repertoire of Islamic symbols and figures to inculcate a secular pan-Arabism that could (and did) appeal to Muslims and non-Muslims alike.

Yet this same reliance on Islamic symbols could just as easily reinforce a sense that the religion that mattered most, at the end of the day, was Islam—and that the Muslims who mattered most were Sunni Arab Muslims. At the level of the Hashemite state, Christian and Jewish minorities may have been "fully" Iraqi in terms of criminal and civil law, but Islam was made the religion of the state in Iraq in 1925 just as it was in Egypt in 1923. Similar to the sectarian state of Lebanon, the modern Iraqi state did not promulgate uniform secular laws of personal status. The opposite occurred: the modern state accepted separate religiously defined marriage, divorce, inheritance, and dowry codes, all of which were adjudicated, contested, and reformed along communal (and tribal) lines.[59] For all his commitment to secular anticolonial nationalism, Husri never once criticized this most sectarian and gendered dualism upon which the elaboration of secular citizenship in the region depended.

Nevertheless, Husri himself desperately wanted to limit the influence of *all* religion in the education of Iraqi schoolchildren. More broadly, he wanted Arab Sunni Muslims to forsake the chauvinistic Islamic tinge of Ottoman nationalism (students affiliated with the Muslim Brotherhood in Syria would later denounce him as "the enemy of God" because of this secularism),[60] he wanted to separate Shi'i Arab Muslims from Iranian influence and from what he felt was the obscurantism of Shi'i clergy, and he wanted Christians to curtail their minoritarian dependency on the colonial West. He also wanted all Iraqi citizens to identify with the wider Arab world, and not merely with citizens of what, after all, was a British-created mandate. For Husri, there was a choice every citizen had to be encouraged to make to place the ecumenical Arab nation at the top of the totem pole of meaningful identifications and above regional, sectarian, tribal, ethnic, and traditional religious loyalties. He advocated compulsory military conscription as a way of forcing a common loyalty to the nation and said, in 1937, "I am an Arab to the core," declaring his devotion to the "religion of Arabism." He also insisted in 1941 that, at moments of crisis, "absolute" individual freedoms had to be sacrificed for the greater national good. Left unsaid by Hursi, who refused to join any political party, was that from his modernizing perch, he believed he could discern better than anyone else where and how this distinction between individual freedom and national liberation lay.[61] At stake in Husri's antisectarianism was a secular anticolonial paternalism that had twentieth-century analogues in Asia, Africa, Latin America, and, of course, Mustafa Kemal's neighboring republican Turkey.

THE LIMITS OF ANTISECTARIAN NATIONALISM

The problem of this paternalism was that it changed the temporality of sectarian fanaticism from being a problem of *self* to be gradually over-come (as nahda reformers such as Bustani and Abduh had largely seen it, and as Chiha himself had accepted in drafting Lebanon's constitution) to being a problem of allegedly backward or reactionary others who had to be emancipated and hauled into modernity willy-nilly by the power of a modernizing secular state. Husri appeared incapable of admitting that the Iraqi state was dominated by Sunni Arabs, perhaps because these were never of a single political outlook. He refused to accept the legitimacy of a purely Iraqi nationalism at the expense of a wider Arab one. He tellingly described those who opposed his national pedagogy as "aberrant sectarians," totally out of touch with the urgent demands of the modern world. Several prominent clerics, as well as inhabitants in Basra and Najaf, openly opposed female education. Husri recalled that when he opened a school in a predominantly Shi'i Baghdad neighborhood, he was unable to staff it initially with the most qualified Arab Christian female teachers because of the prejudice against hiring them.[62] Husri also resented the fact that ministers of education were appointed to placate Shi'i communal aspirations rather than because they were qualified to construct a nationalist curriculum. He condemned what he described as "an intense Iranian tendency" that threatened Arab identity among the Shi'is of the country, and the facility with which Iranian Shi'is traveled to and resided in Iraq. In 1927, he fired a teacher, the future Iraqi poet Muhammad Mahdi al-Jawahiri, because of his alleged sympathy for Iran.[63]

This rejection of sectarianism in the name of Arab unity and secular progress was no less ideological than Chiha's embrace of sectarianism in the name of communal harmony. But Husri's antisectarian zeal worked at cross-purposes to his patron. King Faysal sought stability in a multiethnic and multireligious polity, not anticolonial revolution. He deliberately sought to co-opt major landowning Shi'i tribal leaders, clerics, and urban notables. They, in turn, made communal demands on the resources of the state in the name of national equity. Shi'i ministers thus often sought to staff Iraq's new schools with Shi'i teachers and felt that Shi'i students had been marginalized by Husri's emphasis on building schools in the capital Baghdad. A Shi'i shaykh barged into the Ministry of Education in 1927 and decried a book published on the Umayyad era by a Lebanese teacher who had been hired by Husri. The book was "intolerable" because it allegedly insulted the "Ja'fari [Shi'i] community" of Iraq.[64] Its publication thus violated the putative national unity of the country whose arbiters were defined not by radical modernizers such as Husri, or by the secular law and courts of the new state (to the extent that these actually operated), but by the acknowledged leaders of each community, and ultimately by the king himself.

From the standpoint of his many contemporary critics, Husri's emphasis on national unity rooted in an inculcated modernist antisectarian

Arabism was suffused with arrogance and cultural violence. Husri was not, after all, *from* Iraq. Jawahiri, who came from a distinguished Najafi family, mocked Husri's foreignness and the fact that he, Jawahiri, was required to acquire Iraqi citizenship and fill out an application to become a teacher. According to Jawahiri, the application required him to list his nationality, education, religion, and sect. Asked to list his *shahada madrasiyya* (educational diploma), Jawahiri replied with *the* shahada, the Islamic testament of faith: "La Illah illa Allah." Asked to list his nationality, he wrote "Indian" (Hindi).[65] No matter how consistently Husri rejected the idea of concessions to linguistic, sectarian, tribal, or non-Arab ethnic identifications, he was more often stymied in his efforts to instill in others his rigid secular nationalist ethos. "He emerged victorious in some instances," wrote Rihani empathetically of Husri's struggle to implement nationalist education. "But mostly he was defeated."[66]

Husri resigned from his position as director of Iraqi education in 1927. He was unable to prevent the promulgation of a 1931 Local Languages Law that classified Kurdish as an official language in designated areas of northern Iraq where most Kurdish Iraqis lived and that allowed Kurdish schoolchildren to be taught in Kurdish in those areas.[67] And he was utterly humiliated when younger, highly educated secular Iraqi nationalists convinced the Iraqi government to invite a U.S. educational commission in 1931 to examine the state of Iraqi education. The so-called Monroe Committee was led by Paul Monroe from Columbia University's Teachers College. Historian Sara Pursley explains how the commission embraced the theories of "adaptive" education elaborated by John Dewey, allegedly suited to the needs of different races and exemplified in the work of the segregated Tuskegee Institute of Booker T. Washington. The commission largely ignored Husri and undermined his entire pedagogical approach. Rather than anticolonial nationalism, it advocated a decentralized and gendered curriculum (girls should be taught home economics, not the sex-blind nationalist curriculum) that increased vocational training, legitimated minority education, emphasized tribal and rural education, and limited higher education in the name of the "stability" of the East.[68]

If not spiteful of Husri, these recommendations constituted a withering and paternalistic rebuke of his nationalist project. Husri vehemently and publicly criticized the commission's findings, yet he who had done so much to build up Iraq's educational infrastructure now found himself increasingly marginalized. Although Husri became director of antiquities in 1934, his leading role in Iraqi education was curtailed. Unlike Chiha, Husri never enjoyed the support of a colonial patron. He eventually lost the support of the Hashemite monarchy as well. He was stripped of his Iraqi citizenship and expelled from Iraq in June 1941 following the suppression of an anticolonial revolt led by Iraqi officers and nationalists with whom Husri sympathized. One of the great "sultans of education in the Near East" was overthrown.[69]

THE ASSYRIAN AFFAIR

For all its limitations, Husri's antisectarian Arabism was not artificial—at least no more so than any aspirational work in any other part of the world, whether antiracism in the United States, socialist equality in the early Soviet Union, or anti-communalism in India. It had at its core an emancipatory vision centered on the idea that Arabs of different faiths and sects could indeed coexist without foreign tutelage. His Arabism was unquestionably ideological and had clear blind spots; but in an important sense, it was far more faithful to its Ottoman heritage than the draconian secularism of Mustafa Kemal's Turkey, which had ruthlessly deported well over a million Greek Christians in the name of national liberation and expressly forbade expressions of Kurdish language or Alevi identity. Husri's secular nationalism had not advocated any such mass violence. It had never denied that being Arab was open to a multiplicity of faiths and even, far more ambivalently, to multiple ethnicities (insofar as, say, Armenians or Kurds adopted Arabic language). This inclusiveness, as I have illustrated, was always conditional and highly ambivalent.

The fate of the Assyrians in postcolonial Iraq is an important coda to the story of Husri's rise and fall, for it represented precisely the kind of sectarian problem that secular nationalism had sought to mitigate—and yet also illustrated the very real limitations of this nationalism. Related to the Chaldean Christians native to Iraq, many of those known as the Assyrians were forced out of the Hakkari mountains in Turkey as a result of World War I and settled by the British in Iraq. In a typical colonial twist, British authorities created a separate battalion of Assyrian soldiers from these refugees—known as the Assyrian Levies—who served under British officers and energetically pacified opposition to the mandate. British officials regarded the Assyrians as a "hardy and virile race"[70] and encouraged an Assyrian sense of separateness from Iraqi society. British colonialism in Iraq thus pitted anticolonial nationalists in the mandate created by Britain against minoritarian figures such as the Assyrian patriarch Mar Shimun, whom the British had brought to Iraq in the first place.[71]

The insidiousness of this imperial policy culminated in the Assyrian affair that unfolded immediately after Iraq's formal independence in 1932. Britain relinquished its mandate in that year but reserved the right to use airfields in Iraq to protect its imperial oil interests—concessions that outraged Iraqi nationalists who protested strongly against them. At the same time, the League of Nations insisted that the Iraqi state protect the rights and security of its "minorities," including the Assyrians, in return for ending the mandate and admission to the League of the Nations. These vague pledges did more to offend Iraqi national sensibilities than to mitigate Assyrian insecurity.[72]

The Assyrian patriarch, in the meantime, plunged headlong into supplication before the West. Like many before and after him, he was left bitterly disappointed by the paltry returns on ingratiation. As the Armenians had discovered in the late Ottoman Empire when they appealed in vain for European Christian support, Western government charity was rarely disinterested. Yet like the pro-colonial Syrian Catholic patriarch Ignatius Tappouni, who openly feared the establishment of an Arab nationalist state in neighboring Syria at the end of the French mandate, the Assyrian patriarch Mar Shimun repeatedly distanced himself and his people from the idea of an Arab Iraq and is said to have consistently rejected Iraqi citizenship.[73]

With the end of the British mandate looming, in October 1931, the patriarch and major figures within the Assyrian community in Iraq implored the League of Nations to facilitate their mass emigration from Iraq. In June 1932, Assyrian officers in the Levies resigned en masse to protest the termination of the mandate. Assyrian leaders also petitioned the League of Nations for a "national home" in northern Iraq. They pleaded for a semiautonomous status under the authority of their patriarch, the establishment of separate Assyrian schools and a hospital, and sectarian representation in the Iraqi parliament. They also insisted on retaining their rifles.[74]

From the Iraqi nationalist point of view, these petitions to British officials and the League of Nations raised the specter of foreign intervention. They were reminders of the deeply antagonistic history of the Eastern Question that had seen one Western power after another use the fate of Christians in the East to extract one Ottoman concession after another, whether "free trade," territory, or the abrogation of Ottoman sovereignty. The ostensible protection of minorities was, more immediately, at the heart of the deliberate Anglo-French postwar partitioning of the Middle East. The Assyrian crisis embodied everything the nationalists feared: the Assyrians represented a minority dependent on colonial power; they symbolized sectarianism and separatism; and, by rejecting Iraqi authority, they denoted an obvious curtailment of Iraq's tentative newfound sovereignty.

Sati' al-Husri's son, historian Khaldun Husry (Husri), points out that Iraqi leaders insisted the Assyrian patriarch accept his place as the head of a religious community, while firmly rejecting the notion of an autonomous Assyrian enclave.[75] The escalating tensions between Assyrians and Iraqis came to a head in 1933. King Faysal was in Britain at the time, and the Iraqi government was in the hands of the anticolonial Rashid Ali al-Gaylani. Assyrian tribesmen clashed with Iraqi forces, killing several soldiers. Iraqi authorities accused the Assyrian "rebels" of mutilating the bodies of soldiers and stirred up anti-Assyrian nationalist sentiment across the country. The Iraqi military response was swift. In August 1933, hundreds of Assyrian men were massacred in the village of Simele, and in the wake of this massacre, many more Assyrians were expelled from Iraq. Mar Shimun himself was deported from Iraq to British-occupied Palestine.[76]

Iraqi state violence against the Assyrians was brutal, reminiscent on a much smaller scale of how Abdülhamid II had dealt mercilessly with the Armenians in 1895 and 1896. That it was an Iraqi general of Kurdish descent, Bakr Sidqi, who was generally blamed by the British officers for the massacre of the Assyrians underscored the irony of the mandate. Whereas Kurdish, Jewish, Shi'i Arab, anticolonial nationalist, and tribal affiliations were constantly negotiated and tested, they were not, in this period at least, summarily dismissed or cut off.[77] By being identified so closely with British colonialism and the League of Nations, the Assyrians led by Mar Shimun embodied the specter of further territorial division and minority separatism in a region that had been plagued by both. They elicited a ferocious response from an Iraqi army that, on its own, was unable to evict Britain from Iraq but was more than capable, with British-supplied weaponry, to brutalize some of the Assyrian refugee population in Iraq.

For all its terror, however, the assault on the Assyrians was not a war on the ecumenical frame in Iraq. Rather, it appeared to be a virulent reaction to a politicized form of colonial pluralism cultivated by Western powers in Palestine, Syria, Lebanon, and Iraq. Colonial cynicism courted nationalist indifference. King Faysal flatly denied that any massacre had occurred. Sati' al-Husri did not mention it in his memoirs. His son Khaldun lamented that the history of the Assyrian affair had become "the propaganda of the victims."[78] And even a progressive Arab socialist intellectual, Abdullah 'Alayli in Lebanon, who wrote so evocatively in 1941 about the need for a "natural" religion to bind Arabs of different faiths together, struck an entirely discordant note when it came to the subject of compact minorities. He urged the "dissolution" of the Jews in Palestine, the Assyrians in Iraq, and the Alawis in Syria within the "national melting pot."[79] For all the distant expressions of Western sympathy for the Assyrian victims of the Iraqi army, there was almost none to be spared for them within the Arab world itself.

The further tragedy was that many subjects of the Hashemite state, including Husri's son Khaldun, believed that the army constituted both the sovereignty of the nation and the manifestation of antisectarian national culture. Khaldun was a boy when the Iraqi army was feted in Baghdad and Mosul for protecting the "Fatherland" and defeating "Imperialism," as it returned from its bloody campaign against the Assyrians.[80] He met Sidqi after the massacre and told the Iraqi general that he too wanted to become an officer one day. This veneration of the military pointed to the profound insecurity at the heart of the nationalist ecumenical frame—and anticipated the militarization of society that would ultimately disfigure politics in the postcolonial Arab world.

THE ECUMENICAL FRAME IN THE BALANCE

The Assyrian affair serves as a reminder of the capacity for cruelty within the post-Ottoman ecumenical frame. It occurred nonetheless in a period when most major political constellations in the Arab Mashriq—liberal nationalist, monarchical, conservative, Islamist, or communist—committed themselves to rebuilding, not abolishing, the ecumenical frame. They each understood that the construction of new national communities depended on molding a diverse religious landscape into a coherent national assemblage. As well, they had to determine where and how to distinguish between legitimate religious difference and illegitimate sectarianism. The Assyrians were attacked not because they were Christian, but because they were perceived to be sectarian and separatist; this distinction is fundamental to understanding the nature and limits of the modern ecumenical frame. The Assyrians were depicted as foreign collaborators with British imperialism. They were precisely *not* like Arab Christians—or not like Arab Christians were imagined to be.

The upshot was that by the end of the colonial era in the 1940s, the repudiation of the modern heresy of "sectarianism" in the post-Ottoman Arab political culture was almost total. So strong was this repudiation that, in the 1940s, an Arab Christian named Michel ʿAflaq was able to cofound and lead with a fellow Damascene, Salah al-Din Bitar, one of the most important anticolonial, pan-Arab political parties of the modern era, the Baath Party—something unimaginable even fifty years before. Increasingly, Christian, Muslim, and Jewish Arabs in the Mashriq articulated their aspirations in competing secular languages of political and social rights. The rise of railway, port, and oil workers' unions in Iraq by the 1940s went hand in hand with the emergence of new multiconfessional political parties like the Syrian Social Nationalist Party in Syria and the Muthanna Club and the Communist Party in Iraq.[81] The class interests of these protagonists were different. Their commitments to upholding or overturning the social and economic orders of their day varied enormously, often to the point of factionalism and hatred (such as between the communists of Iraq and the Baathists). The awareness of religious others as compatriots was increasingly taken for granted between the 1920s and the 1950s.

But this political ecumenism was always conditional. The thrust of nationalism was fixated on *denying* (except in Lebanon) the salient political difference of minorities—that is to say, on refuting colonial pluralism. This refutation led to profound awkwardness when it came to *affirming* the reality of the diversity of the Mashriq. The most radical parties and social movements from a secular standpoint—the communists in Lebanon and Iraq, for example—were far from power in the mandate era. Those nationalists in or close to actual power in Lebanon, Iraq, Syria, and Egypt professed genuine ecumenism but practiced it cautiously. They had, if nothing else, to contend with the salience of inherited prejudices and the mobilizing potential of conservative forces that inevitably diluted the inherent ecumenism of anticolonial nationalisms in the Mashriq. But they also had to contend with the structures they had themselves built. Unlike Mustafa Kemal's Turkey, no Arab country dared to promulgate a secular civil code. But also unlike Mustafa Kemal's secular Turkey, no Arab state in the Mashriq embarked on a drastic war against diversity either.

Rather than advocating Islamic states because the majority of their citizens were Muslim, or a Christian state in the case of Maronite-dominated Lebanon, the post-Ottoman nationalisms in the Mashriq legitimated the idea of secular solidarity between Muslim and non-Muslim within clearly demarcated boundaries: overt displays of religious chauvinism were made taboo in the name of combating "sectarianism"; explicitly separatist sectarian movements were stigmatized, especially among non-Muslim communities; economic and land-tenure orders were largely to be maintained, not radically overthrown; religious symbols, especially Muslim ones, were nationalized; and, most obviously, female citizens of every Arab state were placed at the mercy of widely divergent, and invariably inegalitarian, sets of family laws. These separate regimes of personal status guaranteed to members of different religious communities that they would be subject to their "own" family laws; they provided citizens with an assurance that religion remained relevant to intimate aspects of their lives. More materially, they secured for religious functionaries crucial avenues of patronage and employment within the state structure. They also provided Muslims and non-Muslims communal bulwarks against fears of secularism and assimilation, respectively. They were sectarian in practice but not "sectarian" in nationalist ideology. These caveats sustained and shadowed the principle of brotherhood between Muslim and non-Muslim Arabs.

The crucible of the ecumenical national frame ultimately lay, and still lies, in how a commitment to religious diversity could be reconciled with parallel commitments to the rule of law, equal citizenship, social justice, and democracy. As the cases of Chiha's Lebanon and Husri's Iraq attested, constitutional proclamations of equality were one thing, equal access to resources and state patronage another. The two countries equally inherited the intellectually elitist, socially conservative, highly gendered Ottoman-era ecumenical frame. In very different ways and with varying degrees of success, they rebuilt this frame within narrower national Lebanese and Iraqi terms. The main tragedy, however, unfolded where politics broke decisively with the region's Ottoman heritage, and where, as a direct result, the ecumenical frame was shattered. It is to the story of the destruction of Arab Palestine and the beginning of the end of Arab Jewish communities, therefore, that I now turn.

6 Breaking the Ecumenical Frame

ARAB AND JEW IN PALESTINE

We have been in Palestine for twelve years without having
even once made a serious attempt at seeking through negotiations the consent of the indigenous people. . . .
   . . . I believe that it will be possible for us to hold Palestine
and continue to grow for a long time. This will be done first
with British aid and then later with the help of our own bayonets—shamefully called *Haganah* [i.e. defense]. . . . But by
that time we will not be able to do without the bayonets.
The means will have determined the goal.

— Hans Kohn, letter to Berthold Feiwel, 1929

Zionism is a doctrine that had no appeal to oriental
Jewries. Their historical experience was profoundly different from that of the east European Jewries, where Zionism
was invented.

— Elie Kedourie, "Minorities," 1952

The establishment of a Jewish state in 1948 represented a caesura in the
modern history of coexistence in the Mashriq. Sectarian Lebanon, Arab
nationalist Syria, and Hashemite Iraq were logical, though by no means
inevitable or even necessary, continuations of an ecumenical late Ottoman
history. The Zionist idea of a Jewish Palestine was not a continuation. Its
most important proponents and political leaders emerged in Europe. They
regarded religious pluralism in Palestine not so much with ambivalence (as
did Lebanese and Iraqi political elites, as we have seen) but as a major
obstacle to their goal of creating a modern nationalist Jewish state. Because

of its eventual military triumph, the Zionist project in Palestine profoundly affected the nature of the post-Ottoman ecumenical frame. In Palestine it destroyed that frame; in the rest of the Mashriq, Israeli statehood haunted the meaning of modern coexistence between Muslim, Christian, and Jew.

Remarkably, the historiography of the Arab-Israeli conflict has been largely segregated from that of the Ottoman past and from the historiographies of the neighboring mandates of Lebanon and Syria. For understandable reasons, perhaps, much of the critical comparative work on Zionism in Palestine has focused on how Zionism reflects a settler-colonial paradigm, or on the European intellectual provenance of major Zionist intellectuals.[1] But this focus on Europe and colonialism obscures one of the most obvious facets of the story of Zionism in Palestine, namely its insertion into a much broader and already unfolding story of coexistence that had been, in the Ottoman era at least, principally concerned with Muslim and non-Muslim. Zionism, in other words, played out in a historically dense field.[2] Its development in Palestine inaugurated a new sectarian conflict between "Arab" and "Jew."

There was, to be sure, an evident nahda ethos in Palestine on the eve of the British mandate. Like its manifestation in other parts of the Ottoman Mashriq, this ethos was simultaneously national and communal; it was no more or less complex, and no more or less replete with rich and often contradictory elements, than any other part of the Mashriq; and as elsewhere in what remained until 1948 an interconnected region, the ecumenical aspect of this ethos was striking.[3] Christian Arabs played important roles in formulating modern education; among their students were members of a prominent Jerusalemite family, the Husaynis. The mayor of Jerusalem at the outbreak of World War I was the urbane Husayn al-Husayni. Educated in the United States, fluent in English, and respected by all the major religious communities of the city, he was emblematic of the late Ottoman ecumenical frame.[4]

Muslim Arabs formed the vast majority of the native population—over 500,000 of the total population of 650,000 in 1914. Christian Arabs constituted approximately 10 percent of Palestine's total population. The total Jewish population of Palestine stood at roughly 80,000 in 1914.[5] The torchbearers of Zionism were Ashkenazi European Jews who began to settle in Ottoman Palestine in the late nineteenth century. Ottoman Sephardic and

Eastern or Arab Jews made up the indigenous Jewish population. They sought to mediate between their growing attraction to Zionism and their own Ottoman experience.[6] Like other manifestations of the Arabic nahda in the Ottoman period, Palestinian Arab identity was neither strongly nationalist nor militarized. Indeed, the initial Arab responses to the arrival of European Jewish colonists in the 1880s were far from monolithic. Jews and Judaism, after all, had always been a vital part of a multireligious Palestine.

The early Zionist colonists did not possess a unified political structure, nor could they count on the military support of a Western empire. Many of them put their faith in colonization before colonialism, or were themselves seeking shelter from anti-Jewish pogroms in Europe without necessarily articulating or embracing an overtly political Zionist outlook. Some Arab Muslims and Christians, like many Jews in Palestine, could even admire the tenacity and modernity of these pioneering settlers. In his 1904 history of the Jews, Shahin Makarius appreciated the work of Zionist organizations in Palestine that had transformed some areas "from barrenness to fertility."[7] Jurji Zaydan likewise praised new Zionist colonists in Tel-Aviv for their commitment to salubrious modernization.[8] Other Arabs, perhaps most famously Ruhi al-Khalidi and Khalil Sakakini, believed that it was possible for European Jews in Palestine to contribute to a common revival of the East. Initially, therefore, the advent of European Jewish colonists elicited far less general apprehension than it would later.

The problem, in any case, was not the Jewishness of the settlers, but the gradual crystallization of the nationalist Zionist project that regarded Palestine as a Jewish national homeland. Although there were many different forms of Zionism, the decision of the World Zionist Congress at Basel in 1897 to commit to "the creation of a home for the Jewish people in Palestine to be secured by public law," and the arrival of a second wave of more ideologically driven European Jewish immigrants between 1904 and 1914, inevitably exacerbated tensions with the indigenous Palestinians.[9] The foreignness of the colonists was coupled with a more assertive form of Zionism. Their land purchases intended to establish segregated, self-sustaining communities. They regarded Jewish labor as key to a new Jewish, and often socialist, society, often expelling Palestinian laborers from purchased agricultural lands. Some European Jews such as Ahad Ha'am recognized by 1913 that the ill-treatment of the indigenous

Palestinians raised serious questions about the nature of Zionism in Palestine. "If Palestinian Jewry is unable to exercise restraint and decency now that it holds little power," he wondered, "how much worse will it be when we control the land and its Arab inhabitants?"[10]

Consequently, divergent Arab attitudes increasingly converged in a condemnation of Zionism. Beginning with editorials in the local Arabic press, petitions to the Ottoman Sultan Abdülhamid II, and debates within the Ottoman parliament continuing right through the end of Ottoman rule, Palestinian Muslim and Christian parliamentarians, religious leaders, newspaper editors, notables, journalists, and teachers sounded increasingly loud alarms about the colonial enterprise. Jurji Zaydan himself noted in his trip through Palestine in 1913 that if Zionist land purchases and settlement growth were to continue in the face of local apathy and an indifferent government, it would not be long before the entire country would "pass entirely into the hands of the Jews."[11]

So long as the Ottoman Empire remained intact, Zionist aspirations for an independent state were largely contained. The founding father of Zionism, the Viennese Theodor Herzl, was unable to convince the Ottoman state to embrace Zionism. Rival Ottoman Sephardic and other Eastern Jewish non-Zionist currents vied for ideological attention in cities with vibrant and diverse Jewish populations such as Salonika, Baghdad, and Jerusalem. Indeed, some of the sharpest criticisms of the more militant and uncompromising Zionism in the late Ottoman Empire were expressed by Sephardic Ottoman Jews.[12] Zionist individuals and groups thus worked piecemeal to settle in Palestine, relying on their own initiative, on the philanthropic donations of wealthy European Jews such as Baron Edmond Rothschild, and on the Jewish National Fund, founded in 1901 to ensure exclusive Jewish title over land purchases in Palestine. When the Ottoman Empire was defeated, the advent of colonial Zionism began in earnest.

BALFOUR DECLARATION AND THE PASSING OF AN OTTOMAN AGE

The Balfour Declaration of 1917 announced the passing of the Ottoman age in the Mashriq. It tellingly referred to the native Palestinian Arabs by what they were not, for it contrasted the aspirations of "the Jewish people" for a "national home" with the inconvenient reality of "existing non-Jewish communities" in Palestine. Drafted by Zionists led by a Russian-born chemist who resided in England, Chaim Weizmann, then amended and issued by Lord Arthur Balfour, the single-paragraph statement represented a milestone for colonial Zionism.[13] Henceforth, Zionist ambitions in Palestine were yoked directly to the power of the British empire, not to the reality of the indigenous Arab population. At the Paris Peace Conference in 1919, Zionist leaders, including Weizmann and the Polish-born Nahum Sokolow, made a series of extraordinary political demands. They wanted Western recognition of the "historic title of the Jewish people to Palestine" and the "right of Jews to reconstitute in Palestine their National Home." They also demanded that necessary "political, administrative and economic conditions" be put in place, including "fair representation in the executive and legislative bodies in the selection of public and civil servants."[14] The significance of their claims was reinforced by the fact that not one of the Zionist representatives at Paris was actually from Palestine, let alone any of the lands of the former Ottoman Empire. Their political discourse was not only radically out of step with the meaning of the Ottoman Arab ecumenical frame—it was its negation.

Palestine, in these Zionist eyes, was largely "desolate." For the Zionist leadership lobbying the Western powers, therefore, the notion that Muslim, Christian, and non-European Jewish inhabitants could rejuvenate themselves through their own agency—a central assumption of the nahda—was inadmissible, if not unthinkable. Its candid view was that Palestine needed an "enlightened" government that had to be colonial, not simply one that emulated certain aspects of modern Europe. It also needed "an addition to the present population which shall be energetic, intelligent, devoted to the country, and backed by the large financial resources that are indispensable for development. Such a population the Jews alone can supply." Weizmann himself had privately noted to Balfour in 1918 "the treacherous nature of the Arab," who "screams as often as he can and blackmails as much as he can."[15] Weizmann's animus was not only directed at Arab Muslims or Christians. He also scorned the "rich Jews" of Egypt, who at the time were indifferent to Zionism. The local leaders of the Jewish community in Palestine were, in any case, excluded from the decision making of the British-backed Zionist Commission.[16]

The expressly sectarian demands of the Zionist leadership in Paris were unprecedented in their boldness. They were not intended to manage a multireligious polity but to replace it with a Jewish state—to transform the ambiguity of the Balfour Declaration's "national home" into the clarity of Jewish sovereignty. The contrast between the Lebanese sectarian state and the Jewish national home is instructive. Although Christian elites in Lebanon ensured their dominant role in the politics of the country (whose sectarian constitutional clause, as we have seen, was ostensibly temporary), they quickly accepted that Lebanon could not be defined as a Christian state. Having encouraged the French partition of an Ottoman whole, many Lebanese Christian elites worked to reconcile their separate Lebanese state with their Arab Muslim environment. Shi'i, Druze, and Sunni Muslim notables not only came to accept a Lebanese polity, but also actively participated in its constitution, using a language of sectarian rights of their respective communities to contest Maronite political hegemony. These elites could plausibly imagine themselves to be part of the sectarian state even if many of them had initially balked at the French colonial creation of Lebanon.

The idea of a Jewish entity dominated by Western Ashkenazi Jewish—and often Russian-, German-, Yiddish-, or Hebrew-speaking—colonists was fundamentally different. Unlike the native Maronites, most Jewish Ashkenazi colonists in the 1920s were not from Palestine. Yet for Zionist leaders like Weizmann, Jews possessed an eternal indigeneity that they regarded as far more important than the nativeness of the Arabs. In his eyes, centuries of continuous Arab and Islamic life in Palestine might as well have been days: the Arabs merely lived in the place; the Jews eternally belonged there. At a dinner given in April 1918 by the British military governor of Jerusalem, Ronald Storrs, and in front of an audience of Palestinian dignitaries, including the mufti of Jerusalem and the Orthodox Christian vice-mayor, as well as the acting Armenian patriarch, Weizmann reiterated this Zionist mantra of a transcendent nativity. Speaking in English, his speech was translated into Arabic by Storrs. Weizmann sought to reassure Muslim and Christian leaders of his desire for "peace, harmony and cooperation between the communities represented here."

Yet he also informed the gathering that "I am not a stranger to this country, although born and bred in the remote north." Alluding to Biblical narratives and claiming the "inviolable right to this sacred place" of Jews, Weizmann insisted that "we therefore do not come to Palestine: we return to it."[17]

Zionist leaders were inevitably different from one another in temperament, background, and approach to the conundrum of trying to build a Jewish state in a land overwhelmingly inhabited by Palestinian Arabs. Yet they almost all understood that their shared dream of Jewish sovereignty relied heavily on the buttresses of British imperial support. In this, too, they were both similar to, and yet utterly different from, the Lebanese Michel Chiha. Both the Zionists and the ideologue of Lebanese exceptionalism occupied privileged positions within European colonial regimes that encouraged them to transform intellectual fantasies into consequential political projects. Yet, as antithetical as Chiha's pro-colonial francophone milieu was to the anticolonial Arab nationalism of Sati' al-Husri, they nevertheless both emerged from the variegated soil of Ottoman history. Weizmann navigated the corridors of diplomatic power in London, a world away from the realities of Palestine he was so desperate to change. The man who succeeded him as leader of the Jewish community in Palestine in the 1930s was the Polish-born David Ben-Gurion, who had forged his imagination rebelling against the East European shtetl—which had no Ottoman equivalent.[18] Ottoman Christians, Muslims, and Jews of the Arabic nahda had put their faith in the possibility of a national brotherhood to combat the "disease" of sectarianism; they had depended on Ottoman sovereignty. European Zionists such as Weizmann and Ben-Gurion sought Jewish sovereignty and depended entirely at this juncture on the coercive power of British imperialism.

Michel Chiha, of course, also depended on the shield of the French military. But the naked violence of the French mandate in Lebanon was largely confined to its beginnings when Henri Gouraud forcibly carved the state of Lebanon from its Syrian hinterland. In Palestine, the British mandate yoked itself from the outset to the ambitious Zionist fantasy of Jewish redemption and rebirth that had to be first imposed on the Arab majority and then maintained for decades in the face of protracted resistance. To fulfill the terms of this extraordinary enterprise, segregated educational, legal, labor, financial, and immigration systems were established or tolerated by the British. Through the Palestine Zionist Executive and then the Jewish Agency, the Jewish population of the mandate enjoyed a privileged relationship with the British rulers. The first civilian high commissioner, Herbert Samuel, was Jewish and sympathetic to Zionism, and even more so was the first attorney general for the mandate, Norman Bentwich. No Palestinian Muslim or Christian Arab was appointed head of any mandatory government department, and Jewish officials employed by the mandate were paid higher salaries than their non-Jewish Arab counterparts.[19] British colonial officials steadfastly rejected a constitution or basic law analogous to what were put in place in Lebanon and Iraq.

As much as the mandatory government sought to reassure the native Arabs that it would protect their interests, it refused to accept the legitimacy of a politically secular Palestinian Arab national identity.[20] It refused, moreover, to renounce the Balfour Declaration despite consistent Palestinian Arab demands for such a renunciation. Instead, Herbert Samuel created a toothless Advisory Council in 1920 that included four Muslims, three Christians, and three Jews; in 1922, he proposed an equally toothless Legislative Council also composed along sectarian lines. This second council was to be composed of twenty-three members: eleven selected by the British mandatory government and twelve elected from the population in proportion to their ostensible demographic weight— eight Muslims, two Christians, and two Jews.

In his insistence on sectarian representation mediated by European power, Samuel was not different from his French counterparts in the Levant. The key difference now lay in the ultimate purpose of sectarian representation. Colonial Zionism, after all, was not satisfied with affirming and strengthening a Jewish place within a pluralistic Palestine. Instead, it wanted to reverse the situation—that is, to transform Palestine into a Jewish state. It relied on British might to delay democratic representation until unfettered Jewish immigration changed the demographic reality of Palestine—for "the brutal numbers operate against us," admitted Weizmann to Balfour in 1918.[21]

Ben-Gurion and Weizmann wanted nothing less than to build a state for the Jewish people, and only then—as a concession to the historical and demographic reality in Palestine that they fought so hard against—to come to terms, possibly, with the native Arab Muslims and Christians. Until the 1930s, the idea of the removal of the Palestinians was not emphasized as much as was building up the Jewish community through unrestricted immigration to the point where an aspirational Jewish state would become a reality, no matter what the indigenous Arab majority said or did. Certainly, several Zionist political leaders and industrialists understood the potential of a Middle Eastern mass market for Jewish goods. They understood that to thrive economically, the Jewish community in Palestine had ultimately to be integrated into the wider region—as had been the case with Jewish trade networks before the Balfour Declaration.[22] However, the key question was on what, and whose, terms. The explicit and relentless political demand for a "Jewish" home dependent on Western military power foreclosed the possibility of a cultural Zionism that could be reconciled with the nahda ethos of conservative coexistence. It forced a choice of "national" sides in a new existential conflict between "the Jews" and "the Arabs." The Syrian historian Muhammad Kurd Ali noted in 1925 that Zionists "rebel against becoming Arab."[23]

In the face of the capacious, if ambiguous, Ottoman Arab ecumenical frame that Palestinian Muslims, Christians, and Jews had inherited, the post-Ottoman Zionist nationalist frame was more narrowly designed, more militant, and more focused ideologically. The irony here was supreme. At the very moment, by the middle of the 1920s, when the vexed question of Muslim and non-Muslim appeared to have finally exhausted itself, at the cost of great human suffering and displacement in Turkey and the Balkans, British-backed Zionism obsessively and aggressively demarcated Jew from non-Jew. Colonial Zionism, in effect, created an "Arab" question in Palestine and a "Jewish" one in the Mashriq where neither had previously existed.

TAKING SIDES

In the immediate aftermath of the Balfour Declaration, the Ottoman-era ecumenical frame in Palestine remained discernible. Indeed, in the summer of 1918, the mufti of Jerusalem laid one of the cornerstones of the Hebrew University. In that same year, Muslim-Christian associations were formed to emphasize the solidarity and kinship of Muslim and Christian Arabs in the face of official British recognition of the European Zionist Commission led by Weizmann. Since "Jews" had their official body, the "Arabs" now demanded their own. A year later, the first Muslim-Christian Congress convened in Jerusalem.[24] Muslim-Christian solidarity reflected a nascent Palestinian nationalism. More specifically, it was an aspect of many different local responses across Palestine to an international movement that had the express backing of the most powerful empire of its day. But this solidarity was also rooted in the Ottoman-era nahda that had made a modern ecumenical Arab identity meaningful in the first place, and that had forged, in the decades after 1860, an elite consensus across the Mashriq that "true" religion bolstered coexistence between Muslim and non-Muslim. Not surprisingly, as Muslim and Christian Palestinians came together in Palestine to protest the Balfour Declaration and the Zionist demands at the Paris Peace Conference, Muslim reformists Shakib Arslan and Rashid Rida, the latter the famous disciple of Muhammad Abduh and founder of *Al-Manar*, worked closely with Christian Arabs to found the Syro-Palestinian Congress in Geneva in 1921 to protest the mandates.[25]

As the conflict with colonial Zionism escalated, anti-Zionist organizations described Jews with increasing ambivalence. On the one hand, neither the Muslim-Christian associations nor the Syro-Palestinian Congress included Jewish members—as if conceding that Zionism *did* represent Jews at this critical stage. On the other hand, Muslim and Christian intellectuals, journalists, lawyers, mayors, ulema, clerics, and secular dignitaries often distinguished between "Zionists" (*al-sahyuniyyun*), who held Zionism as a nationalist creed, and the "native Jews" (*al-yahud sukkan al-watan al-asliyyun*) of Palestine, "our Jewish brothers, who are the native to the land [unlike European Zionists], they are our brothers in good times and bad, and they have the same rights and responsibilities as we have, and we live together in prosperity and each of us enjoys personal liberty."[26] These associations protested the exclusive Zionist claim to Palestine. In the eyes of Arab Muslim and Christian Palestinians, this claim had to be urgently refuted. They emphasized that the Jewish religious heritage and attachment to Palestine could not possibly supersede Muslim or Christian heritage and attachment to the same land over a thousand years of continuous presence. They also made the point repeat-edly that Palestinian Arabs constituted the overwhelming majority in Palestine.

Colonial Zionism was not simply illegitimate in the eyes of most Arabs. For many of them, it was morally regressive because it represented a nega-tion of the ecumenical spirit of the nahda. Several of the Palestinian peti-tions submitted to the Paris Peace Conference in 1919 explicitly stated that they opposed Zionism because "it incites religious fanaticism and selfish-ness in the twentieth century."[27] Key here was the sense that Zionism was an anachronism. In Arab eyes, colonial Zionism interrupted progress, incited sectarianism, and was antithetical to the common good.

The first major urban intercommunal troubles in Palestine in the mod-ern era occurred because of Zionism—and the contrast between these riots and those of Aleppo and Damascus in 1850 and 1860 is remarkable. Whereas Jews had not been targeted in the nineteenth-century Syrian riots, they were at the heart of twentieth-century ones in Palestine. The Nabi Musa riots of April 4–7, 1920, that broke out in Jerusalem repre-sented the first major Arab-Jewish clash in modern Palestine. According to historian Awad Halabi, the Nabi Musa festival had been one of the most significant religious festivals in Palestine in the nineteenth century, during which Muslim pilgrims would visit the shrine of Moses (Musa) on the road to Jerusalem. In Jerusalem itself, they would pray at Al-Aqsa Mosque. Christians would also participate in the festival. Following the Balfour Declaration, however, the explicit Zionist claims to Palestine, the establishment of British rule in Palestine, and the denial of Arab self-determination immediately raised tensions between Muslim and Jewish inhabitants.

The British military administration believed it had the situation in hand. The militant Russian Zionist Vladimir (Ze'ev) Jabotinsky, mean-while, was training a Jewish militia in anticipation of what he believed was inevitable conflict with the native Palestinian population. In March in Damascus, the Arab nationalist General Syrian Congress proclaimed King Faysal's Arab sovereignty over Greater Syria, including Palestine, and condemned Zionism. The Palestinian educator and reformer Khalil al-Sakakini noted in his diary how what he remembered to have always been a religious festival had now become a "national" one.[28]

On the eve of the San Remo conference in April during which Britain and France would confirm each other's colonial acquisitions in the Mashriq, pilgrims and processions made their way to Jerusalem from all over Palestine. After listening to patriotic speeches at the Arab Club, including those given by the mayor of Jerusalem, Musa al-Husayni, and the Palestinian nationalist Khalil Baydas, pilgrims headed to Al-Aqsa Mosque. As they crossed the Jewish quarter, a melee between pilgrims and Jewish inhabitants rapidly escalated into a major conflagration. The official British report on the riots listed a total of five Jewish and four Muslim deaths, and over two hundred wounded, most of whom were Jews.[29] A year later, in May, another set of riots occurred in Jaffa—and this time the casualties were far greater.

On one side, anticolonial and anti-Zionist passions inevitably commingled with anti-Jewish sentiment; on the other side, anti-Arab convictions mixed with arrogance and an ardent belief in the righteousness of Zionism. As with the Aleppo and Damascus riots of the mid-nineteenth century, a change in the status quo initiated unprecedented intercommunal clashes. The Aleppo riots of 1850 had primarily resisted conscription. The 1920 riots resisted Zionism. According to Sakakini's diary, rioters cried, "The religion of Muhammad was established by the sword." Yet pilgrims, he noted, had also directed slogans specifically against "the Zionist," calling for his departure from "our land."[30] Unlike the protagonists in Aleppo and Damascus, the Arab protestors in Palestine were not invested in upholding putative Muslim privilege, but in lashing out against a new Zionist "government within a government" that was being coercively erected over them in blatant disregard of their wishes. Although he held the British authorities culpable for their negligence, Sakakini insisted that it was "the Jews" who had provoked the rioting, and in response "the Arabs" had attacked Jews. "I hate the Jew if he attacks the Arab," he wrote, "and the Arab if he attacks the Jew, and I hate all of humanity if it is reduced to hatred and enmity." He added: "Jerusalem had not seen such as this for an age."[31]

From Sakakini's local perspective, the riots were not an upwelling of some timeless anti-Semitism, but far more obviously a dramatic escalation of a new conflict. They were, in fact, part of a pattern of resistance to colonial Zionism that had, by 1920, already been expressed in multiple forms, including nonviolent petitions, pleas, discussions, marches, and speeches, none of which had succeeded in undoing Britain's support of colonial Zionism. When Jabotinsky and the Russian-born chairman of the Zionist Commission (and later head of the Jewish National Fund) Menachem Ussishkin described the events of Nabi Musa as a "pogrom," the term was loaded with meaning but also a telling misrecognition.[32] By "pogrom," of course, Jabotinsky and Ussishkin implied government connivance in the anti-Jewish riots—at the very least, a severe dereliction of duty. They elided the significant difference between Jews as victims of a racist and anti-Semitic modern European political culture and the colonial Zionist enterprise in Palestine in which many European Jews were, quite simply, at the forefront of a manifestly exclusionary, and often deeply racist, ideological nationalist project that blatantly discriminated against non-Jews, as well as against so-called oriental Jews. While a few Jewish Zionists urged moderation in the face of open Arab resistance to colonial Zionism, Jabotinsky urged escalation. "Zionist colonization must either stop, or else proceed regardless of the native population," he would write in 1923. "Which means it can proceed and develop only under the protection of a power that is independent of the native population—behind an iron wall which the native population cannot breach."[33]

Given this frank admission, and the actual context of Palestine and its Ottoman history in which Jews in the nineteenth century were neither confined to East European–style ghettoes nor made into the singular exception to Ottoman nationalism, the term "pogrom" itself seemed as out of place as those Zionists who deployed it so insistently. It obfuscated the obvious role of the Zionists in precipitating an intercommunal crisis in Palestine. Sakakini described the same set of events as *hawadith,* or "events," a term whose opacity acknowledged the complicity of all sides in the acts of violence and obliquely recalled other "events" like those of 1860 in Damascus. Sakakini understood the acts of violence as a moment of rupture with the Ottoman Arab past in Palestine and emphasized the degree to which the rioting overturned an established order of things that had long seen Muslims, Christians, and Jews coexist in the city.

The official British report on the Nabi Musa violence—the Palin Commission report—interpreted the riots through a colonial lens. It reproduced a panoply of imperial British discourse about Turkish misrule. It referred to the "Jewish title [to Palestine] based on a tenacious historical memory of the race and a profound religious sentiment," and, inevitably now, it distinguished between "Arabs" and "Jews." The report further distinguished between the "Orthodox Jew" who, it claimed, had not traditionally been an object of Arab distrust, and the "latest [Jewish] immigrants from Eastern Europe" who, it said, were "imbued with all shades of political opinions which have plunged Russia into a welter of anarchy, terrorism, and misery during the past few years." It set up a contrast between the fearful Arab peasant, "apathetic and slow in his intelligence" but rooted to the soil of Palestine, and "the vigorous mental force of the Jew."[34]

Yet as much as it pinned the "racial upstirrings arising out of recent historical events in the Near East" on Zionist "indiscretion and aggression," and on Arab fear of Zionist despoliation that turned into an uncontrolled Arab outburst against innocent Jews, the Palin Commission report nevertheless admitted a single basic point. "Whatever may be alleged against Turkish rule," it asserted, "one fact stands out quite clearly from the evidence. Up to a very recent date the three sects, Moslem, Christians and Jews lived together in a state of complete amity."[35] It also asserted frankly that the Balfour Declaration "is undoubtedly the starting point of the whole trouble" but conceded that no matter what Arab Muslims and Christians said or did, the Balfour Declaration "is a chose jugee [*sic;* i.e., a matter that has been settled] which will most inevitably be executed." It added that the "Administration will nevertheless hold the scales as between all parties with rigid equality."[36]

At the urging of the British High Commissioner Herbert Samuel, the report went unpublished.[37] Its justification of British rule nevertheless reproduced all the elements of modern sectarian discourse. Having created a political context in which an obviously new intercommunal conflict erupted before their eyes, British colonial officials presumed to stand above the "racial" and "religious" fray as if they were not deeply implicated in it. An important element of this discourse was the judgment of sectarian acts as barbaric and their contrast with the allegedly normative, civilized order of British rule. The notion of age-old, immutable "racial" sectarian sentiments functioned to exculpate British responsibility for creating the conditions for inevitable conflict even as the British commissioners admitted that the tensions began with the Balfour Declaration. British colonialism, in short, could not be held responsible for "racial" passions or sectarian hatreds, but only for a failure to manage them in a civilized and firm manner. Thus, in order to remedy these ostensibly deep sectarian manifestations, the British proposed to build a mandate on strict sectarian, not secular, grounds in the name of "rigid equality." Having committed itself to settler-colonialism in an age of self-determination, the British administration desired to balance the interests of "Arab" and "Jew" to the greatest extent allowable under the terms of the Balfour Declaration, and in a manner that preserved its own authority in Palestine.

ISLAMIC PALESTINE

The mandatory government encouraged specifically *Muslim* Palestinian institutions to balance the Jewish privilege inherent in the British mandate. The most famous of these institutions was the so-called Supreme Muslim Council (SMC) of Palestine, headed by the new British-backed "Grand Mufti" of Palestine, Hajj Amin al-Husayni. The SMC was charged with supervising various pious endowments in the mandate and the organization of the sharia court system. It thus had a sizable revenue stream and quickly built a vital patronage network. It was effectively the second-largest employer after the mandate government. The SMC's budget enabled it to renovate religious institutions, construct new schools, open orphanages, provide grants for students, and build clinics throughout the mandate.[38] Hajj Amin's initial prominence in Palestine was proof, in a sense, that the British mandatory government was upholding the Palin Commission's notion of a "rigid equality," albeit along the sectarian lines necessitated by the Balfour Declaration and Zionism. It was also proof that Muslim Arab religious figures, like their Christian Arab counterparts, were often willing to collaborate with colonial authority to consolidate their own authority, even if the two ultimately worked at cross-purposes. Hajj Amin, in this sense, followed in the footsteps of Muhammad Abduh, who had worked closely with Lord Cromer in Egypt. This did not make him a stooge of British imperialism, any more than Abduh's collaboration made him a pawn of the British Empire. It did, however, reinforce the sectarian logic of the mandate in Palestine even as Arab notables, including Hajj Amin himself, repudiated its Zionist underpinnings.

Hajj Amin, in short, exploited Britain's toleration of an Islamic counterweight to the Jewish Agency. He was one of the obvious beneficiaries of the British decision to strengthen rather than weaken communal representation in the name of impartial British colonial rule. In addition to the Supreme Muslim Council, the British administration oversaw the creation of a Muslim millet in Palestine whereby government-supervised "Moslem Religious Courts" were granted jurisdiction over all Muslims in Palestine in the domain of personal status, whereas various courts of the "Christian communities" and the "Rabbincal Courts of the Jewish Community" had "exclusive jurisdiction" over marriage, divorce, alimony, and confirmation of wills for the adherents of their respective communities.[39] Few Muslim or Christian Arabs objected to the continuation, and indeed expansion, of sectarian personal-status laws that segregated Palestine's diverse population. The issue that divided Palestine was not religion per se, and not sectarian personal-status laws that were the norm across the region. The problem remained the privileged status of Jewish colonization. British-backed Zionism's will to create a new political and demographic reality in a multireligious and communal Palestine was the lodestone of Arab discontent. The Jewish population surged to 154,000 in 1927, with about a hundred Jewish settlements built across the country by the end of 1928 and the leading commercial concessions in Jewish hands.[40]

A new set of intercommunal clashes in 1929 confirmed the degree to which the British mandate was unable to contain the sectarian crisis its existence had nurtured. Known in Arabic as Thawrat al-Buraq (The Buraq Uprising), these riots were the third major intercommunal conflagration under British auspices in a decade. Jewish Zionist claims of sovereignty over what they regarded as the Western Wall of the presumed site of Solomon's Temple clashed directly with the fact that the wall was part of the centuries-old Muslim al-Haram al-Sharif complex that houses both Al-Aqsa Mosque and the Dome of the Rock.[41]

As early as 1918, Chaim Weizmann had urged Balfour to give over the Western Wall to Jewish control. In 1926, the Palestine Zionist Executive tried to buy the wall from Muslims in order to demolish adjacent Muslim houses and buildings to create more space for Jewish worshippers. In 1928, the seventh Palestine Arab Congress assembled in Jerusalem with over three hundred Muslim and Christian Palestinian delegates. They appealed to the League of Nations to institute a "democratic parliamentary system of Government" and called for increased public expenditure on education and on the social welfare of Arab workers. Like virtually all Palestinian petitions, this one too was ignored.[42] Hajj Amin, meanwhile, invited several hundred delegates from mostly Arab countries to "defend" the holy Muslim sites in Jerusalem. He then had a muezzin stationed above the Western Wall, which had the effect of disturbing Jewish prayers below.

Both the Zionist and the Palestinian side felt that the other was engaged in intolerable provocations. In August 1929, members of Jabotinsky's Zionist youth organization marched to the Western Wall, raised a Zionist flag, and sang a Zionist anthem. These incidents set off rumors that Jews wanted to attack Al-Aqsa Mosque, sparking intercommunal fighting that eclipsed the sectarian mobilizations of the early 1920s; 133 Jews and 116 Palestinian Arabs were killed.[43] Orthodox Jews were the principal Jewish victims of the rioting in Jerusalem, Hebron, and Safad. Palestinian Arabs were also killed in great numbers, mostly by British soldiers and police. As in the Damascus riots of 1860, some Muslim neighbors sought to protect their Jewish compatriots. Christian Arabs were largely peripheral to the violence—and in several instances, crosses were painted on their houses to mark them as off-limits to looters, which was a telling inversion of the events in Damascus in 1860, when the drawing of crosses preceded the massacre there. Several Palestinian Christians indeed publicly supported the *Arab* Muslim claim to the Buraq Wall.[44] Anti-Christian violence did not simply morph into anti-Jewish violence between 1860 and 1929. Rather, two different disturbances in the status quo, nearly seventy years apart, provoked very different kinds of popular mobilizations in which the ruling authorities lost control of subaltern elements. In 1860, the status quo had been altered in favor of European-instigated reforms that abolished discrimination against Ottoman Christians; in the 1920s, it was being altered in favor of British-backed colonial Zionism.

In the wake of the uprising, Hajj Amin organized the 1931 General Islamic Congress in Jerusalem. The congress reflected the general upsurge across the Mashriq in the discourse of Islamic solidarity in the face of Western missionary threats and Western colonialism that appeared to favor Christian minorities in the Levant. It also exposed the intense competition and divisions among Muslim monarchs, politicians, and intellectuals to grasp the mantle of leadership following the end of the Ottoman Empire. A Muslim World Congress had been convened in Mecca in 1926, and Young Men's Muslim Association chapters had been established throughout Palestine in 1928—the same year the Muslim Brotherhood was founded in Egypt. Three years later, it was clear that for Hajj Amin—as for many of the other participants in the 1931 congress—Arabs and Muslims had to be mobilized urgently in the face of Zionism.

The General Islamic Congress focused Islamic solidarity on Palestine. Delegates from across the Islamic world—from the Maghreb, the Mashriq, Asia, Europe, and Africa—affirmed a pan-Islamic commitment to protect Muslim holy places in Palestine. Many of the figures who attended or supported the congress, from Rashid Rida to Shakib Arslan to Hajj Amin himself, were born in what had been the Ottoman Empire—although many participants also came from India, Morocco, Iran, and other parts of the Muslim world. A Shi'i *mujtahid* from Najaf, Al-Sayyid Muhammad Husayn Al-Kashif al-Ghita', led the Friday prayers at Al-Aqsa Mosque, thus testifying to the spirit of Islamic ecumenism that pervaded the proceedings at the congress.

The explicit concern of the congress with Muslim unity reprised a familiar theme of the nineteenth-century nahda, now injected with the urgency of anti-Zionism. The assembled dignitaries presented a "Muslim" rebuttal to a "Jewish" claim to Palestine. Where Jews had established a Hebrew University campus in Jerusalem in 1925, now Muslims wanted to build a modern Islamic University. Where Jews claimed the Western [Wailing] Wall, Muslims defended the Buraq Wall. Where Jews had established a Jewish National Fund, Muslims wanted to form a Muslim agricultural company. Where Jews wanted to buy land to build a Jewish state, Muslims sought *not* to sell it, in order to preserve what they believed to be Muslim patrimony. Where one envisioned a pan-Jewish Zion, the other saw a pan-Muslim question of Palestine.[45]

This imperative of Muslim unity was interlaced with the imperative of a new anticolonial struggle unfolding in Palestine that demanded the attention of the world. The interwar pan-Islamist Shakib Arslan, for example, saw the congress's support for a modern ecumenical Muslim university as a platform to sustain a self-generated Muslim nahda. He insisted that only Islam, not "atheistic" secular nationalism, could instill the necessary belief in Muslims' own capacity to revive themselves.[46] The Iraqi cleric Kashif al-Ghita' reminded the assembled delegates that in the early period of Islam, Muslims ruled half the world because they were united; now, however, they were subjugated because of their disunity. The congress's Committee for the Holy Places called for a boycott of all "Zionist" products across Islamic lands; it alerted kings, leaders, heads of government, Muslim scholars, and "people of good sense and judgment across the world" about the dangers of Zionism and the immediate need to resist it. The committee demanded the end of land sales to Zionists and the curtailing of Zionist immigration to Palestine.[47] The conferees were prohibited by the British mandate from explicitly calling for the independence of Palestine or condemning the Balfour Declaration. Instead, the congress restricted itself to condemning "any kind of imperialism in any Islamic region" and repudiating "any authority which uses its influence and force to curtail religious freedom, or passes laws to convert the people from their Islamic laws and traditions."[48]

The congress consciously avoided an abrasive sectarian tone. It specifically distinguished between Palestinian Christians, whom it thanked for their support, and foreign missionaries, whom it denounced. This gesture was reciprocated by the staunchly nationalist *El-Carmel* newspaper, owned by the Palestinian Christian Najib Nassar, which repeatedly praised the congress.[49] These public expressions of anti-Zionist nationalist piety by Muslims and Christians were both calculated and sincere—there is no good reason to think otherwise given the context of Palestine. Hajj Amin worked proficiently within the mandate's sectarian frame to dominate this new piety, which expressed itself simultaneously as Palestinian Arab and pan-Islamic. The Palestinian Arab part included Palestinian Christians, who had been a vital part of the development of Palestinian Arab national consciousness up to this point in the early 1930s (which is why many of them supported Hajj Amin), while the pan-Islamic inevitably prioritized Islamic themes and rhetoric. This ambivalence between anticolonial nationalism and anticolonial Islamism marked Palestinian politics until 1948.[50]

FORMS OF RESISTANCE

The rise of Islamic anticolonial solidarity, and the reality of deep divisions among Palestinians about how best to resist Zionism, did not change the fact that Muslim and Christian Palestinians made common cause against this Zionism. The First Congress of Arab Students in Jaffa in August 1929, for instance, saw secondary-school students read nationalist poetry and criticize the mandate and what they viewed as the collaborationist Arab leadership. The Nablus Congress in July 1931, organized by the Nablus Arab Patriotic Society, modeled itself on Gandhian anticolonial civil disobedience and called for a general strike to protest the British creation of "sealed armouries" in various Jewish Zionist settlements. The so-called Istiqlal, or Independence Party, adopted a pan-Arabist line and developed out of an Arab National Congress held in December 1931 in the Jerusalem house of the Palestinian nationalist 'Awni 'Abd al-Hadi.[51] Indeed, Palestinian merchants and businessmen—"men of capital"—built and benefited from a complex political economy that bypassed sectarian lines.[52]

Caught between attempting to accommodate themselves to the mandate's immovable Zionist premise and trying to resist it, Palestinian Muslims and Christians resorted to a variety of secular, pietistic, communalist, and nationalist tactics and organizations that reflected the diverse social and political realities on the ground. The first Palestinian military organization against the British mandate, in fact, was created by Abd al-Qadir Husayni, a relative of the mufti's, and his Christian friend Emile al-Ghuri. They called their organization Al-Jihad al-Muqaddas—the Blessed Struggle.[53] Another anticolonial fighter in this period was the populist Muslim preacher 'Izz al-Din al-Qassam. Originally from Syria, educated at Al-Azhar in Cairo, and resident in Haifa, Qassam brought with him to Palestine his experience of anticolonial struggle in Libya and Syria. Now he urged Hajj Amin to join his violent anti-British and anti-Zionist Islamist struggle: to meet fire with fire.

Hajj Amin demurred, for like many other members of the Palestinian elite, he remained reluctant to break irrevocably with the British mandate, especially at the behest of a populist Muslim from Haifa. In his eyes, there was still far too much to lose by hasty or impulsive actions. This hesitancy, and the wider factionalism it indicated, did little to stem the tide of the Zionist settler movement. The ominous rise of Nazism in Germany resulted in a massive surge of Jewish immigrants into Palestine in the mid-1930s, which in turn made the Zionist movement more determined to create a Jewish state at the expense of the natives, and Palestinians more desperate than ever to resist it. As historian Ilan Pappe put it so well, at this juncture the Palestinians "required unity, not pluralism—a solid national movement, not a national society in its infancy."[54]

They had neither. Yet when Palestinian Arab society finally broke out in open anti-British and anti-Zionist revolt in 1936, Hajj Amin sought to realign himself with an increasingly popular anticolonial national movement. He created the Arab Higher Committee (AHC). The AHC included two prominent Christian Palestinians, Ya'qub Farraj and Alfred Rok. In its founding statement issued from Jerusalem in 1936, the AHC declared: "Nations that aspire to life . . . are those that do not know dissension in their hour of danger." Such nations, it continued, "repudiate trivial differences between communities and individuals. They form a united front made up of closed ranks to face the dangers that surround them."[55] Their emphasis on the Arabness of Palestine was far more self-consciously pluralist than either the discourse of Islamic Palestine (where ecumenism was principally Islamic) or that of Jewish Palestine, against which it desperately set itself.

Unlike the Jerusalem congress's rhetoric of pan-Islamism, the discourse of the AHC in 1936 emphasized national unity and national struggle—*al-jihad al-watani*.[56] It protested land sales to Jews because they were directly associated with colonial Zionism. In Arab eyes, ending the "oppressive immigration" of Jews to Palestine was the sine qua non for any solution. Student committees, women's organizations, guerrilla leaders, and the AHC repeatedly demanded the total prevention of Jewish immigration and the establishment of a "national" democratic and parliamentary government.[57] The emphasis on the "Arabness" of Palestine, and on the "rights of Arabs" set in opposition to "the Jews," further solidified the idea of an Arab Palestine in which Christian Arabs played a prominent role. Hajj Amin specifically pleaded to "the Arab world, both Muslim and Christian, and to the Islamic world as a whole" to heed warnings of the dangers faced by their "brethren in Palestine" from "the oppression of colonialism," and from "the entire Jewish world that drives into these sacred lands with its wealth and manpower."[58]

It was also in 1936, as part of Syrian attempts to negotiate independence from France, that Hajj Amin issued a historic fatwa that recognized the Alawis as true Muslims in order to bolster the cause of anticolonial national unity in Syria.[59] In Palestine, though, given that the Zionist structure was so apparently immovable, the pressing issue for most Arabs was less to articulate an ecumenical idea about the country's future and more to defend its Arabness, past and present. Resistance to Zionist colonization, rather than coexistence with Jews, inevitably became the overriding mantra of Palestinian nationalism.

The constituency and leadership of the AHC exposed the inherent limitations of the landed notable class that continued to put its faith in an eventual compromise with the British. The AHC called for a national strike in 1936 rather than mobilizing for an all-out revolution against the British regime. Hajj Amin still hoped to convince the British of his own indispensability in negotiation. The vast majority of the Palestinians were villagers and peasants—and it was on these men and women that the success of the revolt actually depended. Before he was killed by the British in 1935, the militant Izz al-Din al-Qassam had understood this far more clearly than did most of the AHC leadership.

From 1936 to 1939, the Great Revolt ebbed and flowed. Like most major anticolonial uprisings, this one betrayed many moments of sectarian—and, far more obviously, social, rural, and class—tensions across Palestine. But the revolt's goal was not Islamic revival. It was an uprising against colonial Zionism and the British prevarications that nourished it. Indeed, the constant slippage in Palestinian nationalism (and in virtually all nationalism in the Mashriq) of this period between "national" mobilizations and "Islamic" ones suggests not only a basic dissonance between the two identifications, but also the possibility of rapprochement between them. The popular Palestinian poet Nuh Ibrahim—who admired Qassam, joined the revolt, and was himself slain by the British in 1938—evoked the "invincible" unity of Muslims and Christians to suggest a new ecumenical reality: what Palestinians increasingly held in common—anti-Zionism—was far more constitutive of their national identity than their religious, class, clan, and geographical diversity.[60]

THE SHADOW OF PARTITION

The Great Revolt was crushed by Great Britain. By the time it was finally extinguished in 1939, several thousand Palestinians were incarcerated, wounded, and killed. Hajj Amin found himself in permanent exile, first in Lebanon and then in Iraq, between 1939 and 1941. In July 1937, seeking a way out of the impasse in Palestine but still wedded to the Balfour Declaration, the British Peel Commission, which investigated the reasons for the uprising, recommended partitioning Palestine into separate "Arab" and "Jewish" states. Because the Arab population remained the overwhelming majority of the population, the commissioners admitted plainly that Palestinians would have to give up their lands and homes in order for the notional Jewish state to come into being. They specifically called on Arab "generosity" to help resolve Europe's "Jewish Problem," concluding that "if the Arabs at some sacrifice could help to solve that problem, they would earn the gratitude not of the Jews alone, but of all the Western World."[61] It was everything the Arabs had feared, and everything the British had, for two decades, pledged was not going to happen.

So egregious a proposal ignited nearly two more years of protest and rebellion—but the Palestinian Arabs found themselves in a far more precarious situation after the revolt than before it. Only when the colonial authorities feared their position in the wider Arab world was threatened did they have a change of heart. They summoned both Palestinians and Zionists to London in 1939 to negotiate with the British government. The secretary-general of the Arab delegations was George Antonius. Cambridge-educated and the author of the 1938 English-language book *The Arab Awakening,* the Christian Arab Antonius was emblematic of the dramatic shifts that had taken place in the Mashriq over the past century. He had also been a confidante of Hajj Amin's, but unlike the dragomans of old, Antonius considered himself, and was treated as, Hajj Amin's equal. What had separated them in religious faith was made up for by their shared commitment to saving Arab Palestine.

Far more fluently than Hajj Amin, Antonius was able to express to Western audiences what was at stake in Palestine. His famous book made him the bard of the story of what he described as the "Arab national movement" that had drawn Muslim and non-Muslim Arabs together in

Damascus, Beirut, Baghdad, and Jerusalem. In Antonius's view, this story deserved a positive conclusion, but for that to happen much depended on Britain's next steps in Palestine. He recognized frankly the scourge of anti-Jewish Nazism. But he also insisted that it must not be solved at the expense of the Palestinian Arabs. He called, therefore, for an independent Arab state that safeguarded minority rights, including those of the Jewish community:

> A solution along these lines would be both fair and practicable. It would protect the natural rights of the Arabs in Palestine and satisfy their legitimate national aspirations. It would enable the Jews to have a national home in the spiritual and cultural sense, in which Jewish values could flourish and the Jewish genius have the freest play to seek inspiration in the land of its ancient connexion. It would secure Great Britain's interests on a firm basis of consent. And it would restore Palestine to its proper place, as a symbol of peace in the hearts of Judaism, Christianity and Islam.
>
> No other solution seems practicable, except, possibly at the cost of an unpredictable holocaust of Arab, Jewish and British lives.[62]

FALLING ON DEAF EARS

Antonius's ecumenical plea fell on deaf ears—its romantic gloss lost amid the cynicism of power politics in which Palestinian Arabs held the weakest hand. Instead, the most Britain would do was temporize—again. It announced a white paper in 1939 that restricted Jewish immigration and set aside partition, without acceding to Arab demands for democratic self-determination. As the struggle between the two sides wore on, expressions of compassion and empathy for the other side diminished accordingly. No single figure embodied this diminution on the Arab side more than the exiled Hajj Amin, who turned to Hitler's anti-Semitic Germany in a futile attempt to stop the march of Zionism in his homeland. For him, anticolonialism descended into Judeophobia.[63]

The much-maligned Hajj Amin, however, was no longer relevant to matters on the ground in Palestine. His removal from the scene did little to alleviate the impending threat to the ecumenical frame, for he had never been its principal problem. Indeed, in the 1940s, almost all the formal Arab demands and petitions submitted to the British government were based on the idea that the existing Arab majority should exercise democratic sovereignty over what was, in their eyes, an obviously Arab country, while the Jews who lived there had a right to stay there and be full citizens of this *Arab* state. Almost all these demands were ignored, as they had been consistently for twenty years. When Jamal Husayni, who had been exiled in Rhodesia, appeared before the Anglo-American Committee of Inquiry in 1946, he described how colonial Zionism had violently interrupted an ecumenical trajectory in the Levant. "If these pampered children, if these spoilt children of the British Government, the Zionists," he insisted, "know for once that they are no more to be pampered and spoilt, then the whole condition will be turned to what it has been before the First World War. We will become friends probably."[64]

In turn, Albert Hourani, then with the Arab Office, an organization that was formed in the immediate postwar period to lobby in Western capitals against Zionism, echoed Antonius's recommendation from nearly a decade before. Hourani was born in Manchester to Lebanese parents and educated at Oxford. Moved by the injustice he perceived in Palestine and deeply concerned with the fate of minorities in the Middle East, he expressed to the Anglo-American Committee a fair settlement to the conflict in Palestine embedded in the liberal ideals he personified.[65] He advocated a "self-governing state, with its Arab majority, but with full rights for the Jewish citizens of Palestine." For Hourani, this proposed state conformed to a national ecumenical culture across the Arabic-speaking Levant. It was antisectarian because it rejected the principle of an ethnoreligious partition of Palestine (such as that advocated by the Peel Commission) and because it rejected the notion that any single religious community enjoyed a more privileged relationship to the land than any other. As Hourani declared, Arab leaders pledged that Jews in Palestine could expect "full civil and political rights, control over their own communal affairs, municipal autonomy in districts in which they are mainly concentrated, the use of Hebrew as an additional official language in those districts, and an adequate share of the administration."

What the Palestinian Arabs proposed repeatedly, in short, was not dissimilar to the basic secular nationalisms taking shape in the various mandates: a single, undivided state that would belong to all its citizens. As in Iraq, Syria, and Lebanon, there would be a sectarian exception to secular nationalism in the domain of personal status. Indeed, Hourani's Arab Office formulation made several other communal concessions to reassure Jews of their place in Palestine. Hourani elaborated: "It should be clear from this that there is no question of the Jews being under Arab rule in the bad sense of being thrust into a ghetto, or being cut off from the main stream of life of the community, always shunned and sometimes oppressed. The Arabs are offering not this ghetto status in the bad sense, but membership of the Palestinian community."[66]

The proposed Arab state in Palestine that Hourani outlined would negate colonial Zionism in Palestine, not Jewish life in it. Absent Zionism, his thinking went, Jews could very plausibly be incorporated into an ecumenical nationalist Arab polity in the manner that Christian and Druze—and, indeed, Jewish—communities were incorporated into the neighboring Syrian and Lebanese states. Were it not for colonial Zionism, in fact, the late Ottoman blueprint for a viable state of equal (male) citizens would have been as applicable in Palestine as it was in Syria, Lebanon, and Iraq.

A MINORITY TO BE MADE

The ineluctable problem, from colonial Zionism's point of view, was that a democratic Arab state along the liberal lines proposed by Hourani and the Arab Office was, by definition, antithetical to a Jewish state. David Ben-Gurion, by this time, had become the undisputed leader of the Jewish community in Palestine. After the 1929 riots, Ben-Gurion had flirted with the notion of a federation with "Arabs." Now, in his testimony before the 1946 Anglo-American Committee, he made clear his rejection of a secular Palestinian community that could include Arabs and Jews on equal terms. Ben-Gurion claimed that a Jewish state deserved to come into being because the "Jewish people" had a unique relationship to Palestine—they possessed a "deep passionate love, strong as death, the love of Zion" that had "no parallel . . . in all human history." Ben-Gurion declared that the Zionists wanted to transform that attachment into a state in which Jews could be "100 percent free and 100 percent Jews, which we couldn't be anywhere else." Ben-Gurion admitted that the building of a Jewish "majority" in Palestine was a "stage, a very important one but not final." The goal of colonial Zionism was to build up a Jewish majority in Palestine, he said, in order to build a state that served two functions. The first was to "care for the welfare of the people of this country, all of them, without any difference between Jews, Arabs or others," and the second was to continue to build a "National Home" for the Jews, one in which "our Arab and other non-Jewish neighbors" would have to be treated "as if they were Jews, but [we will] make every effort that they should preserve their Arab characteristics, their language, their Arab culture, their Arab religion, their Arab way of life, while making every effort to make all the citizens of the country equal civilly, socially, economically, politically, intellectually, and gradually raise the standard of life of everyone, Jews and others."[67]

Such was the implacable thrust of colonial Zionism: Ben-Gurion advocated reducing "the Arabs" to a minority in Palestine by massively expanding Jewish colonization because "Arabs" were not Jews. Simultaneously, he vowed to treat the new Arab minority "as if they were Jews." Ben-Gurion, in effect, wanted not so much to reverse engineer the millet system of the Ottoman period, but rather to reinvent in Palestine a modern European national state with a clearly defined Jewish majority and an Arab minority. The Arabs of Palestine would become, figuratively, its Jews—tolerated and politically emancipated but forever different and inassimilable into the modern Jewish body politic. Ben-Gurion pledged that the Arab minority *to be made* would enjoy almost complete autonomy, but also an unbridgeable separateness from the Jews in a Jewish state.

Ben-Gurion's commitment to Jewish nationalism negated the nahda ethos that early Zionists, Ben-Gurion included, had encountered in Palestine. In 1936, he went through the motions of meeting with Arabs who embodied precisely this ethos, including the urbane and worldly George Antonius and Musa Alami.[68] Nevertheless, he had remained convinced of the righteousness and viability of his Zionism. He understood and admitted openly to the Anglo-American Committee that Arabs would resist their own coercive minoritization. Like the ostensibly more radical Jabotinsky, who had advocated, in the early 1920s, building an "iron wall" to crush what he regarded as an inevitable Arab reaction to their impending displacement by Jewish settlers, Ben-Gurion now described Arab resistance to colonial Zionism as "futile." The British mandate had already broken the back of Arab resistance to Zionism by crushing the anticolonial

Great Revolt. Nevertheless, Ben-Gurion's uncompromising vision of a Jewish state in Palestine was a reminder of the cost of creating an exclusivist ethno-religious state in what had historically been a multireligious land.

For Ben-Gurion, the cost to be borne principally by Arabs was justifiable, and even necessary. He was, at least, candid on this point. In his mind, the final goal of a Jewish state, quite simply, was far more important than the fate of Muslim and Christian Arab inhabitants of Palestine. It was also more important than the continuity of centuries-old Jewish life in cities such as Baghdad or Damascus or Cairo. In the Zionist nationalist perspective, the reconstitution of a Jewish state in Palestine, after all, was meant to end the nationless, and thus unnatural, condition of the Jewish diaspora.[69]

A ZIONIST ECUMENICAL FRAME?

There were, however, other Jews who had settled in Palestine who dissented from Ben-Gurion's uncompromising vision. They understood the radical rupture that colonial Zionism had instigated with Arab society and fretted about the implications of this rupture for future relations with the Arabs and for the meaning of Judaism in the world. Like Antonius and Hourani, they tended to be intellectuals and scholars—men and women who grappled with the ethics and dilemmas of colonial Zionism. They suggested what Ben-Gurion himself would not ultimately countenance: adapting their ideal of a Jewish state to the Arab reality of Palestine rather than coercively adapting the reality of Palestine to a Jewish nationalist ideal. This idea was called binationalism.

The binational formula for Palestine sought to reconcile aspects of Zionism within the existing ecumenical frame of the Levant. Binationalism attempted to salvage the Zionist idea of a Jewish national home by abandoning the project of an exclusively Jewish state. The rationale for this retreat from maximalist, nationalist Zionism was basic: a Jewish state in Palestine imposed on the Arab majority was unethical and unworkable in the long run. Ben-Gurion may have believed that the conflict with Arabs was a "passing thing." Binationalists, however, regarded the persistence of the Zionist state project as a prelude to an avoidable, and hence tragic, open-ended war with the Arab world.

The most famous binationalist organization, Brit Shalom, was founded in 1925. It included Hugo Bergman, the German Jewish philosopher; Arthur Ruppin, the German Jewish sociologist who worked with the Zionist Executive; Martin Buber, the eminent German Jewish theologian; and several of Buber's disciples, including the historian Hans Kohn, who was born and raised in Prague during the last decades of the Austro-Hungarian Empire. In 1930, Brit Shalom submitted a memorandum to the Zionist Executive outlining its case for a binational Palestinian state. At its heart was the conviction that there were "two peoples" in Palestine, Arabs and Jews, each of which had to be "free" in their "domestic affairs" but "united in their common political interests, on the basis of complete equality of the rights of each."[70]

Virtually every binational plan put forward in the 1930s and '40s insisted on communal, or sectarian, parity between Arabs and Jews, and between the Arabic and Hebrew languages. This was evident in the numerous memoranda and proposals suggested by Ihud, an organization created in 1942 and led by Martin Buber and the American Jewish founder of the Hebrew University in Jerusalem, Judah Magnes, who jointly defied Ben-Gurion's nationalist orthodoxy to promote their binational idea before the Anglo-American Committee in 1946.

Buber and Magnes described their vision in optimistic terms. They referred to a definition of binationalism that envisioned "two nations hav[ing] equal freedom and independence, equal participation in government and equality of representation" and that differentiated between a "country of nationalities" and "a nationalist country."[71] Their model was Switzerland, where three nationalities constituted equal members of the state, and where none was a minority. But they might have taken, more appropriately, the case of neighboring Lebanon, for like the French mandatory state, Buber and Magnes's proposed Palestinian binational state would guarantee a secular equality through communal representation. The notable difference was that in Lebanon, sectarian representation was specifically a temporary constitutional clause and was, in theory if not actual practice, meant to aid the consolidation of a single, secular Lebanese nationality that bound all Lebanese citizens together as equals despite the profusion of religious communities in the country. Lebanese Muslim, Druze, and Christian politicians actively, if often discordantly, collaborated with one another to build a sectarian state that, for all its many flaws, consolidated an elitist, communal, and conservative nahda ethos of coexistence.

Binationalism was based on the notion of two fundamentally separate political nations, Arabs and Jews. Among the consequences of this idea was the abrogation of the possibility of being an Arab Jew. For Magnes, to be sure, binationalism was an alternative to the violence against Arabs (and, in his eyes, against Judaism) inherent in colonial Zionism. It was also an alternative to the idea of the partition of Palestine first proposed by the British government in 1937 and eventually adopted by the United Nations a decade later. Yet almost every binational proposal floated in the 1930s and '40s, including Buber and Magnes's iterations of the concept, insisted on allowing mass Jewish immigration to Palestine *irrespective* of the political wishes of the Arab majority. Notionally based on the consent of Arabs, binationalism in fact embraced a central Zionist tenet—to change the demographic nature of Palestine under the rubric of a nebulous notion of the "absorptive capacity" of the land, at the same time as it repudiated the overt anti-Arabism of colonial Zionism.

Far more than Jabotinsky and Ben-Gurion, in other words, Buber and Magnes wanted peace with the Arabs. But like the militant Zionists, they willingly worked under the umbrella of British colonialism. Buber's disciple Kohn recognized this contradiction and found it intolerable. He broke with Brit Shalom because he despaired at the unwillingness of its members to take a firm stand against what he described as a "war of the repression of the Arab freedom movement." He believed that as well-meaning as Brit Shalom may have been in principle, in reality it was not ultimately willing to abandon the Balfour Declaration or truly repudiate the oppressive nature of Zionism in Palestine. "Zionism," he insisted, "is not Judaism."[72]

As much as it at least recognized an Arab community in Palestine, binationalism was largely an internal Jewish debate about the ethics of Zionism that raged in Palestine and in Europe.[73] The German-speaking members of Brit Shalom regarded themselves as the conciliatory alternative to the extremism of Jabotinsky, but they were not an actual rival party with a significant constituency in the Zionist Jewish community of Palestine. They were not viable political interlocutors who could engage with

Palestinian Arabs in any official capacity. Binationalism, despite Magnes's scuttling to and fro across the Levant, was not an actual set of political compromises with Arabs—and thus was entirely different from Michel Chiha's vision of Lebanon. In any case, the Arab individuals with whom Magnes and others met repeatedly in the period up until 1948—Adil Jabre, Musa Alami, George Antonius, and 'Awni 'Abd al-Hadi—almost always insisted that they would accept the Jews in situ in Palestine as potential brethren within a single national community. To these Arabs, this was compromise enough, for they acknowledged the fait accompli of decades of Jewish immigration into Palestine that had always been carried out against their collective and demonstrated will. Their experience with the pro-Zionist mandate, and their personal inculcation of the antisectarian ethos of the nahda that clearly marked each one of them, made Magnes's Arab acquaintances deeply resistant to the idea of communalism at the heart of the binational idea. Albert Hourani put this Arab objection most succinctly. Binationalism, he said, would lead "either to a complete deadlock involving perhaps the intervention of foreign powers, or else the domination of the whole life of the state by communal considerations."[74]

Hourani's point, in principle, was unimpeachable. Yet despite its corrosive sectarianism, the Lebanese political system had preserved, not overthrown, the Ottoman-era ecumenical frame. In Palestine, the ecumenical frame was bent by 1946 to the point of breaking.

Sensing the imminence of their victory, Ben-Gurion and the colonial Zionists he led utterly rejected the principle of binationalism and any sort of compromise with Arab Palestinians that obstructed the establishment of a Jewish nationalist state. By the time the leader of the Zionist Jewish community of Palestine appeared before the Anglo-American Committee, Ben-Gurion did not bother with diplomatic niceties. Instead, in the aftermath of the German genocide of European Jews, he and the Zionist movement he presided over prepared for their final triumph over a Palestinian Arab society that had never truly recovered from its sudden and arbitrary detachment from the vast Ottoman Empire, and whose population, in consequence, was overwhelmed by the singular focus and international reach of the British-backed and, increasingly, American-backed Zionist movement.

THE NAKBA

On November 29, 1947, the United Nations voted to partition Palestine into "Jewish" and "Arab" states. Once again, the wishes and desires of the Jewish Zionist minority in Palestine won out over those of the Arab majority, for it was the latter who stood to lose their land and their entire way of life in order to make way for the creation of a Jewish state.[75] War inevitably ensued—with the Zionists determined to establish, and even expand, their Jewish state, and the Arabs desperate to prevent what they had feared all along—that is, a Jewish state being erected forcibly over them.

The shattering defeat of the Arabs collectively in 1948 and the destruction of Arab Palestinian society at the hands of Jewish nationalists is called in Arabic the *nakba*, or "the catastrophe."[76] As a direct consequence of the creation of a Jewish state in Palestine, between 1948 and 1950 the majority of the Arab population, approximately eight hundred thousand Muslim and Christian Palestinians, were deliberately and methodically driven out of their lands, homes, villages, and towns. In several instances, Palestinian villagers and townsfolk were massacred. Their property was expropriated and turned over to Jewish settlers, many of whom were refugees from Europe. The victorious Zionists categorically denied Palestinian Arabs the right to return to their homes and forced the minority of the Palestinians who remained in the new state of Israel to live under military rule. The ethnic cleansing, after all, occurred before, during, and after the "fog of war" in the service of an exclusionary modern political vision of a nation.[77] The devastation of Palestinian lives in 1948 inevitably roiled the rest of the nascent Arab states in the Levant. They were now confronted with a new Palestinian reality: hundreds of thousands of stateless refugees who needed to be fed, clothed, schooled, and sheltered.

The perverse irony of this conflict between Arab and Jew was that it unfolded in the part of the former Ottoman Empire that had been most insulated from the nationalist extremism manifested in the Balkan Wars and in the killing fields of Anatolia. The systematic Jewish Zionist de-Arabization of Palestine in the wake of the 1948 war was also its de-Ottomanization. It had striking parallels with the Turkish Kemalism that had gone to war against the Armenians, Greeks, and Kurds in Anatolia and the Aegean. A significant difference, of course, is that the Turkish nationalists were native to the region; the Zionist leadership was not. Mustafa Kemal wanted Turkey to be like Europe; the Zionists were mostly from Europe. The nakba, in any case, clearly had certain similarities to the outcome of the Balkan Wars of 1912–13, the Armenian genocide of 1915, the fate of Greeks in Turkey in 1922–23, and even the creation of Pakistan in 1947. In each case, an exclusive modern idea of nationalism violently and irrevocably disrupted and effaced centuries of uneven, yet equally undeniable, complex coexistence. In each of the episodes, as well, the creation of new states precipitated huge and coercive population shifts.[78]

These nation-states were secular but anti-ecumenical. They undid the diversity that made secularism in its broadest and most interesting sense meaningful, and yet they were not theocratic states at all. Ben-Gurion's reading of the Israeli Declaration of Independence on May 14, 1948, emphasized this precise point. Together with the thirty-six other signatories of the declaration—all but two of whom were from Central or Eastern Europe—Ben-Gurion insisted that the new state of Israel belonged to the "sovereign Jewish people settled in its own land"; that it was "open for Jewish immigration and for the Ingathering of the Exiles"; and that it would ensure "complete equality of social and political rights to all its inhabitants irrespective of religion, race or sex."[79] Just as the Balkan states of Greece and Bulgaria drew heavily on romantic narratives of the ancient and medieval past to build modern ethno-national states, so too did the newly established ethno-national Jewish state see itself as far more than a reincarnation of the putative Biblical Hebrew kingdom. Yet in the new state of Israel, Orthodox Judaism was privileged legally over all other forms of Judaism (American Reform Judaism remains unrecognized). Jews were clearly privileged over the remaining non-Jews who survived the nakba of 1948.

Like the other post-mandate states, moreover, Israel maintained segregated sectarian personal-status spheres and rejected the possibility of civil marriage within its jurisdiction. In this one sense, it mimicked its regional environment. But unlike the other mandate states, this sectarian principle affirmed the irreducible Jewish character of the state and, by definition, affirmed the primacy of the category of Jew over that of secular Israeli citizen and, indeed, over the principle of equality. Historian Shira Robinson has described how citizenship was designed expressly to exclude as many Palestinian Muslims and Christians as possible.[80] The mandate states of Iraq and Syria fought hard to limit the idea of "minorities" in their midst in order to emphasize, in principle at least, a common nationality; the Lebanese sectarian system was ostensibly aimed at transcending sectarian loyalties in favor of a secular Lebanese one; the Jewish state, however, rejected the very idea of a secular Israeli nationality. It made the category of being Jewish central to its legal and ideological fabric.

Israel viewed its remaining, utterly disempowered Palestinian population as an unwanted minority impeding the realization of a nationalist ideal, yet also as a necessary marker of belonging to the allegedly tolerant and civilized modern family of nations.[81] In this, it was indeed like several other states in the world. But in Israel's case, the fulfillment of this nationalist ideal required constant additional Jewish immigration and colonization—Ben-Gurion's reference to the "Ingathering of Exiles" is key here—to bolster a newly made majority. It also encouraged a search for minorities in the Middle East, both to create affinities in the region and to undermine the potential for anti-Zionist secular Arab unity. The new state created a Jewish-led Minorities Unit in its armed forces made up of Druze, Bedouin, and Circassian soldiers and tolerated different minorities in order to separate "Druze" from "Arab" and both of them from Jews. In this particular cultivation of non-Jewish diversity, the new state revealed its indebtedness to its colonial European heritage.[82]

ARAB JEWS AND THE DOUBLE TRAGEDY OF THE NAKBA

The double tragedy of the nakba was that Arab Jews were inevitably ensnared by the political maelstrom of 1948. Zionism devastated Palestine, and Arab reactions to Zionism also did grievous damage to ecumenical culture in the rest of the Arab world. As early as 1941, Jews in Baghdad were subjected to an unprecedented massacre known as the *farhud*. The brutal British suppression of the anticolonial revolt in Palestine in 1936 had already galvanized anti-Zionist sentiment across the Arab world, and had stigmatized Arab Jews as potential agents of Zionism. The arrival of Hajj Amin al-Husayni in Baghdad in 1939 and the influx of other

Palestinian exiles ratcheted up anti-Zionist and anticolonial discourse in Iraq. Active German propaganda also contributed to tensions.[83] The proximate cause of the riot was a breakdown in order following the fall of an Iraqi nationalist government in late May 1941. The British military had overthrown this government by force and was about to restore the pliant Hashemite monarchy to Baghdad when the rioting began.

Rumor had it that the Jews of Baghdad welcomed the fall of the anticolonial nationalist government. On the first two days of June 1941, members of the Jewish community in Baghdad were terrorized as their homes and property were looted. A mob made up of paramilitaries, policemen, recent migrants, and others killed approximately 180 Jews and wounded many more. Historian Orit Bashkin, who describes this terrible episode as the "first pogrom in a modern Arab state," insists that the farhud interrupted the incorporation of Arabized Baghdadi Jews into a wider Iraqi Arab identity in the first half of the twentieth century.[84] Bashkin's authoritative account goes to great lengths to illustrate the complexity of the events and to note how many Muslims protected their Jewish neighbors even as others attacked them. A similar pattern, of course, was evident in Damascus in 1860. For this reason, Bashkin's description of the event as the "first pogrom in a modern Arab state" seems entirely inadequate. The farhud has no obvious connection to the history of Eastern Europe, and the blatant anti-Jewishness of the rioters was manifestly not tied to a wider anti-Jewish culture or to a state-building project that had excluded Jews. If anything, the Baghdadi Jewish community had been among the most integrated Jewish communities in the region. The anti-Jewish riot revealed the unspoken reality of nahda ecumenism: unity and equality were fundamentally aspirational projects that required enormous will and conviction. They were manifestly *not* an uncomplicated expression of historical fraternity.

The farhud, in any case, was not the major turning point in the modern history of the Jews in the Mashriq. Zionism in Palestine was. Syrian Christians, after all, had recovered from the trauma of 1860 and used it to spur a new nahda ecumenical culture. They were aided both by the political imperatives of the Ottoman state and by Arab Muslim sentiment. Iraqi Jews were in no position to spur a similar humanism after the farhud. Politics and circumstances conspired against them. The Iraqi government commissioned a report on the events and hanged several rioters. But it then consigned the event to official oblivion. The Iraqi reaction to the establishment of Israel in 1948, to the defeat of the Iraqi contingent that had been sent to defend Arab Palestine, and to clandestine Zionist activity in Iraq, was far more damaging to the future of the Jews of Iraq.

The systematic scapegoating of Iraqi Jews began with the expulsion of Jews from various positions in the government and in state-owned enterprises in 1948 and 1949. It continued with the execution of a Jewish businessman in Basra in September 1948 on apparently trumped-up charges. And it culminated with the denationalization and subsequent freezing of the assets of those Iraqi Jews who emigrated, mostly to Israel, in the early 1950s—although some Iraqi and Arab nationalists protested denationalization.[85] Neither the Lebanese nor the Syrian government followed Iraq's example in hounding their respective Jewish communities, but across the Arab world, Jewish citizens were far too easily, almost inevitably, conflated with the state that claimed to speak in their name.

The Hashemite Iraqi state did not publicly embrace a doctrine of anti-Semitism, nor did it claim that it wanted Jews to leave Iraq. Yet the emigration of Iraqi Jews was quietly coordinated with the new state of Israel—"one of these tacit, monstrous complicities not entirely unknown to history," as the orientalist Elie Kedourie acerbically noted in 1952.[86] Kedourie was himself from an Iraqi Jewish background. He understood, as well as anyone could, how the stigmatization of Iraqi Jews, and indeed of Jews throughout the Middle East, accelerated in the aftermath of Zionism's arrival on the Middle Eastern scene. He had never had much faith in what he labeled the "absurd attempt to form a nation" in Iraq, but he recognized how the salvific promise of the Jewish state answered specific European questions and was not at all resonant with the lived experiences of the Jewish populations of the Mashriq—particularly the Iraqi Jews of Baghdad. "One's first impulse in the face of all this," wrote Kedourie in the aftermath of the creation of Israel, "is to say, No good can come out of it."[87] For in response to the nakba, Hashemite Iraq reinforced Zionism's main sectarian nationalist premise, that Jews belonged *apart* from Muslims and Christians. The oppression of Palestinian Muslims and Christians was reinforced by the oppression of Iraqi Jews. They were two facets of a single tragedy.

THE AFTERMATH OF 1948

1948 was the annus horribilis for coexistence between Arabs and Jews in the Arab world. Rather than a temporary rupture of the type indicated by the violent, clearly anarchic, events of 1860 in Damascus or 1941 in Baghdad, one of the tragedies of colonial Zionism in Palestine was that it constituted a categorical blow against ecumenical culture in the Mashriq. Inevitably, defeat raised difficult questions about why the Arabs had failed to defend Palestine, about the key to overturning colonial Zionism, and about the meaning of being Arab. The sense of crisis expressed by many Arab writers reflected a clear *nahdawist* sensibility: Why were "we" defeated? What went wrong? How can "we" change ourselves in the face of a victorious, and clearly modern, Zionism? Some answers to these difficult questions were squarely secular nationalist; others, like those proposed by the Egyptian Muslim Brotherhood, were quite clearly more Islamist, and still others were communist or socialist.[88]

The 1948 defeat in Palestine catalyzed rather than diminished a commitment among many Arabs to an ecumenical nationalist frame insofar as Muslim-Christian understanding was concerned. The prevailing sentiment was not that the nahda ideas of progress or brotherhood had been wrong but that they needed far more urgent, anticolonial, systematic, sovereign nationalization. The great defeat of 1948 thus called for root-and-branch reform. The palpable sense of danger that surrounded the Arab world was mirrored by the belief that the response to this danger could best be—indeed had to be—articulated by Arabs themselves.

Among the most famous postmortems of the Palestine disaster was provided by the Syrian educator, historian, and nationalist intellectual Constantine Zurayk, who coined the term *nakba* in his 1948 book *Maʿna al-nakba* (The Meaning of the Catastrophe). In the wake of the Arab defeat, Zurayk, who taught at the American University of Beirut, called for a separation of religion from politics, for reform and development, for national consciousness that transcended current social conditions, and for systematic Arab unity overseen by a progressive elite. These refrains were all typical of the nahda.[89] In the wake of the loss of Palestine, however, this nahdawist juxtaposition of a moribund tradition with modernity was infused with a political urgency and an Arab nationalist focus unseen in the nineteenth century.

As much as Zurayk worked within an established tradition of a nearly century-old ecumenical frame, he was also well aware of how the success of Zionism threatened to undermine this tradition. The very ambiguity, diversity, and capaciousness of the ecumenical frame had counted against it; the will to coexistence without power had been exposed by the will to power that deliberately effaced coexistence. The question for Zurayk was not merely the obvious need for a revitalized Arab sovereignty in order to translate the cultural and intellectual nahda into viable political practice: it was also what kind of modern sovereignty was imagined in the first instance.

For Zurayk, the struggle against Zionism was the defining ethical and ecumenical act of the modern Arab word, for the clash at hand was not one between Arabs and Jews per se, but between two fundamentally antithetical mobilizations of religion and nation-state: a Jewish Zionist nationalist formation against an ecumenical Arab nationalist one beset by its own ongoing major internal problems that Zurayk enumerated as "feudalism," "tribalism," "sectarianism," and "fatalism." Zionism, in other words, did more than obliterate Palestinian self-determination. It constituted a counter-nahda by inserting religion into nationalism in a part of the world already rife with politicized religious difference. Like other Arabs of this period, Zurayk acknowledged that the Zionists had built a modern organization and that they had single-mindedly worked for "years, nay generations," to influence and mobilize the great powers of the world behind their cause. To the great misfortune of the Arabs, colonial Zionism had "descended upon a nation still at the beginning of its own nahda" following centuries of Ottoman despotism. Zurayk warned that the viability of "the Arab world" hinged on an Arab ability to reverse the Zionist idea "to build nationalism on the basis of religion and faith, in opposition to what history, political theory and sociology have established."[90] The struggle *against* the establishment of a Zionist state was for Zurayk a struggle *for* a modern, ecumenical Arab world. The antithesis to the Jewish state was not the Muslim or Christian state, but the ecumenical Arab one.

By the time Zurayk wrote his seminal treatise, Israeli Zionists had already driven out hundreds of thousands of Palestinians. Although he invoked a long history of coexistence between Arabs and Jews and maintained that the Arabs "are still prepared to coexist with the Jews on the basis of a single democratic rule," the reality on the ground pointed to a bleaker future. Within two decades, the Arab world had lost the vast majority of its Jewish populations. Zurayk, in fact, personified how the palpable Christian-Muslim solidarity evident in the language of Arab nationalism was henceforth sharply distinguished from the equally palpable Jewish solidarity with Israel. Neither solidarity was inherent or immutable or uncontested; in fact, both were quintessentially modern affiliations that bore distinctive costs.

Arabism was inherently more ecumenical than Zionism and far more faithful to the region's Ottoman past. Zionism, however, was far more successful as a sovereign political project. What was sacrificed on both sides of the 1948 divide was the idea of being a Jewish Arab or an Arab Jew. No matter how complex was the Jewish experience in the Arab and Islamic world, the loss of Jewish communities to the Arab world carried far more weight than most people at the time understood. Their absence was as significant as their original presence. It would become one of the unspokens of anticolonial Arab nationalism. For the Jewish nationalism of Israel this identification of being an Arab Jew was an unacceptable anomaly that had to be erased as quickly as possible, together with Palestine's Arab past and present.[91]

More clearly than ever, the events of 1948 exposed how vulnerable the Arab ecumenical frame in the Mashriq was to the shifts in the geopolitical context of the post-Ottoman Middle East. In their immediate aftermath, there were a series of military nationalist revolutions in Egypt, Iraq, and Syria. The question that remained to be answered was whether the post-1948 nationalisms in the revolutionary Arab world would ultimately be any different from the historic but terribly flawed and violent experiments of Kemalism and Zionism—would they, in any of their iterations, provide a sounder and more stable home for the damaged but resilient ecumenical frame?

Epilogue

It is the white man who creates the Negro. But it is the Negro who creates negritude.

— Frantz Fanon, *A Dying Colonialism* (1959)

What became of the ecumenical frame in the postcolonial era? The rise of anticolonial revolutions in the Arab East swept away the monarchies of Egypt and Iraq in the 1950s, but they did not herald the end of the ecumenical frame. Instead, they maintained its conservative design as contradictory narratives about liberation and competing social movements fought with one another for political dominance. We still lack an adequately nuanced and empathetic intellectual, political, and social history of the Arab world when the Mashriq was finally freed from the shackles of the mandate system.[1]

Like their Asian and African corollaries, the now discarded Arab political writings from that era were suffused with a sense of possibility, or what the Syrian-Jordanian Arab nationalist Munif al-Razzaz noted was the "new consciousness that is Arab as it has never been before."[2] The Egyptian revolution of 1952 and the emergence of Gamal Abdel Nasser as a pan-Arab popular hero was a massive fillip to the hopes for genuine Arab sovereignty across the Mashriq and beyond. Razzaz wrote his major work, *Ma'alim al-hayat al-'arabiyya al-jadida* (Signposts of the New Arab Life), in Nasser's shadow. Already in its fourth edition by 1960, Razzaz's book extolled the importance of the Egyptian revolution: its land reform, expansion of education, major infrastructural development, nationalization of the Suez Canal, and anti-imperialist Third-Worldism. But from Razzaz's perspective, the Egyptian revolution vindicated, most of all, an Arab national idea that transcended blood ties, religion, language, and geography.

Despite Palestinian catastrophe, Razzaz firmly believed, like Zurayk and Husri before him, that the destiny of the divided and colonized Arab world still lay firmly in Arab hands. He wrote poignantly that it was either "for us to write history or for history to be written for us."[3] At the same time, Razzaz was no fool. He recognized that the Arabs had inherited, from the mandate era, rampant economic and social inequality in which workers and peasants suffered at the hands of unscrupulous factory owners and feudal landowners, women had few political rights, oil resources were being squandered by way of unfavorable concessions, democracy was reduced to the ritual of hollow parliamentary elections (if that), and neither strong trade unions nor cooperative societies existed. He realized that Nasser's charisma notwithstanding, a basic divide across the Mashriq continued to separate most Arab rulers and states, including the revolutionary ones, from the masses with their pent-up desire for liberation and material progress. Perhaps most presciently, he feared the dawning of a postcolonial "police state" that relied on "internal security" to compensate for its estrangement from its own citizens.[4]

In truth, Razzaz's exhortations in 1960 reflected an extraordinary postcolonial political energy evident across the region. Historian Hanna Batatu maintains that in Iraq the 1950s was a period when Sunni and Shi'i Islamic ideas were "in a state of progressive decomposition."[5] In Egypt, the Muslim Brotherhood regarded itself as fighting a desperate war for survival in a secular era dominated by the intoxicating figure of Nasser. Beyond the struggle against Zionism, the political question in the Mashriq was encapsulated by the contest among various forms of nationalism—Nasserism against Baathism, principally—and between communism and nationalism. Sunni, Shi'i, and Christian Arabs were represented on all sides. The internecine battles to determine the political fate of the postcolonial Mashriq were often bitter, but all the main political tendencies involved in these battles were committed to maintaining the ecumenical frame. The increasingly obvious mid-century estrangement of the Jewish populations from the Arab fold was primarily a consequence of Zionism and the struggle over Palestine; it was the exception to the rule, or so it appeared.

The pieties of this anticolonial world were not sectarian, but rather nationalist or communist. The *jihad* that motivated men and women was the anticolonial nationalist struggle for political and economic independence.[6] For example, George Habash, a Christian expelled from Lydd, Palestine, in 1948, played a major role in shaping radical Arab politics around the question of Palestine through founding and leading the Movement of Arab Nationalists; Zaki al-Arsuzi, a Alawi from Syria, was one of the most eloquent mid-century advocates of antisectarian Arab nationalism; and the Chaldean Christian Iraqi Yusuf Salman Yusuf, known simply as Comrade Fahd, was the principal organizer in the 1940s of the Iraqi Communist Party, which also included Armenian Christians, Sunni Kurds, Arab Sunnis, Alawis and Shi'is, and Jews. When he was hanged by the Iraqi state in 1949, two fellow communists, the Shi'i Muhammad Husayn al-Shabibi and the Sunni Zaki Basim, were executed with him. The Christian Arab Michel Aflaq cofounded the Baath Party, and a Shi'i Iraqi, Fuad al-Rikabi, was the leading Baathist in Iraq in the 1950s. Arab Sunnis and Shi'is (until 1963) made up the greatest percentage of members of the national pan-Arab command of the Baath Party between 1954 and 1970, but Alawis, Druze, Orthodox Christians, and Catholics were all overrepresented in proportion to their demographic weight in Syria, Iraq, Jordan, and Lebanon.[7]

THE AUTHORITARIAN ECUMENICAL FRAME

The most consequential question of the independence era was the army's role in the affairs of state, not that of religion. Postcolonial Arab life came to be dominated, well into the twenty-first century, by the one-party states that Munif al-Razzaz feared, but also by military men from fairly humble roots who were often products of the mandate-era military academies of Syria, Iraq, and Egypt.[8] Besides Gamal Abdel Nasser in Egypt, who was the most famous, these military men included Abdel Karim Qasim in Iraq and Salah Jadid in Syria. They personified the rise to power of the middle and lower classes that shaped the revolutionary movements and militaries of the 1950s and '60s.[9]

The military nationalist revolutionaries in Iraq, Egypt, and Syria proffered a basic bargain to their respective citizenries: in return for an allegedly powerful sovereignty denied them by British and French colonialism, they demanded a monopoly on power to fulfill the promise of this sovereignty. They offered material development including, but not limited to, electrification, centralized planning, and increasing government employment. They promoted free education and redistribution of land. They nationalized the Suez Canal in 1956 and the Iraq Petroleum Company in 1961. They expanded women's rights, including suffrage, as well as healthcare infrastructure. But they also abolished meaningful opposition parties, undercut constitutionalism and freedom of the press, and repressed dissidents far more ferociously and systematically than the monarchical or early nationalist regimes had done. Similar to Peronism in Latin America and to the leadership of decolonizing states in many other parts of the world, Arab rulers sacrificed political democracy in favor of redistributive states. At first, this bargain may have seemed like a rational answer to the mid-century crisis that had devastated Palestine and to the desperate need for land reform and economic transformation in the Arab East. Strongmen appeared to be best positioned to thwart Western colonialism and Zionism, and to decisively overthrow the old order of things with its "feudal" interests and religious obscurantists.

The most senior of the Iraqi Free Officers who toppled the Hashemite monarchy in July 1958, Abdel Karim Qasim, was himself the product of a mixed Arab Sunni-Shi'i Kurdish marriage. Qasim's vision of a revolutionary Iraq was radically different from the pro-Western outlook adopted by the Hashemite monarchy. He provided, to be sure, already privileged military officers with even more privileges—houses, schools, markets, bakeries, cinemas, and swimming pools—in a bid to ensure their loyalty. Qasim also stripped landed shaykhs of huge estates, instituted the Iraqization of the foreign-dominated oil industry by insisting on hiring Iraqis in positions of technical expertise and not simply as oil-field workers, and sought to end British-era tribal regulations.[10] His regime eschewed pan-Arabism and increased the adoption of Kurdish as a language of instruction in intermediate and secondary schools in northern Iraq. It also oversaw a major reform of the personal-status regime for *all* Muslims, Sunni and Shi'a, in Iraq—although, significantly, Muslim women were still not allowed to marry non-Muslim men, and Muslim men were not allowed to marry women who were not of the Abrahamic faiths. Following the work of a committee that included several prominent Iraqi women lawyers and activists, the new Personal Status Law 188 of 1959 made polygamy far more difficult, fixed the legal age of consent for marriage at eighteen years for both men and women, and granted female and male heirs equal shares of property governed by intestate inheritance. Both the Shi'i religious establishment in Iraq and the Iraqi (Sunni) Muslim Brotherhood denounced these reforms.[11]

The flip side of these reforms was their obvious reliance on revolutionary authority. Immediately after Qasim was overthrown in 1963, in fact, the new Baathist regime repealed some of the most progressive aspects of his Law 188, such as the provision for equal inheritance.[12] The greatest single political persecution of this period of Iraqi history targeted communists, hundreds of whom the Baathist army and security services, with the aid of the United States, hunted down, imprisoned, tortured, and slaughtered in February 1963.[13] In Egypt, it was the communists and the Islamists who were jailed and killed. In Syria, the Baathists turned on each other after crushing Islamists, communists, and Nasserists. The particular religion or ideology of dissenter was almost a secondary concern— leftist or rightist, conservative or communist, Islamist or secular, party-affiliated or independent, Sunni or Shi'i, Kurdish or Arab, it seemed to matter little. Rather, these bloody internecine battles pitted "traitors" and "sectarians" against "nationalists" and "patriots," "collaborators" against "anti-imperialists."

The tragedy of the military nationalists in Iraq, Syria, and Egypt was that their commitment to revolution was far more energetically manifested in their construction of postcolonial security regimes than it was in building postcolonial democratic secular states. Beginning in the 1950s, it is true, the Mashriq became a setting for the Cold War and an active Arab-Israeli conflict in which Western states sided with Israel. Yet it is also apparent that the radical governments of the 1950s and '60s were not able or willing to initiate a secular cultural revolution that paralleled the boldness of their nationalization of large estates or the Suez Canal, or their overthrowing of pro-Western monarchical regimes.

Nasser may have ideologically rejected and derided Islamists as part of his attempt to crush them politically, but he maintained Islam as the state religion of Egypt and was quick to rekindle what historian Paul Sedra has described as the unequal "millet partnership" with the Coptic Church that reinforced the absolute communal authority of the Coptic patriarch.[14] Coptic Christians remained unable to build a new church in Egypt without presidential permission—this remains the case in Egypt until today.[15] Independent Syria, which had fought so hard against French colonial pluralism, included a constitutional stipulation in 1950 that *only* a Muslim could become president of the republic. The revolutionary nationalists who followed in the 1960s maintained this stipulation. Every revolutionary state in the Mashriq reformed, but did not abandon, sectarian personal-status regimes. Yet unlike the violent republicanism of Kemalist Turkey, these states engaged neither in radical cultural engineering nor in dramatic religious or ethnic cleansing of their populations.

SECURITY SECULARISM AND SECTARIANISM

Munif al-Razzaz spent the last five years of his life under house arrest in Baghdad, where he died in 1984. What he could not foresee in 1960 was the degree to which the revolutionary Arab states, from Nasser's Egypt to the Syrian and Iraqi Baathist regimes, would transform, bit by bit, the ecumenical frame of the modern Arab world into a prop for their authoritarianism. Pluralism and freedom in any meaningful political sense withered away under antidemocratic sovereignties. The irony lay in how Baathist regimes in Syria and Iraq that were manifestly and avowedly antisectarian and pan-Arabist strengthened the very sectarian sentiments against which they claimed to stand.

This happened at first far more by contingency than by design—and it was certainly not because Arab nationalism was an avatar for "Sunni" identity. The armies in Egypt, Iraq, and Syria, after all, were subject to the same class cleavages and divergent ideologies that competed for hegemony in the wider political sphere: communist, Islamist, nationalist, and pan-Arabist. The fact that the officer corps was predominantly Arab Sunni should not obscure the reality that the Free Officers in Iraq, inspired by Egypt's Nasser, conspired against a monarchy ruled by a Sunni Arab king and his coterie during the 1958 revolt. The king and the regent were killed by the army during the revolt. So great was anticolonial sentiment and loathing of the pro-British prime minister Nuri al-Sa'id that he was also killed in the course of the revolution. Protesters disinterred and burned his body and attacked the British embassy. What is crucial to note is that the great animus at work in those revolutionary days was clearly anti-imperialist and antimonarchical, not sectarian.[16]

Nevertheless, when the Baathist coup d'état deposed Qasim in February 1963 and had him summarily executed, the predominantly Sunni neighborhoods sided with the Baathists, and the predominantly Shi'i neighborhoods offered the most protracted resistance to the coup, although these happened to also be the poorest areas of the city, in which the communists—among whose fold were many Sunnis—had substantial organization. More ominously, by 1968 the Baath Party in Iraq, which had originated as a pan-Arab project that had attracted both Sunni and Shi'i youth in the 1940s and '50s, was dominated by Sunni Arabs, and its leadership was dominated by men from the Tikrit and surrounding towns. They brought in and trusted their own. They repressed any individual or group that threatened their grasp on power.[17]

A similar story repeated itself in Syria, where the rural and historically marginalized Alawis of the country had been encouraged to enter the military during the French mandate. Several of these Alawi military officers were inspired by the ideas of Arab nationalism and joined the Baath Party. After a series of coups, purges, and power struggles in the 1960s, some Alawi officers found themselves in an extraordinary and unprecedented position of influence.[18] They took advantage of these circumstances as any other group might have done, taking control of Syria after 1966. Razzaz found this "sectarian agglomeration" abhorrent because he saw it as contrary to the spirit, rationale, and history of the Baath itself.[19] The more difficult truth is that both Sunni Arab Tikriti Iraqis and Alawi Arab Syrians were, at one point, genuine nationalists deeply shaped by aspirations of meaningful postcolonial *Arab* sovereignty, and yet they were also haunted by the possibility of being overthrown from within and without.

There is no reason to believe that they did not intend to uphold the basic parameters of the conservative ecumenical frame.

A LESS ECUMENICAL AGE

Somewhere along the line, however, the belief in the viability of the ecumenical frame was shaken profoundly. The shattering 1967 Arab defeat by Israel, Anwar Sadat's cultivation of Islamists in Egypt in the 1970s, the seismic Iranian Revolution of 1979, the oil wealth that fueled Saudi Wahabism, and U.S. support for the anti-Soviet jihad in Afghanistan all played their part in sapping the fundaments of the modern Arab ecumenical frame. Collectively, these events undermined the optimism that had sustained a century of politics in the Mashriq. They cast a pall over the idea of ecumenical Arabism that had provided a common frame of reference in which Muslim and Christian Arabs might reconcile the quest for modern life with the reality of religious difference.[20]

So much was staked on Gamal Abdel Nasser's confrontation with the imperialist West that his sudden death in 1970 left a gaping hole, a vacuum of legitimacy that was bound to be filled by some force that appeared to fulfill the dashed aspirations of people in the region. At first, Palestinian guerrilla movements such as Fateh, led by Yasser Arafat, rushed to seal the breach. But these movements were too weak and, above all, totally lacking any real sovereignty to effect a sustained example for other Arabs to follow. Yet it was significant that when Arafat spoke before the United Nations in 1974, he presented a poignant ecumenical vision for Palestine. He called for a liberated democratic and multireligious Palestine that would include Muslims, Christians, and Jews as equal citizens: "one democratic state where Christian, Jew and Muslim live in justice, equality, fraternity."[21]

After specifically hailing the new states of Bangladesh, Guinea-Bissau, and Grenada, Arafat declared that the "old world order" of racism and colonialism was inevitably giving way to a brighter new one of genuine self-determination. In his view, a modern ecumenical, liberated Palestine, the cradle of the Abrahamic faiths, would embody this new world order.

The point to bear in mind here is the degree to which Arafat's vision of Palestine was itself more than an expression of third-world decoloniza- tion, anti-Zionism, and anti-imperialism. In his repudiation of an exclu- sively Jewish Zionist state, Arafat also drew directly on the legacy of the ecumenical frame. The Palestinian leader echoed the pleas of the earliest Muslim-Christian associations that had sprung up in reaction to the imposition of British military rule in Palestine. His call, moreover, corre- sponded quite closely with the Arab Christian theologians' declaration after 1967 that urged the creation in Palestine of a pluralist secular state in which Muslims, Christians, and Jews would live together as equal citi- zens. Arafat, in short, understood that the idea of liberating Palestine appealed to virtually every sector of the modern Arab world; it made Arabs *Arabs* in the broadest possible sense.[22]

The reality, however, was that after 1967 the United States was far more significant in shaping the future of the Arab world than the stateless Palestinian leader. U.S. hegemony in the Middle East rested on three inher- ently anti-ecumenical propositions: overwhelming military, economic, political, and financial support for the Jewish state of Israel; support for the pro-Western petroleum order dominated by Wahabist Saudi Arabia; and, I think less appreciated outside the Arab world, an unrelenting war against the idea of a Palestine-centric ideal of secular Arab unity as mis- guided, if not delusional. As a 1969 U.S. State Department study put it, what was required for progress in the Middle East was the "de-Arabiza- tion" of Arabs, and by that, quite simply, was meant abandoning the idea of secular anticolonial Arabism as a ruinous fantasy.[23]

THE DIMINISHMENT OF ARABISM

Within a year of Arafat's speech, a civil war began in Lebanon in 1975, a country that had been sheltering hundreds of thousands of Palestinian refugees since 1948. By the early 1970s, the Palestine Liberation Organization had also established its headquarters in Lebanon. Chiha's confessional Lebanese political experiment had already been shaken by a brief civil war in 1958, but two decades later it collapsed along violent ideological and sectarian lines.

The outbreak of fighting in Lebanon galvanized the clearest expressions of sectarian and antisectarian identities. The former inevitably have received the lion's share of attention in accounts of the war; the latter, however, echoed Bustani's calls in *Nafir Suriyya* in the aftermath of the 1860 debacle. On one side of the war were those, mostly Christian militias, who fought for a sectarian future; on the other side were those movements, whose membership drew from all religious communities, committed to the Arabism of Lebanon, not to the elimination of the religious other. In the midst of the carnage enveloping Lebanon, 1976 saw some of the clearest demands for the wholesale reformation of state and society, including calls for the abolition of "political sectarianism" and the secularization of laws of personal status. But these efforts were more desperate than programmatic. The guns, in any case, underscored a different reality. Unlike a century earlier, the question was no longer how the ecumenical frame was going to change, but whether it would survive at all.[24]

The Lebanese war reflected, in truth, the great diminishment of the Arab idea as a unifying political force. In the shadow of the Arab defeat in 1967, Baathist Syria and Iraq strode down their own roads to open despotism. The primary function of once radical nationalist projects became to perpetuate increasingly insecure regimes—dominated by Saddam Hussein in the case of Iraq and by Hafiz al-Asad in Syria. Both rulers insisted until their deaths that they remained Arab nationalists. Sati' al-Husri's Arabic primer, for example, continued to be used in Iraq, albeit adorned with illustrations of Saddam Hussein with these lines to be repeated by dutiful students: "I love the Leader / I love the Leader and Commander / The Hero Saddam Hussein / He loves us and we love him / The Leader visits us in our school and in our house / We are all soldiers of the Commander Saddam Hussein / May God Preserve our Commander for us."[25]

It is not only the cult of personality being foisted upon the students that is noteworthy, but also the ecumenical nationalist "we" the students were still instructed to read. Like his Baathist rival Asad in Syria, Hussein remained committed to a certain form of ecumenical nationalist subjectivity. In the Iraqi case, this subjectivity was marked by the inclusion of a Christian foreign minister, Tariq Aziz, in government. Both Hussein and Asad fanned the fears of Christian minorities and appealed to their countrymen as nationalist leaders who could rise above all sectarian considerations at the same time that they entrenched kinship networks at the highest levels of state. They classified their opponents as terrorists or sectarians.[26] Both leaders sought to make themselves indispensable personifications of an ecumenical Arab sovereignty. If they were killed, or otherwise removed from power, they suggested, it would be as if the idea of Arabism would die with them.

The enveloping of the ecumenism of modern Arab history within the folds of unrelenting despotism was no different, in a sense, from the connection between liberal ideology and colonialism. One did not necessarily lead to the other, but the two proved easily reconcilable. Despotism, like colonialism, often presented itself as a guardian of pluralism. But colonialism in the Arab East helped generate an ecumenical nationalist opposition that was keenly aware of its presence on a global stage and desperate to prove its political maturity. The same could not be said of Arab military regimes. In both Iraq and Syria, the ruling regimes became so identified with one sect or group that they caused grievous damage to the ecumenical frame. The most perverse aspect of these once radical nationalist states is that they exacerbated sectarianism by using antisectarianism as a weapon of containment and counterrevolution. The Syrian dissident Yassin al-Haj Saleh, who was imprisoned for sixteen years for being a communist, has argued passionately for an understanding of the sectarian dynamics of contemporary Syria. He discerns a false secular, "outer" Syrian state—the official slogans, the nationalist educational system, and the state bureaucracy—and a real "inner" sectarian state reflected in the security services and the highest echelons of the army and state dominated by the Alawis.[27]

This categorical view of the bifurcated state illuminates one aspect of the contemporary struggle in Syria. But it also ignores why the regime deploys the language of antisectarianism in the first instance. It does not reckon with a century of work that had made Arab nationalism, including Baathism, legible and credible or with the vital fact that many Syrians, and Arabs more broadly (of all faiths, including Alawis), have invested in the ecumenical frame for decades. Saleh's ahistorical notion of "absolute Arabism" nevertheless underscores how malleable is the language of antisectarianism, and how quickly it can be emptied of emancipatory potential and transformed into a weapon in the arsenal of post-Ottoman states. His description is also, I fear, a symptom of the inevitable backlash against despotism by a long-suffering Iraqi and Syrian citizenry. This backlash has threatened not only to remove the regime, as in the nationalist coups of the 1950s and '60s, but to destroy the modern ecumenical frame altogether in the name of "majority" rule, often defined largely in fixed sectarian and religious terms.

EULOGIZING THE NAHDA

The irony in the Arab East was that as jails filled up with dissidents in Syria, Iraq, and Egypt in the final decades of the twentieth century (and into our own time), the idea of a nahda as a secular Arab nationalist project was most systematically elaborated and, at the same time, eulogized. The Center for Arab Unity Studies in Beirut was founded in 1975 and run by the Iraqi Khair El-Din Haseeb, who had served as governor of the Central Bank of Iraq and then was tortured and jailed by the Baathist regime before going into exile in Beirut. His center published volume after volume of nationalist politics and criticism in an effort to reinforce the idea that Arab unity, irrespective of religious affiliation, was viable and necessary. Far more single-mindedly, the Syrian author Muhammad al-Khatib produced documentary works and commentaries in the 1980s and '90s in an effort to canonize the nahda as an age of national reform that began in 1800. At stake for him was two centuries of work that had made the emancipatory Arab political imagination possible.[28]

Khatib was hardly the first to read the nahda in nationalist terms, nor was he the first to observe a basic tension within the Arab world between its secular and Islamist orientations. For Khatib, the nahda had never been only an idealist intellectual project, although it certainly was that as well, but was a reflection of changing social, material, and economic conditions. The nahda had coincided with capitalist incorporation into a global economy to which Arabs had made little contribution, save for the export of manpower and petroleum resources. He believed that the idealism of the nahda was undercut by the chaotic patterns of development that marked modern Arab cities, in which new professions of modern medicine, engineering, law, university teaching, journalism, and writing proliferated in an unstable political and economic environment. Khatib insisted that the effects of colonialism—including the creation of Israel, unemployment, population growth, and migrations that produced misery belts around every major Arab city—inevitably affected the viability of the nahda.

Khatib blamed both structural conditions and the military men, including Nasser, for bringing about this state of affairs. He wrote that the secular reformist impetus within the postcolonial Arab world had been overwhelmed by the "officer's cap and the shaykh's turban."[29] While the military men destroyed modern Arab politics, Islamists threatened to destroy modern Arab culture. Military officers allowed the mosque and church to stand, and yet they smashed the independent political party and trade union. Khatib, who needed an official permit to publish his works in Syria, could not specifically condemn the Asad regime by name, but it was clear that he included military Baathism in his criticism. The serial destruction of all forms of civic life by authoritarian Arab regimes inadvertently bolstered the Islamists, because they, unlike their secular-minded compatriots, could fall back on and exploit what Khatib described as archaic solidarities that predated the nahda and the age of Western hegemony in which the nahda had been inextricably inscribed.

The upshot for Khatib was a chilling realization. The optimistic, naive, and forward-looking missives of nineteenth-century Muslim and Christian reformers such as Butrus al-Bustani, Muhammad Abduh, and Jurji Zaydan, and the more obviously political mid-twentieth-century exhortative works of Taha Husayn, Constantine Zurayq, and Munif al-Razzaz, had given way to a lachrymose narrative of the Arab world and its internal ills. In 1998, the famous Syrian poet and critic Adonis captured this sense of despair by writing that "we are today less religious and tolerant and more sectarian and fanatical, less united and more divided, less open and accepting of the Other and more unjust and isolated." For Adonis, the Arab "nation" had become a travesty. Rather than a herald of unity, it had become a military barracks, a sectarian enclave, and a tribal encampment. "Thirty years," declared Adonis, reflecting on the initial publication of his book *Preface to the End of a Century,* "and everything gets worse."[30] Adonis may as well have been the embittered orientalist Elie Kedourie. Although they

affiliated very differently with the Arab world, both men looked back from
exile at the ruination of societies of which they had once been a part.

THE ISLAMIC TURN

The failure of the project of secular Arabism was underscored by the surge
to prominence of Islamism after the Iranian Revolution in 1979. This
Islamist surge has always had its own internal diversity, represented by a
spectrum of divergent intellectual and social movements—from the
Muslim Brotherhood in Egypt, to Hizbullah in Lebanon, to the Da'wa in
Iraq, to Wahabism in the Gulf. Whereas the Muslim Brotherhood and
Hizbullah are very much part of the history of the ecumenical frame I
have charted in this book, the Saudi Wahabis are not, largely because they
repudiate its basic tenets. These movements share, nevertheless, a fundamental commitment to embracing publicly and politically an assertive
Islamic identity within Arab society. In Egypt, Syria, and Iraq, Islamists
have been hardened by persecution and emboldened by the continual ero-
sion of the legitimacy of the military dictatorships that have ruled in these
countries with an iron fist for decades.

For all its diversity, political Islamism assumes a location from which
different religious communities and individual citizens must exist according to Islamic precepts, from which there can be no transcendence. At
best, because it sees itself as the expression of the "majority" and of God,
political Islamism underscores Islam's toleration of "people of the book,"
affirming their constitutional citizenship with the understanding that
they "respect" the sensitivities of the majority: that is, that they accept living in an Islamic society and state.[31] At worst, this Islamism solidifies a
chauvinism and entitlement that threatens to utterly undo the cultural
achievements of a century of ecumenical work in the name of defending
allegedly sacrosanct spaces, texts, lands, and symbols. It contributes to a
lack of empathy with others, whether non-Muslim or heterodox communities or Muslims who are deemed to have transgressed or flouted Islamic
norms. The infamous trial of the "apostate" Nasr Hamid Abu Zayd in
Cairo in 1994 was a flagrant example of this. Abu Zayd, who worked at
Cairo University, was accused of defaming Islam in his academic work. An

Egyptian court annulled his marriage in 1995 on account of the accusation that he had apostatized from Islam. Abu Zayd and his wife were forced into exile.[32]

But this Islamist turn is *not* a total assault on the ecumenical frame; rather, it is a reminder of its original, conservative limits. The Abu Zayd trial, after all, occurred not in an Islamic theocracy, but in the U.S.-backed authoritarian, antidemocratic, and military-dominated Egypt of Husni Mubarak that jailed Islamists as well as secular dissenters. Abu Zayd's trial is a reminder that religion in the modern era has not been privatized but nationalized across the region. Hence the ongoing acceptance across the Mashriq and Maghreb (with the possible exception of Tunis, where Muslim women finally won the right to marry non-Muslim men in 2017) of religiously segregated laws of personal status; hence the various clauses privileging Islam that remain in most Arab constitutions; hence the Lebanese sectarian system dominated by warlords that continues to make sectarian affiliation the basis for political representation in the name of safeguarding "coexistence"; and hence the constant attempts by both conservative Christians and Muslims to ban "indecent" books, plays, and films throughout the century. That religious clerics or overtly pious individuals have more stridently entered the public sphere in our time is not so much a violation of an ethos of the original nahda but an exaggeration of one of its key aspects that had consistently nationalized "true" religion, especially Islam. The problem of Islamism, in short, resides within the terms of the ecumenical frame, not outside of it.

SALVAGING THE ECUMENICAL FRAME

But the Abu Zayd trial illustrates something else as well. Throughout the twentieth century and up to the present moment, countless individuals like Abu Zayd have embodied the persistence of the ecumenical frame. These individuals come from all faiths and communities of the region. They reflect a facet of the modern Arab world that is often obscured by contemporary events. More accurately, this persistence is its own unheralded contemporary event: scholars, writers, artists, public intellectuals, mobilized youth, teachers, journalists, politicians, lawyers, workers, and men and women from all walks of life *do* continue to inhabit the ecumenical frame. Whether they are secular or pietistic is hardly as important a question as whether and how they are committed to equality and emancipation in societies that remain diverse. Not all, or even most, of these individuals are involved in public spectacle or courtroom drama like Abu Zayd. In myriad other ways that require exploration and acknowledgment, people in and from the Arab world, I believe, persevere in a way of life that recalls or insists on the will to coexist in the most generous and dynamic sense of this term, not in its most cynical, conservative, and formulaic invocation.

The major mobilizations of Arab youth against tyranny across the region during the revolutionary upheavals of 2010 and 2011 are evidence of this perseverance; the ongoing Palestinian quest to secure freedom on the basis of secular equality is also evidence, and so too are some efforts to reimagine what being an Arab Jew means. I could dwell on the failures of the revolutionary protests within the Arab world, and on how they have been brutally crushed and sectarianized by counterrevolutionary forces. I could say how daunting is the prospect of Palestinian liberation, or how nostalgic the attempt to rediscover and rethink what being Arab and Jewish means in the aftermath of 1948. But this would be to miss their combined significance. That they continue to occur at all is the point.

These efforts at emancipation remind us that the history of the ecumenical frame does not disappear; nor is it "just there." Rather, it exists as separate moments, artifacts, and memories of the past waiting to be put together to tell a coherent and meaningful story of the present and to chart a vision for the future. There is, therefore, no "end" to the story of the ecumenical frame, but there was a beginning. Today, I admit, we are confronted with looming wars in a ravaged Arab world—in Iraq, Syria, Bahrain, Yemen, Saudi Arabia, and Lebanon. We are left with the aftermath of decades of massive U.S. military, political, and economic interference in the region, epitomized by the invasion of Iraq in 2003. We are confronted, moreover, by "secular" regimes in Egypt and Syria that have gone to war against their own people in a desperate bid to cling to undemocratic power. We witness the apparent military triumph of the Western-backed "Jewish state" of Israel that subjugates millions of Palestinians. We have beheld the ephemeral spectacle of the so-called "Islamic State" in the

Levant, whose name alone should evoke the bitterest irony of modern history: that the one region of the late nineteenth-century Ottoman Empire that seemed to escape the convulsions of rabid nationalism has been laid low in the twenty-first century by the scourge of those who facilitate and sponsor—or actually fight, die, and kill—for the fantasy of an Islamic state.

Can the ecumenical frame be salvaged? Perhaps, although massacres and invasions cannot be undone, and forced population movements and emigration will be difficult to reverse. Can there again be Arab Jews? Perhaps, at least as a form of dissenting identification. Is there a future for Christian Arabs? Possibly, but the same question has to include Muslim Arabs. They face no less an existential crisis about their location in the world and what kind of world they ultimately want to live in. These questions highlight the degree to which the surviving ecumenical frame will have to be reimagined and reconstituted on radically new terms if and when the violent wars that today devastate the Middle East finally run their terrible course.

We are still far from any honest reckoning with the complexity of diversity and its modern history in the Arab world—and still far away from a genuine understanding of what it might mean to develop a political culture that can embrace fully and equally the concept of equality irrespective of race, religion, and gender without equivocation or denial. This self-reflection need not be an exercise in self-flagellation as routinely practiced by Adonis and countless other modern Arab critics who have despaired at the current state of the region. There is little point in asserting that the West is "better" or more "modern." It should be evident by now that Western countries suffer their own ailments and inequalities and have their own calamities and their own racial, gendered, and religious taboos.

One of the principal messages of this book is to recognize the existence of a modern antisectarian tradition that goes all the way back to 1860 and yet has barely been studied as a tradition. Another key message is that to understand the Arab world empathetically is also to acknowledge that its travails have parallels in every other part of the world, including the United States, Europe, and South Asia. No honest person can possibly believe that the problem of race and racism in the West is resolved. Nor, by the same token, is sectarianism resolved in the Middle East. Or communalism in South Asia. The question is how one affiliates with and responds to these ugly expressions of human work—how to use our knowledge of the past so that we can be prepared to recognize the contemporary meaning and implications of what William Blake described as "mind-forg'd manacles." The other question is how to identify with those figures past and present, in the East and West, belonging to different faiths but not necessarily different traditions, who have tried to build a better and more just world free from those manacles.

Notes

INTRODUCTION

1. Bruce Masters, *Christians and Jews in the Ottoman Arab World: The Roots of Sectarianism* (Cambridge: Cambridge University Press, 2001), 40.

2. Karen E. Fields and Barbara J. Fields, *Racecraft: The Soul of Inequality in American Life* (London: Verso, 2012); Patrick Wolfe, *Traces of History: Elementary Structures of Race* (London: Verso, 2016); George M. Fredrickson, *White Supremacy: A Comparative History in American and South African History* (Oxford: Oxford University Press, 1981); Edmund S. Morgan, *American Slavery, American Freedom* (New York: W.W. Norton, 1975); David Roediger, *The Wages of Whiteness: Race and the Making of the American Working Class* (London: Verso, 1991).

3. The historian Marshall Hodgson long ago suggested that Islam arose in what he described as the "Oikoumene," or the vast area of interrelations between different peoples within the Afro-Eurasian region. See Marshall G.S. Hodgson, *The Venture of Islam: Conscience and History in a World Civilization, vol. 1: The Classical Age of Islam* (Chicago: University of Chicago Press, 1974), 109–110; see also Fred M. Donner, "How Ecumenical Was Early Islam?" (The Farhat J. Ziadeh Distinguished Lecture in Arab and Islamic Studies, Department of Near Eastern Languages and Civilizations at the University of Washington, April 29, 2013).

4. Brian Stanley, *The World Missionary Conference, Edinburgh 1910* (Grand Rapids, MI: William B. Eerdmans, 2009), 18–20; and Ruth Rouse, ed., *A History*

of the Ecumenical Movement 1517-1948 (London: SPCK, 1954). There are, in addition, older designations of "ecumenical" that refer to the patriarch of the Orthodox church as well as the "ecumenical" councils of late antiquity, such as that of Nicaea in 325 A.D. that had a strictly ecclesiastical remit to reconcile conflicting doctrinal interpretations of the nature of Jesus Christ.

5. Muhammad 'Abed al-Jabri, *Arab-Islamic Philosophy: A Contemporary Critique*, trans. Aziz Abbassi (Austin: University of Texas Press, 1999), 23. Historian Aziz al-Azmeh suggests that the modern Islamist/fundamentalist turn across the Arab world willfully denied its own obvious debt to secular global modernism; see Aziz al-Azmeh, *Al-'almaniyya min mandhur mukhtalif* (Beirut: Markaz dirasat al-wahda al-'arabiyya, 1992), 175.

6. They did not merely play the traditional "politics of notables" famously defined by Albert Hourani; see Hourani, "Ottoman Reform and the Politics of the Notables," in *Beginnings of Modernization in the Middle East: The Nineteenth Century*, ed. William R. Polk and Richard L. Chambers (Chicago: University of Chicago Press, 1968), 41–68.

7. I draw here on Michelle Campos's suggestion of a "civic Ottomanism"—that is, the effort in the late Ottoman age to construct an Ottoman political identity that transcended particular religious loyalties. Michelle U. Campos, *Ottoman Brothers: Muslims, Christians, and Jews in Early Twentieth-Century Palestine* (Stanford, CA: Stanford University Press, 2011).

8. Michael A. Meyer, ed., *German-Jewish History in Modern Times, vol. 2: Emancipation and Acculturation, 1780-1871* (New York: Columbia University Press, 1997) and *vol. 3: Integration in Dispute, 1871-1918* (New York: Columbia University Press, 1998); David Mislin, *Saving Faith: Making Religious Pluralism an American Value at the Dawn of the Secular Age* (Ithaca, NY: Cornell University Press, 2015); Neilesh Bose, *Recasting the Region: Language, Culture, and Islam in Colonial Bengal* (New Delhi: Oxford University Press, 2014).

9. For the comparison with Russia, see Michael A. Reynolds, *Shattering Empires: The Clash and Collapse of the Ottoman and Russian Empires, 1908-1918* (Cambridge: Cambridge University Press, 2011). For a comparison with Austria, see Omar Bartov and Eric D. Weitz, eds., *Shatterzone of Empires: Coexistence and Violence in the German, Habsburg, Russian, and Ottoman Borderlands* (Bloomington: Indiana University Press, 2013). For the United States and empire, see Paul A. Kramer, "Power and Connection: Imperial Histories of the United States in the World," *American Historical Review* 116 (2011): 1348–1391; see also Bradford Perkins, *The Cambridge History of American Foreign Relations, vol. 1: The Creation of a Republican Empire, 1776-1865* (Cambridge: Cambridge University Press, 1993).

10. For antiblack violence, see W. Fitzhugh Brundage, *Lynching in the New South: Georgia and Virginia, 1880-1930* (Urbana: University of Illinois Press, 1993); Steven Hahn, *A Nation under Our Feet: Black Political Struggles in the*

Rural South from Slavery to the Great Migration (Cambridge, MA: Belknap Press of Harvard University Press, 2003); David W. Blight, *Race and Reunion: The Civil War in American Memory* (Cambridge, MA: Belknap Press of Harvard University Press, 2001), especially ch. 4.

11. Fouad Ajami, *The Arab Predicament: Arab Political Thought and Practice since 1967* (Cambridge: Cambridge University Press, 1981), 3.

12. Mahmood Mamdani, *Citizen and Subject: Contemporary Africa and the Legacy of Late Colonialism* (Princeton, NJ: Princeton University Press, 1996), 7.

13. Kamal Salibi, *A House of Many Mansions: The History of Lebanon Reconsidered* (London I.B. Tauris, 1988), is probably one of the most important English-language studies. For an important criticism of the naturalization of the "sectarian community," see Mahdi ʿAmil, *Fi al-dawla al-taʾifiyya* (Beirut: Dar al-Farabi, 2003 [1986]). For an Arabic-language compendium of mid-twentieth-century views on sectarianism in Lebanon, see *Lubnan wa al-bunya al-taʾifiyya* (Beirut: Muʾassasat al-abhath al-ʿarabiyya, 1985). For a defense of the sectarian system, see Farid el Khazen, *The Breakdown of the State in Lebanon, 1967–1976* (Cambridge, MA: Harvard University Press, 2000).

14. For recent Ottoman literature, see Masters, *Christians and Jews in the Ottoman Arab Lands;* M. Şükrü Hanioğlu, *A Brief History of the Late Ottoman Empire* (Princeton, NJ: Princeton University Press, 2008); Leila Tarazi Fawaz, *An Occasion for War: Civil Conflict in Lebanon and Damascus in 1860* (London: Centre for Lebanese Studies and I.B. Tauris, 1994); Caesar E. Farah, *The Politics of Interventionism in Ottoman Lebanon 1830–1861* (London: Centre for Lebanese Studies and I.B. Tauris, 2000). For an older orientalist literature, see Moshe Maoz, *Ottoman Reform in Syria and Palestine 1840–1861: The Impact of the Tanzimat on Politics and Society* (Oxford: Oxford University Press, 1968).

15. See Dina Rizk Khoury, *Iraq in Wartime: Soldiering, Martyrdom, and Remembrance* (Cambridge: Cambridge University Press, 2013); Dina Rizk Khoury, "The Security State and the Practice and Rhetoric of Sectarianism in Iraq," *International Journal of Contemporary Iraqi Studies* 4 (2010): 325–338. Other works that have likewise delved into sectarianism include Max Weiss, *In the Shadow of Sectarianism: Law, Shiʿism, and the Making of Modern Lebanon* (Cambridge, MA: Harvard University Press, 2010); Laura Robson, *Colonialism and Christianity in Mandate Palestine* (Austin: University of Texas Press, 2011); Orit Bashkin, *The Other Iraq: Pluralism and Culture in Hashemite Iraq* (Stanford, CA: Stanford University Press, 2009); and Fanar Haddad, *Sectarianism in Iraq: Antagonistic Visions of Unity* (London: Hurst and Company, 2011). See also Omar H. AlShehabi, *Contested Modernity: Sectarianism, Nationalism, and Colonialism in Bahrain* (London: Oneworld, 2019); and Madawi al-Rasheed, "Sectarianism as Counter-Revolution: Saudi Responses to the Arab Spring," *Studies in Ethnicity and Nationalism* 11 (2011): 513–526. For recent Arabic literature on sectarianism, see the review essay by Fanar Haddad, "'Sectarianism'

and Its Discontents in the Study of the Middle East," *Middle East Journal* 71 (2017): 363–382; Fadil Rubay'i and Wahjih Kawtharani, *Al-ta'ifiyya wa al-harb* (Damascus: Dar al-Fikr, 2011); Muhammad Jamal Barut, ed., *Al-mas'ala al-ta'ifiyya wa sina'at al-aqliyyat fi al-watan al-'arabi* (Doha: Arab Center for Research and Policy Studies, 2017); and Abdulilah Bilqziz, ed., *Al-ta'ifiyya wa al-tasamuh wa al-'adala al-intiqaliyya: min al-fitna ila dawlat al-qanun* (Beirut: Markaz dirasat al-wahda al-'arabiyya, 2013).

16. Talal Asad, *Formations of the Secular: Christianity, Islam, Modernity* (Stanford, CA: Stanford University Press, 2003), 15, 183–184.

17. William T. Cavanaugh, *The Myth of Religious Violence: Secular Ideology and the Roots of Modern Conflict* (Oxford: Oxford University Press, 2009).

18. Saba Mahmood, *Religious Difference in a Secular Age: A Minority Report* (Princeton, NJ: Princeton University Press, 2016); Wendy Brown, *Regulating Aversion: Tolerance in the Age of Identity and Empire* (Princeton, NJ: Princeton University Press, 2006).

19. Asad, *Formations of the Secular,* 198. For an important critique of the criticisms of Arab nationalism, see Aziz al-Azmeh, "Nationalism and the Arabs," *Arab Studies Quarterly* 17 (1995): 1–17.

20. Mahmood, *Religious Difference in a Secular Age,* 79.

21. For a discussion of this problem of too rigid a segregation of secular and Islamic thought, see Marwa Elshakry, *Reading Darwin in Arabic: 1860–1950* (Chicago: University of Chicago Press, 2013), 9; and Omnia El Shakry, "'History without Documents': The Vexed Archives of Decolonization in the Middle East," *American Historical Review* 120 (2015), 925. But both understate the key feature of Albert Hourani's classic *Arabic Thought in the Liberal Age, 1798–1939* (Cambridge: Cambridge University Press, 1983 [1962]), which argued that Muslim and Christian Arabs belonged in the same interpretative frame that he described (although he later regretted the term) as "liberal." For a recent reinterpretation of Hourani's legacy, see Jens Hanssen and Max Weiss, eds., *Arabic Thought beyond the Liberal Age: Towards an Intellectual History of the Nahda* (Cambridge: Cambridge University Press, 2016).

22. Aziz al-Azmeh, *Islams and Modernities,* 3rd ed. (London: Verso, 2009), 74; Samuli Schielke, "Second Thoughts about the Anthropology of Islam, or How to Make Sense of Grand Schemes in Everyday Life," *Working Papers, Zentrum Moderner Orient,* no. 2 (2010): 1–16.

23. Bernard Heyberger, *Chrétiens du monde arabe: Un archipel en terre d'Islam* (Paris: Éditions Autrement, 2003).

24. See Morris's interview by Ari Shavit, "Survival of the Fittest? An Interview with Benny Morris," www.logosjournal.com/morris.htm.

25. Adonis, *Fatiha li-nihayat al-qarn* (Beirut: Dar al-nahar lil-nashr, 1998), 11–13.

26. At least according to Sadiq al-Azm, who insisted that is how the events were referred to in Damascus, in conversation with the author at the Wissenschaftskolleg zu Berlin, 2012–13. For conspiracy, see the memoirs of Al-amir Muhammad Sa'id al-Jaza'iri, *Mudhakkirati 'an al-qadaya al-'arabiyya wa al-'alam al-islami* (Algiers: Dar al-yaqdha al-'arabiyya, 1968), 18; for "haditha" see Abd al-Aziz al-Azmah, *Mir'at al-Sham: Tarikh Dimashq wa ahluha* (Damascus: Dar al-fikr, 2002), 316–326.

27. For example, Tariq al-Bishri, *Al-muslimun wa al-aqbat fi itar al-jama'a al-wataniyya*, revised ed. (Cairo: Dar al-shuruq, 2004).

28. This point about Western academic scholars is one that Abdullah Laroui noted decades ago in the context of writing about the Maghreb. See his *The History of the Maghrib: An Interpretive Essay*, trans. Ralph Manheim (Princeton, NJ: Princeton University Press, 1977 [1970]), 4–5.

29. Edward W. Said, *Culture and Imperialism* (New York: Knopf, 1993), 51.

30. Thomas Bender, "Historians, the Nation, and the Plentitude of Narratives," in *Rethinking American History in a Global Age*, ed. Thomas Bender (Berkeley: University of California Press, 2002), 11.

31. Bernard Lewis, *The Jews of Islam* (Princeton, NJ: Princeton University Press, 1984). Avigdor Levy, ed., *Jews, Turks, Ottomans: A Shared History, Fifteenth through the Twentieth Century* (Syracuse, NY: Syracuse University Press, 2002). For a more recent approach, see Marc David Baer, *The Dönme: Jewish Converts, Muslim Revolutionaries, and Secular Turks* (Stanford, CA: Stanford University Press, 2010).

32. Orit Bashkin, *New Babylonians: A History of Jews in Modern Iraq* (Stanford, CA: Stanford University Press, 2012).

1. RELIGIOUS DIFFERENCE IN AN IMPERIAL AGE

1. Evliya Çelebi, *The Intimate Life of an Ottoman Statesman: Melek Ahmed Pasha (1588–1662) as Portrayed in Evliya Çelebi's Book of Travels*, trans. and commentary by Robert Dankoff (Albany: State University of New York Press, 1991), 167–172. The information about Evliya's family is drawn from the introduction to this translation by Rhoads Murphey.

2. Bruce Masters, *Christians and Jews in the Ottoman Arab World: The Roots of Sectarianism* (Cambridge: Cambridge University Press, 2001), 39.

3. Cited in Colin Imber, *Ebu's-su'ud: The Islamic Legal Tradition* (Stanford, CA: Stanford University Press, 1997), 75. The list of Sultanic attributes is far longer.

4. Najwa al-Qattan, "Dhimmis in the Muslim Court: Legal Autonomy and Religious Discrimination," *International Journal of Middle East Studies* 31

(1999): 429–444; Qattan, "The Damascene Jewish Community in the Latter Decades of the Eighteenth Century," in Thomas Philipp, ed., *The Syrian Land in the 18th and 19th Century* (Stuttgart, Germany: F. Steiner, 1992); Masters, *Christians and Jews*, 32; Elyse Semerdjian, "Naked Anxiety: Bathhouses, Nudity, and the Dhimmi Woman in 18th Century Aleppo," *International Journal of Middle East Studies* 45 (2013): 651–676. Leslie Peirce, in her *Morality Tales: Law and Gender in the Ottoman Court of Aintab* (Berkeley: University of California Press, 2003), 382–283, makes the point that Muslim judges, although bound by structural discriminatory codes against non-Muslims and women, also could encourage the women's use of the court system.

5. For a concise definition of the millet system, see Jane Hathaway, *The Arab Lands under Ottoman Rule, 1516–1800* (Harlow, UK: Pearson, 2008), 191–194. For an older account, see Stanford J. Shaw, *History of the Ottoman Empire and Modern Turkey, vol. 1: Empire of the Gazis: The Rise and Decline of the Ottoman Empire 1280–1808* (Cambridge: Cambridge University Press, 1976), 59.

6. Shaw, *History of the Ottoman Empire, vol. 1*, 84. The dates regarding when an Ottoman sultan bestowed status among various Christian ecclesiastical leaders are approximate.

7. For the role of the Orthodox Church in sixteenth-century tax farming, see Tom Papademetriou, *Render unto the Sultan: Power, Authority, and the Greek Orthodox Church in the Early Ottoman Centuries* (New York: Oxford University Press, 2014).

8. Tijana Krstic, *Contested Conversions to Islam: Narratives of Religious Change in the Early Modern Ottoman Empire* (Stanford, CA: Stanford University Press, 2011). For Ottoman Shi'ism, see Stefan Winter, *The Shi'ites of Lebanon under Ottoman Rule 1516–1788* (Cambridge: Cambridge University Press, 2010).

9. Karen Barkey, *Empire of Difference: The Ottomans in Comparative Perspective* (New York: Cambridge University Press, 2008), 120; emphasis in original. See also Marc David Baer, *Honored by the Glory of Islam: Conversion and Conquest in Ottoman Europe* (Oxford: Oxford University Press, 2008).

10. Cited in Ussama Makdisi, *Artillery of Heaven: American Missionaries and the Failed Conversion of the Middle East* (Ithaca, NY: Cornell University Press, 2008), 43.

11. For an important discussion of anachronistic terms to describe "minority" communities in the Ottoman Empire, see Aaron Rodrigue, "Difference and Tolerance in the Ottoman Empire: Interview by Nancy Reynolds," *Stanford Electronic Humanities Review* 5 (1996), http://web.stanford.edu/group/SHR/5-1/text/rodrigue.html.

12. Barkey, *Empire of Difference*, 124.

13. Imber, *Ebu's-su'ud*, 86.

14. Derin Terzioğlu, "Where 'Ilm-i Hal Meets Catechism: Islamic Manuals of Religious Instruction in the Ottoman Empire in the Age of Confessionalization,"

Past and Present 220 (2013): 79–114; see also Baki Tezcan, *The Second Ottoman Empire: Political and Social Transformation in the Early Modern World* (Cambridge: Cambridge University Press, 2010).

15. Abdul-Rahim Abu-Husayn, *The View from Istanbul: Ottoman Lebanon and the Druze Emirate* (Oxford: Centre for Lebanese Studies in association with I. B. Tauris, 2004), 55.

16. Cited in Çelebi, *Intimate Life of an Ottoman Statesman*, 167–168.

17. Barkey, *Empire of Difference*, 179.

18. Christine M. Philliou, *Biography of an Empire: Governing Ottomans in an Age of Revolution* (Berkeley: University of California Press, 2011), 11, 57–60.

19. Haydar Ahmad al-Shihabi, *Lubnan fi 'ahd al-umera' al-shihabiyyin, vol. 3*, ed. Asad Rustum and Fu'ad Efram al-Bustani (Beirut: Manshurat al-maktaba al-bulusiyya, 1984), 553.

20. Shihabi, *Lubnan fi 'ahd al-umera'*, vol. 3, 553.

21. For an account of this moment, see Baer, *Honored by the Glory of Islam*.

22. For more on Shabbatai Zvi, see Marc David Baer, *The Dönme: Jewish Converts, Muslim Revolutionaries, and Secular Turks* (Stanford, CA: Stanford University Press, 2010), 1–5; see also Gabor Agoston and Bruce Masters, *Encyclopedia of the Ottoman Empire* (New York: Facts on File, 2009), 525.

23. Masters, *Christians and Jews*, 80–97. For reactions to Protestant missionaries, see Makdisi, *Artillery of Heaven*, 98–99.

24. Masters, *Christians and Jews*, 98–104; Bernard Heyberger, *Les Chrétiens du Proche-Orient au temps de la Réforme Catholique* (Rome: École Française de Rome, 1994).

25. Cited in Masters, *Christians and Jews*, 105.

26. Masters, *Christians and Jews*, 81.

27. Masters, *Christians and Jews*, 101. Masters describes the missionaries as "Frankish priests."

28. Masters, *Christians and Jews*, 98; Heyberger, *Chrétiens du Proche-Orient*.

29. Masters, *Christians and Jews*, 105–106.

30. Mikhayil Mishaqa, *Jawab 'ala iqtirah al-ahbab* translated as *Murder, Mayhem, Pillage, and Plunder: The History of the Lebanon in the 18th and 19th Centuries*, trans. Wheeler M. Thackston Jr. (Albany: State University of New York Press, 1988), 120.

31. Heyberger, *Chrétiens du Proche-Orient*, 185–208; Bernard Heyberger, "Terre Sainte et mission au XVIIe siècle," in *Dimensioni e problemi della ricerca storica, vol. 2* (Rome: Université "La Sapienza," 1994), 127–153.

32. Michel Febvre, *Théâtre de la Turquie, où sont representées les choses les plus remarquables qui s'y passent aujourd'hui touchant les Moeurs, le Gouvernement, les Coûtumes & la Religion des Turcs, & de treize autres*

sortes de Nations qui habitent dans l'Empire Ottoman (Paris: Edme Couterot, 1682), 345.

33. Eli Smith, *Toleration in the Turkish Empire* (Boston: T. R. Marvin, 1846).

2. THE CRUCIBLE OF SECTARIAN VIOLENCE

1. Christine Philliou makes this astute criticism in "The Paradox of Perceptions: Interpreting the Ottoman Past through the Nationalist Present," *Middle Eastern Studies* 44 (2008): 661–675.

2. See "'Fight for Faith and Motherland': Alexandros Ypsilantis's Proclamation of Revolt in the Danubian Principalities, 24 February 1821," in Richard Clogg, ed., *The Movement for Greek Independence 1770–1821: A Collection of Documents* (London: Macmillan, 1976), 202. On Greek nationalism, see Paschalis M. Kitromilides, "'Imagined Communities' and the Origins of the National Question in the Balkans," reprinted in *Enlightenment, Nationalism, Orthodoxy: Studies in the Culture and Political Thought of South-Eastern Europe* (Aldershot, UK: Variorum, 1994), 149–192.

3. As with other nationalist historiographies, partisanship and denial are evident in the work of Salahi R. Sonyel, "How the Turks of the Peloponnese were Exterminated during the Greek Rebellion," *Belleten* 62 (1998): 121–135; and Justin McCarthy, *Death and Exile: The Ethnic Cleansing of Ottoman Muslims 1821–1922* (Princeton, NJ: Darwin Press, 1995).

4. Here again is a problem. McCarthy, *Death and Exile*, 339, records twenty-five thousand Muslim deaths and ten thousand refugees, though he admits these to be "rough estimates."

5. Kitromilides, "Imagined Communities," 159.

6. Kitromilides, "Imagined Communities," 179, 177, 186; see also Victor Roudometof, "From Rum Millet to Greek Nation: Enlightenment, Secularization, and National Identity in Ottoman Balkan Society, 1453–1821," *Journal of Modern Greek Studies* 16 (1998): 11–48.

7. Quotations and analysis of Sultan Mahmud II's response to the Greek uprising are drawn from Huseyin Sukru Ilicak, "A Radical Rethinking of Empire: Ottoman State and Society during the Greek War of Independence (1821–1826)," PhD diss., Harvard University, 2011.

8. Christine M. Philliou, *Biography of an Empire: Governing Ottomans in an Age of Revolution* (Berkeley: University of California Press, 2011), 68–72.

9. From *Tarih-i Şanizade, vol. 2*, ed. Ziya Yılmazer (Istanbul: Çamlıca, 2008), 1122–1123. I thank Sukru Ilicak for alerting me to this text.

10. Hakan Erdem, "'Do Not Think of the Greeks as Agricultural Laborers': Ottoman Responses to the Greek War of Independence," in Faruk Birtek and

Thalia Dragonas, eds., *Citizenship and Nation-State in Greece and Turkey* (London: Routledge, 2005), 69; Ilicak, "Radical Rethinking," 161.

11. Cited in Erdem, "Do Not Think of the Greeks as Agricultural Laborers," 77.

12. Thomas Philipp, *Acre: The Rise and Fall of a Palestinian City, 1730–1831* (New York: Columbia University Press, 2001), 183.

13. Philliou, *Biography of an Empire*, 107–117.

14. Philliou, *Biography of an Empire*, 109–111.

15. Donald Quataert, "Clothing Laws, State, and Society in the Ottoman Empire, 1720–1829," *International Journal of Middle East Studies* 29 (1997): 403–425.

16. Şevket Pamuk and Jeffery G. Williamson, "Ottoman De-industrialization, 1800–1913: Assessing the Magnitude, Impact, and Response," *Economic History Review* 64 (2011): 159–184.

17. J.C. Hurewitz, ed., *The Middle East and North Africa in World Politics: A Documentary Record*, vol. 1 (New Haven, CT: Yale University Press, 1975), 316–318.

18. Butrus Abu-Manneh, "The Islamic Roots of the Gülhane Rescript," *Die Welt des Islams* 34 (1994): 173–203. Roderic H. Davison's *Reform in the Ottoman Empire 1856–1876* (New York: Gordian Press, 1973 [1963]) remains a classic interpretation.

19. Bruce Masters, *Christians and Jews in the Ottoman Arab World: The Roots of Sectarianism* (Cambridge: Cambridge University Press, 2001), 137–142.

20. Treaty of Paris, reproduced in Hurewitz, *Middle East and North Africa in World Politics, vol. 1*, 320.

21. For Aleppo, see Masters, *Christians and Jews*, 158; for Damascus, see Caesar E. Farah, *The Politics of Interventionism in Ottoman Lebanon, 1830–1861* (London: Centre for Lebanese Studies and I.B. Tauris, 2000), 592; Leila Tarazi Fawaz, *An Occasion for War: Civil Conflict in Lebanon and Damascus in 1860* (London: Centre for Lebanese Studies and I.B. Tauris, 1994), 132; Fawaz cites reports of casualties between five hundred and ten thousand. There is no way to verify the accuracy of these casualty figures, most of which were provided by British or French consular sources. They are presumably exaggerated.

22. Masters, *Christians and Jews*, 132.

23. Hidemitsu Kuroki, "The 1850 Aleppo Disturbance Reconsidered," in Markus Köhbach, Gisela Procházka-Eisl, and Claudia Römer, eds., *Acta Viennensia Ottomanica* (Vienna, 1999), 223. The qualification of "black" is based on Masters's discussion of these demands in *Christians and Jews*, 159; see also his warning against a decontextualized analysis of the Aleppo riots in Bruce Masters, "The 1850 Events in Aleppo: An Aftershock of Syria's Incorporation into the Capitalist World System," *International Journal of Middle East Studies* 22 (1990): 3–20.

24. Firas Krimsti, "The 1850 Uprising in Aleppo: Reconsidering the Explanatory Power of Sectarian Argumentation," in Ulrike Freitag, Nelida Fuccaro, Claudia Ghrawi, and Nora Lafi, eds., *Urban Violence in the Middle East: Changing Cityscapes in the Transition from Empire to Nation State* (New York: Berghahn Books, 2015), 141–163.

25. See Ussama Makdisi, *Culture of Sectarianism: Community, History, and Violence in Nineteenth-Century Ottoman Lebanon* (Berkeley: University of California Press, 2000), 118–145.

26. Abdel Karim Rafeq, "New Light on the 1860 Riots in Ottoman Damascus," *Die Welt des Islams* 28 (1988): 412–430; Fawaz, *Occasion for War*, 99–100. Linda Schatkowski Schilcher, *Families in Politics: Damascene Factions and Estates of the 18th and 19th Centuries* (Stuttgart, Germany: F. Stein, 1985), 97, cites the number of Christian looms destroyed as nearly three thousand. This is based on a British consular report. This, in turn, reflects the interpretation of the Aleppo riot in Masters, "1850 Events in Aleppo."

27. Fawaz, *Occasion for War*, 89; Schilcher, *Families in Politics*, 87.

28. There is still no study that draws on Ottoman documents to further shed light on the Damascus massacre of 1860. For Mount Lebanon, see Makdisi, *Culture of Sectarianism*.

29. Virginia Aksan has described this as the "new absolutism" of the nineteenth-century Ottoman Empire. See Virginia H. Aksan, *Ottoman Wars 1700-1870: An Empire Besieged* (Harlow, UK: Pearson Education, 2007), 259.

30. For an Ottoman figure of "rebel" dead, see Masters, *Christians and Jews*, 161. Ottoman authorities restored plundered property to Christians, arrested and publicly humiliated the alleged ringleaders of the rebellious rioters, and reaffirmed conscription. They also insisted that the bishops of each sect in the city nominate an individual to sit on an administrative council. See Kuroki, "1850 Aleppo Disturbance Reconsidered," 224.

31. The following section draws from an interpretation of the events of 1860 that I published in an essay entitled "Diminished Sovereignty and the Impossibility of 'Civil War' in the Modern Middle East," *American Historical Review* 120 (2015), 1739–1752.

32. Cited in Makdisi, *Culture of Sectarianism*, 149; Farah, *Politics of Interventionism in Ottoman Lebanon*, 611; see also Cevdet Paşa, *Tezâkir* (Ankara: Türk Tarih Kurumu Basımevi, 1991), 110.

33. For executions, see Fawaz, *Occasion for War*, 139–141; for fines and other punishments, see Farah, *Politics of Interventionism in Ottoman Lebanon*, 612–613; Fawaz, *Occasion for War*, 156–163.

34. See, for example, the wonderfully rich and underutilized records of the meetings of the commission of 1860–61 in Antoin Daw, ed., *Hawadith 1860 fi Lubnan wa Dimashq: Lajnat Bayrut al-duwaliyya, al-mahadir al-kamila, 1860-1862*, 2 vols. (Beirut: Mukhtarat, 1996). See also Davide Rodogno, *Against*

Massacre: Humanitarian Interventions in the Ottoman Empire, 1815–1914: The Emergence of a European Concept and International Practice (Princeton, NJ: Princeton University Press, 2012).

35. See, for instance, "Note de la Sublime Porte aux Ambassadeurs de France et de la Grande-Bretagne" (Ottoman Note to the Ambassadors of France and Great Britain), dated July 20, 1860, reproduced in Gabriel Effendi Noradoung-hian, ed., *Recueil d'actes internationaux de l'empire ottoman, vol. 3: 1865–1878* (Paris, 1902), 124; see also Rodogno, *Against Massacre*, 114–117.

36. Philliou, *Biography of an Empire*, 115; Makdisi, *Culture of Sectarianism*, 57–62.

37. For more information on British attitudes, see Selim Deringil, *Conversion and Apostasy in the Late Ottoman Empire* (Cambridge: Cambridge University Press, 2012), 67–69.

38. Stratford Canning to the Earl of Abderdeen, March 2, 1843, reproduced in Adel Ismail, ed., *Documents diplomatiques et consulaires relatifs a l'histoire du Liban: Les sources Anglaises, vol. 41* (Beirut: Éditions des Oeuvres Politiques et Historiques, 2000), 34; emphasis added.

39. See plan for reorganizing Mount Lebanon submitted in March 1861, reproduced in Daw, *Hawadith 1860, vol. 1*, 270–275. A French copy is to be found in Dufferin to Bulwer, April 26, 1861, reproduced in Ismail, *Documents diplomatiques et consulaires, vol. 45*, 303. See also Rodogno, *Against Massacre*, 113–114.

40. See Becklard's memorandum on the proposed partition plan for Mount Lebanon dated March 20, 1861, reproduced in Daw, *Hawadith 1860, vol. 1*, 276–277.

41. For an English-language translation, see Hurewitz, *Middle East and North Africa in World Politics, vol. 1*, 346–349.

42. For antecedents, see Philliou, *Biography of an Empire*, 114–117; Stanford J. Shaw, "The Origins of Representative Government in the Ottoman Empire: An Introduction to Provincial Councils, 1839–1876," in R. Bayly Winder, ed., *Near Eastern Round Table, 1967–68* (New York: Near East Center and the Center for International Studies, New York University, 1969), 53–142, 60–62.

43. These recommendations were not necessarily applied in practice and seem to have been devised with the predominantly Christian Balkans in mind. See Stanford S. Shaw and Ezel Kural Shaw, *History of the Ottoman Empire and Modern Turkey, vol. 2: Reform, Revolution and Republic/The Rise of Modern Turkey 1808–1975* (Cambridge: Cambridge University Press, 1977), 89.

44. Butrus al-Bustani, *Nafir Suriyya*. I have drawn here on both the Arabic originals reprinted and edited by Yusuf Quzma Khuri (Beirut: Dar al-Hamra', 1990) and the English translation provided by Jens Hanssen and Hicham Safieddine, *The Clarion of Syria: A Patriot's Call against the Civil War of 1860* (Oakland: University of California Press, 2019). The English translations are

all drawn from Hanssen and Safieddine unless noted otherwise. I have changed their translation of *abna' al-watan* to "sons of the nation" rather than their "children of the homeland." Citations below refer to the number and date of the specific epistle quoted.

45. *Nafir Suriyya*, no. 4, October 25, 1860.

46. Philliou, *Biography of an Empire*, 153–154; Serif Mardin, *The Genesis of Young Ottoman Thought: A Study in the Modernization of Turkish Political Ideas* (Princeton, NJ: Princeton University Press, 1962); Adam Mestyan, *Arab Patriotism: The Ideology and Culture of Power in Late Ottoman Egypt* (Princeton, NJ: Princeton University Press, 2017), 75–77; Steven Sheehi, "Butrus al-Bustani: Syria's Ideologue of the Age," in Adel Beshara, ed., *The Origins of Syrian Nationhood: History, Pioneers and Identity* (New York: Routledge, 2011), 70.

47. *Nafir Suriyya*, no. 7, November 19, 1860.

48. *Nafir Suriyya*, no. 2, October 8, 1860.

49. For more on sectarianization, see Nader Hashemi and Danny Postel, eds., *Sectarianization: Mapping the New Politics of the Middle East* (London: Hurst, 2017).

50. *Nafir Suriyya*, no. 4, October 25, 1860. My translation. Safieddine translates this as "confessional fanaticism." This point was made by the first significant modern English-language interpreter of Bustani's *Nafir*, George Antonius, in *The Arab Awakening: The Story of the Arab National Movement* (London: Hamish Hamilton, 1938), 49–51; see also Albert Hourani, *Arabic Thought in the Liberal Age, 1798–1939* (Cambridge: Cambridge University Press, 1983 [1962]), 100–102.

51. *Nafir Suriyya*, no. 5, November 1, 1860. See also Ussama Makdisi, "After 1860: Debating Religion, Reform, and Nationalism in the Ottoman Empire," *International Journal of Middle Eastern Studies* 34 (2002): 601–617; see also Nadia Bou Ali, "In the Hall of Mirrors: The Arab Nahda, Nationalism, and the Question of Language," D.Phil. diss., Oxford University, 2012; Peter Hill, "Utopia and Civilisation in the Arab Nahda," D.Phil. diss., Oxford University, 2015.

52. *Nafir Suriyya*, no. 5, November 1, 1860.

53. See *Nafir Suriyya*, no. 7, November 19, 1860.

54. *Nafir Suriyya*, no. 9, January 14, 1861.

55. For more on the school's ethos of coexistence, see Yusuf Q. Khoury, *Rajul sabiq li 'asrihi: al-mu'allim Butrus al Bustani, 1819–1883* (Beirut: Bisan, 1995), 53–68; see also Aleksandra Kobiljski, "Un modèle américain? Les collèges protestants de Beyrouth et Kyoto, 1860–1975," *Monde(s)* 6 (2014): 171–193; Jens Hanssen, *Fin de Siècle Beirut: The Making of an Ottoman Provincial Capital* (Oxford: Oxford University Press, 2005), 164–168; Hanssen notes the American missionary couple enrolling its sons.

56. *Nafir Suriyya*, no. 9, January 14, 1861.

57. *Nafir Suriyya*, no. 9, January 14, 1861.

58. *Nafir Suriyya*, no. 6, November 8, 1860. I thank Dr. George Sabra for this observation about Ezekiel 34:2 and its relationship to the *Nafir;* email communication, April 3, 2017.

59. *Nafir Suriyya*, no. 7, November 19, 1860. For "barrier," see *Nafir Suriyya*, no. 10, February 22, 1861.

60. *Nafir Suriyya*, no. 9, January 14, 1861.

3. COEXISTENCE IN AN AGE OF GENOCIDE

1. Donald Bloxham, *The Great Game of Genocide: Imperialism, Nationalism and the Destruction of the Ottoman Armenians* (Oxford: Oxford University Press, 2005).

2. Ronald Grigor Suny, Fatma Müge Göçek, and Norman M. Naimark, eds., *A Question of Genocide: Armenians and Turks at the End of the Ottoman Empire* (Oxford: Oxford University Press, 2011), 3–52.

3. Ryan Gingeras, *Fall of the Sultanate: The Great War and the End of the Ottoman Empire, 1908-1922* (Oxford: Oxford University Press, 2016), 64–68. For an elaboration of a reading of the Ottoman experience from the northern part of the empire, see Christine Philliou, "Nationalism, Internationalism and Cosmopolitanism: Comparison and Commensurability," *Comparative Studies of South Asia, Africa and the Middle East* 36 (2016): 455–464.

4. A point that was made first by C. Ernest Dawn, *From Ottomanism to Arabism: Essays on the Origins of Arab Nationalism* (Urbana: University of Illinois Press, 1973), and then by Hasan Kayali, *Arabs and Young Turks: Ottomanism, Arabism, and Islamism in the Ottoman Empire, 1908-1918* (Berkeley: University of California Press, 1997), and most recently by Bruce Masters, *The Arabs of the Ottoman Empire, 1516-1918: A Social and Cultural History* (Cambridge: Cambridge University Press, 2013), 229–231.

5. Isa Blumi, *Reinstating the Ottomans: Alternative Balkan Modernities, 1800-1912* (New York: Palgrave, 2011); İpek Yosmaoğlu, *Blood Ties: Religion, Violence and the Politics of Nationhood in Ottoman Macedonia, 1878-1908* (Ithaca, NY: Cornell University Press, 2014).

6. James J. Reid, *Crisis of the Ottoman Empire: Prelude to Collapse 1839-1878* (Stuttgart, Germany: F. Steiner, 2000), 319. The Ottomanist Justin McCarthy claims that 260,000 Bulgarian Muslims perished as a result of the conflict; see McCarthy, *Death and Exile: The Ethnic Cleansing of Ottoman Muslims 1821-1922* (Princeton, NJ: Darwin Press, 1995), 91. It is very difficult to verify the accuracy of such figures. The anthropologist Dawn Chatty cites McCarthy in her *Displacement and Dispossession in the Modern Middle East* (Cambridge: Cambridge University Press, 2010), 73.

7. Fatma Müge Göçek, *Rise of the Bourgeoisie, Demise of Empire: Ottoman Westernization and Social Change* (New York: Oxford University Press, 1996), 138–141.

8. Cecilie Endresen, *Is the Albanian's Religion Really "Albanianism"? Religion and Nation according to Muslim and Christian Leaders in Albania* (Wiesbaden, Germany: Harrassowitz, 2012); Edin Hajdarpasic, *Whose Bosnia? Nationalism and Political Imagination in the Balkans, 1840–1914* (Ithaca, NY: Cornell University Press, 2015).

9. Kent F. Schull, M. Safa Saraçoğlu, and Robert Zens, eds., *Law and Legality in the Ottoman Empire and the Republic of Turkey* (Bloomington: Indiana University Press, 2016).

10. Sibel Zandi-Sayek, *Ottoman Izmir: The Rise of a Cosmopolitan Port, 1840–1880* (Minneapolis: University of Minnesota Press, 2012); Zeynep Çelik, *The Remaking of Istanbul: Portrait of an Ottoman City in the Nineteenth Century* (Berkeley: University of California Press, 1986); Bruce Masters, *The Arabs of the Ottoman Empire, 1516–1918* (Cambridge: Cambridge University Press, 2013), 195; Keith David Watenpaugh, *Being Modern in the Middle East: Revolution, Nationalism, Colonialism, and the Arab Middle Class* (Princeton, NJ: Princeton University Press, 2006); Malek Sharif, *Imperial Norms and Local Realities: The Ottoman Municipal Laws and the Municipality of Beirut, 1860–1908* (Beirut: Orient-Institut, 2014), 181–209; Jens Hanssen, *Fin de Siècle Beirut: The Making of an Ottoman Provincial Capital* (Oxford: Clarendon Press, 2005), 236–263.

11. Murat C. Yildiz, "Institutions and Discourses of Sports in the Modern Middle East," in Nicholas S. Hopkins and Sandrine Gamblin, eds., *Sports and Society in the Middle East* (Cairo Papers in Social Science: American University in Cairo Press, 2016), 12–47. Göçek, *Rise of the Bourgeoisie, Demise of Empire,* 124–125.

12. Kemal H. Karpat, *Ottoman Population 1830–1914: Demographic and Social Characteristics* (Madison: University of Wisconsin Press, 1985), 151. Seventeen million was the total tabulated; Karpat's larger figure of thirty-nine million includes estimates of populations in administrative areas and special and autonomous provinces not included in the census.

13. For Ottoman "image management," see Selim Deringil, *The Well-Protected Domains: Ideology and the Legitimation of Power in the Ottoman Empire, 1876–1909* (London: I. B. Tauris, 1999), 135–150. See also Cemil Aydin, *The Idea of the Muslim World: A Global Intellectual History* (Cambridge, MA: Harvard University Press, 2017).

14. For marriage, see Karen M. Kern, *Imperial Citizen: Marriage and Citizenship in the Ottoman Frontier Provinces of Iraq* (Syracuse, NY: Syracuse University Press, 2011), 90. See also Kemal H. Karpat, *The Politicization of Islam: Reconstructing Identity, State, Faith, and Community in the Late Ottoman*

State (Oxford: Oxford University Press, 2001), 200; Sabri Ateş, *The Ottoman-Iranian Borderlands: Making a Boundary, 1843-1914* (New York: Cambridge University Press, 2013). Moreover, Isa Blumi points out, in *Reinstating the Ottomans*, 160-161, that in Albania there were clear tensions between Bektashi devotees and the Hamidian Sunni Islamist project.

15. Midhat Pasha, "The Past, Present, and Future of Turkey," *The Nineteenth Century* XVI (June 1878): 982-983.

16. Ali Haydar Midhat Bey, *The Life of Midhat Pasha: A Record of His Services, Political Reforms, Banishment, and Judicial Murder* (London: John Murray, 1903), 287, 291.

17. Carter Vaughn Findley, *Turkey, Islam, Nationalism, and Modernity: A History, 1789-2007* (New Haven, CT: Yale University Press, 2010), 142.

18. Janet Klein, *The Margins of Empire: Kurdish Militias in the Ottoman Tribal Zone* (Stanford, CA: Stanford University Press, 2011). See also Hans-Lukas Kieser, "Réformes ottomanes et cohabitation entre chrétiens et Kurdes (1839-1915)," *Études rurales* 186 (July-December 2010): 43-60; Stephan H. Astourian, "The Silence of the Land: Agrarian Relations, Ethnicity, and Power," in Suny et al., *Question of Genocide*, 62-64.

19. Edhem Eldem, "L'écrivain engagé et le bureaucrate zélé: La prise de la Banque ottomane et les "événements" de 1896 selon Victor Bérard et Hüseyin Nazım Pacha," in Sophie Basch, ed., *Portraits de Victor Bérard* (Athens: École française d'Athènes, 2015), 209-215; Julia Phillips Cohen, *Becoming Ottomans: Sephardi Jews and Imperial Citizenship in the Modern Era* (Oxford: Oxford University Press, 2014), 74-78.

20. Bloxham, *Great Game of Genocide*, 51.

21. See Vahakn N. Dadarian, "The 1894 Sassoun Massacre: *A Juncture in the Escalation of the Turko-Armenian Conflict*," *Armenian Review* 47 (*2001*): 5-39; on p. 33, Dadarian calls the Sassoun massacre a "watershed event" because of its genocidal aspects. See also Bedross Der Matossian, *Shattered Dreams of Revolution: From Liberty to Violence in the Late Ottoman Empire* (Stanford, CA: Stanford University Press, 2014).

22. M. Şükrü Hanioğlu, *A Brief History of the Late Ottoman Empire* (Princeton, NJ: Princeton University Press, 2008), 147.

23. The most exhaustive study of the Young Turks in opposition is that of M. Şükrü Hanioğlu, *The Young Turks in Opposition* (New York: Oxford University Press, 1996); see also Hanioğlu, *Brief History of the Late Ottoman Empire*, 145.

24. Information on the Adana riot is drawn from Bedross Der Matossian, "From Bloodless Revolution to Bloody Counterrevolution: The Adana Massacres of 1909," *Genocide Studies and Prevention* 6 (2011): 152-173; Nazan Maksudyan, "New 'Rules of Conduct' for State, American Missionaries, and Armenians: 1909 Adana Massacres and the Ottoman Orphanage (Darü'l-Eytam-ı Osmani)," in François Georgeon, ed., *"L'ivresse de la liberté": La revolution de 1908 dans*

l'Empire ottoman (Paris: CNRS, 2012), 137–171; and Taner Akçam, *A Shameful Act: The Armenian Genocide and the Question of Turkish Responsibility* (New York: Henry Holt, 2006), 69. For "regrettable," see Grand Vizier Hilmi Pasha's statement, available online at www.imprescriptible.fr/rhac/tome3/p1d3. I thank Professor Maksudyan for this reference.

25. Cited by Hans-Lukas Kieser, "From 'Patriotism' to Mass Murder: Dr. Mehmed Reşid (1873–1919)," in Suny et al., *Question of Genocide*, 137.

26. Achille Mbembe, "Necropolitics" *Public Culture* 15 (2003): 11–40; for more on the Armenian genocide, see Taner Akçam, *The Young Turks' Crime against Humanity: The Armenian Genocide and Ethnic Cleansing in the Ottoman Empire* (Princeton, NJ: Princeton University Press, 2012).

27. For more on this period's violence, see Ryan Gingeras, *Sorrowful Shores: Violence, Ethnicity, and the End of the Ottoman Empire 1912–1923* (Oxford: Oxford University Press, 2009); Uğur Ümit Üngör, *The Making of Modern Turkey: Nation and State in Eastern Anatolia, 1913–1950* (Oxford: Oxford University Press, 2011); Dominik J. Schaller and Jürgen Zimmerer, "Late Ottoman Genocides: The Dissolution of the Ottoman Empire and Young Turkish Population and Extermination Policies—Introduction," *Journal of Genocide Research* 10 (2008), 7–14.

28. Nadir Özbek, "Defining the Public Sphere during the Late Ottoman Empire: War, Mass Mobilization and the Young Turk Regime (1908–18)," *Middle Eastern Studies* 43 (2007): 795–809.

29. Bloxham, *Great Game of Genocide*, 165.

30. Michael Provence, *The Last Ottoman Generation and the Making of the Modern Middle East* (Cambridge: Cambridge University Press, 2017), 18–55.

31. See Waïl S. Hassan, *Immigrant Narratives: Orientalism and Cultural Translation in Arab American and Arab British Literature* (Oxford: Oxford University Press, 2011), 38–77; Carol Hakim, *The Origins of the Lebanese National Idea 1840–1920* (Berkeley: University of California Press, 2013), 171.

32. See, in particular, Malek Sharif's nuanced reading of the 1903 flare-up in his "The 1903 'Massacre of Christians' in Beriut and Its Immediate Aftermath Revisited," in Hidemitsu Kuroki, ed., *Human Mobility and Multiethnic Coexistence in Middle Eastern Urban Societies 2: Tehran, Cairo, Istanbul, Aleppo, and Beirut* (Tokyo: ILCAA, 2018), 225–245.

33. Leila Tarazi Fawaz, *Merchants and Migrants in Nineteenth-Century Beirut* (Cambridge, MA: Harvard University Press, 1983), 123; Sharif, *Imperial Norms and Local Realities*, 115–142; Hanssen, *Fin de Siècle Beirut*, 1–54.

34. Fawaz, *Merchants and Migrants*, 96–98; Hanssen, *Fin de Siècle Beirut*, 95–96, 109.

35. Philippe de Tarazi, *Tarikh al-sahafa al-'arabiyya*, 2 vols. (Beirut: Al-matba'a al-adabiyya, 1913–1914). For literacy rates, see Ziad Fahmy, *Ordinary Egyptians: Creating the Modern Nation through Popular Culture* (Stanford, CA:

Stanford University Press, 2011), 6; for Palestine, see Ami Ayalon, *Reading Palestine: Printing and Literacy, 1900–1948* (Austin: University of Texas Press, 2004), 16–17.

36. Nadya Sbaiti, "If the Devil Taught French: Strategies of Language and Learning in French Mandate Beirut," in Osama Abi-Mershed, ed., *Trajectories of Education in the Arab World: Legacies and Challenges* (New York: Routledge, 2010), 66; Hanssen, *Fin de Siècle Beirut*, 166–187.

37. Philip S. Khoury, *Syria and the French Mandate: The Politics of Arab Nationalism, 1920–1945* (Princeton, NJ: Princeton University Press, 1987), 410.

38. For the case of the Egyptian press, see Adam Mestyan, *Arab Patriotism: The Ideology and Culture of Power in Late Ottoman Egypt* (Princeton, NJ: Princeton University Press, 2017), 185.

39. Ann-Laure Dupont, *Gurgi Zaydan 1861–1914: Écrivain réformiste et témoin de la Renaissance Arabe* (Damascus: IFPO, 2006), 178, 218–220.

40. Jurji Zaydan, *Tarikh adab al-lugha al-'arabiyya, vol. 4* (Cairo: Dar al-Hilal, 1957 [1914]). For more on Zaydan's history writing, see Dupont, *Gurgi Zaydan*, 336–337; see also Lewis Beier Ware, "Jurji Zaydan: The Role of Popular History in the Formation of a New Arab World-View," PhD diss., Princeton University, 1973, 163; and Yoav Di Capua, *Gatekeepers of the Arab Past: Historians and History Writing in Twentieth-Century Egypt* (Berkeley: University of California Press, 2008), 33–43.

41. Zaydan, *Tarikh adab al-lugha al-'arabiyya, vol. 4*, 16. The nahda has primarily been studied in terms of Albert Hourani's classic formulation of an Arabic "liberal age"—a notion that Hourani explicitly premised on the existence of an untainted original European liberalism from which the mimetic Arabic version of the nahda derived. See Albert Hourani, *Arabic Thought in the Liberal Age, 1798–1939* (Cambridge: Cambridge University Press, 1983 [1962]). For a recent review of the main outlines of the nahda, see Elizabeth Suzanne Kassab, *Contemporary Arab Thought: Cultural Critique in Comparative Perspective* (New York: Columbia University Press, 2010), 17–47. See also Jens Hanssen and Max Weiss, eds., *Arabic Thought beyond the Liberal Age: Toward an Intellectual History of the Nahda* (Cambridge: Cambridge University Press, 2016).

42. Sami Ayoub, "The Mecelle, Sharia, and the Ottoman State: Fashioning and Refashioning of Islamic Law in the Nineteenth and Twentieth Centuries," in Schull et al., *Law and Legality in the Ottoman Empire*, 129–131.

43. The vast majority of writings about the nahda have focused on these writings, the most recent of which is Marwa Elshakry's *Reading Darwin in Arabic, 1860–1950* (Chicago: University of Chicago Press, 2013).

44. Suleyman al-Bustani, *'Ibra wa dhikra aw al-dawla al-'uthmaniyya qabla al-dustur wa ba'dahu* (Cairo: Matba'at al-Akhbar, 1908), 6–10. For an incisive analysis of such a discourse of brotherhood, see Campos's aptly named *Ottoman*

Brothers, which focuses on Ottoman Palestine: Michelle U. Campos, *Ottoman Brothers: Muslims, Christians and Jews in Early Twentieth-Century Palestine* (Stanford, CA: Stanford University Press, 2011).

45. Bustani, *'Ibra wa dhikra*, 6, 90-98.

46. Yusuf al-Dibs, *Tarikh Suriyya, vol. 8: Fi-tarikh Suriyya fi ayyam al-salatin al-'uthmaniyyin al-'izam* (Piscataway, NJ: Gorgias Press, 2009), 673.

47. For wage versus newspaper cost, see Elizabeth M. Holt, *Fictitious Capital: Silk, Cotton, and the Rise of the Arabic Novel* (New York: Fordham University Press, 2017), 55-56; for property qualifications for municipal elections, see Sharif, *Imperial Norms and Local Realities*, 81.

48. Ilham Khuri-Makdisi, "The *Nahda* Revisited: Socialism and Radicalism in Beirut and Mount Lebanon, 1900-1914," in Christoph Schumann, ed., *Liberal Thought in the Eastern Mediterranean: Late 19th Century until the 1960s* (Leiden, The Netherlands: Brill, 2008), 147-174; Ilham Khuri-Makdisi, *The Eastern Mediterranean and the Making of Global Radicalism, 1860-1914* (Berkeley: University of California Press, 2010), 35-59.

49. See, for example, most of the figures described in Khuri-Makdisi, *The Eastern Mediterranean and the Making of Global Radicalism*. See also Hourani, *Arabic Thought*, 259.

50. Jurji Zaydan, "Community of Interest: The Source of All Other Communities and the Primary Motivation for Undertaking Great Deeds," trans. Paul Starkey and reproduced in Thomas Philipp, *Jurji Zaydan and the Foundations of Arab Nationalism* (Syracuse, NY: Syracuse University Press, 2010), 330-337.

51. "Tarikh Ibn Rushd wa falsafatahu," *Al-Jami'a* 3 (1902), 524; Michel Jiha, ed., *Al-munazara al-diniyya bayna al-shaykh Muhammad Abduh wa Farah Antun* (Beirut: Bisan, 2014), 121-131 (for "twins," see 124).

52. Umar Ryad, *Islamic Reformism and Christianity: A Critical Reading of the Works of Muḥammad Rashīd Riḍā and His Associates (1898-1935)* (Leiden, The Netherlands: Brill, 2009), 87; and for actual letter, see appendix V.

53. Vivian Ibrahim, *The Copts of Egypt: The Challenges of Modernisation and Identity* (London: I. B. Tauris, 2013), 64.

54. For the contrast between filiation and affiliation, see Edward W. Said, "Secular Criticism," in *The World, the Text, and the Critic* (Cambridge, MA: Harvard University Press, 1983), 1-30.

55. Unlike what Hourani asserts in *Arabic Thought*, 254, 259. Hourani uses the term "master" to describe Antun's relationship to Renan but, oddly, does not mention Renan's racial philology and anti-Islamism. Hourani, however, also acknowledges that Antun's writings reflected the first shoots of "the expression of an active political consciousness among the Arab Christians."

56. For more on the role of Syrian Christians in Egypt, see Donald M. Reid, *The Odyssey of Farah Antun: A Syrian Christian's Quest for Secularism* (Minneapolis, MN: Bibliotheca Islamica, 1975), 30-33. For Copts, see Muhammad

Sayyid Kilani, *Al-adab al-qibti qadiman wa hadithan* (Cairo: Dar al-qawmiyya al-'arabiyya lil-tiba'a, 1963), 70–71; Ibrahim, *Copts of Egypt*, 39–67.

57. For example, see Mikhayil Mishaqa, *Jawab 'ala iqtirah al-ahbab*, trans. Wheeler M. Thackston Jr. as *Murder, Mayhem, Pillage, and Plunder: The History of the Lebanon in the 18th and 19th Centuries* (Albany: State University of New York Press, 1988), 250–251; see also Bustani, *'Ibra wa dhikra*, 95, 102.

58. Cited in Leyla Dakhli, "The Mahjar as Literary and Political Territory in the First Decades of the Twentieth Century: The Example of Amin Rihani (1876–1940)," in Dyala Hamzah, ed., *The Making of the Arab Intellectual: Empire, Public Sphere and the Colonial Coordinates of Selfhood* (London: Routledge, 2013), 167.

59. Louis Cheikho, "Al-tasahul al-dini," *Al-Machriq* 4 (1901): 373–377. For more on Cheikho, see Robert Bell Campbell, "The Arabic Journal, *Al-Machriq*: Its Beginnings and First Twenty-Five Years under the Editorship of Père Louis Cheikho, S. J.," PhD diss., University of Michigan, 1972.

60. Michael Laffan, "'Another Andalusia': Images of Colonial Southeast Asia in Arabic Newspapers," *Journal of Asian Studies* 66 (2007): 689–722; Aydin, *Idea of the Muslim World*; Ryad, *Islamic Reformism and Christianity*; Dyala Hamzah, *Muhammad Rashid Rida (1865–1935) ou le "Tournant salafiste"— Intérêt général, Islam et opinion publique dans l'Égypte coloniale* (Paris: Éditions du CNRS, forthcoming, 2019).

61. The description of reconciliation is Umar Ryad's in his "A Printed Muslim 'Lighthouse' in Cairo: *Al-Manar*'s Early Years, Aspiration and Reception (1898–1903)," *Arabica* 56 (2009): 42.

62. Rashid Rida, *Tarikh al-ustadh al-imam al-shaykh Muhammad Abduh*, vol. 1, part 1 (Beriut: Dar al-Fadila, 2003), 392. For the welcome of Copts, see Ibrahim, *Copts of Egypt*, 102. For attending of Coptic charity association, see Samir Seikaly, "Coptic Communal Reform: 1860–1914," *Middle Eastern Studies* 6 (1970): 252; for 'Urabi revolution, see Juan R. I. Cole, *Colonialism and Revolution in the Middle East: Social and Cultural Origins of Egypt's 'Urabi Movement* (Princeton, NJ: Princeton, 1993), 247.

63. Ryad, *Islamic Reformism and Christianity*, appendix IV.

64. For Qabbani, see Tarek El-Ariss, ed., *The Arab Renaissance: A Bilingual Anthology of the Nahda* (New York: Modern Language Association of America, 2018), 340–344. Abdelkader is cited in Itzchak Weismann, *Taste of Modernity: Sufism, Salafiyya, and Arabism in Late Ottoman Damascus* (Leiden, The Netherlands: Brill, 2001), 160.

65. Mestyan, *Arab Patriotism*, 277.

66. Rida, *Tarikh al-ustadh al-imam*, vol. 1, part 1, 415.

67. This is from Charles C. Adams, *Islam and Modernism in Egypt: A Study of the Modern Reform Movement Inaugurated by Muhammad 'Abduh* (New York: Russell & Russell, 1933), 116–117.

68. Muhammad Abduh, *Al-Islam wa al-nasraniyya* (Cairo: Matba'at majalat al-Manar, 1905), 13–14.

69. Rida, *Tarikh al-ustadh al-imam, vol. 1, part 1*, 403.

70. Aziz al-Azmeh, *Al-'almaniyya min manthur mukhtalif* (Beirut: Markaz al-dirasat al-wahda al-arabiyya, 2008), 151.

71. Mustafa Kamil, *Kitab al-mas'ala al-sharqiyya* (Cairo: Al-Adab, 1898), 9, 279–280, does not actually refer to Copts but to Eastern Christians such as Armenians, whom he denounced for rebelling against Ottoman authority but said could still be included in a Muslim sovereignty if they obeyed and appreciated their status; for Coptic inclusion, see Hourani, *Arabic Thought*, 207; Ibrahim, *Copts of Egypt*, 51.

72. Ibrahim, *Copts of Egypt*, 45–49, 54–55.

73. Ryad, *Islamic Reformism and Christianity*, 109.

74. At least according to Thomas Philipp's biography of Zaydan, *Jurji Zaydan and the Foundations of Arab Nationalism*, 46–47.

75. For Abduh's assessment of Christianity as intolerant, see Abduh, *Al-Islam wa al-nasraniyya*, 7–55. The crux of Shibili Nu'mani's criticisms against Zaydan was that Zaydan was, quite simply, unqualified to write a history of Islamic civilization: his choice of texts was suspect, his reading of them was outrageously selective, and his refusal to accept the testimony of the acknowledged Muslim chroniclers in scripting the history of Islam was scandalous. Nu'mani accused Zaydan of falsification, deceit, and dishonoring Arabs and Muslims: he made the incidental central, the minor major, and the specific general. Nu'mani's criticism was originally printed in Rida's journal *Al-Manar* and was reprinted in Rashid Rida, ed., *Kitab intiqad kitab tarikh al-tamaddun al-islami* (Cairo: Al-Manar, 1912), 1–76; for Cheikho's piece that was reprinted from *Al-Machriq*, see 127–146.

76. Jiha, *Al-munazara*, 121–122; for "religious books," 123; for "fanaticism," 126; see also Elshakry, *Reading Darwin*, 185–189.

77. Jiha, *Al-munazara*, 130.

78. Jiha, *Al-munazara*, 183–184.

79. Jiha, *Al-munazara*, 131.

80. Hourani, *Arabic Thought*, 255–256.

81. See also the Farid Kamil and Abdelaziz Jawish controversy in 1908 about Muslim and Coptic "fanaticism" in Kilani, *Al-adab al-qubti*, 72–80.

82. Paul Sedra, "Class Cleavages and Ethnic Conflict: Coptic Christian Communities in Modern Egyptian Politics," *Islam and Christian-Muslim Relations* 10 (1999): 224; see also Ibrahim, *Copts of Egypt*, 21–27; Seikaly, "Coptic Communal Reform"; for judicial affairs, see Magdi Guirguis, *Al-qada' al-qibti fi Misr: dirasa tarikhiyya* (Cairo: Mirit, 1999), 107–113.

83. Dakhli, "Mahjar as Literary and Political Territory in the First Decades of the Twentieth Century," 167–170.

84. Qasim Amin, *The Liberation of Women: A Document in the History of Egyptian Feminism*, trans. Samiha Sidhom Peterson (Cairo: American University in Cairo Press, 1992), 64, 66–67.

85. Toufoul Abou-Hodeib, *A Taste for Home: The Modern Middle Class in Ottoman Beirut* (Stanford, CA: Stanford University Press, 2017), 113–144; and Omnia Shakry, "Schooled Mothers and Structured Play: Child Rearing in Turn-of-the-Century Egypt," in Lila Abu-Lughod, ed., *Remaking Women: Feminism and Modernity in the Middle East* (Princeton, NJ: Princeton University Press, 1998), 126–170.

86. For Labiba Ahmad, see Beth Baron, *Egypt as Woman: Nationalism, Gender, and Politics* (Berkeley: University of California Press, 2005), 189–213. For Moyal, see Lital Levy, "Partitioned Pasts: Arab Jewish Intellectuals and the Case of Esther Azhari Moyal (1873–1948)," in Hamzah, *Making of the Arab Intellectual*, 128–163; Beth Baron, *The Women's Awakening in Egypt: Culture, Society, and the Press* (New Haven, CT: Yale University Press, 1997), 20–21.

87. Kenneth M. Cuno, *Modernizing Marriage: Family, Ideology, and Law in Nineteenth-and Early Twentieth-Century Egypt* (Syracuse, NY: Syracuse University Press, 2015); Chibli Mallat, *Introduction to Middle Eastern Law* (Oxford: Oxford University Press, 2007), 355–405.

88. See Article 58 of Ottoman Hukuk-i Aile Kararnamesi of 1917. However, all marriages now had to be reported and registered by the state. See Darina Martykanova, "Matching Sharia and 'Governmentality': Muslim Marriage Legislation in the Late Ottoman Empire," in Andrea Gémes, Florence Peyrou, and Ioannis Xydopolous, eds., *Institutional Change and Stability: Conflicts, Transitions and Social Values* (Pisa, Italy: PLUS-Pisa University Press, 2009), 153–175. For an older interpretation that stresses the law's conservatism, see Judith E. Tucker, "Revisiting Reform: Women and the Ottoman Law of Family Rights, 1917," *Arab Studies Journal* 4 (1996): 4–17.

89. John Rawls, "The Idea of an Overlapping Consensus," *Oxford Journal of Legal Studies* 7 (1987): 1–25.

90. Cited in Fatma Müge Göçek, ed., *Social Constructions of Nationalism in the Middle East* (Albany: State University of New York Press, 2002), 54; Abdurrahman Atçıl, "Decentralization, Imperialism, and Ottoman Sovereignty in the Arab Lands before 1914: Shakib Arslan's Polemic against the Decentralization Party," *Die Welt des Islams* 53 (2013): 26–49.

91. Yusuf al-Bustani, *Tarikh harb al-balqan al-ula* (n.p., 1913). Dyala Hamzah makes this same point about Bustani's contributors in her essay "From *'Ilm* to *Sihafa* or the Politics of the Public Interest (*Maslaha*): Muhammad Rashid Rida and His Journal *Al-Manar* (1898–1935)," in Hamzah, *Making of the Arab Intellectual*, 95. See also Eyal Ginio, "Making Sense of the Defeat of the Balkan Wars," in M. Hakan Yavuz and Isa Blumi, eds., *War and Nationalism: The*

Balkan Wars, 1912–1913, and Their Sociopolitical Implications (Salt Lake City: University of Utah Press, 2013), 594–617.

92. Compare Bustani and his interlocutors with the Carnegie Commission; for example, see Carnegie Endowment, *Report of the International Commission to Inquire into the Causes and Conduct of the Balkan Wars*, republished as *The Other Balkan Wars: A 1913 Carnegie Endowment in Retrospect* (Washington, DC: Carnegie Endowment, 1993 [1914]). For Ottoman officials, see Eyal Ginio, "Paving the Way for Ethnic Cleansing: Eastern Thrace during the Balkan Wars (1912–1913) and Their Aftermath," in Omer Bartov and Eric D. Weitz, eds., *Shatterzone of Empires: Coexistence and Violence in the German, Habsburg, Russian, and Ottoman Borderlands* (Bloomington: Indiana University Press, 2013), 283–297.

93. Cited in Bustani, *Tarikh harb al-balqan*, 322.

4. COLONIAL PLURALISM

1. *Al-Qibla,* Monday 15 Shawwal, 1334 (August 14, 1916), Issue 1. The editor of *Al-Qibla* was Muhhib al-Din al-Khatib, who would go on to found the Young Muslim Men's Association in Egypt and open the Salafist Nur bookstore in Cairo.

2. For a text of the Husayn-McMahon correspondence, see George Antonius, *The Arab Awakening: The Story of the Arab National Movement* (London: Hamish Hamilton, 1938), 413–427.

3. Yusuf Q. Khoury [Khuri], ed., *Al-Dasatir fir al-'alam al-'arabi: nusus wa ta'dilat: 1839–1987* (Beirut: Dar al-Hamra', 1989), 23–24; Elizabeth F. Thompson, "Rashid Rida and the 1920 Syrian-Arab Constitution: How the French Mandate Undermined Islamic Liberalism," in Cyrus Schayegh and Andrew Arsan, eds., *The Routledge Handbook of the History of the Middle East Mandates* (Milton Park, UK: Routledge, 2015), 244–257.

4. "The Mandate for Syria and Lebanon, July 24th, 1922," reproduced in A. H. Hourani, *Syria and Lebanon: A Political Essay* (Oxford: Royal Institute of International Affairs and Oxford University Press, 1946), 310.

5. On the politics of minorities, see Laura Robson, *States of Separation: Transfer, Partition, and the Making of the Modern Middle East* (Oakland: University of California Press, 2017), 30–34; and Carole Fink, *Defending the Rights of Others: The Great Powers, the Jews, and International Minority Protection* (Cambridge: Cambridge University Press, 2004). On the non-application of "minority" treaties in the mandates, see Benjamin Thomas White, *The Emergence of Minorities in the Middle East: The Politics of Community in French Mandate Syria* (Edinburgh: Edinburgh University Press, 2011), 132–133; see also Karen Barkey and George Gavrilis, "The Ottoman Millet System: Non-

territorial Autonomy and Its Contemporary Legacy," *Ethnopolitics* 15 (2016): 24–42.

6. Michael Provence, "Liberal Colonialism and Martial Law in French Mandate Syria," in Christoph Schumann, ed., *Liberal Thought in the Eastern Mediterranean: Late 19th Century until the 1960s* (Leiden, The Netherlands: Brill, 2008), 62.

7. Mahmood Mamdani, *Citizen and Subject: Contemporary Africa and the Legacy of Late Colonialism* (Princeton, NJ: Princeton University Press, 1996), 38–39.

8. Gérard D. Khoury, "Robert de Caix et Louis Massignon: Deux visions de la politique française au Levant en 1920," in Nadine Méouchy and Peter Sluglett, eds., *The British and French Mandates in Comparative Perspectives* (Leiden, The Netherlands: Brill, 2004), 169. My translation.

9. N. E. Bou-Nacklie, "Les Troupes Spéciales: Religious and Ethnic Recruitment, 1916–46," *International Journal of Middle East Studies* 25 (1993): 645–660; Daniel Neep, *Occupying Syria under the French Mandate: Insurgency, Space and State Formation* (Cambridge: Cambridge University Press, 2012), 34. In the words of historian Keith Watenpaugh, the Armenian survivors of the Ottoman Turkish genocide entered into a dynamic "survivors' bargain" that, in Watenpaugh's view, was essential to the preservation of the Armenian community. Keith D. Watenpaugh, "Towards a New Category of Colonial Theory: Colonial Cooperation and the Survivors' Bargain—the Case of the Post-Genocide Armenian Community of Syria under the French Mandate," in Méouchy and Sluglett, *British and French Mandates*, 603.

10. Philip S. Khoury, *Syria and the French Mandate: The Politics of Arab Nationalism, 1920-1945* (Princeton, NJ: Princeton University Press, 1987), 206; see also 53, 81. For more on the cultivation and patronage of minorities in the mandates, see Seda Altug, "Sectarianism in the Syrian Jazira: Community, Land, and Violence in the Memories of World War One and the French Mandate," PhD diss., Utrecht University, 2011, 68–70, 166–196; Elizabeth Thompson, *Colonial Citizens: Republican Rights, Paternal Privilege, and Gender in French Syria and Lebanon* (New York: Columbia University Press, 2000), 82.

11. Uğur Üngör, *The Making of Modern Turkey: Nation and State in Eastern Anatolia, 1913-1950* (Oxford: Oxford University Press, 2011); Zeynep Turkyilmaz, "Maternal Colonialism and Turkish Woman's Burden in Dersim: Educating the 'Mountain Flowers' of Dersim," *Journal of Women's History* 28 (2016): 162–186.

12. Roger Owen and Şevket Pamuk, *A History of Middle East Economies in the Twentieth Century* (London: I. B. Tauris, 1998), 51–75. See also Asher Kaufman, *Contested Frontiers in the Syria-Lebanon-Israel Region: Cartography, Sovereignty, and Conflict* (Baltimore: Johns Hopkins University Press, 2013).

13. Recent work has emphasized, in fact, how hundreds of Arab officers in the Ottoman army had invested in an Ottoman future. Many of these officers were integrated into the new national armies of Syria and Iraq. See Laila Parsons, *The Commander: Fawzi Al-Qawuqji and the Fight for Arab Independence 1914–1948* (New York: Hill and Wang, 2016); and Michael Provence, *The Last Ottoman Generation and the Making of the Modern Middle East* (Cambridge: Cambridge University Press, 2017).

14. For more on these debates and the complexity of Maronite intellectual and political perspectives before the establishment of the mandate, see Carol Hakim, *The Origins of the Lebanese National Idea 1840–1920* (Berkeley: University of California Press, 2013). For a detailed discussion of the case of Kurds and Christians and the question of minorities in Syria during the mandate, see Altug, "Sectarianism in the Syrian Jazira," 225–228, 244–246. For Jewish responses, see Robson, *States of Separation*, 142–145.

15. Michel Aflaq, *Fi Sabil al-Ba'th*, cited in Hanna Batatu, *The Old Social Classes and the Revolutionary Movements of Iraq: A Study of Iraq's Old Landed and Commercial Classes and of Its Communists, Ba'thists and Free Officers* (Princeton, NJ: Princeton University Press, 1978), 737.

16. Amin Rihani, "Al-nahda al-sharqiyya al-haditha," *Al-Muqtataf* (May 1927), 490. I thank Esmat Elhalaby for this reference. The prior reference to the "green baize table" is, of course, from Frantz Fanon, *The Wretched of the Earth* (New York: Grove Weidenfeld, 1963), 61.

17. Rihani, "Al-nahda al-sharqiyya al-haditha," 489–490.

18. Khoury, *Syria and the French Mandate;* Keith David Watenpaugh, *Being Modern in the Middle East: Revolution, Nationalism, Colonialism, and the Arab Middle Class* (Princeton, NJ: Princeton University Press, 2006), 245.

19. Will Hanley, "Grieving Cosmopolitanism in Middle East Studies," *History Compass* 6 (2008): 1346–1367; Vivian Ibrahim, "Beyond the Cross and the Crescent: Plural Identities and the Copts in Contemporary Egypt," *Ethnic and Racial Studies* 38 (2015): 2584–2597; for an older criticism of nationalism, see James L. Gelvin, *Divided Loyalties: Nationalism and Mass Politics in Syria at the Close of Empire* (Berkeley: University of California Press, 1998).

5. SECTARIANISM AND ANTISECTARIANISM

1. This is drawn directly from Albert Hourani, *A History of the Arab Peoples*, 2nd ed. (Cambridge, MA: Belknap Press of Harvard University Press, 2002), 333–345.

2. For the complexity in the lead-up to the creation of Greater Lebanon in 1920, see Carol Hakim, *The Origins of the Lebanese National Idea 1840–1920* (Berkeley: University of California Press, 2013); and Kamal Salibi, *A House of*

Many Mansions: The History of Lebanon Reconsidered (London: I. B. Tauris, 1988).

3. Edmond Rabbath, *La formation historique du Liban politique et constitutionnel: Essai de synthèse,* nouvelle édition (Beirut: Publications de l'Université Libanaise, 1986), 371–373; for an example of opposition, see Wadad Makdisi Cortas, *A World I Loved: The Story of an Arab Woman* (New York: Nation Books, 2009), 15–16, 80–81.

4. For the famine politics, see Melanie S. Tanielian, *The Charity of War: Famine, Humanitarian Aid, and World War I in the Middle East* (Stanford, CA: Stanford University Press, 2017); see also Maïssa Jalloul, "Une histoire en clair-obscur: 1860 dans La Revue phénicienne (1919)," in Dima de Clerc, Carla Eddé, Naila Kaidbey, and Souad Slim, eds., *1860: Histoires et mémoires d'un conflit* (Beirut: IFPO, 2015), 363–386.

5. Cited in Asher Kaufman, *Reviving Phoenicia: The Search for Identity in Lebanon* (London: I. B. Tauris, 2004), 91–92. The translation from French is my own.

6. Jalloul, "Une histoire en clair-obscur," 364, where Jalloul attributes the phrase "récit chrétien de la victimisation" to Nadine Picaudou. On Corm, see also Kaufman, *Reviving Phoenicia.*

7. For collaboration, see Michel Chiha, "Contre la servilité," *Le Jour* (December 12, 1934), http://michelchiha.org/editorials/1934/29/6/. For a critical evaluation of Michel Chiha, see Michelle Hartmann and Alessandro Olsaretti, "'The First Boat and the First Oar': Inventions of Lebanon in the Writings of Michel Chiha," *Radical History Review* 86 (2003): 37–65. See also Fawwaz Traboulsi, *Silat bila wasl: Michel Chiha wa al-idiyulujiyya al-lubnaniyya* (Beirut: Riad el-Rayyes Books, 1999), which I have drawn on.

8. For Thomas Jefferson, see First Inaugural Address (March 4, 1801), The Avalon Project at Yale Law School, http://avalon.law.yale.edu/19th_century/jefinau1.asp. On Chiha and minorities, see Hartmann and Olesseti, "First Boat and the First Oar," 49. See also Benjamin Thomas White, *The Emergence of Minorities in the Middle East: The Politics of Community in French Mandate Syria* (Edinburgh: Edinburgh University Press, 2011); and Laura Robson, *States of Separation: Transfer, Partition, and the Making of the Modern Middle East* (Oakland: University of California Press, 2017); both of the latter deal with the question of minorities from the perspective of the French colonial officials and the League of Nations, respectively.

9. Michel Chiha, *Politique intérieure* (Beirut: Éditions du Trident, 1964), 135. See also Michel Chiha, *Liban d'aujourd'hui* (Beirut: Fondation Chiha, 1994 [1949]), 42–43, 59, 65.

10. Claude Doumet-Serhal and Michèle Hélou-Nahas, eds., *Michel Chiha: 1891–1954* (Beirut: Fondation Michel Chiha, 2001), 76–91.

11. For one of the earliest explorations of the term, see Adib Farhat, "Al-ta'ifiyya wa adwariha," *Al-'Irfan* 22 (1931): 17–31.

12. Edmond Rabbath, *La constitution libanaise: Origines, textes, et commentaires* (Beirut: Publications de l'Université Libanaise, 1982), 26. Translation mine.

13. Rabbath, *La constitution libanaise*, 27. For another perspective that echoes Rabbath, see Mark Farha, "Secularism in a Sectarian Society? The Divisive Drafting of the Lebanese Constitution of 1926," in Aslı Ü. Bali and Hanna Lerner, eds., *Constitution Writing, Religion and Democracy* (Cambridge: Cambridge University Press, 2017), 101–130.

14. Muhammad Dakrub, *Judhur al-sindiyana al-hamra'*, 3rd ed. (Beirut: Farabi, 2007 [1974]). For "nonsectarianism," p. 471; for "greatest obstacle," p. 482.

15. Shafiq Jiha, ed., *Al-dustur al-lubnani* (Beirut: Dar al-'ilm lil-malayin, 1991), 117.

16. Chiha, *Politique intérieure*, 116.

17. Chiha, *Politique intérieure*, 305.

18. Rabbath, *La constitution libanaise*, 518–519.

19. Meir Zamir, *Lebanon's Quest: The Road to Statehood 1926–1939* (London: I. B. Tauris, 2000), 47.

20. See, for instance, the complaint of the Shi'i Yusuf Zayn in parliamentary session of January 1, 1928, regarding the formation of Bishara Khuri's government in Yusuf Q. Khoury [Khuri], *Al-bayanat al-wizariyya al-lubnaniyya wa munaqashatuha fi majli al-nuwwab, 1926–1984, vol. 1* (Beirut: mu'assasat al-dirasat al-lubnaniyya, 1986), 10–11; see also Zamir, *Lebanon's Quest*, 58.

21. Cited in Ahmad Beydoun, *Al-sira' 'ala tarikh lubnan: aw al-hawiyya wa al-zaman fi a'mal mu'arrikhina al-mu'asirin* (Beirut: Publications de l'université libanaise, 1989), 172, n. 55. Max Weiss, *In the Shadow of Sectarianism: Law, Shi'ism, and the Making of Modern Lebanon* (Cambridge, MA: Harvard University Press, 2010), 122, 126–129, argues strongly for Shi'i sectarianization from above (prompted by the mandate) and from below and illustrates how Shi'i institutionalization (especially judicial institutionalization) increased dramatically during the mandate; see also Linda Sayed, "Sectarian Homes: The Making of Shi'i Families and Citizens under the French Mandate 1918–1943," PhD diss., Columbia University, 2013.

22. Farid al-Khazen, *The Communal Pact of National Identities: The Making and Politics of the 1943 National Pact* (Oxford: Centre for Lebanese Studies, 1991). See also, for a criticism of this pact, Michael Johnson, *All Honorable Men: The Social Origins of War in Lebanon* (London: Centre for Lebanese Studies and I. B. Tauris, 2001).

23. Rabbath, *La formation historique du Liban*, 543. This is the same backroom deal that political scientist Arend Lijphart hailed in 1969 as a model for "consociational democracy." See Arend Lijphart, "Consociational Democracy," reprinted in *Thinking about Democracy: Power Sharing and Majority Rule in Theory and Practice* (London: Routledge, 2008), 24–41.

24. Cabinet Declaration of September 25, 1943, www.pcm.gov.lb/arabic/subpg .aspx?pageid = 268; see also Johnson, *All Honorable Men,* 143; Fawwaz Traboulsi, *A History of Modern Lebanon,* 2nd ed. (London: Pluto Press, 2007), 110–112.

25. Reproduced at www.pcm.gov.lb/arabic/subpg.aspx?pageid = 268. For other political programs calling for the abolition of political sectarianism, see Yusuf Q. Khoury [Khuri], ed., *Al-ta'ifiyya fi Lubnan min khilal munaqashat majlis al-nuwwab 1923-1987* (Beirut: Dar al-Hamra', 1989); see p. 71 for Riyad al-Sulh's cabinet declaration of 1947.

26. A point well made by Mahdi Amil, *Fi al-dawla al-ta'ifiyya* (Beirut: Dar al-Farabi, 1986), 21–24.

27. Chiha, *Politique intérieure,* 303–306. See Maya Mikdashi, "Sectarianism: Notes on Studying the Lebanese State," in Amal Ghazal and Jens Hanssen, eds., *The Oxford Handbook of Contemporary Middle-Eastern and North African History* (Oxford: Oxford University Press, published online June 2018, DOI: 10.1093 /oxfordhb/9780199672530.013.24). This distinction between "modern" and "traditional" domains of law recalls Mamdani's argument in *Citizen and Subject.*

28. Rabbath, *La constitution libanaise,* 517.

29. Rania Maktabi, "The Lebanese Census of 1932 Revisited. Who Are the Lebanese?" *British Journal of Middle Eastern Studies* 26 (1999): 219–241.

30. The two most interesting accounts of this war date back to the late 1980s. See Salibi, *House of Many Mansions;* and Beydoun, *Al-sira' 'ala tarikh lubnan.*

31. For more on mandate-era education, see Jennifer M. Dueck, *The Claims of Culture at Empire's End: Syria and Lebanon under French Rule* (Oxford: Oxford University Press, 2010), 91–111.

32. Chiha, *Politique intérieure,* 109.

33. See Lamia Shehadi, Suad Slim, Maher Jarrar, and Nader al-Bizri, eds., *Asad Rustum: Mu'assis 'ilm al-tarikh fi al-'alam al-'arabi* (Beirut: AUB and Dar al-Farabi, 2015), 56–58, 182. See also Asher Kaufman (*Reviving Phoenicia,* 117–119), who says that the Rustum and Bustani book was widely adopted; and Salibi (*House of Many Mansions,* 203–204), who asserts that Muslim opposition prevented its "official adoption" in state schools.

34. Asad Rustum and Fouad Efram Bustani, *Tarikh lubnan al-mujaz* (Beirut: al-matba'a al-kathulikiyya, 1937), 114; see also Dima de Clerck, "Histoire officelle et mémoires en conflit dans le Sud du Mon-Liban: Les affrontements druzo-chrétiens du XIXe siècle," *Revue des mondes musulmans et de la Méditerranée* 135 (2014): 171–190.

35. Zaki al-Naqqash and 'Umar Farrukh, *Tarikh Suriyya wa Lubnan al-musawwar* (Beirut: Matba'at al-Kashshaf, 1933), 131–132.

36. Fawwaz Traboulsi, *History of Modern Lebanon,* 118; see also Hartmann and Olsaretti, "First Boat and the First Oar," 43, for a criticism of Chiha's ideology and its links to the nexus of a financial bourgeoisie and landowning class of Lebanon.

37. Pierre Gemayel, "Lebanese Nationalism and Its Foundations: The Phalangist Viewpoint," in Kemal H. Karpat, ed., *Political and Social Thought in the Contemporary Middle East* (New York: Praeger, 1968), 112–113.

38. For example, see Antun Saadeh, "Al-hizbiyya al-diniyya la'natu al-umma," *Kull shay'* (Beirut), April 1, 1949, reproduced online at http://antoun-saadeh .com. See also *Mithaq al-hizb al-taqaddumi al-ishtiraki* (Beirut: Dar al-Ahad, n.d.), 69, 66.

39. One of the very few books that attempt to deal with labor mobilization in the mandate era is Malek Abisaab, *Militant Women of a Fragile Nation* (Syracuse, NY: Syracuse University Press, 2010).

40. The definitive biography of Sati' al-Husri remains William L. Cleveland, *The Making of an Arab Nationalist: Ottomanism and Arabism in the Life and Thought of Sati' al-Husri* (Princeton, NJ: Princeton University Press, 1971). For Husri's educational project, see Sara Pursley, *Familiar Futures: Time, Selfhood, and Sovereignty in Iraq* (Stanford, CA: Stanford University Press, 2019), 57–105.

41. The criticism of Husri as merely "Sunni" or "sectarian" has been especially in vogue since the U.S. invasion of Iraq. See Eric Davis, *Memories of State: Politics, History, and Collective Identity in Modern Iraq* (Berkeley: University of California Press, 2005), 57; see also Robson, *States of Separation,* 89. For an older view on the allegedly pernicious influences of the "populist Germanophile Arab nationalism" of Husri, see Bassam Tibi, *Arab Nationalism: Between Islam and the Nation-State,* 3rd ed. (London: Macmillan, 1997), 118. For a more nuanced perspective, see Fanar Haddad, *Sectarianism in Iraq: Antagonistic Visions of Unity* (London: Hurst, 2011), 43.

42. Amin Rihani, *Qalb al-Iraq: Rihalat wa tarikh* (Beirut: Dar al-jil, n.d.), 221.

43. See Dina Rizk Khoury, "Reflections on Nationality and Sect in Iraqi History," The Fourteenth Annual Wadie Jwaideh Memorial Lecture, Department of Near Eastern Languages and Cultures, University of Indiana, Bloomington, IL, October 15, 2015.

44. Pursley, *Familiar Futures,* 34; Peter Sluglett, *Britain in Iraq: Contriving King and Country* (New York: Columbia University Press, 2007), 193–209; Toby Dodge, *Inventing Iraq: The Failure of Nation Building and a History Denied* (New York: Columbia University Press, 2003); Orit Bashkin, *The Other Iraq: Pluralism and Culture in Hashemite Iraq* (Stanford, CA: Stanford University Press, 2009), 231.

45. Hanna Batatu, *The Old Social Classes and the Revolutionary Movements of Iraq: A Study of Iraq's Old Landed and Commercial Classes and of Its Communists, Ba'thists and Free Officers* (Princeton, NJ: Princeton University Press, 1978), 23–28; Sluglett, *Britain in Iraq,* 42–64.

46. "La Da'i lil-ya's," reprinted in Abu Khaldun Sati' al-Husri, *Safahat min al-madi al-qarib* (Beirut: Markaz dirasat al-wahda al-'arabiyya, 1985 [1948]), 74.

47. Abu Khaldun Sati' al-Husri, *Naqd taqrir lajnat Munru* (Baghdad: Matba'at al-najah, 1932), 27–28.

48. Sati' al-Husri, *Mudhakirrati fil Iraq, 1921–1941, vol. 1* (Beirut: Dar al-tali'a, 1967), 318–319; Husri, *Naqd taqrir lajnat Munru*, 48.

49. Husri openly admired the eighteenth-century Swiss democratic educator Johann Pestalozzi, whose bust he kept in his office in Baghdad; see Cleveland, *Making of an Arab Nationalist*, 87. For "sectarian passions," see Husri, *Naqd taqrir lajnat munru*, 48.

50. For numbers of schools, see 'Abd al-Razzaq al-Hilali, *Tarikh al-ta'lim fi al-Iraq fi 'ahd al-intidab al-britani 1921–1932* (Baghdad: Dar al-shu'un al-thaqafiyya al-'amma, 2000), 105, 117–118.

51. Iraq's budget allocation increased from around 1 percent of the budget in 1919 to 10 percent in 1935. Cited in Hilary Falb Kalisman, "Bursary Scholars at the American University of Beirut: Living and Practicing Arab Unity," *British Journal of Middle Eastern Studies* 42 (2015): 602, n. 14.

52. Pursley, *Familiar Futures*, 48, 57–58.

53. Ni'am K. El-Hashimi, "The Higher Teachers College, Baghdad: A History, 1923–1958," master's thesis, American University of Beirut, 1963, 109, indicates that these regulations were in place by 1930. See also Roderic D. Matthews and Matta Akrawi, *Education in Arab Countries of the Near East: Egypt, Iraq, Palestine, Transjordan, Syria, Lebanon* (Washington, DC: American Council on Education, 1949), 189, who indicate that these regulations were in practice by 1945.

54. See "Letter Ten," published on October 9, 1932, in Husri, *Naqd taqrir lajnat Munru*, 125–129. See also Pursley, *Familiar Futures*, 77, 94.

55. For rejection of racial or ethnic nationalism, see Adrien Zakar, "The End of Ottoman Positivism: The Gökalp-al-Husri Debate of 1916," *International Journal of Middle East Studies* 47 (2015): 580–583; and Tibi, *Arab Nationalism*, 161–163. For a nuanced discussion of language in Husri, see Yasir Suleiman, *The Arabic Language and National Identity: A Study in Ideology* (Edinburgh: Edinburgh University Press, 2003), 126–146.

56. Bashkin, *Other Iraq*, 182–184.

57. Husri, *Mudhakirrati fil Iraq, 1921–1941, vol. 1*, 80.

58. Darwish al-Miqdadi, *Tarikh al-umma al-'arabiyya* (Baghdad: Dar al-tiba'a al-haditha, 1936), 2.

59. For family law and "tribalization" of women in Iraq, see Noga Efrati, *Women in Iraq: Past Meets Present* (New York: Columbia University Press, 2012), 40–47.

60. Cleveland, *Making of an Arab Nationalist*, 79.

61. For "religion of Arabism," see Cleveland, *Making of an Arab Nationalist*, 70; for support of conscription in 1934, see pp. 166–167. For "total" freedom, see Husri's speech about the collapse of France to Germany, in which he wondered why so many Arabs sympathized with their French colonial oppressor; he

insisted that German nationalism was mischaracterized, especially by "parasitic," presumably Jewish, refugees in France. This was, I believe, one of the most jarring notes in Husri's speeches and writings. See Abu Khaldun Sati' al-Husri, "Hawla inhiyar Faransa," in *Safahat min al-madi al-qarib*, 25–42.

62. Husri, *Mudhakkirati fi al-Iraq, vol. 1;* for "sectarians," see p. 566; for prejudice against female Christian teachers, see p. 413. For opposition to female teaching in Basra and Najaf, see Hilali, *Tarikh al-ta'lim fi al-Iraq*, 120–124; Ali al-Wardi, *Dirasa fi tabi'at al-mujtama' al-'iraqi* (Baghdad: Mataba'at al-'ani, 1965), 346–349.

63. See Husri, *Mudhakkirati fi al-Iraq, vol. 1*, 597, for the word "intense," which he used in reference to Jawahiri's poem. For the firing of Jawahiri, see Bashkin, *Other Iraq*, 170. For resentment of ministers of education, see Cleveland, *Making of an Arab Nationalist*, 68.

64. Husri, *Mudhakkirati fi al-Iraq, vol. 1*, 564; see also Bashkin, *Other Iraq*, 48–49.

65. For this aspect of the Jawahiri incident, see Muhammad Mahdi al-Jawahri, *Dhikrayati, vol. 1* (Damascus: Dar al-Rafidayn, 1988), 141–142.

66. Rihani, *Qalb al-Iraq*, 221.

67. Bashkin, *Other Iraq*, 182–185.

68. Pursley, *Familiar Futures*, 84–89.

69. Rihani, *Qalb al-Iraq*, 220.

70. *Report by His Britannic Majesty's Government on the Administration of 'Iraq for the Period April 1923–December 1924* (Geneva: League of Nations, 1925), 22.

71. Robson, *States of Separation*, 39–56.

72. For an interpretation of these events that focuses on the League of Nations perspective, see Robson, *States of Separation*, 83–90.

73. The refusal to take citizenship is according to Khaldun S. Husry, "The Assyrian Affair of 1933 (I)," *International Journal of Middle East Studies* 5 (1974): 170. See also Sami Zubaida, "Contested Nations: Iraq and the Assyrians," *Nations and Nationalism* 6 (2000): 363–382.

74. Robson, *States of Separation*, 86–87; Husry, "Assyrian Affair of 1933 (I)," 168–172. Sargon George Donabed, *Reforging a Forgotten History: Iraq and the Assyrians in the Twentieth Century* (Edinburgh: Edinburgh University Press, 2015), 96–100; for rifles, see *Iraq Administration Reports 1914–1932, vol. 10: 1931–1932* (Archived Editions, 1992), 476.

75. Husry, "Assyrian Affair of 1933 (I)," 169, 172.

76. Robson, *States of Separation*, 87–88; for an Iraqi government perspective, see Al-Sayyid 'Abd al-Razzaq al-Husayni, *Tarikh al-wizarat al-'iraqiyya fi al-'ahd al-malaki, vol. 3* (Baghdad: Dar al-shu'un al-thaqafiyya al-'amma, 1988), 254–306.

77. Sami Zubaida, "The Fragments Imagine the Nation: The Case of Iraq," *International Journal of Middle East Studies* 34 (2002): 205–215.

78. Husry, "Assyrian Affair of 1933 (I)," 161.

79. Abdullah al-'Alayli, *Dustur al-'arab al-qawmi* (Beirut: Dar al-jadid, 1996 [1941]), 178.

80. Khaldun S. Husry, "The Assyrian Affair of 1933 (II)," *International Journal of Middle East Studies* 5 (1974): 352. See also Bashkin, *Other Iraq*, 52–86; Donabed, *Reforging a Forgotten History*, 122.

81. Christoph Schumann, "The Generation of Broad Expectations: Nationalism, Education and Autobiography in Syria and Lebanon, 1930–1958," and Peter Wein, "Waiting for the Superman: A New Generation of Arab Nationalists in 1930s Iraq," in Dyala Hamzah, ed., *The Making of the Arab Intellectual* (London: Routledge, 2013); for the case of Iraq, see Eric Davis, "The Political Economy of Modern Iraq," in David S. Sorenson, ed., *Interpreting the Middle East: Essential Themes* (New York: Westview Press, 2010), 344; for Egypt, see Joel Beinin and Zachary Lockman, *Workers on the Nile: Nationalism, Communism, Islam, and the Egyptian Working Class, 1882–1954* (Cairo: American University in Cairo Press, 1998).

6. BREAKING THE ECUMENICAL FRAME

1. See Shira Robinson's excellent study of the "liberal settler state," *Citizen Strangers: Palestinians and the Birth of Israel's Liberal Settler State* (Stanford, CA: Stanford University Press, 2013); see also Gabriel Piterberg, *The Returns of Zionism: Myths, Politics and Scholarship in Israel* (London: Verso, 2008); Jacqueline Rose, *Question of Zion* (Princeton, NJ: Princeton University Press, 2005); and Patrick Wolfe, *Traces of History: Elementary Structures of Race* (London: Verso, 2016).

2. The vital work of Michelle U. Campos situates the Ottoman landscape of this coexistence in Palestine; see Campos, *Ottoman Brothers: Muslims, Christians, and Jews in Early-Twentieth Century Palestine* (Stanford, CA: Stanford University Press, 2011). See also Yuval Ben-Bassat and Eyal Ginio, eds., *Late Ottoman Palestine: The Period of Young Turk Rule* (London: I. B. Tauris, 2011).

3. Salim Tamari, *Mountain against the Sea: Essays on Palestinian Society and Culture* (Berkeley: University of California Press, 2009); Rashid Khalidi, *Palestinian Identity: The Construction of Modern National Consciousness* (New York: Columbia University Press, 1997); and Cyrus Schayegh, *The Middle East and the Making of the Modern World* (Cambridge, MA: Harvard University Press, 2017).

4. Ilan Pappe, *The Rise and Fall of a Palestinian Dynasty: The Husaynis 1700–1948* (Berkeley: University of California Press, 2010), 167. For Christian teachers, see 137–138.

5. Figures are approximate. Charles D. Smith, *Palestine and the Arab-Israeli Conflict: A History with Documents,* 9th ed. (Boston: Bedford/St. Martin's, 2017), 25; Laura Robson, *Colonialism and Christianity in Mandate Palestine* (Austin: University of Texas Press, 2011), 165, n. 3.

6. Campos, *Ottoman Brothers;* see also Ben-Bassat and Ginio, *Late Ottoman Palestine;* Abigail Jacobson and Moshe Naor, *Oriental Neighbors: Middle Eastern Jews and Arabs in Mandatory Palestine* (Waltham, MA: Brandeis University Press, 2016) settle on the term "oriental" to describe Arab Jews but also use terms such as "Arab-Jewish" identity and illustrate how Sephardic and Oriental Jewish leaders were increasingly concerned to show loyalty to the Ashkenazi-dominated Yishuv during the Mandate.

7. Shahin Makaryus, *Tarikh al-Isra'iliyyin* (Cairo: Matba'at al-Muqtataf, 1904), 202–203; Jonathan Marc Gribetz, *Defining Neighbors: Religion, Race, and the Early Zionist-Arab Encounter* (Princeton, NJ: Princeton University Press, 2014); Ben-Bassat and Ginio, *Late Ottoman Palestine.* See also Khalidi, *Palestinian Identity,* 75, 80–81, for the case of Yusuf Diya' al-Khalidi and Ruhi al-Khalidi. See also Gershon Shafir, *Land, Labor and the Origins of the Israeli-Palestinian Conflict, 1882–1914* (Cambridge: Cambridge University Press, 1989); Tom Segev, *One Palestine, Complete: Jews and Arabs under the British Mandate,* trans. Haim Watzman (New York: Metropolitan Books, 2000), 105. For an older interpretation, see Neville J. Mandel, *The Arabs and Zionism before World War I* (Berkeley: University of California Press, 1976), 32–57.

8. Jurji Zaydan, "Al-musta'marat al-yahudiyya fi Filastin," *Al-Hilal* 22 (1914): 518–520; and translated by Anne-Laure Dupont, *Ğurğī Zaydān (1861–1914): Écrivain réformiste et témoin de la Renaissance arabe* (Damascus: Institut Français du Proche-Orient, 2006), 705–709.

9. Smith, *Palestine and the Arab-Israeli Conflict,* 31.

10. Cited in Steven J. Zipperstein, *Elusive Prophet: Ahad Ha'am and the Origins of Zionism* (Berkeley: University of California Press, 1993), 246–247.

11. Zaydan, "Al musta'marat al-yahudiyya," *Al-Hilal* 22 (1914): 520. See Gribetz, *Defining Neighbors,* for an elaboration of the transformation of attitudes; see also Smith, *Palestine and the Arab-Israeli Conflict,* 33–38.

12. Campos, *Ottoman Brothers,* 158–165; Julia Phillips Cohen, *Becoming Ottomans: Sephardi Jews and Imperial Citizenship in the Modern Era* (Oxford: Oxford University Press, 2014); Orit Bashkin, *New Babylonians: A History of Jews in Modern Iraq* (Stanford, CA: Stanford University Press, 2012), 20–22.

13. James Renton, "Flawed Foundations: The Balfour Declaration and the Palestine Mandate," in Rory Miller, ed., *Britain, Palestine and Empire: The Mandate Years* (Farnham, UK: Ashgate, 2010), 15–38; Jehuda Reinharz, "The Balfour Declaration and Its Maker: A Reassessment," *Journal of Modern History* 64 (1992): 455–499.

14. "The Zionist Organization's Memorandum to the Supreme Council at the Peace Conference, 3 February 1919," in J. C. Hurewitz, ed., *The Middle East and North Africa in World Politics: A Documentary Record, vol. 2*, 2nd ed. (New Haven, CT: Yale University Press, 1979), 138–141.

15. Chaim Weizmann to Arthur Balfour, May 30, 1918, reproduced in Dvorah Barzilay and Barnett Litvinoff, eds., *The Letters and Papers of Chaim Weizmann, Series A Papers, vol. 8: November 1917–October 1918* (Rutgers, NJ: Transaction Books, 1977), 198.

16. For "rich Jews," see Weizmann to Balfour, May 30, 1918, 199. For Sephardic Jews, see Abigail Jacobson, *From Empire to Empire: Jerusalem between Ottomanism and British Rule* (Syracuse, NY: Syracuse University Press, 2011), 150–151.

17. Chaim Weizmann, "Plea for Friendship and Peace," April 27, 1918, reproduced in *The Letters and Papers of Chaim Weizmann, Series B Papers, vol. 1, August 1898–July 1931* (New Brunswick, NJ: Transaction Books, 1983), 182–183.

18. Anita Shapira, "Ben-Gurion and the Bible: The Forging of an Historical Narrative?" *Middle Eastern Studies* 33 (1997): 649.

19. Smith, *Palestine and the Arab-Israeli Conflict*, 116.

20. Robson, *Colonialism and Christianity in Mandate Palestine*, 46.

21. See Weizmann to Balfour, May 30, 1918, 201.

22. Schayegh, *Middle East the Making of the Modern World*, 154–155.

23. Muhammad Kurd Ali, *Kitab Khitat al-Sham, vol. 1* (Damascus: al-matba'a al-haditha, 1925), 70. He wondered, however, whether after two or three generations they would eventually learn Arabic and become Arab or force the Arabs of Palestine to learn Hebrew.

24. Bayan Nuwayhed al-Hout, *Al-qiyadat wa al-mu'assasat al-siyasiyya fi Filastin 1917–1948* (Beirut: Mu'assasat al-dirasat al-filastiniyya, 1981), 95–100; Jacobson, *From Empire to Empire*, 156–157; Robson, *Colonialism and Christianity in Mandate Palestine*, 40–41. For "cornerstone," see Pappe, *Rise and Fall of a Palestinian Dynasty*, 191.

25. Shakib Arslan, *A'mal al-wafd al-suri al-filastini* (Beirut: Al-dar al-taqaddumiyya, 2008).

26. "Protest of Exiled Palestinians to the Paris Peace Conference and to the British Foreign Office about Zionism and the Situation in Palestine, 12 December, 1918," reproduced in 'Abd al-Wahab al-Kayyali, ed., *Watha'iq al-muqawama al-filastiniyya al-'arabiyya* (Beirut: Mu'assasat al-dirasat al-filastiniyya, 1988 [1968]), 2. Inevitably, anti-Zionist associations also spoke about "the Jews" (*al-yahud*) as a singular group, blurring the very important distinction they also made between native Jews (*wataniyyin*) and foreign Zionist Jews (*al-sayhuniyyun* or *al-ajanib*). Gribetz (*Defining Neighbors*, 235–237) makes this point about

hardening boundaries, but it seems fairly clear that these associations were responding to the extreme privileging of Jews over non-Jews in the Balfour Declaration and the radical demands presented by Zionist organizations at the Paris Peace Conference.

27. "Protest of Exiled Palestinians," 2. See also "Petition of Muslim-Christian Association to Paris Peace Conference, March 3, 1919," reproduced in Kayyali, *Watha'iq*, 9, for the same phrase about Zionism's instigation of "religious fanaticism" in the "twentieth century."

28. Khalil al-Sakakini, *Yawmiyyat Khalil al-Sakakini, vol. 3: "Ikhtibar" al-intidab wa as'ilat al-hawiyya, 1919-1922* (Ramallah and Jerusalem: Khalil Sakakini Cultural Centre and Institute of Jerusalem Studies, 2004), 219. See also Awad Halabi, "Islamic Ritual and Palestinian Nationalism: al-Hajj Amin al-Husayni and the Nabi Musa Festival in Jerusalem, 1921-1937," in Lena Jayyusi, ed., *Jerusalem Interrupted: Modernity and Colonial Transformation 1917-Present* (Northampton, MA: Olive Branch Press, 2015), 139-152. For Jabotinsky marching, see "Report of the Court of Inquiry Convened by Order of H.E. The High Commissioner and Commander-in-Chief, Dated the 12th Day of April, 1920," reproduced in Isaiah Friedman, ed., *The Rise of Israel: Riots in Jerusalem—San Remo Conference April 1920* (New York: Garland, 1987), 111, 127; hereafter cited as "Palin Commission Report"; all quotations from the report are from this source unless noted otherwise. For more on Jabotinsky, see Segev, *One Palestine, Complete*, 132-133.

29. Palin Commission Report, 134-135.

30. Sakakini, *Yawmiyyat Khalil al-Sakakini*, 210, 214, 219.

31. The term "government within a government" is one that Sakakini uses to describe how the local British administration viewed the Zionist Commission's role in the country. Sakakini, *Yawmiyyat Khalil al-Sakakini*, 218; for "age," 217.

32. Segev, *One Palestine, Complete*, 131, 137.

33. Ze'ev [Vladimir] Jabotinsky, "The Iron Wall," originally published in Russian on November 4, 1923. I have used the translation available online at http://en.jabotinsky.org/media/9747/the-iron-wall.pdf.

34. Palin Commission Report, 71, 74,

35. Palin Commission Report, 63, 60, 139.

36. Palin Commission Report, 68, 139.

37. Sahar Huneidi, *A Broken Trust: Herbert Samuel, Zionism and the Palestinians 1920-1925* (London: I. B. Tauris, 2001), 41.

38. Basheer M. Nafi, *Arabism, Islamism and the Palestine Question, 1908-1941: A Political History* (Reading, UK: Ithaca Press, 1998), 92.

39. Robson, *Colonialism and Christianity in Mandate Palestine*, 58, 72; and The Palestine Order in Council, August 10, 1922, available online at www.un.org/unispal/document/mandate-for-palestine-the-palestine-order-in-lon-council-mandatory-order/.

40. Gudrun Krämer, *A History of Palestine: From Ottoman Conquest to the Founding of the State of Israel*, trans. Graham Harman and Gudrun Krämer (Princeton, NJ: Princeton University Press, 2008), 224; Pappe, *Rise and Fall of a Palestinian Dynasty*, 239.

41. See Hillel Cohen, *Year Zero of the Arab-Israeli Conflict 1929*, trans. Haim Watzman (Waltham, MA: Brandeis University Press, 2015), for a recent liberal Zionist perspective; see also Rena Barakat, "*Thawrat al-Buraq* in British Mandate Palestine: Jerusalem, Mass Mobilization, and Colonial Politics, 1928–1930," PhD diss., University of Chicago, 2007.

42. Cited in Hans Cohn, *Nationalism and Imperialism in the Hither East* (London: George Routledge and Sons, 1932), 146.

43. Cohen, *Year Zero*, xxi; see also Smith, *Palestine and the Arab-Israeli Conflict*, 123–128; Pappe, *Rise and Fall of a Palestinian Dynasty*, 238; Barakat, "*Thawrat al-Buraq* in British Mandate Palestine: Jerusalem, Mass Mobilization, and Colonial Politics, 1928–1930."

44. Noah Haiduc-Dale, *Arab Christians in the British Palestine Mandate: Communalism and Nationalism, 1917–1948* (Edinburgh: Edinburgh University Press, 2013), 101–102.

45. Nafi, *Arabism, Islamism and the Palestine Question*, 117–127. For an older perspective, see Y. Porath, *The Emergence of the Palestinian Arab National Movement 1918–1929* (London: Frank Cass, 1974), 293–303.

46. Shakib Arslan, *Zaman al-'uruba al-abtar* (Mukhtara: Al-dar al-taqadummiyya, 2011), 66–67, 185–190.

47. "Al-mu'tamar al-islami al-'am," *El-Carmel*, Wednesday, December 16, 1931; Nafi, *Arabism, Islamism and the Palestine Question*, 121.

48. Cited in Weldon C. Matthews, "Pan-Islam or Arab Nationalism? The Meaning of the 1931 Jerusalem Islamic Congress Reconsidered," *International Journal of Middle East Studies* 35 (2003): 15.

49. "Al-mu'tamar al-islami: asas banyan al-jami'a al-jadid," *El-Carmel*, December 16, 1931; I thank Abdel Razzaq Takriti for this reference. See Haiduc-Dale, *Arab Christians in the British Palestine Mandate*, 110, for Husayni attempting to assuage Christian Arab anxieties.

50. The ambivalence between nationalism and communalism is a point made by both Noah Haiduc-Dale and Laura Robson in their accounts of Arabs Christians during the mandate. Robson, in *Colonialism and Christianity in Mandate Palestine*, argues that British mandate policies led to the inculcation of a Christian sectarian consciousness and mobilization in the 1930s.

51. Weldon C. Matthews, "Pan-Islam or Arab Nationalism?" 5–11. For "sealed armouries," see "Report by His Majesty's Government in the United Kingdom of Great Britain and Northern Ireland to the Council of the League of Nations on the Administration of Palestine and Trans-Jordan for the Year 1931," available at http://unispal.un.org/UNISPAL.NSF/0/C2567D9C6F6CE5D8052565D9006EFC72.

52. Sherene Seikaly, *Men of Capital: Scarcity and Economy in Mandate Palestine* (Stanford, CA: Stanford University Press, 2016).

53. Pappe, *Rise and Fall of a Palestinian Dynasty,* 295.

54. Pappe, *Rise and Fall of a Palestinian Dynasty,* 259.

55. Kayyali, *Watha'iq,* 378.

56. See, for instance, the speech by Hajj Amin al-Husayni at the opening of the congress of nationalist committees in Jerusalem, reproduced in Kayyali, *Watha'iq,* 388–393; see also the statement of the SMC on June 26, 1936, reproduced in Kayyali, *Watha'iq,* 413. The contrast between the populist Qassam and the elitist Husayni was made eloquently by Pappe, *Rise and Fall of a Palestinian Dynasty,* 268–272.

57. For "oppressive immigration," see Kayyali, *Watha'iq,* 443.

58. Kayyali, *Watha'iq,* 393.

59. Yvette Talhamy, "The *Fatwas* and the Nusayri/Alawis of Syria," *Middle Eastern Studies* 46 (2012): 185.

60. Poem cited in Haiduc-Dale, *Arab Christians,* 144–145; Samih Shabeeb, "Poetry of Rebellion: The Life, Verse and Death of Nuh Ibrahim during the 1936–39 Revolt," *Jerusalem Quarterly* 25 (2006): 65–78.

61. For the text of the Peel Commission report, see https://unispal.un.org /DPA/DPR/unispal.nsf/561c6ee353d740fb8525607d00581829/08e38a7182014 58b052565700072b358?OpenDocument.

62. George Antonius, *The Arab Awakening: The Story of the Arab National Movement* (London: Hamish Hamilton, 1938), 410–411.

63. Nafi, *Arabism, Islamism and the Palestine Question,* 360–384.

64. Cited in Amicham Nachmani, *Great Power Discord in Palestine* (London: Frank Cass, 1987), 168.

65. For an elaboration, see Jens Hanssen, "Albert's World: Historicism, Liberal Imperialism and the Struggle for Palestine, 1936–1948," in Jens Hanssen and Max Weiss, eds., *Arabic Thought beyond the Liberal Age: Towards an Intellectual History of the Nahda* (Cambridge: Cambridge University Press, 2016), 62–92.

66. Albert Hourani, "The Case against a Jewish State in Palestine: Albert Hourani's Statement to the Anglo-American Committee of Enquiry of 1946," *Journal of Palestine Studies* 35 (2005): 81, 87.

67. "Statement of Mr. David Ben-Gurion," reproduced in *The Jewish Case before the Anglo-American Committee of Inquiry on Palestine as Presented by the Jewish Agency for Palestine: Statements & Memoranda* (Jerusalem: The Jewish Agency, 1947), 61, 65, 71–73.

68. Segev, *One Palestine, Complete,* 376–377.

69. Amnon Raz-Krakotzkin, "Jewish Memory between Exile and History," *Jewish Quarterly Review* 97 (2007): 530–543; Shapira, "Ben-Gurion and the Bible."

70. Susan Lee Hattis, *The Bi-national Idea in Palestine during Mandatory Times* (Haifa: Shikmona, 1970), 51–52. See also Shalom Ratzabi, *Between Zionism and Judaism: The Radical Circle of Brith Shalom, 1925–1930* (Leiden, The Netherlands: Brill, 2002).

71. Martin Buber and Judah Leon Magnes, *Arab-Jewish Unity: Testimony before the Anglo-American Inquiry Commission for the Ihud (Union) Association by Judah Magnes and Martin Buber* (London: Victor Gollancz, 1947), 12. Buber and Magnes were citing with approval a definition of binationalism from 1931.

72. See Adi Gordon, "'Nothing but a Disillusioned Love': Hans Kohn's Break with the Zionist Movement," in Ezra Mendelsohn, Stefani Hoffman, and Richard I. Cohen, eds., *Against the Grain: Jewish Intellectuals in Hard Times* (New York: Berghahn, 2014), 125–126, 135.

73. Hannah Arendt's writings on binationalism, for example, rarely mention any Arab individual. On binationalism, see Hannah Arendt, *The Jewish Writings,* ed. Jerome Kohn and Ron H. Feldman (New York: Schocken Books, 2007). Jens Hanssen, "Kafka and the Arabs," *Critical Inquiry* 39 (2012): 167–197, further illuminates this point with reference to Kafka. The irony, if anything, is how many Arabic-speaking Sephardic and Arab Jews used their actual knowledge of Arab culture, politics, and people to work for the Zionist project in Palestine. See Jacobson and Naor, *Oriental Neighbors,* 60–73, 105.

74. Hourani, "Case against a Jewish State in Palestine," 83.

75. Smith, *Palestine and the Arab-Israeli Conflict,* 188–189.

76. For the latest history of the nakba and one of the very few from the perspective of the Arab victims of Zionism, see Adel Manna, *Nakbatun wa baqa': hikayatu filastiniyiin zallu fi Haifa wa al-Jalil (1948–1956)* (Beirut: Markaz al-dirasat al-filastiniyya, 2016).

77. Manna, *Nakbatun wa baqa';* Ilan Pappe, *The Ethnic Cleansing of Palestine* (Oxford: Oneworld, 2006); Benny Morris, *The Birth of the Palestinian Refugee Problem Revisited,* 2nd ed. (Cambridge: Cambridge University Press, 2004 [1988]).

78. Robson, *States of Separation,* charts some of the similarities and linkages between various League of Nations–era transfer schemes in the Middle East.

79. "Declaration of Israel's Independence 1948" (May 14, 1948), The Avalon Project at Yale Law School, http://avalon.law.yale.edu/20th_century/israel.asp.

80. Robinson, *Citizen Strangers,* 105–112.

81. See Nadim N. Rouhana and Sahar S. Huneidi, eds., *Israel and Its Palestinian Citizens: Ethnic Privileges in a Jewish State* (Cambridge: Cambridge University Press, 2017), and especially Nimer Sultany's contribution entitled "The Legal Structures of Subordination: The Palestinian Minority and Israeli Law," 191–237.

82. Robinson, *Citizen Strangers,* 56–57, 82, 108.

83. Bashkin, *New Babylonians*, 100–115; Peter Wien, *Iraqi Arab National-ism: Authoritarian, Totalitarian, and Pro-Fascist Inclinations, 1932–1941* (London: Routledge, 2006), 108–112; Wien argues that youth mobilizations played a role.

84. Bashkin, *New Babylonians*, 17, 26–27, 57.

85. This section is taken from Bashkin, *New Babylonians*, 183–237.

86. Elie Kedourie, "Minorities," in *The Chatham House Version and Other Middle-Eastern Studies*, new edition (Hanover, NH: University Press of New England, 1984 [1970]), 312. See also Yehouda Shenhav, "The Jews of Iraq, Zionist Ideology, and the Property of the Palestinian Refugees of 1948: An Anomaly of National Accounting," *International Journal of Middle East Studies* 31 (1999): 605–630.

87. Kedourie, "Minorities," 306, 315.

88. Frances Hasso, "Modernity and Gender in Arab Accounts of the 1948 and 1967 Defeats," *International Journal of Middle East Studies* 32 (2000): 491–510; and Nadine Picaudou, "The Historiography of the 1948 Wars," *Online Encyclo-pedia of Mass Violence*, November 1, 2008, www.sciencespo.fr/mass-violence-war-massacre-resistance/en/document/historiography-1948-wars.

89. Constantine Zurayk, *Ma'na al-nakba*, reproduced in *Al-a'mal al-fikriyya al-'amma lil-duktur Constantine Zurayk, vol. 1* (Beirut: Markaz Dirasat al-wahda al-'arabiyya, 1996), 229–230. Also available in English as *The Meaning of the Disaster*, trans. R. Bayly Winder (Beirut: Khayat's, 1956).

90. For "nahda," Zurayk, *Ma'na al-nakba*, 202; for "nationalism," Zurayk, *Ma'na al-nakba*, 259. This is an addendum to *Ma'na al-nakba* that was origi-nally delivered as a radio address on May 31, 1948.

91. Orit Bashkin, *Impossible Exodus: Iraqi Jews in Israel* (Stanford, CA: Stan-ford University Press, 2017), 3–20.

EPILOGUE

1. Elizabeth Suzanne Kassab's study, *Contemporary Arab Thought: Cultural Critique in Comparative Perspective* (New York: Columbia University Press, 2010), focuses on the post-1967 era.

2. Munif al-Razzaz, *Ma'alim al-hayat al-'arabiyya al-jadida* (Beirut: Dar al-'ilm lil-malayin, 1960), 12.

3. Razzaz, *Ma'alim al-hayat al-'arabiyya al-jadida*, 38.

4. Razzaz, *Ma'alim al-hayat al-'arabiyya al-jadida*, 93.

5. Hanna Batatu, *The Old Social Classes and the Revolutionary Movements of Iraq: A Study of Iraq's Old Landed and Commercial Classes and of Its Commu-nists, Ba'thists, and Free Officers* (Princeton, NJ: Princeton University Press, 1978), 480.

6. Razzaz, *Ma'alim al-hayat al-'arabiyya al-jadida*, 23.

7. Batatu, *Old Social Classes*, 746–748.

8. For the case of Iraq, see Batatu, *Old Social Classes*, 778–783; see also Hanna Batatu, *The Egyptian, Syrian, and Iraqi Revolutions: Some Observations on Their Underlying Causes and Social Character* (Washington, DC: Center for Contemporary Arab Studies, Georgetown, 1984).

9. Batatu, *Old Social Classes*, 807.

10. Batatu, *Old Social Classes*, 843.

11. Sara Pursley, *Familiar Futures: Time, Selfhood, and Sovereignty in Iraq* (Stanford, CA: Stanford University Press, 2019), 175–197, provides an insightful criticism of the limitations and assumptions of the personal-status law; see also Noga Efrati, "Negotiating Rights in Iraq: Women and the Personal Status Law," *Middle East Journal* 59 (2005): 577–595. For opposition, see Khalil F. Osman, *Sectarianism in Iraq: The Making of State and Nation since 1920* (London: Routledge, 2015), 75.

12. Batatu, *Old Social Classes*, 1018.

13. Weldon C. Matthews, "The Kennedy Administration, Counterinsurgency, and Iraq's First Ba'thist Regime," *International Journal of Middle East Studies* 43 (2011): 635–653.

14. Paul Sedra, "Class Cleavages and Ethnic Conflict: Coptic Christian Communities in Modern Egyptian Politics," *Islam and Christian-Muslim Relations* 10 (1999): 219–235; see also Paul Sedra, "Church-State Relations in Egypt," Middle East Institute, February 24, 2014, www.mei.edu/content/church-state-relations-egypt.

15. Laure Guirguis, *Copts and the Security State: Violence, Coercion and Sectarianism in Contemporary Egypt* (Stanford, CA: Stanford University Press, 2017), 17–19.

16. Batatu, *Old Social Classes*, 764–807.

17. Batatu, *Old Social Classes*, 1085–1086.

18. Hanna Batatu, *Syria's Peasantry, the Descendants of Its Lesser Rural Notables, and Their Politics* (Princeton, NJ: Princeton University Press, 1999), 157–160. For an analysis of the Alawis that crucially contextualizes the diversity of their modern historical experiences, see Stefan Winter, *A History of the 'Alawis: From Medieval Aleppo to the Turkish Republic* (Princeton, NJ: Princeton University Press, 2016), 218–268.

19. Munif al-Razzaz, "Al-tajriba al-murra," in *Al-a'mal al-fikriyya wa al-siyasiyya, vol. 2* (Amman: mu'assasat Munif al Razzaz lil-dirasat al-qawmiyya, 1986), 158–160.

20. This has led some Arab authors to question the trope of the nahda in the aftermath of the Arab defeat in the 1967 war. See Zeina G. Halabi, *The Unmaking of the Arab Intellectual: Prophecy, Exile and the Nation* (Edinburgh: Edinburgh University Press, 2017), 38–59.

21. "Palestine at the United Nations: The Speech of Yasser Arafat," *Journal of Palestine Studies* 4 (1975), 191.

22. Jean Corbon, George Khodr, Samir Ka'fity, and Albert Lahham, "What Is Required of the Christian Faith Concerning the Palestine Problem," *Biblical and Theological Concerns* (Limassol, Cyprus: Middle East Council of Churches, n.d.), 11–13, cited in Samuel J. Kuruvilla, *Radical Christianity in Palestine and Israel: Liberation and Theology in the Middle East* (London: I. B. Tauris, 2013), 105–114.

23. The report is cited in Matthew F. Jacobs, *Imagining the Middle East: The Building of an American Foreign Policy, 1918–1967* (Chapel Hill: University of North Carolina Press, 2011), 140–142.

24. Among many other unstudied documents about secularism from this era, see *Lubnan al-akhar, mu'tamar hawla al-'almana wa al-hawiyya al-'arabiyya* (Beirut: Mu'assasat al-dirasat wa al-abhath al-lubnaniyya, 1976), 32–37.

25. Abu Khaldun Sati' al-Husri, *Mabadi' al-qira'a al-khalduniyya*, 27th ed. (Baghdad: Ministry of Education, 1987–1988). Needless to say, this is an edition published long after Husri's death, and the words are obviously not his own.

26. See Dina Rizk Khoury, "The Security State and the Practice and Rhetoric of Sectarianism in Iraq," *International Journal of Contemporary Iraqi Studies* 4 (2010): 325–338; and Dina Rizk Khoury, *Iraq in Wartime: Soldiering, Martyrdom, and Remembrance* (Cambridge: Cambridge University Press, 2013).

27. Yassin al-Haj Saleh, *The Impossible Revolution: Making Sense of the Syrian Tragedy* (London: C. Hurst, 2017), 229.

28. Muhammad Kamil al-Khatib, *Takwin al-nahda al-'arabiyya 1800–2000* (Damascus: Matba'at al-Yaziji, 2001).

29. Khatib, *Takwin al-nahda*, 105.

30. Adonis, *Fatiha li-niyahat al-qarn* (Beriut: Dar al-nahar lil-nashr, 1998), 11.

31. Yusuf al-Qaradawi, *Non-Muslims in the Islamic Society*, trans. Khalil Muhammad Hamad and Sayed Mahboob Ali Shah (Indianapolis, IN: American Trust, 1985); Tarek Bishri, *Al-muslimun wa al-aqbat fi itar al-jama'a al-wataniyya* (Cairo: Dar al-shuruq, 2004 [1980]).

32. Georges Tamer, "Nasr Hamid Abu Zayd," *International Journal for Middle East Studies* 43 (2011): 193–195.

Works Cited

Abdo, Geneive. *The New Sectarianism: The Arab Uprisings and the Rebirth of the Shi'a-Sunni Divide*. Washington, DC: Brookings, 2013.

Abduh, Muhammad. *Al-Islam wa al-nasraniyya*. Cairo: Matba'at majalat al-Manar, 1905.

Abisaab, Malek. *Militant Women of a Fragile Nation*. Syracuse, NY: Syracuse University Press, 2010.

Abou Hodeib, Toufoul. *A Taste for Home: The Modern Middle Class in Ottoman Beirut*. Stanford, CA: Stanford University Press, 2017.

Abu-Husayn, Abdul-Rahim. *The View from Istanbul: Ottoman Lebanon and the Druze Emirate*. Oxford: Centre for Lebanese Studies and I. B. Tauris, 2004.

Abu-Manneh, Butrus. "The Islamic Roots of the Gülhane Rescript." *Die Welt des Islams* 34 (1994): 173–203.

Adams, Charles C. *Islam and Modernism in Egypt: A Study of the Modern Reform Movement Inaugurated by Muhammad 'Abduh*. New York: Russell & Russell, 1933.

Adonis. *Fatiha li-niyahat al-qarn*. Beriut: Dar al-nahar lil-nashr, 1998.

Agoston, Gabor, and Bruce Masters, eds. *Encyclopedia of the Ottoman Empire*. New York: Facts on File, 2009.

Ajami, Fouad. *The Arab Predicament: Arab Political Thought and Practice since 1967*. Cambridge: Cambridge University Press, 1981.

Akçam, Taner. *The Young Turks' Crime against Humanity: The Armenian Genocide and Ethnic Cleansing in the Ottoman Empire*. Princeton, NJ: Princeton University Press, 2012.

Aksan, Virginia H. *Ottoman Wars 1700–1870: An Empire Besieged*. Harlow, UK: Pearson Education, 2007.

'Alayli, Abdullah al-. *Dustur al-'arab al-qawmi*. Beirut: Dar al-jadid, 1996 [1941].

AlShehabi, Omar H. *Contested Modernity: Sectarianism, Nationalism, and Colonialism in Bahrain*. London: Oneworld, 2019.

Altug, Seda. "Sectarianism in the Syrian Jazira: Community, Land, and Violence in the Memories of World War One and the French Mandate." PhD diss., Utrecht University, 2011.

'Amil, Mahdi. *Fi al-dawla al-ta'ifiyya*. Beirut: Dar al-Farabi, 2003 [1986].

Amin, Qasim. *The Liberation of Women: A Document in the History of Egyptian Feminism*, trans. Samiha Sidhom Peterson. Cairo: American University in Cairo Press, 1992.

Antonius, George. *The Arab Awakening: The Story of the Arab National Movement*. London: Hamish Hamilton, 1938.

Antun, Farah. "Tarikh Ibn Rushd wa falsafatahu." *Al-Jami'a* 3 (1902): 517–540.

Arafat, Yasser. "Palestine at the United Nations: The Speech of Yasser Arafat." *Journal of Palestine Studies* 4 (1975): 181–192.

Arendt, Hannah. *The Jewish Writings*, ed. Jerome Kohn and Ron H. Feldman. New York: Schocken Books, 2007.

Ariss, Tarek El-, ed. *The Arab Renaissance: A Bilingual Anthology of the Nahda*. New York: Modern Language Association of America, 2018.

Arslan, Shakib. *A'mal al-wafd al-suri al-filastini*. Beirut: Al-dar al-taqaddumiyya, 2008.

———. *Zaman al-'uruba al-abtar*. Mukhtara: Al-dar al-taqadummiyya, 2011.

Asad, Talal. *Formations of the Secular: Christianity, Islam, Modernity*. Stanford, CA: Stanford University Press, 2003.

Astourian, Stephan H. "The Silence of the Land: Agrarian Relations, Ethnicity, and Power," in Ronald Grigor Suny, Fatma Müge Göçek, and Norman M. Naimark, eds., *A Question of Genocide: Armenians and Turks at the End of the Ottoman Empire*. Oxford: Oxford University Press, 2011, 55–81.

Atcil, Abdurrahman. "Decentralization, Imperialism and Sovereignty in the Late Ottoman Empire: Shakib Arslan's Polemic against the Decentralization Party." *Die Welt des Islams* 53 (2013): 26–49.

Ateş, Sabri. *The Ottoman-Iranian Borderlands: Making a Boundary, 1843–1914*. New York: Cambridge University Press, 2013.

Ayalon, Ami. *Reading Palestine: Printing and Literacy, 1900–1948*. Austin: University of Texas Press, 2004.

Aydin, Cemil. *The Idea of the Muslim World: A Global Intellectual History*. Cambridge, MA: Harvard University Press, 2017.

Ayoub, Sami. "The Mecelle, Sharia, and the Ottoman State," in Kent F. Schull, M. Saraçoğlu, and Robert Zens, eds., *Law and Legality in the Ottoman Empire and the Republic of Turkey*. Bloomington: Indiana University Press, 2016, 129–131.

'Azmah, 'Abd al-'Aziz al-. *Mir'at al-Sham: Tarikh Dimashq wa ahluha*. Damascus: Dar al-fikr, 2002.

Azmeh, Aziz al-. *Al-'almaniyya min mandhur mukhtalif*. Beirut: Markaz dirasat al-wahda al-'arabiyya, 2008 [1992].

———. *Islams and Modernities*, 3rd ed. London: Verso, 2009.

———. "Nationalism and the Arabs." *Arab Studies Quarterly* 17 (1995): 1–17.

Baer, Marc David. *The Dönme: Jewish Converts, Muslim Revolutionaries, and Secular Turks*. Stanford, CA: Stanford University Press, 2010.

———. *Honored by the Glory of Islam: Conversion and Conquest in Ottoman Europe*. Oxford: Oxford University Press, 2008.

Barakat, Rena. "*Thawrat al-Buraq* in British Mandate Palestine: Jerusalem, Mass Mobilization, and Colonial Politics, 1928–1930." PhD diss., University of Chicago, 2007.

Barkey, Karen. *Empire of Difference: The Ottomans in Comparative Perspective*. New York: Cambridge University Press, 2008.

Barkey, Karen, and George Gavrilis. "The Ottoman Millet System: Non-territorial Autonomy and Its Contemporary Legacy." *Ethnopolitics* 15 (2016): 24–42.

Baron, Beth. *Egypt as Woman: Nationalism, Gender, and Politics*. Berkeley: University of California Press, 2005.

———. *The Women's Awakening in Egypt: Culture, Society, and the Press*. New Haven, CT: Yale University Press, 1997.

Bartov, Omar, and Eric D. Weitz, eds. *Shatterzone of Empires: Coexistence and Violence in the German, Habsburg, Russian, and Ottoman Borderlands*. Bloomington: Indiana University Press, 2013.

Barut, Muhammad Jamal, ed. *Al-mas'ala al-ta'ifiyya wa sina'at al-aqliyyat fi al-watan al-'arabi*. Doha: Arab Center for Research and Policy Studies, 2017.

Barzilay, Dvorah, and Barnett Litvinoff, eds. *The Letters and Papers of Chaim Weizmann, vol. 8*. Rutgers, NJ: Transaction Books, 1977.

Bashkin, Orit. *Impossible Exodus: Iraqi Jews in Israel*. Stanford, CA: Stanford University Press, 2017.

———. *New Babylonians: A History of Jews in Modern Iraq*. Stanford, CA: Stanford University Press, 2012.

———. *The Other Iraq: Pluralism and Culture in Hashemite Iraq*. Stanford, CA: Stanford University Press, 2009.

Batatu, Hanna. *The Egyptian, Syrian, and Iraqi Revolutions: Some Observations on Their Underlying Causes and Social Character*. Washington, DC: Center for Contemporary Arab Studies, Georgetown, 1984.

———. *The Old Social Classes and the Revolutionary Movements of Iraq: A Study of Iraq's Old Landed and Commercial Classes and of Its Communists, Ba'thists, and Free Officers.* Princeton, NJ: Princeton University Press, 1978.

———. *Syria's Peasantry, the Descendants of Its Lesser Rural Notables, and Their Politics.* Princeton, NJ: Princeton University Press, 1999.

Beinin, Joel, and Zachary Lockman. *Workers on the Nile: Nationalism, Communism, Islam, and the Egyptian Working Class, 1882–1954.* Cairo: American University in Cairo Press, 1998.

Ben-Bassat, Yuval, and Eyal Ginio, eds. *Late Ottoman Palestine: The Period of Young Turk Rule.* London: I. B. Tauris, 2011.

Bender, Thomas. "Historians, the Nation, and the Plentitude of Narratives," in Thomas Bender, ed., *Rethinking American History in a Global Age.* Berkeley: University of California Press, 2002.

Beydoun, Ahmad. *Al-sira' 'ala tarikh lubnan: aw al-hawiyya wa al-zaman fi a'mal mu'arrikhina al-mu'asirin.* Beirut: Publications de l'université libanaise, 1989.

Bilqziz, 'Abdulilah, ed. *Al-ta'ifiyya wa al-tasamuh wa al-'adala al-intiqaliyya: min al-fitna ila dawlat al-qanun.* Beirut: Markaz dirasat al-wahda al-'arabiyya, 2013.

Bishri, Tariq al-. *Al-muslimun wa al-aqbat fi itar al-jama'a al-wataniyya.* Cairo: Dar al-shuruq, 2004 [1980].

Blight, David W. *Race and Reunion: The Civil War in American Memory.* Cambridge, MA: Belknap Press of Harvard University Press, 2001.

Bloxham, Donald. *The Great Game of Genocide: Imperialism, Nationalism and the Destruction of the Ottoman Armenians.* Oxford: Oxford University Press, 2005.

Blumi, Isa. *Reinstating the Ottomans: Alternative Balkan Modernities, 1800–1912.* New York: Palgrave, 2011.

Bose, Neilesh. *Recasting the Region: Language, Culture, and Islam in Colonial Bengal.* New Delhi: Oxford University Press, 2014.

Bou Ali, Nadia. "In the Hall of Mirrors: The Arab Nahda, Nationalism, and the Question of Language." D.Phil diss., Oxford University, 2012.

Boulatta, Kamal. *Palestinian Art: From 1850 to the Present.* London: Saqi, 2009.

Bou-Nacklie, N. E. "Les Troupes Spéciales: Religious and Ethnic Recruitment, 1916–46." *International Journal of Middle East Studies* 25 (1993): 645–660.

Brown, Wendy. *Regulating Aversion: Tolerance in the Age of Identity and Empire.* Princeton, NJ: Princeton University Press, 2006.

Brundage, W. Fitzhugh. *Lynching in the New South: Georgia and Virginia, 1880–1930.* Urbana: University of Illinois Press, 1993.

Buber, Martin, and Judah Leon Magnes. *Arab-Jewish Unity: Testimony before the Anglo-American Inquiry Commission for the Ihud (Union) Association by Judah Magnes and Martin Buber.* London: Victor Gollancz, 1947.

Bustani, Butrus al-. *Nafir Suriyya*, ed. Yusuf Q. Khuri. Beirut: Dar al-Hamra', 1990.

Bustani, Suleyman al-. *'Ibra wa dhikra aw al-dawla al-'uthmaniyya qabla al-dustur wa ba'dahu.* Cairo: Matba'at al-akhbar, 1908.

Bustani, Yusuf al-. *Tarikh harb al-balqan al-awwal.* n.p., 1913.

Campbell, Robert Bell. "The Arabic Journal, *Al-Machriq:* Its Beginnings and First Twenty-Five Years under the Editorship of Père Louis Cheikho, S.J." PhD diss., University of Michigan, 1972.

Campos, Michelle U. *Ottoman Brothers: Muslims, Christians, and Jews in Early Twentieth-Century Palestine.* Stanford, CA: Stanford University Press, 2011.

Cavanaugh, William T. *The Myth of Religious Violence: Secular Ideology and the Roots of Modern Conflict.* Oxford: Oxford University Press, 2009.

Çelebi, Evliya. *The Intimate Life of an Ottoman Statesman: Melek Ahmed Pasha 1588–1662 as Portrayed in Evliya Çelebi's Book of Travels,* trans. and commentary by Robert Dankoff. Albany: State University of New York Press, 1991.

Çelik, Zeynep. *The Remaking of Istanbul: Portrait of an Ottoman City in the Nineteenth Century.* Berkeley: University of California Press, 1986.

Cevdet Paşa. *Tezâkir.* Ankara: Türk Tarih Kurumu Basımevi, 1991.

Chatty, Dawn. *Displacement and Dispossession in the Modern Middle East.* Cambridge: Cambridge University Press, 2010.

Cheikho, Louis. "Al-tasahul al-dini." *Al-Machriq* 4 (1901): 373–377.

———. *Tarikh al-adab al-'arabiyya fi al-qarn al-tasi' 'ashar wa al-rub' al-awwal min al-qarn al-'ishrin.* Piscataway, NJ: Gorgias Press, 2008 [1924].

———. *Wuzara' al-nasraniyya wa kuttabuha fi al-Islam.* Juniya: Al-maktaba al-bulusiyya, 1987.

Chiha, Michel. "Contre la servilité." *Le Jour,* December 12, 1934.

———. *Fi al-siyasa al-dakhiliyya,* trans. Ahmad Beydoun. Beirut: Dar al-Nahar, 2004.

———. *Liban d'aujourd'hui.* Beirut: Fondation Chiha, 1994 [1949].

———. *Politique intérieure.* Beirut: Éditions du Trident, 1964.

Clerck, Dima de. "Histoire officelle et mémoires en conflit dans le Sud du Mon-Liban: Les affrontements druzo-chrétiens du XIXe siècle." *Revue des mondes musulmans et de la Méditerranée* 135 (2014): 171–190.

Cleveland, William L. *The Making of an Arab Nationalist: Ottomanism and Arabism in the Life and Thought of Sati' al-Husri.* Princeton, NJ: Princeton University Press, 1971.

Clogg, Richard, ed. *The Movement for Greek Independence 1770–1821: A Collection of Documents.* London: Macmillan, 1976.

Cohen, Hillel. *Year Zero of the Arab-Israeli Conflict 1929*, trans. Haim Watzman. Waltham, MA: Brandeis University Press, 2015.

Cohen, Julia Phillips. *Becoming Ottomans: Sephardi Jews and Imperial Citizenship in the Modern Era*. Oxford: Oxford University Press, 2014.

Cohn, Hans. *Nationalism and Imperialism in the Hither East*. London: George Routledge and Sons, 1932.

Cole, Juan R. I. *Colonialism and Revolution in the Middle East: Social and Cultural Origins of Egypt's 'Urabi Movement*. Princeton, NJ: Princeton University Press, 1993.

Corbon, Jean, George Khodr, Samir Kafity, and Albert Lahham. "What Is Required of the Christian Faith Concerning the Palestine Problem," in *Biblical and Theological Concerns*. Limassol, Cyprus: Middle East Council of Churches, n.d.

Cortas, Wadad Makdisi. *A World I Loved: The Story of an Arab Woman*. New York: Nation Books, 2009.

Cromer, Evelyn Baring, Earl of. *Modern Egypt*, 2 vols. New York: Macmillan, 1909.

Cuno, Kenneth M. *Modernizing Marriage: Family, Ideology, and Law in Nineteenth- and Early Twentieth-Century Egypt*. Syracuse, NY: Syracuse University Press, 2015.

Dadarian, Vahakn N. "The 1894 Sassoun Massacre: *A Juncture in the Escalation of the Turko-Armenian Conflict*." *Armenian Review* 47 (2001): 5–39.

Dakhli, Leyla. "The Mahjar as Literary and Political Territory in the First Decades of the Twentieth Century: The Example of Amin Rihani 1876–1940," in Dyala Hamzah, ed., *The Making of the Arab Intellectual: Empire, Public Sphere and the Colonial Coordinates of Selfhood*. New York: Routledge, 2013, 164–187.

Dakrub, Muhammad. *Judhur al-sindiyana al-hamra'*, 3rd ed. Beirut: Farabi, 2007 [1974].

Darwish, Mahmoud. *If I Were Another*, trans. Fady Joudah. New York: Farrar, Straus and Giroux, 2009.

Davis, Eric. *Memories of State: Politics, History, and Collective Identity in Modern Iraq*. Berkeley: University of California Press, 2005.

———. "The Political Economy of Modern Iraq," in David S. Sorenson, ed., *Interpreting the Middle East: Essential Themes*. New York: Westview Press, 2010, 337–362.

Davison, Roderic H. *Reform in the Ottoman Empire 1856–1876*. New York: Gordian Press, 1973.

Daw, Antoin, ed. *Hawadith 1860 fi Lubnan wa Dimashq: Lajnat Bayrut al-duwaliyya, al-mahadir al-kamila, 1860–1862*, 2 vols. Beirut: Mukhtarat, 1996.

Dawn, C. Ernest. *From Ottomanism to Arabism: Essays on the Origins of Arab Nationalism*. Urbana: University of Illinois Press, 1973.

Deringil, Selim. *Conversion and Apostasy in the Late Ottoman Empire.* Cambridge: Cambridge University Press, 2012.

———. *The Well-Protected Domains: Ideology and the Legitimation of Power in the Ottoman Empire, 1876–1909.* London: I. B. Tauris, 1999.

Der Matossian, Bedross. "From Bloodless Revolution to Bloody Counterrevolution: The Adana Massacres of 1909." *Genocide Studies and Prevention* 6 (2011): 152–173.

———. *Shattered Dreams of Revolution: From Liberty to Violence in the Late Ottoman Empire.* Stanford, CA: Stanford University Press, 2014.

Devji, Faisal. *Muslim Zion: Pakistan as a Political Idea.* Cambridge, MA: Harvard University Press, 2013.

Dibs, Yusuf al-. *Tarikh Suriyya, vol. 8: Fi-tarikh Suriyya fi ayyam al-salatin al-'uthmaniyyin al-'izam.* Piscataway, NJ: Gorgias Press, 2009.

Di Capua, Yoav. *Gatekeepers of the Arab Past: Historians and History Writing in Twentieth-Century Egypt.* Berkeley: University of California Press, 2008.

Dodge, Toby. *Inventing Iraq: The Failure of Nation Building and a History Denied.* New York: Columbia University Press, 2003.

Donabed, Sargon George. *Reforging a Forgotten History: Iraq and the Assyrians in the Twentieth Century.* Edinburgh: Edinburgh University Press, 2015.

Donner, Fred M. "How Ecumenical Was Early Islam?" The Farhat J. Ziadeh Distinguished Lecture in Arab and Islamic Studies, Department of Near Eastern Languages and Civilizations at the University of Washington, April 29, 2013.

Doumet-Serhal, Claude, and Michèle Hélou-Nahas, eds. *Michel Chiha: 1891–1954.* Beirut: Fondation Michel Chiha, 2001.

Dueck, Jennifer M. *The Claims of Culture at Empire's End: Syria and Lebanon under French Rule.* Oxford: Oxford University Press, 2010.

Dupont, Anne-Laure. *Ǧurǧī Zaydān (1861–1914): Écrivain réformiste et témoin de la Renaissance arabe.* Damascus: Institut Français du Proche-Orient, 2006.

Efrati, Noga. "Negotiating Rights in Iraq: Women and the Personal Status Law." *Middle East Journal* 59 (2005): 577–595.

———. *Women in Iraq: Past Meets Present.* New York: Columbia University Press, 2012.

Eldem, Edhem. "L'écrivain engagé et le bureaucrate zélé: la prise de la Banque ottomane et les "événements" de 1896 selon Victor Bérard et Hüseyin Nazım Pacha," in Sophie Basch, ed., *Portraits de Victor Bérard.* Athens: École française d'Athènes, 2015, 209–215.

Elshakry, Marwa. *Reading Darwin in Arabic, 1860–1950.* Chicago: University of Chicago Press, 2013.

Endresen, Cecilie. *Is the Albanian's Religion Really "Albanianism"? Religion and Nation according to Muslim and Christian Leaders in Albania.* Wiesbaden, Germany: Harrassowitz, 2012.

Erdem, Hakan. "'Do Not Think of the Greeks as Agricultural Laborers': Ottoman Responses to the Greek War of Independence," in Faruk Birtek and Thalia Dragonas, eds., *Citizenship and Nation-State in Greece and Turkey*. London: Routledge, 2005.

Fahmy, Ziad. *Ordinary Egyptians: Creating the Modern Nation through Popular Culture*. Stanford, CA: Stanford University Press, 2011.

Fanon, Frantz. *A Dying Colonialism*. New York: Grove Press, 1967 [1959].

———. *The Wretched of the Earth*. New York: Grove Weidenfeld, 1963.

Farah, Caesar E. *The Politics of Interventionism in Ottoman Lebanon 1830–1861*. London: Centre for Lebanese Studies and I. B. Tauris, 2000.

Farha, Mark. "Secularism in a Sectarian Society? The Divisive Drafting of the Lebanese Constitution of 1926," in Aslı Ü. Bali and Hanna Lerner, eds., *Constitution Writing, Religion and Democracy*. Cambridge: Cambridge University Press, 2017, 101–130.

Farhat, Adib. "Al-ta'ifiyya wa adwariha." *Al'Irfan* 22 (1931): 17–31.

Fawaz, Leila Tarazi. *Merchants and Migrants in Nineteenth-Century Beirut*. Cambridge, MA: Harvard University Press, 1983.

———. *An Occasion for War: Civil Conflict in Lebanon and Damascus in 1860*. London: Centre for Lebanese Studies and I. B. Tauris, 1994.

Febvre, Michel. *Théâtre de la Turquie, où sont representées les choses les plus remarquables qui s'y passent aujourd'hui touchant les Moeurs, le Gouvernement, les Coûtumes & la Religion des Turcs, & de treize autres sortes de Nations qui habitent dans l'Empire Ottoman*. Paris: Edme Couterot, 1682.

Fields, Karen E., and Barbara J. Fields. *Racecraft: The Soul of Inequality in American Life*. London: Verso, 2012.

Findley, Carter Vaughn. *Turkey, Islam, Nationalism, and Modernity: A History, 1789–2007*. New Haven, CT: Yale University Press, 2010.

Fink, Carole. *Defending the Rights of Others: The Great Powers, the Jews, and International Minority Protection*. Cambridge: Cambridge University Press, 2004.

Fredrickson, George M. *White Supremacy: A Comparative History in American and South African History*. Oxford: Oxford University Press, 1981.

Friedman, Isaiah, ed. *The Rise of Israel: Riots in Jerusalem—San Remo Conference April 1920*. New York: Garland, 1987.

Gelvin, James L. *Divided Loyalties: Nationalism and Mass Politics in Syria at the Close of Empire*. Berkeley: University of California Press, 1998.

Gemayel, Pierre. "Lebanese Nationalism and Its Foundations: The Phalangist Viewpoint," in Kemal H. Karpat, ed., *Political and Social Thought in the Contemporary Middle East*. New York: Praeger, 1968.

Gingeras, Ryan. *Fall of the Sultanate: The Great War and the End of the Ottoman Empire, 1908–1922*. Oxford: Oxford University Press, 2016.

————. *Sorrowful Shores: Violence, Ethnicity, and the End of the Ottoman Empire 1912–1923.* Oxford: Oxford University Press, 2009.

Ginio, Eyal. "Making Sense of the Defeat of the Balkan Wars," in M. Hakan Yavuz and Isa Blumi, eds., *War and Nationalism: The Balkan Wars, 1912–1913, and Their Sociopolitical Implications.* Salt Lake City: University of Utah Press, 2013, 594–617.

————. "Paving the Way for Ethnic Cleansing: Eastern Thrace during the Balkan Wars 1912–1913 and Their Aftermath," in Omer Bartov and Eric D. Weitz, eds., *Shatterzone of Empires: Coexistence and Violence in the German, Habsburg, Russian, and Ottoman Borderlands.* Bloomington: Indiana University Press, 2013, 283–297.

Göçek, Fatma Müge. *Rise of the Bourgeoisie, Demise of Empire: Ottoman Westernization and Social Change.* New York: Oxford University Press, 1996.

————, ed. *Social Constructions of Nationalism in the Middle East.* Albany: State University of New York Press, 2002.

Gordon, Adi. "'Nothing but a Disillusioned Love': Hans Kohn's Break with the Zionist Movement," in Ezra Mendelsohn, Stefani Hoffman, and Richard I. Cohen, eds., *Against the Grain: Jewish Intellectuals in Hard Times.* New York: Berghahn, 2014, 117–142.

Gribetz, Jonathan Marc. *Defining Neighbors: Religion, Race and the Early Zionist-Arab Encounter.* Princeton, NJ: Princeton University Press, 2014.

Guirguis, Laure. *Copts and the Security State: Violence, Coercion and Sectarianism in Contemporary Egypt.* Stanford, CA: Stanford University Press, 2017.

Guirguis, Magdi. *Al-qada' al-qibti fi Misr: dirasa tarikhiyya.* Cairo: Mirit, 1999.

Haddad, Fanar. "'Sectarianism' and Its Discontents in the Study of the Middle East." *Middle East Journal* 71 (2017): 363–382.

————. *Sectarianism in Iraq: Antagonistic Visions of Unity.* London: Hurst, 2011.

Hahn, Steven. *A Nation under Our Feet: Black Political Struggles in the Rural South from Slavery to the Great Migration.* Cambridge, MA: Belknap Press of Harvard University Press, 2003.

Haiduc-Dale, Noah. *Arab Christians in the British Palestine Mandate: Communalism and Nationalism, 1917–1948.* Edinburgh: Edinburgh University Press, 2013.

Hajdarpasic, Edin. *Whose Bosnia? Nationalism and Political Imagination in the Balkans, 1840–1914.* Ithaca, NY: Cornell University Press, 2015.

Hakim, Carol. *The Origins of the Lebanese National Idea 1840–1920.* Berkeley: University of California Press, 2013.

Halabi, Awad. "Islamic Ritual and Palestinian Nationalism: al-Hajj Amin al-Husayni and the Nabi Musa Festival in Jerusalem, 1921–1937," in Lena Jayyusi, ed., *Jerusalem Interrupted: Modernity and Colonial Transformation 1917–Present.* Northampton, MA: Olive Branch Press, 2015, 139–152.

Halabi, Zeina G. *The Unmaking of the Arab Intellectual: Prophecy, Exile and the Nation*. Edinburgh: Edinburgh University Press, 2017.

Hamzah, Dyala. "From *'Ilm* to *Sihafa* or the Politics of the Public Interest (*Maslaha*): Muhammad Rashid Rida and His Journal *al-Manar* 1898–1935," in Dyala Hamzah, ed., *The Making of the Arab Intellectual: Empire, Public Sphere and the Colonial Coordinates of Selfhood*. New York: Routledge, 2013, 90–127.

———, ed. *The Making of the Arab Intellectual: Empire, Public Sphere and the Colonial Coordinates of Selfhood*. New York: Routledge, 2013.

———. *Muhammad Rashid Rida (1865–1935) ou le "Tournant salafiste"—Intérêt général, Islam et opinion publique dans l'Égypte coloniale*. Paris: Éditions du CNRS. Forthcoming, 2019.

Hanioğlu, M. Şükrü. *A Brief History of the Late Ottoman Empire*. Princeton, NJ: Princeton University Press, 2008.

———. *The Young Turks in Opposition*. New York: Oxford University Press, 1996.

Hanley, Will. "Grieving Cosmopolitanism in Middle East Studies." *History Compass* 6 (2008): 1346–1367.

Hanssen, Jens. "Albert's World: Historicism, Liberal Imperialism and the Struggle for Palestine, 1936–1948," in Jens Hanssen and Max Weiss, eds., *Arabic Thought beyond the Liberal Age: Towards an Intellectual History of the Nahda*. Cambridge: Cambridge University Press, 2016, 62–92.

———. *Fin de Siècle Beirut: The Making of an Ottoman Provincial Capital*. Oxford: Oxford University Press, 2005.

———. "Kafka and Arabs." *Critical Inquiry* 39 (2012): 167–197.

Hanssen, Jens, and Hicham Safieddine. *The Clarion of Syria: A Patriot's Call against the Civil War of 1860*. Oakland: University of California Press, 2019.

Hanssen, Jens, and Max Weiss, eds. *Arabic Thought against the Authoritarian Age: Towards an Intellectual History of the Present*. Cambridge: Cambridge University Press, 2018.

———. *Arabic Thought beyond the Liberal Age: Towards an Intellectual History of the Nahda*. Cambridge: Cambridge University Press, 2016.

Hartmann, Michelle, and Alessandro Olsaretti. "'The First Boat and the First Oar': Inventions of Lebanon in the Writings of Michel Chiha." *Radical History Review* 86 (2003): 37–65.

Hashemi, Nader, and Danny Postel, eds. *Sectarianization: Mapping the New Politics of the Middle East*. London: Hurst, 2017.

Hashimi, Ni'am K. El-. "The Higher Teachers College, Baghdad: A History, 1923–1958." Master's thesis, American University of Beirut, 1963.

Hassan, Waïl S. *Immigrant Narratives: Orientalism and Cultural Translation in Arab American and Arab British Literature*. Oxford: Oxford University Press, 2011.

Hasso, Frances. "Modernity and Gender in Arab Accounts of the 1948 and 1967 Defeats." *International Journal of Middle East Studies* 32 (2000): 491–510.

Hathaway, Jane. *The Arab Lands under Ottoman Rule, 1516–1800*. Harlow, UK: Pearson, 2008.

Hattis, Susan Lee. *The Bi-national Idea in Palestine during Mandatory Times*. Haifa: Shikmona, 1970.

Heyberger, Bernard. *Chrétiens du monde arabe: Un archipel en terre d'Islam*. Paris: Éditions Autrement, 2003.

———. *Les Chrétiens du Proche-Orient au temps de la Réforme Catholique*. Rome: École Française de Rome, 1994.

———. "Terre Sainte et mission au XVIIe siècle." *Dimensioni e problemi della ricerca storica*. Rome: Université "La Sapienza," 1994.

Hilali, 'Abd al-Razzaq al-. *Tarikh al-ta'lim fi al-Iraq fi 'ahd al-intidab al-britani 1921–1932*. Baghdad: Dar al-shu'un al-thaqafiyya al-'amma, 2000.

Hill, Peter. "Utopia and Civilisation in the Arab Nahda." D.Phil. diss., Oxford University, 2015.

Hodgson, Marshall G. S. *The Venture of Islam: Conscience and History in a World Civilization, vol. 1: The Classical Age of Islam*. Chicago: University of Chicago Press, 1974.

Holt, Elizabeth. *Fictitious Capital: Silk, Cotton and the Rise of the Arabic Novel*. New York: Fordham University Press, 2017.

Hourani, Albert. *Arabic Thought in the Liberal Age, 1798–1939*. Cambridge: Cambridge University Press, 1983 [1962].

———. "The Case against a Jewish State in Palestine: Albert Hourani's Statement to the Anglo-American Committee of Enquiry of 1946." *Journal of Palestine Studies* 35 (2005): 80–90.

———. *A History of the Arab Peoples*, 2nd ed. Cambridge, MA: Belknap Press of Harvard University Press, 2002.

———. "Ottoman Reform and the Politics of the Notables," in William R. Polk and Richard L. Chambers, eds., *Beginnings of Modernization in the Middle East: The Nineteenth Century*. Chicago: University of Chicago Press, 1968.

———. *Syria and Lebanon: A Political Essay*. Oxford: Royal Institute of International Affairs and Oxford University Press, 1946.

Hout, Bayan Nuwayhed al-. *Al-qiyadat wa al-mu'assasat al-siyasiyya fi Filastin 1917–1948*. Beirut: Mu'assasat al-dirasat al-filastiniyya, 1981.

Huneidi, Sahar. *A Broken Trust: Herbert Samuel, Zionism and the Palestinians 1920–1925*. London: I. B. Tauris, 2001.

Hurewitz, J. C., ed. *The Middle East and North Africa in World Politics: A Documentary Record*, 2 vols. New Haven, CT: Yale University Press, 1975 and 1979.

Husayni, Al-Sayyid ʿAbd al-Razzaq al-, ed. *Tarikh al-wizarat al-ʿiraqiyya fi al-ʿahd al-malaki*, 4 vols. Baghdad: Dar al-shuʾun al-thaqafiyya al-ʿamma, 1988.

Husri, Abu Khaldun Satiʿ al-. *Mabadiʾ al-qiraʾa al-khalduniyya*, 27th ed. Baghdad: Ministry of Education, 1987–1988.

———. *Mudhakirrati fil Iraq, 1921–1941*, 2 vols. Beirut: Dar al-taliʿa, 1967.

———. *Naqd taqrir lajnat Munru*. Baghdad: Matbaʿat al-najah, 1932.

———. *Safahat min al-madi al-qarib*. Beirut: Markaz dirasat al-wahda al-ʿarabiyya, 1985 [1948].

Husry, Khaldun S. "The Assyrian Affair of 1933 (I)." *International Journal of Middle East Studies* 3 (1974): 161–176.

Ibrahim, Vivian. "Beyond the Cross and the Crescent: Plural Identities and the Copts in Contemporary Egypt." *Ethnic and Racial Studies* 38 (2015): 2584–2597.

———. *The Copts of Egypt: The Challenges of Modernisation and Identity*. London: I. B. Tauris, 2013.

Ilicak, Huseyin Sukru. "A Radical Rethinking of Empire: Ottoman State and Society during the Greek War of Independence 1821–1826." PhD diss., Harvard University, 2011.

Imber, Colin. *Ebuʾs-suʿud: The Islamic Legal Tradition*. Stanford, CA: Stanford University Press, 1997.

Ismail, Adel, ed. *Documents diplomatiques et consulaires relatifs a l'histoire du Liban: Les sources Anglaises*. Beirut: Éditions des Oeuvres Politiques et Historiques, 2000.

Jabri, Muhammad ʿAbed al-. *Al-mashruʾ al-nahdawi al-ʿarabi: murajaʾah naqdiyya*. Beirut: Al-Muʾsasat al-ʿarabiyya li al-dirisat wa al-nashir, 1996.

———. *Arab-Islamic Philosophy: A Contemporary Critique*, trans. Aziz Abbassi. Austin: University of Texas Press, 1999.

Jacobs, Matthew F. *Imagining the Middle East: The Building of an American Foreign Policy, 1918–1967*. Chapel Hill: University of North Carolina Press, 2011.

Jacobson, Abigail. *From Empire to Empire: Jerusalem between Ottomanism and British Rule*. Syracuse, NY: Syracuse University Press, 2011.

———. *Oriental Neighbors: Middle Eastern Jews and Arabs in Mandatory Palestine*. Waltham, MA: Brandeis University Press, 2016.

Jalloul, Maïssa. "Une histoire en clair-obscur: 1860 dans La Revue phénicienne 1919," in Dima de Clerc, Carla Eddé, Naila Kaidbey, and Souad Slim, eds., *1860: Histoires et mémoires d'un conflit*. Beirut: Institut Français du Proche-Orient, 2015, 363–386.

Jawahri, Muhammad Mahdi al-. *Dhikrayati*, 2 vols. Damascus: Dar al-Rafidayn, 1988.

Jaza'iri, Al-amir Muhammad Sa'id al-. *Mudhakkirati 'an al-qadaya al-'arabiyya was al-'alam al-islami*. Algiers: Dar al-yaqdha al-'arabiyya, 1968.

Jefferson, Thomas. First Inaugural Address, March 4, 1801. The Avalon Project at Yale Law School. http://avalon.law.yale.edu/19th_century/jefinau1.asp.

Jiha, Michel, ed. *Al-munazara al-diniyya bayna al-shaykh Muhammad Abduh wa Farah Antun*. Beirut: Bisan, 2014.

Jiha, Shafiq, ed. *Al-dustur al-lubnani*. Beirut: Dar al'ilm lil-malayin, 1991.

Johnson, Michael. *All Honorable Men: The Social Origins of War in Lebanon*. London: Centre for Lebanese Studies and I. B. Tauris, 2001.

Kalisman, Hilary Falb. "Bursary Scholars at the American University of Beirut: Living and Practicing Arab Unity." *British Journal of Middle Eastern Studies* 42 (2015): 599–617.

Kamil, Mustafa. *Kitab al-mas'ala al-sharqiyya*. Cairo: Al-Adab, 1898.

Karpat, Kemal H. *Ottoman Population 1830–1914: Demographic and Social Characteristics*. Madison: University of Wisconsin Press, 1985.

———. *The Politicization of Islam: Reconstructing Identity, State, Faith and Community in the Late Ottoman State*. Oxford: Oxford University Press, 2001.

Kassab, Elizabeth S. *Contemporary Arab Thought: Cultural Critique in Comparative Perspective*. New York: Columbia University Press, 2010.

Kaufman, Asher. *Contested Frontiers in the Syria-Lebanon-Israel Region: Cartography, Sovereignty, and Conflict*. Baltimore: Johns Hopkins University Press, 2013.

———. *Reviving Phoenicia: The Search for Identity in Lebanon*. London: I. B. Tauris, 2004.

Kayali, Hasan. *Arabs and Young Turks: Ottomanism, Arabism, and Islamism in the Ottoman Empire, 1908–1918*. Berkeley: University of California Press, 1997.

Kayyali, 'Abd al-Wahab al-, ed. *Watha'iq al-muqawama al-filastiniyya al-'arabiyya*. Beirut: Mu'assasat al-dirasat al-filastiniyya, 1988 [1968].

Kedourie, Elie. *The Chatham House Version and Other Middle-Eastern Studies*, new ed. Hanover, NH: University Press of New England, 1984 [1970].

Kern, Karen M. *Imperial Citizen: Marriage and Citizenship in the Ottoman Frontier Provinces of Iraq*. Syracuse, NY: Syracuse University Press, 2011.

Khalidi, Rashid. *Palestinian Identity: The Construction of Modern National Consciousness*. New York: Columbia University Press, 1997.

Khatib, Muhammad Kamil. *Takwin al-nahda al-'arabiyya 1800–2000*. Damascus: Matba'at al-Yaziji, 2001.

Khazen, Farid el. *The Breakdown of the State in Lebanon, 1967–1976*. Cambridge, MA: Harvard University Press, 2000.

———. *The Communal Pact of National Identities: The Making and Politics of the 1943 National Pact*. Oxford: Centre for Lebanese Studies, 1991.

Khoury, Dina Rizk. *Iraq in Wartime: Soldiering, Martyrdom, and Remembrance.* Cambridge: Cambridge University Press, 2013.

———. "Reflections on Nationality and Sect in Iraqi History." The Fourteenth Annual Wadie Jwaideh Memorial Lecture. Department of Near Eastern Languages and Cultures, University of Indiana, Bloomington, IN, October 15, 2015.

———. "The Security State and the Practice and Rhetoric of Sectarianism in Iraq." *International Journal of Contemporary Iraqi Studies* (2010) 4: 325–338.

Khoury, Gérard D. "Robert de Caix et Louis Massignon: Deux visions de la politique française au Levant en 1920," in Nadine Méouchy and Peter Sluglett, eds., *The British and French Mandates in Comparative Perspectives.* Leiden, The Netherlands: Brill, 2004, 165–184.

Khoury, Philip S. *Syria and the French Mandate: The Politics of Arab Nationalism, 1920–1945.* Princeton, NJ: Princeton University Press, 1987.

Khoury [Khuri], Yusuf Q. *Al-bayanat al-wizariyya al-lubnaniyya wa munaqashatuha fi majli al-nuwwab, 1926–1984,* 3 vols. Beirut: mu'assasat al-dirasat al-lubnaniyya, 1986.

———, ed. *Al-Dasatir fi al-'alam al-'arabi: nusus wa ta'dilat: 1839–1987.* Beirut: Dar al-Hamra', 1989.

———. *Al-ta'ifiyya fi Lubnan min khilal munaqashat majlis al-nuwwab 1923–1987.* Beirut: Dar al-Hamra', 1989.

———. *Rajul sabiq li 'asrihi: al-mu'allim Butrus al Bustani, 1819–1883.* Beirut: Bisan, 1995.

Khuri-Makdisi, Ilham. *The Eastern Mediterranean and the Making of Global Radicalism, 1860–1914.* Berkeley: University of California Press, 2010.

———. "The *Nahda* Revisited: Socialism and Radicalism in Beirut and Mount Lebanon, 1900–1914," in Christoph Schumann, ed., *Liberal Thought in the Eastern Mediterranean: Late 19th Century until the 1960s.* Leiden, The Netherlands: Brill, 2008, 147–174.

Kieser, Hans-Lukas. "From 'Patriotism' to Mass Murder: Dr. Mehmed Reşid 1873–1919," in Ronald Grigor Suny, Fatma Müge Göçek, and Norman M. Naimark, eds., *A Question of Genocide: Armenians and Turks at the End of the Ottoman Empire.* Oxford: Oxford University Press, 2011, 126–150.

———. "Réformes ottomanes et cohabitation entre chrétiens et Kurdes 1839–1915." *Études rurales* 186 (2010): 43–60.

Kilani, Muhammad Sayyid. *Al-adab al-qibti qadiman wa hadithan.* Cairo: Dar al-qawmiyya al-'arabiyya lil-tiba'a, 1963.

Kitromilides, Paschalis M. "'Imagined Communities' and the Origins of the National Question in the Balkans," in *Enlightenment, Nationalism, Orthodoxy: Studies in the Culture and Political Thought of South-Eastern Europe.* Aldershot, UK: Variorum, 1994.

Klein, Janet. *The Margins of Empire: Kurdish Militias in the Ottoman Tribal Zone*. Stanford, CA: Stanford University Press, 2011.

Kobiljski, Aleksandra. "Un modèle américain? Les collèges protestants de Beyrouth et Kyoto, 1860–1975." *Monde(s)* 6 (2014): 171–193.

Krämer, Gudrun. *A History of Palestine: From Ottoman Conquest to the Founding of the State of Israel*, trans. Graham Harman and Gudrun Krämer. Princeton, NJ: Princeton University Press, 2008.

Kramer, Paul A. "Power and Connection: Imperial Histories of the United States in the World." *American Historical Review* 116 (2011): 1348–1391.

Krimsti, Firas. "The 1850 Uprising in Aleppo: Reconsidering the Explanatory Power of Sectarian Argumentation," in Ulrike Freitag, Nelida Fuccaro, Claudia Ghrawi, and Nora Lafi, eds., *Urban Violence in the Middle East: Changing Cityscapes in the Transition from Empire to Nation State*. New York: Berghahn Books, 2015.

Krstic, Tijana. *Contested Conversions to Islam: Narratives of Religious Change in the Early Modern Ottoman Empire*. Stanford, CA: Stanford University Press, 2011.

Kurd 'Ali, Muhammad. *Kitab Khitat al-Sham, vol. 1*. Damascus: al-matba'a al-haditha, 1925.

Kuroki, Hidemitsu. "The 1850 Aleppo Disturbance Reconsidered," in Markus Köhbach, Gisela Procházka-Eisl, and Claudia Römer, eds., *Acta Viennensia Ottomanica: Proceedings of the 13th CIEPO Symposium, Vienna*, 1999.

Kuruvilla, Samuel J. *Radical Christianity in Palestine and Israel: Liberation and Theology in the Middle East*. London: I. B. Tauris, 2013.

Laffan, Michael. "'Another Andalusia': Images of Colonial Southeast Asia in Arabic Newspapers." *Journal of Asian Studies* 66 (2007): 689–722.

Laroui, Abdullah. *History of the Maghrib: An Interpretive Essay*, trans. Ralph Manheim. Princeton, NJ: Princeton University Press, 1977 [1970].

Levy, Avigdor, ed. *Jews, Turks, Ottomans: A Shared History, Fifteenth through the Twentieth Century*. Syracuse, NY: Syracuse University Press, 2002.

Levy, Lital. "Partitioned Pasts: Arab Jewish Intellectuals and the Case of Esther Azhari Moyal 1873–1948," in Dyala Hamzah, ed., *The Making of the Arab Intellectual: Empire, Public Sphere and the Colonial Coordinates of Selfhood*. New York: Routledge, 2013, 128–163.

Lewis, Bernard. *The Jews of Islam*. Princeton, NJ: Princeton University Press, 1984.

Lieven, Dominic. *Empire: The Russian Empire and Its Rivals*. New Haven, CT: Yale University Press, 2002.

Lubnan al-akhar, mu'tamar hawla al-'almana wa al-hawiyya al-'arabiyya. Beirut: Mu'assasat al-dirasat wa al-abhath al-lubnaniyya, 1976.

Mahmood, Saba. *Religious Difference in a Secular Age: A Minority Report*. Princeton, NJ: Princeton University Press, 2016.

Makarius, Shahin. *Tarikh al-Isra'iliyyin*. Cairo: Matba'at al-Muqtataf, 1904.

Makdisi, Ussama. "After 1860: Debating Religion, Reform, and Nationalism in the Ottoman Empire." *International Journal of Middle Eastern Studies* 34 (2002): 601–617.

———. *Artillery of Heaven: American Missionaries and the Failed Conversion of the Middle East*. Ithaca, NY: Cornell University Press, 2008.

———. *Culture of Sectarianism: Community, History, and Violence in Nineteenth-Century Ottoman Lebanon*. Berkeley: University of California Press, 2000.

———. "Diminished Sovereignty and the Impossibility of 'Civil War' in the Modern Middle East." *American Historical Review* 120 (2015): 1739–1752.

Maksudyan, Nazan. "New 'Rules of Conduct' for State, American Missionaries, and Armenians: 1909 Adana Massacres and the Ottoman Orphanage Darü'l-Eytam-ı Osmani," in François Georgeon, ed., *"L'ivresse de la liberté": La revolution de 1908 dans l'Empire ottoman*. Paris: CNRS, 2012, 137–171.

Maktabi, Rania. "The Lebanese Census of 1932 Revisited. Who Are the Lebanese?" *British Journal of Middle Eastern Studies* 26 (1999): 219–241.

Mallat, Chibli. *Introduction to Middle Eastern Law*. Oxford: Oxford University Press, 2007.

Mamdani, Mahmood. *Citizen and Subject: Contemporary Africa and the Legacy of Late Colonialism*. Princeton, NJ: Princeton University Press, 1996.

Mandel, Neville J. *The Arabs and Zionism before World War I*. Berkeley: University of California Press, 1976.

Manna, Adel. *Nakbatun wa baqa': hikayatu filastiniyiin zallu fi Haifa wa al-Jalil (1948–1956)*. Beirut: Markaz al-dirasat al-filastiniyya, 2016.

Maoz, Moshe. *Ottoman Reform in Syria and Palestine 1840–1861: The Impact of the Tanzimat on Politics and Society*. Oxford: Oxford University Press, 1968.

Martykanova, Darina. "Matching Sharia and 'Governmentality': Muslim Marriage Legislation in the Late Ottoman Empire," in Andrea Gémes, Florence Peyrou, and Ioannis Xydopolous, eds., *Institutional Change and Stability: Conflicts, Transitions and Social Values*. Pisa, Italy: PLUS-Pisa University Press, 2009, 153–175.

Masters, Bruce. *The Arabs of the Ottoman Empire, 1516–1918: A Social and Cultural History*. Cambridge: Cambridge University Press, 2013.

———. *Christians and Jews in the Ottoman Arab World: The Roots of Sectarianism*. Cambridge: Cambridge University Press, 2001.

Matthews, Roderic D., and Matta Akrawi. *Education in Arab Countries of the Near East: Egypt, Iraq, Palestine, Transjordan, Syria, Lebanon*. Washington, DC: American Council on Education, 1949.

Matthews, Weldon C. "The Kennedy Administration, Counterinsurgency, and Iraq's First Ba'thist Regime." *International Journal of Middle East Studies* 43 (2011): 635–653.

―――. "Pan-Islam or Arab Nationalism? The Meaning of the 1931 Jerusalem Islamic Congress Reconsidered." *International Journal of Middle Eastern Studies* 35 (2003): 1–22.

Mazza, Roberto. "Transforming the Holy City: From Communal Clashes to Urban Violence, the Nebi Musa Riots in 1920," in Ulrike Freitag, Nelida Fuccaro, Claudia Ghrawi, and Nora Lafi, eds., *Urban Violence in the Middle East: Changing Cityscapes in the Transition from Empire to Nation State.* New York: Beghahn, 2015, 179–194.

McCarthy, Justin. *Death and Exile: The Ethnic Cleansing of Ottoman Muslims 1821–1922.* Princeton, NJ: Darwin Press, 1995.

Mestyan, Adam. *Arab Patriotism: The Ideology and Culture of Power in Late Ottoman Egypt.* Princeton, NJ: Princeton University Press, 2017.

Meyer, Michael A., ed. *German-Jewish History in Modern Times, vol. 2: Emancipation and Acculturation, 1780–1871.* New York: Columbia University Press, 1997.

―――. *German-Jewish History in Modern Times, vol. 3: Integration in Dispute, 1871–1918.* New York: Columbia University Press, 1998.

Midhat Bey, Ali Haydar. *The Life of Midhat Pasha: A Record of His Services, Political Reforms, Banishment, and Judicial Murder.* London: John Murray, 1903.

Midhat Pasha. "The Past, Present, and Future of Turkey." *The Nineteenth Century* XVI (June 1878): 982–983.

Mikdashi, Maya. "Sectarianism: Notes on Studying the Lebanese State," in Amal Ghazal and Jens Hanssen, eds., *The Oxford Handbook of Contemporary Middle-Eastern and North African History.* Oxford: Oxford University Press. Published online June 2018. DOI: 10.1093/oxfordhb/9780199672530.013.24.

Mikhayil, Kyriakos. *Copts and Moslems under British Control: A Collection of Facts and a Résumé of Authoritative Opinions on the Coptic Question.* London: Smith, Elder, 1911.

Miqdadi, Darwish. *Tarikh al-umma al-'arabiyya.* Baghdad: Dar al-tiba'a al-haditha, 1936.

Mishaqa, Mikhail. *Murder, Mayhem, Pillage and Plunder: The History of the Lebanon in the 18th and 19th Centuries,* trans. Wheeler M. Thackston Jr. Albany: State University of New York Press, 1988.

Mislin, David. *Saving Faith: Making Religious Pluralism an American Value at the Dawn of the Secular Age.* Ithaca, NY: Cornell University Press, 2015.

Morgan, Edmund S. *American Slavery, American Freedom.* New York: W.W. Norton, 1975.

Morris, Benny. *The Birth of the Palestinian Refugee Problem Revisited,* 2nd ed. Cambridge: Cambridge University Press, 2004 [1988].

Nachmani, Amicham. *Great Power Discord in Palestine.* London: Frank Cass, 1987.

Nafi, Basheer M. *Arabism, Islamism and the Palestine Question, 1908-1941: A Political History.* Reading, UK: Ithaca Press, 1998.

Naqqash, Zaki al-, and ʻUmar Farrukh. *Tarikh Suriyya wa Lubnan al-musawwar.* Beirut: Matbaʻat al-Kashshaf, 1933.

Neep, Daniel. *Occupying Syria under the French Mandate: Insurgency, Space and State Formation.* Cambridge: Cambridge University Press, 2012.

Noradounghian, Gabriel Effendi, ed. *Recueil d'actes internationaux de l'empire ottoman, vol. 3: 1865-1878.* Paris, 1902.

Osman, Khalil F. *Sectarianism in Iraq: The Making of State and Nation since 1920.* London: Routledge, 2015.

Owen, Roger, and Şevket Pamuk. *A History of Middle East Economies in the Twentieth Century.* London: I. B. Tauris, 1998.

Özbek, Nadir. "Defining the Public Sphere during the Late Ottoman Empire: War, Mass Mobilization and the Young Turk Regime 1908-18." *Middle Eastern Studies* 43 (2007): 795-809.

Pamuk, Şevket, and Jeffery G. Williamson. "Ottoman De-industrialization, 1800-1913: Assessing the Magnitude, Impact, and Response." *Economic History Review* 64 (2011): 159-184.

Papademetriou, Tom. *Render unto the Sultan: Power, Authority, and the Greek Orthodox Church in the Early Ottoman Centuries.* New York: Oxford University Press, 2014.

Pappe, Ilan. *The Ethnic Cleansing of Palestine.* Oxford: Oneworld, 2006.

———. *The Rise and Fall of a Palestinian Dynasty: The Husaynis 1700-1948.* Berkeley: University of California Press, 2010.

Parsons, Laila. *The Commander: Fawzi Al-Qawuqji and the Fight for Arab Independence 1914-1948.* New York: Hill and Wang, 2016.

Peirce, Leslie. *Morality Tales: Law and Gender in the Ottoman Court of Aintab.* Berkeley: University of California Press, 2003.

Perkins, Bradford. *The Cambridge History of American Foreign Relations, vol. 1: The Creation of a Republican Empire, 1776-1865.* Cambridge: Cambridge University Press, 1993.

Philipp, Thomas. *Acre: The Rise and Fall of a Palestinian City, 1730-1831.* New York: Columbia University Press, 2001.

———. *Jurji Zaydan and the Foundations of Arab Nationalism.* Syracuse, NY: Syracuse University Press, 2010.

Philliou, Christine M. *Biography of an Empire: Governing Ottomans in an Age of Revolution.* Berkeley: University of California Press, 2011.

———. "Nationalism, Internationalism and Cosmopolitanism: Comparison and Commensurability." *Comparative Studies of South Asia, Africa and the Middle East* 36 (2016): 455-464.

———. "The Paradox of Perceptions: Interpreting the Ottoman Past through the Nationalist Present." *Middle Eastern Studies* 44 (2008): 661-675.

Picaudou, Nadine. "The Historiography of the 1948 Wars." *Online Encyclopedia of Mass Violence*, November 1, 2008, www.sciencespo.fr/mass-violence-war-massacre-resistance/en/document/historiography-1948-wars.

Piterberg, Gabriel. *The Returns of Zionism: Myths, Politics and Scholarship in Israel*. London: Verso, 2008.

Porath, Y. *The Emergence of the Palestinian Arab National Movement 1918–1929*. London: Frank Cass, 1974.

Provence, Michael. *The Last Ottoman Generation and the Making of the Modern Middle East*. Cambridge: Cambridge University Press, 2017.

———. "'Liberal Colonialism' and Martial Law in French Mandate Syria," in Christoph Schumann, ed., *Liberal Thought in the Eastern Mediterranean: Late 19th Century until the 1960s*. Leiden, The Netherlands: Brill, 2008, 51–74.

Pursley, Sara. *Familiar Futures: Time, Selfhood, and Sovereignty in Iraq*. Stanford, CA: Stanford University Press, 2019.

Qaradawi, Yusuf al-. *Non-Muslims in the Islamic Society*, trans. Khalil Muhammad Hamad and Sayed Mahboob Ali Shah. Indianapolis, IN: American Trust, 1985.

Qattan, Najwa al-. "The Damascene Jewish Community in the Latter Decades of the Eighteenth Century," in Thomas Philipp, ed., *The Syrian Land in the 18th and 19th Century*. Stuttgart, Germany: F. Steiner, 1992.

———. "Dhimmis in the Muslim Court: Legal Autonomy and Religious Discrimination." *International Journal of Middle East Studies* 31 (1999): 429–444.

Quataert, Donald. "Clothing Laws, State, and Society in the Ottoman Empire, 1720–1829." *International Journal of Middle East Studies* 29 (1997): 403–425.

Rabbath, Edmond. *La constitution libanaise: Origines, textes, et commentaires*. Beirut: Publications de l'Université Libanaise, 1982.

———. *La formation historique du Liban politique et constitutionnel: Essai de synthèse*, nouvelle édition. Beirut: Publications de l'Université Libanaise, 1986.

Rafeq, Abdel Karim. "New Light on the 1860 Riots in Ottoman Damascus." *Die Welt des Islams* 28 (1988): 412–430.

Rasheed, Madawi al-. "Sectarianism as Counter-Revolution: Saudi Responses to the Arab Spring." *Studies in Ethnicity and Nationalism* 11 (2011): 513–526.

Ratzabi, Shalom. *Between Zionism and Judaism: The Radical Circle of Brith Shalom, 1925–1930*. Leiden, The Netherlands: Brill, 2002.

Rawls, John. "The Idea of an Overlapping Consensus." *Oxford Journal of Legal Studies* 7 (1987): 1–25.

Raz-Krakotzkin, Amnon. "Jewish Memory between Exile and History." *Jewish Quarterly Review* 97 (2007): 530–543.

Razzaz, Munif al-. *Al-a'mal al-fikriyya wa al-siyasiyya*, 2 vols. Amman: mu'assasat Munif al Razzaz lil-dirasat al-qawmiyya, 1986.

——. *Ma'alim al-hayat al-'arabiyya al-jadida.* Beirut: Dar al-'ilm lil-malayin, 1964.

Reid, Donald M. *The Odyssey of Farah Antun: A Syrian Christian's Quest for Secularism.* Minneapolis, MN: Bibliotheca Islamica, 1975.

Reid, James J. *Crisis of the Ottoman Empire: Prelude to Collapse 1839–1878.* Stuttgart, Germany: F. Steiner, 2000.

Reinharz, Jehuda. "The Balfour Declaration and Its Maker: A Reassessment." *Journal of Modern History* 64 (1992): 455–499.

Renton, James. "Flawed Foundations: The Balfour Declaration and the Palestine Mandate," in Rory Miller, ed., *Britain, Palestine and Empire: The Mandate Years.* Farnham, UK: Ashgate, 2010, 15–38.

Report by His Britannic Majesty's Government on the Administration of 'Iraq for the Period April 1923–December 1924. Geneva: League of Nations, 1925.

Reynolds, Michael A. *Shattering Empires: The Clash and Collapse of the Ottoman and Russian Empires, 1908–1918.* Cambridge: Cambridge University Press, 2011.

Rida, Rashid, ed. *Kitab intiqad kitab tarikh al-tamaddun al-islami.* Cairo: Al-Manar, 1912.

——. *Tarikh al-ustadh al-imam al-shaykh Muhammad Abduh, vol. 1, part 1.* Beirut: Dar al-Fadila, 2003.

Rihani, Amin. "Al-nahda al-sharqiyya al-haditha." *Al-Muqtataf* (1927): 488–492.

——. *Kashkul al-khawatir: khamsun maqala majhula,* ed. Jan Daye. Beirut: Fajr al-nahda, 2014.

——. *Qalb al-Iraq: Rihalat wa tarikh.* Beirut: Dar al-jil, n.d.

Robinson, Shira. *Citizen Strangers: Palestinians and the Birth of Israel's Liberal Settler State.* Stanford, CA: Stanford University Press, 2013.

Robson, Laura. *Colonialism and Christianity in Mandate Palestine.* Austin: University of Texas Press, 2011.

——. *States of Separation: Transfer, Partition, and the Making of the Modern Middle East.* Oakland: University of California Press, 2017.

Rodogno, Davide. *Against Massacre: Humanitarian Interventions in the Ottoman Empire, 1815–1914.* Princeton, NJ: Princeton University Press, 2012.

Rodrigue, Aaron. "Difference and Tolerance in the Ottoman Empire: Interview by Nancy Reynolds." *Stanford Electronic Humanities Review* 5 (1996), http://web.stanford.edu/group/SHR/5-1/text/rodrigue.html.

Roediger, David. *The Wages of Whiteness: Race and the Making of the American Working Class.* London: Verso, 1991.

Rose, Jacqueline. *Question of Zion.* Princeton, NJ: Princeton University Press, 2005.

Roudometof, Victor. "From Rum Millet to Greek Nation: Enlightenment, Secularization, and National Identity in Ottoman Balkan Society, 1453–1821." *Journal of Modern Greek Studies* 16 (1998): 11–48.

Rouhana, Nadim N., and Sahar S. Huneidi, eds. *Israel and Its Palestinian Citizens: Ethnic Privileges in a Jewish State*. Cambridge: Cambridge University Press, 2017.

Rouse, Ruth, ed. *A History of the Ecumenical Movement 1517–1948*. London: SPCK, 1954.

Rubay'i, Fadil, and Wahjih Kawtharani. *Al-ta'ifiyya wa al-harb*. Damascus: Dar al-Fikr, 2011.

Rustum, Asad, and Fouad Efram Bustani. *Tarikh lubnan al-mujaz*. Beirut: al-matba'a al-kathulikiyya, 1937.

Ryad, Umar. *Islamic Reformism and Christianity: A Critical Reading of the Works of Muhammad Rashīd Riḍā and His Associates 1898–1935*. Leiden, The Netherlands: Brill, 2009.

———. "A Printed Muslim 'Lighthouse' in Cairo: Al-Manar's Early Years, Aspiration and Reception 1898–1903." *Arabica* 56 (2009): 27–60.

Saadeh, Antun. "Al-hizbiyya al-diniyya la'natu al-umma," *Kull shay'* (Beirut), April 1, 1949, reproduced online at http://antoun-saadeh.com.

Said, Edward W. *Culture and Imperialism*. New York: Knopf, 1993.

———. *The World, the Text, and the Critic*. Cambridge, MA: Harvard University Press, 1983.

Sakakini, Khalil al-. *Yawmiyyat Khalil al-Sakakini, vol. 3: "Ikhtibar" al-intidab wa as'ilat al-hawiyya, 1919–1922*. Ramallah and Jerusalem: Khalil Sakakini Cultural Centre and Institute of Jerusalem Studies, 2004.

Saleh, Yassin al-Haj. *The Impossible Revolution: Making Sense of the Syrian Tragedy*. London: C. Hurst, 2017.

Salibi, Kamal. *A House of Many Mansions: The History of Lebanon Reconsidered*. London: I. B. Tauris, 1988.

Sayed, Linda. "Sectarian Homes: The Making of Shi'i Families and Citizens under the French Mandate 1918–1943." PhD diss., Columbia University, 2013.

Sbaiti, Nadya. "If the Devil Taught French: Strategies of Language and Learning in French Mandate Beirut," in Osama Abi-Mershed, ed., *Trajectories of Education in the Arab World: Legacies and Challenges*. New York: Routledge, 2010.

Schaller, Dominik J., and Jürgen Zimmerer. "Late Ottoman Genocides: The Dissolution of the Ottoman Empire and Young Turkish Population and Extermination Policies—introduction." *Journal of Genocide Research* 10 (2008): 7–14.

Schayegh, Cyrus. *The Middle East and the Making of the Modern World*. Cambridge, MA: Harvard University Press, 2017.

Schielke, Samuli. "Second Thoughts about the Anthropology of Islam, or How to Make Sense of Grand Schemes in Everyday Life." *Working Papers, Zentrum Moderner Orient*, no. 2 (2010): 1–16.

Schilcher, Linda Schatkowski. *Families in Politics: Damascene Factions and Estates of the 18th and 19th Centuries*. Stuttgart, Germany: F. Steiner, 1985.

Schull, Kent F., M. Safa Saraçoğlu, and Robert Zens, eds. *Law and Legality in the Ottoman Empire and the Republic of Turkey*. Bloomington: Indiana University Press, 2016.

Schumann, Christoph. "The Generation of Broad Expectations: Nationalism, Education and Autobiography in Syria and Lebanon, 1930–1958," in Dyala Hamzah, ed., *The Making of the Arab Intellectual: Empire, Public Sphere and the Colonial Coordinates of Selfhood*. New York: Routledge, 2013, 188–211.

Sedra, Paul. "Church-State Relations in Egypt." *Middle East Institute*, February 24, 2014, www.mei.edu/content/church-state-relations-egypt.

———. "Class Cleavages and Ethnic Conflict: Coptic Christian Communities in Modern Egyptian Politics." *Islam and Christian-Muslim Relations* 10 (1999): 219–235.

Segev, Tom. *One Palestine Complete: Jews and Arabs under the British Mandate*, trans. Haim Watzman. New York: Metropolitan Books, 2000.

Seikaly, Samir. "Coptic Communal Reform: 1860–1914." *Middle Eastern Studies* 6 (1970): 247–275.

Seikaly, Sherene. *Men of Capital: Scarcity and Economy in Mandate Palestine*. Stanford, CA: Stanford University Press, 2016.

Semerdjian, Elyse. "Naked Anxiety: Bathhouses, Nudity, and the Dhimmi Woman in 18th Century Aleppo." *International Journal of Middle East Studies* 45 (2013): 651–676.

Shabeeb, Samih. "Poetry of Rebellion: The Life, Verse and Death of Nuh Ibrahim during the 1936–39 Revolt." *Jerusalem Quarterly* 25 (2006): 65–78.

Shafir, Gershon. *Land, Labor and the Origins of the Israeli-Palestinian Conflict, 1882–1914*. Cambridge: Cambridge University Press, 1989.

Shakry, Omnia El. "'History without Documents': The Vexed Archives of Decolonization in the Middle East." *American Historical Review* 120 (2015): 920–934.

———. "Schooled Mothers and Structured Play: Child Rearing in Turn-of-the-Century Egypt," in Lila Abu-Lughod, ed., *Remaking Women: Feminism and Modernity in the Middle East*. Princeton, NJ: Princeton University Press, 1998, 126–170.

Shapira, Anita. "Ben-Gurion and the Bible: The Forging of an Historical Narrative?" *Middle Eastern Studies* 33 (1997): 645–674.

Sharif, Malek. "The 1903 'Massacre of Christians' in Beriut and Its Immediate Aftermath Revisited," in Hidemitsu Kuroki, ed., *Human Mobility and Multiethnic Coexistence in Middle Eastern Urban Societies 2: Tehran, Cairo, Istanbul, Aleppo, and Beirut*. Tokyo: ILCAA, 2018, 225–245.

———. *Imperial Norms and Local Realities: The Ottoman Municipal Laws and the Municipality of Beirut, 1860–1908*. Beirut: Orient-Institut, 2014.

Shavit, Ari. "Survival of the Fittest? An Interview with Benny Morris." *Logos: A Journal of Modern Society & Culture* 3 (2004). www.logosjournal.com /morris.htm.

Shaw, Stanford J. *History of the Ottoman Empire and Modern Turkey, vol. 1: Empire of the Gazis: The Rise and Decline of the Ottoman Empire 1280– 1808*. Cambridge: Cambridge University Press, 1976.

———. "The Origins of Representative Government in the Ottoman Empire: An Introduction to Provincial Councils, 1839–1876," in R. Bayly Winder, ed., *Near Eastern Round Table, 1967–68*. New York: Near East Center and the Center for International Studies, New York University, 1969.

Shaw, Stanford J., and Ezel Kural Shaw. *History of the Ottoman Empire and Modern Turkey, vol. 2: Reform, Revolution, and Republic; the Rise of Modern Turkey 1808–1975*. Cambridge: Cambridge University Press, 1977.

Sheehi, Steven. "Butrus al-Bustani: Syria's Ideologue of the Age," in Adel Beshara, ed., *The Origins of Syrian Nationhood: History, Pioneers and Identity*. New York: Routledge, 2011.

Shehadi, Lamia, Suad Slim, Maher Jarrar, and Nader al-Bizri, eds. *Asad Rustum: Mu'assis 'ilm al-tarikh fi al-'alam al-'arabi*. Beirut: AUB and Dar al-Farabi, 2015.

Shenhav, Yehouda. "The Jews of Iraq, Zionist Ideology, and the Property of the Palestinian Refugees of 1948: An Anomaly of National Accounting." *International Journal of Middle Eastern Studies* 31 (1999): 605–630.

Shihabi, Haydar Ahmad al-. *Lubnan fi 'ahd al-umera' al-shihabiyyin*, 3 vols., ed. Asad Rustum and Fu'ad Efram al-Bustani. Beirut: Manshurat al-maktaba al-bulusiyya, 1984.

Sluglett, Peter. *Britain in Iraq: Contriving King and Country*. New York: Columbia University Press, 2007.

Smith, Charles D. *Palestine and the Arab-Israeli Conflict: A History with Documents*, 9th ed. Boston: Bedford/St. Martin's, 2017.

Smith, Eli. *Toleration in the Turkish Empire*. Boston: T. R. Marvin, 1846.

Sonyel, Salahi R. "How the Turks of the Peloponnese Were Exterminated during the Greek Rebellion." *Belleten* 62 (1998): 121–135.

Stanley, Brian. *The World Missionary Conference, Edinburgh 1910*. Grand Rapids, MI: William B. Eerdmans, 2009.

Suleiman, Yasir. *The Arabic Language and National Identity: A Study in Ideology*. Edinburgh: Edinburgh University Press, 2003.

Sultany, Nimer. "The Legal Structures of Subordination: The Palestinian Minority and Israeli Law," in Nadim N. Rouhana and Sahar S. Huneidi, eds., *Israel and Its Palestinian Citizens: Ethnic Privileges in a Jewish State*. Cambridge: Cambridge University Press, 2017.

Suny, Ronald Grigor, Fatma Müge Göçek, and Norman M. Naimark, eds. *A Question of Genocide: Armenians and Turks at the End of the Ottoman Empire.* Oxford: Oxford University Press, 2011.

Talhamy, Yvette. "The *Fatwas* and the Nusayri/Alawis of Syria." *Middle Eastern Studies* 46 (2010): 175–194.

Tamari, Salim. *Mountain against the Sea: Essays on Palestinian Society and Culture.* Berkeley: University of California Press, 2009.

Tamer, Georges. "Nasr Hamid Abu Zayd." *International Journal for Middle East Studies* 43 (2011): 193–195.

Tanielian, Melanie S. *The Charity of War: Famine, Humanitarian Aid, and World War I in the Middle East.* Stanford, CA: Stanford University Press, 2017.

Tarazi, Philippe de. *Tarikh al-sahafa al-'arabiyya.* Beirut: n.p., 1913–1914.

Terzioğlu, Derin. "Where 'Ilm-i Hal Meets Catechism: Islamic Manuals of Religious Instruction in the Ottoman Empire in the Age of Confessionalization." *Past and Present* 220 (2013): 79–114.

Teveth, Shabtai. *Ben-Gurion: The Burning Ground, 1886–1948.* Boston: Houghton Mifflin, 1987.

Tezcan, Baki. *The Second Ottoman Empire: Political and Social Transformation in the Early Modern World.* Cambridge: Cambridge University Press, 2010.

The Other Balkan Wars: A 1913 Carnegie Endowment in Retrospect. Washington, DC: Carnegie Endowment, 1993 [1914].

Thompson, Elizabeth F. *Colonial Citizens: Republican Rights, Paternal Privilege, and Gender in French Syria and Lebanon.* New York: Columbia University Press, 2000.

———. "Rashid Rida and the 1920 Syrian-Arab Constitution: How the French Mandate Undermined Islamic Liberalism," in Cyrus Schayegh and Andrew Arsan, eds., *The Routledge Handbook of the History of the Middle East Mandates.* Milton Park, UK: Routledge, 2015, 244–257.

Tibi, Bassam. *Arab Nationalism: Between Islam and the Nation-State,* 3rd ed. London: Macmillan, 1997.

Traboulsi, Fawwaz. *A History of Modern Lebanon,* 2nd ed. London: Pluto Press, 2007.

———. *Silat bila wasl: Michel Chiha wa al-idiyulujiyya al-lubnaniyya.* Beirut: Riad el-Rayyes Books, 1999.

Tucker, Judith E. "Revisiting Reform: Women and the Ottoman Law of Family Rights, 1917." *Arab Studies Journal* 4 (1996): 4–17.

Turkyilmaz, Zeynep. "Maternal Colonialism and Turkish Woman's Burden in Dersim: Educating the 'Mountain Flowers' of Dersim." *Journal of Women's History* 28 (2016): 162–186.

Üngör, Uğur Ümit. *The Making of Modern Turkey: Nation and State in Eastern Anatolia, 1913–1950.* Oxford: Oxford University Press, 2011.

Wardi, Ali al-. *Dirasa fi tabi'at al-mujtama' al-'iraqi*. Baghdad: Mataba'at al-'ani, 1965.

Ware, Lewis Beier. "Jurji Zaydan: The Role of Popular History in the Formation of a New Arab World-View." PhD diss., Princeton University, 1973.

Watenpaugh, Keith David. *Being Modern in the Middle East: Revolution, Nationalism, Colonialism, and the Arab Middle Class*. Princeton, NJ: Princeton University Press, 2006.

———. "Towards a New Category of Colonial Theory: Colonial Cooperation and the Survivors' Bargain—the Case of the Post-Genocide Armenian Community of Syria under the French Mandate," in Nadine Méouchy and Peter Sluglett, eds., *The British and French Mandates in Comparative Perspective*. Leiden, The Netherlands: Brill, 2004, 597–622.

Weiss, Max. *In the Shadow of Sectarianism: Law, Shi'ism, and the Making of Modern Lebanon*. Cambridge, MA: Harvard University Press, 2010.

Weizmann, Chaim. *The Letters and Papers of Chaim Weizmann, Series B Papers, vol. 1, August 1898–July 1931*. New Brunswick, NJ: Transaction Books, 1983.

White, Benjamin Thomas. *The Emergence of Minorities in the Middle East: The Politics of Community in French Mandate Syria*. Edinburgh: Edinburgh University Press, 2011.

Wien, Peter. *Iraqi Arab Nationalism: Authoritarian, Totalitarian, and Pro-Fascist Inclinations, 1932–1941*. London: Routledge, 2006, 108–112.

———. "Waiting for the Superman: A New Generation of Arab Nationalists in 1930s Iraq," in Dyala Hamzah, ed., *The Making of the Arab Intellectual: Empire, Public Sphere and the Colonial Coordinates of Selfhood*. New York: Routledge, 2013, 212–244.

Winter, Stefan. *A History of the 'Alawis: From Medieval Aleppo to the Turkish Republic*. Princeton, NJ: Princeton University Press, 2016.

———. *The Shi'ites of Lebanon under Ottoman Rule 1516–1788*. Cambridge: Cambridge University Press, 2010.

Wolfe, Patrick. *Traces of History: Elementary Structures of Race*. London: Verso, 2016.

Yildiz, Murat C. "Institutions and Discourses of Sports in the Modern Middle East," in Nicholas S. Hopkins and Sandrine Gamblin, eds., *Sports and Society in the Middle East*. Cairo: American University in Cairo Press, 2016, 12–47.

Yosmaoğlu, İpek. *Blood Ties: Religion, Violence, and the Politics of Nationhood in Ottoman Macedonia, 1878–1908*. Ithaca, NY: Cornell University Press, 2014.

Zakar, Adrien. "The End of Ottoman Positivism: The Gökalp-al-Husri Debate of 1916." *International Journal of Middle East Studies* 47 (2015): 580–583.

Zamir, Meir. *Lebanon's Quest: The Road to Statehood 1926–1939*. London: I. B. Tauris, 2000.

Zandi-Sayek, Sibel. *Ottoman Izmir: The Rise of a Cosmopolitan Port, 1840–1880*. Minneapolis: University of Minnesota Press, 2012.

Zaydan, Jurji. "Al-musta'marat al-yahudiyya fi Filastin." *Al-Hilal* 22 (1914): 518–520.

———. "Community of Interest: The Source of All Other Communities and the Primary Motivation for Undertaking Great Deeds," trans. Paul Starkey and reproduced in Thomas Philipp, *Jurji Zaydan and the Foundations of Arab Nationalism*. Syracuse, NY: Syracuse University Press, 2010, 330–337.

———. *Tarikh adab al-lugha al-'arabiyya, vol. 4*. Cairo: Dar al-Hilal, 1957 [1914].

———. *Tarikh al-tamaddun al-islami*, 2 vols. Beirut: Dar Maktabat al-Hayat, n.d. [1912].

Zipperstein, Steven J. *Elusive Prophet: Ahad Ha'am and the Origins of Zionism*. Berkeley: University of California Press, 1993.

Zubaida, Sami. "Contested Nations: Iraq and the Assyrians." *Nations and Nationalism* 6 (2000): 363–382.

———. "The Fragments Imagine the Nation: The Case of Iraq." *International Journal of Middle East Studies* 34 (2002): 205–215.

Zurayk, Constantine. *Al-a'mal al-fikriyya al-'amma lil-duktur Constantine Zurayk*, 4 vols. Beirut: Markaz dirasat al-wahda al-'arabiyya, 1996.

———. *The Meaning of the Disaster*, trans. R. Bayly Winder. Beirut: Khayat's, 1956.

Index

'Abd al-Hadi, 'Awni, 182, 193
Abdelkader ['Abd al-Qadir] (prince), 95, 97
Abduh ['Abdu], Muhammad, 97–99, 101, 102, 145, 172, 214
Abdülhamid II (Sultan), 79, 82, 101, 158, 166
Abdülmecid (Sultan), 66
Abu Zayd, Nasr Hamid, 215–17
Academy of Arabic Language, 97
Adana, 82
Adonis, 214, 218
al-Afghani, Jamal al-Din, 79
Afghanistan, 209
'Aflaq, Michel, 160, 204
AHC. *See* Arab Higher Committee
Ahliyya (National Civic) school, 87
Ahmad, Labiba, 106
Al-Ahram (newspaper), 94
Ajami, Fouad, 13
Akçura, Yusuf, 81
Alami ['Alami], Musa, 189, 193
Alawis ['Alawis], 184, 208
al-'Alayli, Abdullah, 147, 159
Aleppo: contrast wtih Nabi Musa riots of 1920, 173–74; riots in 1850, 54–55, 57
Ali (Caliph), 27
Amin, Qasim, 105

Anatolia, 20, 75, 77; Armenians in, 80–81; nationalism in, 76. *See also* Eastern Anatolia
Anglo-American Committee, 189, 191, 193
Anglo-Iraqi treaty of 1922, 148
antiblack riots, 55
anti-British rebellion of 1920, 125
anti-Catholic riots, 55
anticlericalism, 105
anticolonialism, 119, 174, 182–84, 186; Arab nationalism and, 17
anticolonial uprisings, 116
anti-conscription riots, 54, 55
anti-Jewish riots, 174–75, 197
anti-Jewish sentiment, 55
antisectarianism, 20, 47, 102, 212; Bustani, B., and, 67, 71–73; Husri and, 154; sectarianism disguised as, 146
antisectarian nationalism: Husri and, 147–53; limits of, 153–56
antisectarian reformism, 102
anti-Semitism, 11, 17, 174, 186, 198
anti-Zionism, 172, 174, 181, 184, 196–97, 253n26; revolts, 183
Antonius, George, 185–87, 189, 193
Antun, Farah, 92–94, 96, 97, 101, 102, 109; on tolerance, 103